FROM ADAM TO NOAH

PUBLICATIONS OF THE
PERRY FOUNDATION FOR BIBLICAL RESEARCH
IN THE HEBREW UNIVERSITY OF JERUSALEM

A COMMENTARY ON THE BOOK OF GENESIS

by

U. CASSUTO

Late Professor of Bible at the Hebrew University of Jerusalem

Translated from the Hebrew by

ISRAEL ABRAHAMS

Professor of Hebrew, University of Cape Town

PART I

FROM ADAM TO NOAH

GENESIS I — VI 8

JERUSALEM

THE MAGNES PRESS, THE HEBREW UNIVERSITY

מ. ד. קאסוטו: מאדם עד נח

First published in Hebrew, Jerusalem 1944
Reprinted in 1953, 1959, 1965, 1969, 1974, 1978, 1983 and 1986

First English Edition, Jerusalem 1961
Reprinted 1972, 1978, 1989, 1998

ISBN 965-223-480-X

Printed in Israel

PART ONE

FROM ADAM TO NOAH

A Commentary on Genesis I—VI 8

TRANSLATOR'S FOREWORD

IT MUST be an everlasting source of regret to all lovers of the Bible that Professor Umberto Cassuto died before he was able to complete his *magnum opus,* the Commentary on the Pentateuch. In the words of Bialik: 'The song of his life was cut off in the middle . . . And lo! the hymn is lost for ever!'

But even the 'unfinished symphony' shows all the qualities of the master. He illumines every passage of the Bible that he annotates. With profound insight he reveals the inner meaning of Scriptural teaching against the background of history. He enables us to see the fascinating process of the evolution of ideas in the ancient world; and he sets the Biblical contribution to the progress of our conception of God and His providence, of the mystery and wonders of creation, of the unfoldment of the moral law within the human heart, in their true perspective. In doing all this, Prof. Cassuto, we are conscious, not only uncovers some of the noblest foundations of modern civilization, but he orients our minds anew to Hebraic ideals, which have their roots in antiquity, but the golden fruit of whose unending yield has much to offer Jew and Gentile alike in solving the contemporary crisis, frought with so much danger to mankind as a whole, and in helping to formulate the constitution of the brave new world envisioned by the prophets.

Cassuto brought a wealth of scholarship to bear on his work. His almost unrivalled knowledge of ancient Semitic literature, his authoritative understanding of all branches of Biblical inquiry, and his outstanding critical acumen marked him as one of the great Bible exegetes of our age. Endowed with a mind of unusual originality, he pioneered novel scientific methods of interpretation that amounted to a new approach to some of the major exegetical problems of the Book of books, and enabled him to batter the foundations on which the Graf-Wellhausen school rested their documentary theories and expositions. Cassuto's strictures in regard to one particular point of interpretation (p. 190) aptly summarize his criticism of the prevailing expository method as a whole. 'This method, he writes, 'which establishes a given principle *a priori,* without taking into consideration what is expressly stated in the text, and then, placing the passage upon the Procrustean bed of that principle, hacks off the textual limbs that do not fit into the bed, can hardly be accepted as valid.'

It is true that Cassuto had precursors, and that inevitably his own theories were subjected to thorough-going criticism. Nevertheless, if today the documentary hypothesis is seriously challenged, no small measure of tribute for this revolt against the unwarranted 'vivisection' of the Bible on the basis of flimsy analysis is due to Cassuto, who met the Higher Critics with a panoply of scholarly apparatus that fully matched their own.

In view of the intrinsic value of our author's distinguished contribution to the elucidation of the Torah, one cannot but wish that his writings were known to a far wider public. The pellucid clarity of his exposition and the purity of his classic Hebrew style made his Pentateuchal commentaries immediate best sellers in Israel. But outside the Jewish State, only the higher echelons of Bible scholars were able to read his Hebrew works. To the ordinary student of Scripture — both Jewish and non-Jewish — his writings remained a sealed book, and his very name is unknown outside a limited circle of students.

It was, therefore, with a sense of unfeigned privilege that I accepted the invitation to render the Cassuto commentaries into English. I am convinced that the general reader as well as the scholar will welcome the opportunity of becoming acquainted with the illuminating results of this great exegete's researches. I can but humbly hope that the translation will not obscure the many excellencies of the original.

From the outset I realized that I was at a great disadvantage in not being able to consult the author on various questions inherent in turning a work of this character from one language into another. One example must suffice to illustrate a host of analagous problems:

in the course of his annotations, Cassuto often buttresses his argument with references to Biblical passages that are themselves in certain details the subject of exegetical controversy. The Hebrew quotation carries no commitment in respect of its obscurity; but the English translation must of necessity decide in matters that do not always admit of simple solutions. I was often without any guide as to the way in which our author would have expounded the verses he cites.

Generally, however, I followed the rendering of *The Revised Standard Version of the Old Testament* as the basis of my Biblical translation, deviating from it whenever required by Cassuto's interpretation. It will thus be noted that, as in *The Revised Standard Version,* I have dispensed with the use of *thou* and *thee* (except in reference to the Deity), and I have avoided other archaic expressions found in the older English versions.

With regard to the principles that guided me in the work of translation as a whole, I may perhaps be permitted to cite Maimonides' advice to Samuel Ibn Tibbon, when the latter undertook to translate his *Guide for the Perplexed*:

> Let me premise one canon. Whoever wishes to translate, and purposes to render each word literally, and at the same time to adhere slavishly to the order of the words and sentences in the original, will meet with much difficulty. This is not the right method. The translator should first try to grasp the sense of the subject thoroughly, and then state the theme with perfect clearness in the other language. This, however, cannot be done without changing the order of the words, putting many words for one word, or *vice versa,* so that the subject be perfectly intelligible in the language into which he translates.

To this I would add Samuel Johnson's dictum:

> He will deserve the highest praise who can give a representation at once faithful and pleasing, who can convey the same thoughts with the same graces, and who, when he translates, changes nothing but the language.

Such was my aim. I endeavoured to keep the translation as true to the Hebrew as the requirements of idiomatic English usage (including punctuation) would permit. * But alas! —

Between the idea
And the reality...
Falls the shadow.

Doubtless I have lived up to the familiar adage that 'translators are traitors', and I have betrayed the author here and there by failing to convey some nuance or emphasis. My only plea in self-exculpation is that the betrayal was committed unwittingly.

Cassuto was not only a meticulous scholar but, as a perfectionist, he also demanded the highest standards from his printers. Nevertheless it is difficult, if not impossible, to keep the printer's gremlin completely under control. I have corrected such typographical errors and wrong references as I noticed, and I have indicated the Hebrew as well as the English number of every verse where these differ in the two versions. The nature of the work also made it necessary for me to add an occasional gloss, or to give the meaning of a Semitic root or word that had to be retained in its original language. These explanatory notes are enclosed in square brackets.

In order to assist the reader who has little or no knowledge of Semitic languages, it was decided to give, in addition to the original, the transliteration of all Hebrew, Aramaic and Arabic words quoted; but the Sumerian, Babylonian and Ugaritic words, being in cuneiform in the original, always appear in transcription only. Long vowels in the Hebrew are uniformly indicated by a horizontal line over the vowel; the circumflex accent (^), which is often used to mark essentially long vowels (either naturally so or by contraction), has, for the sake of simplicity, been dispensed with. In the case of Assyrian and Babylonian words, however, it was deemed advisable to retain this symbol. The key to the transliteration will be found at the end of this Foreword.

It should also be noted that in the case of Ugaritic citations, and at times when the roots of other tongues are referred to, the con-

* This rule has been broken in the translation of Genesis v, where the numbers follow the Hebrew order contrary to the normal English idiom. The purpose of this deviation is to indicate the ascending and descending order of the numerals; see the commentary on v 3.

sonants alone are represented in the transcription; vowels are provided only in those instances where Cassuto has indicated these himself. Likewise the Tetragrammaton is always transcribed without vowels, thus: *YHWH.* For Biblical names (including the books of the Bible) and rabbinic works and authorities, the customary spelling, even though not strictly scientific, has been retained.

Considerable use has been made of italics. These indicate not only words emphasized by the author but also all passages quoted from the Bible. In addition the following two symbols have been employed: the end of each Scriptural text to be annotated is marked by]; but if the quotation is immediately followed by square brackets, a slanting stroke (/) is placed between them and the subsequent comment. This stroke is also used to indicate the caesura in the Biblical lines.

I would conclude with a brief, but deepfelt, word of thanks to all who helped me in various ways to carry out my work of translation, and enabled it to be published in its present form.

First, I desire to convey my gratitude to Mr. Silas S. Perry, after whom the Perry Foundation for Biblical Research in the Hebrew University is named, for his unfailing encouragement, invaluable suggestions, and consistent help in numerous directions; were it not for his generous idealism and friendship this translation would never have seen the light of day.

My warm thanks are tendered to Professor Isaac L. Seeligmann for his gracious assistance in solving a number of problems. Lack of adequate library facilities in South Africa compelled me to submit to him a whole series of queries (involving, *inter alia,* the tracing of a number of references), to which he replied with painstaking care characteristic of his fine scholarship. His courtesy and counsel to one who was a complete stranger to him will always remain with me a fragrant memory.

I am likewise indebted to Dr. Milka Cassuto-Salzmann, the daughter of the author, for her valuable assistance. Apart from reading the proofs and preparing the indexes with exemplary skill and patience, she also rendered a great service to the undertaking by many helpful suggestions and was instrumental in assuring the accuracy of the rendering at various points.

My grateful thanks are also due to a number of experts who put their special knowledge at my disposal: to Dr. M. Spitzer for repeated guidance in typographical matters, which conduced to the aesthetic appearance of the work; to Dr. S. E. Loewenstamm for his erudite advice on questions appertaining to Ugaritic literature; and to the Central Printing Press for the conscientious and meticulous manner in which they carried out their task.

Finally, my thanks go out to the Hebrew University for bestowing its imprimatur on the translation and arranging for it to be printed by the Magnes Press, an honour of which I am deeply conscious and for which I am truly grateful. I am especially indebted to Professor B. Mazar, the President of the University, for the personal interest he has taken in the enterprise. It was in no small measure due to his understanding of the permanent significance of Cassuto's Commentaries for our knowledge of Scripture that this translation came to fruition. In helping to make this monumental work of Biblical scholarship and exegesis available to a far wider circle of readers than the original could have reached, the Hebrew University is putting the world once again in its debt by deepening our knowledge of the Torah and by spreading its moral and spiritual truths to the ends of the earth.

ISRAEL ABRAHAMS

Cape Town.
January, 1959.
Tebeth, 5719.

KEY TO THE TRANSLITERATION

Hebrew

(a) Consonants

א	= ʾ	ל	= l
בּ	= b	מ, ם	= m
ב	= bh	נ, ן	= n
גּ	= g	ס	= s
ג	= gh	ע	= ʿ
דּ	= d	פּ	= p
ד	= dh	פ, ף	= ph
ה	= h	צ, ץ	= ṣ
ו	= w	ק	= q
ז	= z	ר	= r
ח	= ḥ	שׂ	= ś
ט	= ṭ	שׁ	= š
י	= y	תּ	= t
כּ, ךּ	= k	ת	= th
כ, ך	= kh		

Note: (1) Unsounded ה at the end of a word is not represented in the transcription;

(2) the customary English spelling is retained for Biblical names and rabbinic works and authorities.

(b) Vowels

Long		*Short*	
◌ָ *(Qāmeṣ gādhōl)*	= ā	◌ַ	= a
◌ִי . . . *(Ḥireq gādhōl)*	= ī	◌ֶ	= e
◌ֵי .. ◌ֵ ..	= ē	◌ִ *(Ḥireq qāṭān)*	= i
◌ֹ ,וֹ	= ō	◌ָ *(Qāmeṣ qāṭān)*	= o
וּ	= ū	◌ֻ	= u

◌ְ *(Šᵉwāʾ)*	= ᵉ
◌ֲ	= ă
◌ֳ	= ŏ
◌ֱ	= ĕ

Note: Capital E represents ◌ֵ , ◌ֶ and ◌ֱ ; thus אֱלֹהִים is transliterated *ʾElōhīm,* and אֵל is transcribed *El.*

Arabic and other languages

The method commonly used in scientific works was followed in the transliteration of Arabic, Akkadian, Egyptian and Ugaritic words.

CONTENTS

Translator's Foreword VII

Key to transliteration XIII

List of Abbreviations XVII

Preface 1

SECTION ONE: The Story of Creation (i 1–ii 3)

Introduction 7

Introductory verse (i 1) 19

First Paragraph: The Story of the First Day (i 2–5) . . . 21

Second Paragraph: The Story of the Second Day (i 6–8) . . 31

Third Paragraph: The Story of the Third Day (i 9–13) . . 35

Fourth Paragraph: The Story of the Fourth Day (i 14–19) . . 42

Fifth Paragraph: The Story of the Fifth Day (i 20–23) . . 47

Sixth Paragraph: The Story of the Sixth Day (i 24–31) . . 52

Seventh Paragraph: The Seventh Day; end of the Section (ii 1–3) 60

SECTION TWO: The Story of the Garden of Eden (ii 4–iii 24)

Introduction 71

Introductory verse, Transition from Previous Section (ii 4) . 96

First Paragraph: Creation of Man (ii 5–7) 100

Second Paragraph: The Planting of the Garden of Eden (ii 8–14) 106

Third Paragraph: Adam's Task in the Garden of Eden (ii 15–17) 121

Fourth Paragraph: Creation of Woman (ii 18–25) 126

Fifth Paragraph: Adam's Sin (iii 1–7) 138

Sixth Paragraph: The Judgment and the Sentence (iii 8–21) . 149

Seventh Paragraph: The Expulsion from the Garden of Eden (iii 22–24) 172

CONTENTS

SECTION THREE: The Story of Cain and Abel (iv 1–26)

Introduction 178
First Paragraph: The Birth and Occupations of Cain and Abel (iv 1–2) 196
Second Paragraph: The Story of the Murder (iv 3–8) 204
Third Paragraph: The Murderer's Sentence (iv 9–16) 216
Fourth Paragraph: The Descendants of Cain (iv 17–22) . . . 228
Fifth Paragraph: Lamech's Song (iv 23–24) 239
Sixth Paragraph: The Birth of Seth and Enosh (iv 25–26) . . . 244

SECTION FOUR: The Book of the History of Adam (v 1–vi 8)

Introduction 249
Rubric of Section (v 1a) 273
First Paragraph: Adam (v 1b–5) 273
Second Paragraph: Seth (v 6–8) 278
Third Paragraph: Enosh (v 9–11) 279
Fourth Paragraph: Kenan (v 12–14) 279
Fifth Paragraph: Mahalalel (v 15–17) 280
Sixth Paragraph: Jared (v 18–20) 281
Seventh Paragraph: Enoch (v 21–24) 281
Eighth Paragraph: Methuselah (v 25–27) 286
Ninth Paragraph: Lamech (v 28–31) 287
Tenth Paragraph: Noah (v 32) 290
Eleventh Paragraph: The Story of the Sons of God and the Daughters of Men (vi 1–4) 290
Twelfth Paragraph: Punishment is decreed on the Generation of the Flood, but Grace is shown to Noah (vi 5–8) 301

INDEXES

I. Biblical References 309
II. Other Literary References 317
III. Notabilia 320

BIBLIOGRAPHICAL ABBREVIATIONS

I REFER to the commentaries on the Book of Genesis only by the author's name (e.g., Dillmann, Gunkel, Jacob). Below I list the works (almost all periodicals) that I cite by their initial letters. More obvious abbreviations — for instance, *Ephemeris, Jew. Enc.* and the like — are not given here.

AJSL	American Journal of Semitic Languages and Literature
AfO	Archiv für Orientforschung
ARW	Archiv für Religionswissenschaft
BASOR	Bulletin of the American Schools of Oriental Research
BJPES	Bulletin of the Jewish Palestine Exploration Society [Hebrew]
BZ	Biblische Zeitschrift
BZAW	Beihefte zur Zeitschrift für die alttestamentliche Wissenschaft
GGN	Nachrichten von der k. Gesellschaft der Wissenschaften ... zu Göttingen
HThR	Harvard Theological Review
GSAI	Giornale della Società Asiatica Italiana
HUCA	Hebrew Union College Annual
JAOS	Journal of the American Oriental Society
JBL	Journal of Biblical Literature
JPOS	Journal of the Palestine Oriental Society
JRAS	Journal of the Royal Asiatic Society
MdW	Masoreten des Westens, Stuttgart 1927–1930
MGWJ	Monatsschrift für Geschichte und Wissenschaft des Judentums
NRTh	Nouvelle revue théologique
RB	Revue Biblique
Rech.Sc.Rel.	Recherches de science religieuse
RHPhR	Revue d'histoire et de philosophie religieuses
SMSR	Studi e materiali di storia delle religioni
ZA	Zeitschrift für Assyriologie
ZAW	Zeitschrift für die alttestamentliche Wissenschaft
ZDMG	Zeitschrift der deutschen morgenländischen Gesellschaft

[BDB F. Brown, S. R. Driver and C. A. Briggs, *A Hebrew and English Lexicon of the Old Testament* . . . based on the Lexicon of W. Gesenius

Gesenius–Kautzsch[2] Gesenius' *Hebrew Grammar* as edited and enlarged by the late E. Kautzsch, Second English Edition]

OTHER ABBREVIATIONS

J	=	Jahwist	S	=	Seir
E	=	Elohist	P	=	Priestly Code

E.V. = English Version of the O.T.

PREFACE

THE AIM of this commentary is to explain, with the help of an historico-philological method of interpretation, the simple meaning of the Biblical text, and to arrive, as nearly as possible, at the sense that the words of the Torah were intended to have for the reader at the time when they were written. Although the homiletical method is, without doubt, of great importance, in as much as it interprets the Bible in every generation according to the spirit and needs of the age, nevertheless every verse has its primary signification, and Scripture merits our effort to fathom its original intent.

The lines along which I have worked will become self-apparent to the reader as he studies the book; there is no need, therefore, for me to go into detail here. I shall draw attention only to a few basic principles by which I have been guided throughout.

The first chapters of the Book of Genesis, which form the subject of this commentary, deal with topics about which — and their like — there were numerous sagas in the ancient East, both among the Israelites and among the Gentiles. Hence, it is not possible to understand the purpose of the Torah in these chapters without constant reference to the lore and learning, the doctrines and traditions, of the neighbouring peoples, and of Israel itself, concerning these and related matters. For this reason, I paid greater attention than earlier commentators to the literature of the nations of the ancient East and to all the archaeological data that might possibly throw light on the subject — in all, a vast and variegated body of material, which, thanks to a number of fortunate discoveries, has, in recent years, grown considerably. Moreover, I gave consideration not only to the parallels between Israel and the other peoples, but also to the divergences between them; for the differences are likewise instructive, perhaps even more so than the similarities.

In order to determine the content of the traditions that were current among the *Israelites,* and their origin and development, I sought to gather and examine the scattered references in the other books of the Bible to the subjects under discussion; and since even the Apocrypha and Rabbinic Literature, though written at a later date, incorporate ancient elements capable of shedding light on the Israelite traditions that were extant in the earliest period, I made use of them, too, in my researches.

I investigated the history and principles of the *literary tradition* with no less care than the development of the *thematic tradition.* For to gain an exact understanding of a Biblical passage it is very important to observe the way in which literary expression is given to the thought. In this respect, too, I found it invaluable to compare the writings of the neighbouring nations, and more particularly those of the Canaanites (see my Hebrew essay, 'Biblical and Canaanite Literature', in *Tarbiz,* xiii, pp. 197–212 and xiv, pp. 1–10). I have attempted to establish the detailed rules followed by the Bible in its use of particular syntactical forms, rhetorical style, repetitions with certain modifications, synonymous and antithetic parallelism, as well as the laws governing the structure of verses, paragraphs and sections; at no time, however, did I lose sight of the fact that the peoples of the ancient East did not think along the same lines, or express themselves in the same manner, as the European races. I also made every effort to note accurately all the linguistic details of the text, its grammatical niceties, its allusions, even its play upon words; and this thoroughgoing study was of great help to me in determining the precise meaning of Scripture.

The study of the history of the traditional themes is bound up with the study of the *sources.* I have given a general exposition of my views concerning the sources of the Book of Genesis in my Italian treatise, *La Questione della Genesi,* (Florence, 1934), pp. 393–398, and in the Hebrew abridgement thereof, called תּוֹרַת הַתְּעוּדוֹת וְסִדּוּרָם שֶׁל סִפְרֵי הַתּוֹרָה *Tōrath Hatteʿūdhōth Wesiddūrām Šel Siphrē Hattōrā* [*The Documentary Hypothesis and Composition of the Pentateuch*], Jerusalem, 1942 (English translation, Jerusalem, 1961, pp. 101 ff.). Anyone who has studied these volumes will know that, in my opinion, the sources are very different from the documents J (Jahwist), E (Elohist), P (Priestly Code), postulated by the commonly-held theory. In the present work, I proceed to give a detailed example of a comprehensive commentary based on my view of the original documents.

Seeing that this is the first commentary ever written on these sections of the Pentateuch in accordance with the principles that I have outlined above and in the light of my aforementioned views on the question of the sources, it follows that my exposition is, in its entirety, completely new and original. I have taken constant care, however, to avoid any hypotheses that are not well-founded. I have endeavoured throughout not to forsake the firm basis of the facts; I did not bend the Bible to make it fit in with my theories, but rather fitted my theories to the Biblical text.

Needless to say, I consulted such earlier commentaries as were available to me, as well as all the scientific works bearing on the subject; I have also appended to each section a detailed bibliography. But since it was not my wish to make the commentary, which in any case had assumed no inconsiderable proportions, longer than was necessary, and as, moreover, it was not my intention to enter into polemics but simply to give what appeared to me to be the correct exposition of the text, I refrained, as a rule, from citing the interpretations of other exegetes; only if warranted by exceptional reasons, did I refer, in the briefest terms, to the explanations of other expositors. I was invariably careful, however, to quote the author of any statement that was not my own; but should my book, by chance, be found to contain any observation that is also made by another commentator, without his name being indicated, it signifies (unless I have been guilty of an oversight) that I had already made this point in a previous book or article, and that I am to be regarded as the originator thereof, even though the other annotator failed to mention my name.

In the bibliographies appended before each section, I have not included the works already listed in my Italian treatise mentioned above, but I have started from the year of its publication (1934). The earlier bibliographical references are available in my Italian work; where this is not to hand, bibliographical guidance on preceding literature will be found in the books and articles published during the last decade, which I mention in this volume. *

When I began my scientific researches on the Book of Genesis eighteen years ago, I approached my task without any bias, and I was prepared, from the start, to accept all the results of my investigations, be they what they might. I adopted a similar attitude when I began my work on the present commentary; I was willing to accept the conclusion, if necessary, that what I had myself previously written was erroneous. It was not my object to defend any particular viewpoint or any particular exegetical method, but only to arrive at a thorough understanding of the Torah's meaning, whatever that might be.

Possibly this attitude will not be acceptable to those who hold, from the outset, that certain views are not open to doubt. There are those, on the one hand, who are accustomed to read the Scriptures in the light of homiletical interpretation and think it wrong to deviate from the explanations that they received from their teachers and from the approach to which they have become used since childhood; and, on the other hand, there are those who see in the documentary hypothesis an assured and enduring achievement of science, an impregnable structure. I would ask both these schools of thought not to be hasty and pass judgment on my book before they have read it completely and have examined what it states in detail. I venture to hope that in the end even though they may not agree with me on all points — full agreement, of course, is not to be expected — they will both concede at least the correctness of my method and of most of my conclusions. The one group, which is well acquainted with the rabbinic dictum that every verse retains its simple meaning, must admit that the sincere endeavour to comprehend the words of the Torah according to their primary sense, and to fathom the ultimate purport of Scripture, cannot be regarded as something contrary to the spirit of the Bible itself. The other group, which is well aware that science has no dogmas, must grant that there is no scientific theory, however much it may be favoured, which is entitled to permanent acceptance and may not be criticised or replaced by another theory. On the contrary, the investigator is not only permitted, but is obliged, to submit the earlier theories to constant re-examination, and if it appears to him that the view that was formerly considered correct does not correspond to the established facts or to the new data discovered by science, it is his duty to abandon it and attempt to put forward, in its stead, another hypothesis that will better fit the existing facts and the new data.

PREFACE

The commentary I present here on the first chapters of Genesis, which belong to the difficult and obscure portions of the Pentateuch, will serve, in a way, as a touchstone for my method. I trust that it will stand the test.

It is my pleasant duty to express my thanks to Dr. J. L. Magnes, the Director of the Hebrew University Press Association, and to his fellow-members of the Editorial Board, for kindly including this book in the Association's series of publications. I am also grateful to the various libraries in which I worked on the preparation of my commentary, to wit, the National and University Library, the library of the Government Department of Antiquities, the library of the American School of Oriental Research, the library of the Dominican School of Bible and Archaeology, the Schocken Library, and the library of the Museum of Jewish Antiquities; I am indebted to the directors and staff of these institutions for their courteous assistance. Finally, my thanks are due to the printers, Raphael Hayyim Ha-Cohen and Sons, who always endeavoured to fulfil my every request and to give me the utmost satisfaction with their work.

JERUSALEM, ELUL, 5704 (1944)

U. C.

* No attempt has been made to bring the bibliographies up to date, since it is felt that this is a task that only the author, had he lived, could properly have performed (*Translator*).

SECTION ONE

THE STORY OF CREATION

CHAPTER I, VERSE 1 — CHAPTER II, VERSE 3

INTRODUCTION

§ 1. THE PURPOSE of the Torah in this section is to teach us that the whole world and all that it contains were created by the word of the One God, according to His will, which operates without restraint. It is thus opposed to the concepts current among the peoples of the ancient East who were Israel's neighbours; and in some respects it is also in conflict with certain ideas that had already found their way into the ranks of our people. The language, however, is tranquil, undisturbed by polemic or dispute; the controversial note is heard indirectly, as it were, through the deliberate, quiet utterances of Scripture, which sets the opposing views at nought by silence or by subtle hint.

§ 2. All kinds of wondrous stories about the creation of the world were wide-spread throughout the lands of the East, and many of them assumed a literary form in epic poems or other compositions. In the course of our exposition we shall have repeated occasion to refer to a number of matters found in these sources and to translate several verses from their texts. Here it will suffice to indicate briefly their general character. They began, as a rule, with a theogony, that is, with the origin of the gods, the genealogy of the deities who preceded the birth of the world and mankind; and they told of the antagonism between this god and that god, of frictions that arose from these clashes of will, and of mighty wars that were waged by the gods. They connected the genesis of the world with the genesis of the gods and with the hostilities and wars between them; and they identified the different parts of the universe with given deities or with certain parts of their bodies. Even the elect few among the nations, the thinkers who for a time attained to loftier concepts than those normally held in their environment, men like Amenhotep IV — the Egyptian king who attributed the entire creation to one of the gods, the sun-god Aten — and his predecessors (the discoveries of recent years prove that he was not the first to hold this doctrine), even they pictured this god to themselves as but one of the gods, be he the very greatest, as a deity linked to nature and identifiable with one of its component parts. Then came the Torah and soared aloft, as on eagles' wings, above all these notions. Not many gods but One God; not theogony, for a god has no family tree; not wars nor strife nor the clash of wills, but only One Will, which rules over everything, without the slightest let or hindrance; not a deity associated with nature and identified with it wholly or in part, but a God who stands absolutely above nature, and outside of it, and nature and all its constituent elements, even the sun and all the other entities, be they never so exalted, are only His creatures, made according to His will.

§ 3. Among the Israelites, too, there existed, prior to the Biblical account, narrative poems about the creation and the beginning of the world's history. Although these poems have not come down to us, having perished in the course of time, evidence of their existence is to be found both in this section and in other parts of Scripture. Frequently the prophets and the Bible poets allude to matters appertaining directly or indirectly to the creation of the world that are not mentioned in our section at all, for example, the story of Rahab, the prince of the sea, who rose up in revolt against God, and in the end God subdued him and slew him (see below, on i 9); but the brevity of these references leaves the impression that the authors were touching on topics that were well-known to the people they addressed. At times the Scriptural allusions closely resemble what we are told in the legends of the non-Israelites; yet it is difficult to imagine that these particular myths influenced them directly. Generally speaking, it is inconceivable that the prophets and poets of Israel intended to seek support for their views in the pagan mythological works, which they undoubtedly detested and abominated; nor is it thinkable that they mentioned the heathen legends as something that the Israelites knew and accepted. Furthermore, whilst these allusions show certain resemblances—quite striking, at times — to the sagas of the Gentiles, they also exhibit distinct differences: the actions credited to the various deities in the pagan literature are attributed in the Hebrew Scriptures to the God of Israel, and are portrayed in a form more in keeping with Israel's religious conscience. It follows that we have to assume the existence of intermediate links in the chain of development, which bridged the gap between the poems of the non-Israelites and the myths alluded to in the Bible. It seems that the intermediaries between the heathen peoples and Israel were the groups of Sages, the exponents of international 'Wisdom', who, it is known, were prone to obscure the religious elements peculiar to each individual nation. It may confidently be surmised that the said links included epic poems of Israel, Israelite cycles in which the ancient Eastern tradition took on a form that was generally in harmony with the national spirit of Israel and its religious convictions. I have dealt at length with this subject in my Hebrew essay on 'The Epic Poetry of Israel', which appeared in *Keneseth,* dedicated to H. N. Bialik, Vol. viii, 1943; I shall not, therefore, repeat what I have written there. Here I shall refer only to matters that concern our section as a whole, and in the course of my annotations on the individual verses, I shall mention the points that have a bearing on those verses in particular.

Allusions to the creation-story that are unrelated to our section are found, for instance, in Job xxxviii 4–7:

Where were you when I laid the foundation of the earth?
Tell me, if you have understanding.
Who determined its measurements — surely you know!
Or who stretched the line upon it?
On what were its bases sunk, or who laid its cornerstone,
When the morning stars sang together, and all the sons of God shouted for joy?

There is a clear indication here of a tradition concerning the creation of the earth on a bright morning, whilst the stars and God's angels sang a paean. Undoubtedly, the author of the book of Job did not fabricate these details. Nor did he invent such concepts or terms as *lay the foundations, measurements, line, bases, cornerstone.*

Similarly, we read in Isaiah xl 12, 21–22:

Who has measured the waters in the hollow of his hand and marked off the heavens with a span,
enclosed the dust of the earth in a measure and weighed the mountains in scales and the hills in a balance?

. . . .

Have you not known? Have you not heard?
Has it not been told you from the beginning?
Have you not understood from the foundations of the earth?
It is He who sits above the circle of the earth,
and its inhabitants are like grasshoppers;
who stretches out the heavens like a curtain,
and spreads them like a tent to dwell in.

The two passages probably derive from a common poetic source. It may be noted in regard to the root יָסַד *yāsadh* ['lay the foundations'], which occurs in both texts in relation to the earth, that it is used a number of times in the Bible in this sense, although it does not appear in our section at all. The same applies to the verb נָטָה *nāṭā* ['stretch out'] in connection with the heavens, which is found in Isaiah *ibid.,* and in another passage of Job (ix 8); this word, too, occurs frequently in Scripture but not in our section. At times, moreover, both expressions — *to lay the foundations of the earth* and *to stretch out the heavens* — are found in juxtaposition. It cannot, therefore, be doubted that we have here an ancient literary tradition, and apparently this tradition has its roots in Israel's epic poetry. There are also other literary characteristics that appear to belong to the vocabulary and phraseology of the ancient poetic tradition regarding the creation, and serve to prove the existence of such a poetic tradition among the Israelites: for instance, the expression *spread forth the earth;* the simile of a *tent-curtain,* or some synonym thereof, employed in connection with the stretching out of the heavens; the figure of *chambers* or *upper chambers,* signifying the heavens in relation to the earth beneath them; the verb הַמְקָרֶה *hamᵉqāre* ['who hast laid the beams'] in Psa. civ 3, which corresponds to an Akkadian expression (see below, on verse 6); the root כון *kūn* ['establish'] followed by the words בַּל יִמּוֹט *bal yimmōṭ* or בַּל תִּמּוֹט *bal timmōṭ* ['shall not be moved']; the verb חוֹלֵל *ḥōlēl* in the sense of *created;* the adverb טֶרֶם *ṭerem* ['not yet'] or the conjunction בְּטֶרֶם *bᵉṭerem* ['before'], used with reference to the pre-creation period (a similar usage is also common in non-Israelite writings), and many more examples of this kind.

As far as our own section is concerned, a poetic construction like חַיְתוֹ אֶרֶץ *ḥayᵉthō ʾereṣ* ['beasts of the earth'] (i 24) next to the corresponding prose form חַיַּת הָאָרֶץ *ḥayyath hā'āreṣ* (i 25, 30); or verses with poetic rhythm like i 27:

So God created man in His own image,
in the image of God He created him;
male and female He created them.

and a number of other poetic features, which we shall discuss in the course of our exposition, also point to a poetic tradition among the Israelites anterior to the Book of Genesis. The metre of the verse, *So God created man* ... — tetrameter —, which is also found in other verses of our section, is the most usual in the epic poetry of the Eastern peoples of antiquity, and was probably employed to a large extent in the epic poetry of Israel, too. There is no necessity to assume that the Torah took these verses verbatim from an earlier epic poem. Admittedly this is possible; but it is simpler to suppose that wherever, in the course of the Biblical story, which is mainly in prose, the special importance of the subject led to an exaltation of style approaching the level of poetry, the thought took on of its own accord, as it were, an aspect conforming to the traditional pattern of narrative poetry — an aspect, at all events, that was in keeping with ancient poetic tradition.

§ 4. Although the epic poetry of Israel gave the traditional material, as has been stated, a form that was generally in harmony with the spirit and conscience of the nation, it nevertheless retained certain elements in which echoes of their origin in a foreign environment could still be heard. The saga, for example, of the revolt of 'the lord of the sea' against God belonged to this category. The same applies to the reference in Job xxxviii 7, to the morning stars that sang and to the sons of God who shouted for joy when God laid the cornerstone of the earth. It is not surprising, therefore, that the attitude of the Torah to these elements was not sympathetic. The prophets and the Biblical poets, who were accustomed to clothe their ideas in poetic garb and to elucidate them with the help of similes, and generally to employ the familiar devices of poesy, were not, to be sure, deterred from using what they found to hand in Israel's epic poetry. But the Torah, which is not written in verse but in prose, and employs as a rule simple, not figurative, language, and weighs every word scrupulously, was careful not to introduce ingredients that were not completely in accord with its doctrines.

Nay more, whenever necessary it voiced, in its own subtle way, its objection in principle to concepts suggestive of an alien spirit as, for instance, the myth of the revolt of the sea against its Creator (see below on i 6, 9, 14–15, 21).

Nevertheless, the Torah did not refrain from taking over other components of Israel's poetic tradition, in so far as these did not militate against its spirit. We have already seen above that here and there the style of our section assumes an elevated poetic form, and that it is precisely the metre of epic poetry that is reflected in some of its sentences. This applies also to the content of the story, which has likewise absorbed certain elements of Israel's ancient poetry. The truth that the Torah wished to convey in this section, to wit, that the world in its entirety was created by the word of the One God, could not be stated in abstract terms, simply as a theoretical concept. Semitic thought avoids general statements. Particularly in the case of a book like ours, which was not intended for the thinkers and the elect few only, but for the people as a whole, including also its common folk, it was proper that its ideas should be embodied in the language of concrete description. Hence, the Torah made use of the concrete traditions that found expression in the 'Wisdom' literature and in the ancient heroic poetry of Israel, and drew from them material for its structure. Choosing only what it deemed worthy, it refined and purified the selected matter, and moulded the entire narrative to a pattern of its own — a pattern befitting its purpose and educational aim. In the light of this hypothesis, the parallels between our section and the traditions current in the ancient Orient become perfectly clear.

§ 5. The structure of our section is based on a system of numerical harmony. Not only is the number *seven* fundamental to its main theme, but it also serves to determine many of its details. Both to the Israelites and to the Gentiles, in the East and also in the West — but especially in the East — it was the number of *perfection* and the basis of ordered arrangement; and particular importance attached to it in the symbolism of numbers. The work of the Creator, which is marked by absolute perfection and flawless systematic orderliness, is distributed over seven days: six days of labour and a seventh day set aside for the enjoyment of the completed task. On the significance and use of the number *seven* see the works I have listed in *Tarbiz,* xiii, p. 207, notes 31–32, and my remarks *ibid.,* pp. 206–207 [Hebrew], as well as the examples that I have cited there from Akkadian and Ugaritic literature, which prove that a series of *seven consecutive days* was considered a perfect *period* [unit of time] in which to develop an important work, the action lasting six days and reaching its conclusion and outcome on the seventh day. Possibly the Torah perceives in the importance attributed to the number seven by non-Israelites a kind of indistinct echo of the story of creation.

It is worth noting in this connection that in the case of actions lasting the above-mentioned length of time, it was customary to divide the six days of labour into three pairs, and to relate the story somewhat as follows: on the first day and on the second such-and-such a work was done; so, too, on the third day and on the fourth that work was done; likewise on the fifth day and on the sixth the same work was done. Thereafter, when the work had been completed on the sixth day, came the seventh day, a day of conclusion and change of situation (see the Akkadian and Ugaritic examples that I quote *ibid.*). In our section the division of the days is, as we shall see later, rather different, to wit, two series of three days each. But the prevailing pattern is implicit in the rabbinic saying: 'It (the Sabbath day) has no partner: there is the first of the Sabbath [i.e. week], the second of the Sabbath; the third, the fourth, the fifth, the eve of the Sabbath; but the Sabbath itself remains unpaired' (Bereshith Rabba, xi 8; for the different readings and parallels see Theodor's edition).

In view of the importance ascribed to the number seven generally, and particularly in the story of Creation, this number occurs again and again in the structure of our section. The following details are deserving of note:

(a). After the introductory verse (i 1), the section is divided into *seven* paragraphs, each of which appertains to one of the seven days. An obvious indication of this division is to be seen in the recurring sentence, *And there was evening and there was morning, such-and-such a day.* Hence the Masoretes were right in placing an open paragraph [i.e. one that begins on a new line] after each of these verses. Other ways of dividing the section suggested by some modern scholars are unsatisfactory.

(b–d). Each of the three nouns that occur in the first verse and express the basic concepts of the section, *viz God* [אֱלֹהִים *'Elōhīm*] *heavens* [שָׁמַיִם *šāmayim*], *earth* [אֶרֶץ *'ereṣ*], are repeated in the section a given number of times that is a multiple of *seven*: thus the name of *God* occurs thirty-five times, that is, five times *seven* (on the fact that the Divine Name, in one of its forms, occurs seventy times in the first four chapters, see below); *earth* is found twenty-one times, that is, three times seven; similarly *heavens* (or *firmament*, רָקִיעַ *rāqīa'*) appears twenty-one times.

(e). The ten sayings with which, according to the Talmud, the world was created (Aboth v 1; in B. Rosh Hashana 32a and B. Megilla 21b only nine of them are enumerated, the one in i 29, apparently, being omitted) — that is, the ten utterances of God beginning with the words, *and . . . said* — are clearly divisible into two groups: the first group contains *seven* Divine fiats enjoining the creation of the creatures, to wit, 'Let there be light', 'Let there be a firmament', 'Let the waters be gathered together', 'Let the earth put forth vegetation', 'Let there be lights', 'Let the waters bring forth swarms', 'Let the earth bring forth'; the second group comprises three pronouncements that emphasize God's concern for man's welfare (*three* being the number of emphasis), namely, 'Let us make man' (not a command but an expression of the will to create man), 'Be fruitful and multiply', 'Behold I have given unto you every plant yielding seed'. Thus we have here, too, a series of *seven* corresponding dicta.

(f). The terms *light* and *day* are found, in all, *seven* times in the first paragraph, and there are *seven* references to *light* in the fourth paragraph.

(g). *Water* is mentioned *seven* times in the course of paragraphs two and three.

(h). In the fifth and sixth paragraphs forms of the word חַיָּה *ḥayyā* [rendered 'living' or 'beasts'] occur *seven* times.

(i). The expression *it was good* appears *seven* times (the seventh time — *very good*).

(j). The first verse has *seven* words.

(k). The second verse contains fourteen words — twice *seven*.

(1). In the *seventh* paragraph, which deals with the *seventh* day, there occur the following three consecutive sentences (three for emphasis), each of which consists of *seven* words and contains in the middle the expression *the seventh day*:

And on THE SEVENTH DAY *God finished His work which He had done, and He rested on* THE SEVENTH DAY *from all His work which He had done.*

So God blessed THE SEVENTH DAY *and hallowed it.*

(m). The words in the seventh paragraph total thirty-five — five times *seven.*

To suppose that all this is a mere coincidence is not possible.

§ 6. This numerical symmetry is, as it were, the golden thread that binds together all the parts of the section and serves as a convincing proof of its unity against the view of those — and they comprise the majority of modern commentators — who consider that our section is not a unity but was formed by the fusion of two different accounts, or as the result of the adaptation and elaboration of a shorter earlier version. According to the prevailing view, the division of the work of creation in the original text differed from that found in the present recension, eight — or ten — creative acts, or seven days of work (man being formed on the seventh), or some other scheme being envisaged; only in the last redaction, it is assumed, was the division into six days of work introduced and the idea of the Sabbath added. The final edition is attributed by most scholars to the source P; the different theories concerning the source of the first version need not detain us here. I have already dealt with this matter fully in the second part of my essay, 'La creazione del mondo nella Genesi' (the creation of the world according to the Book of Genesis), published in *Annuario di studi ebraici,* Vol. i (1934) pp. 47–49. The reader who wishes to delve more deeply into the subject will find there the requisite details as well as a bibliography; here a summary account of the position must suffice. Following are the main arguments advanced by the scholars referred to:

(1). Internal contradictions: the existence of day and night before the creation of the luminaries; the presence of plants before the sun came into being.

(2). Signs of inconsistency and the absence of a unified system in the phrasing and formulation of the account: sometimes the expression *and it was so* is used, sometimes a different wording; on most of the days we are told *it was good,* but not on the second day; the acts of creation are described in different ways (at times God issues an order and His order is carried out; at other times it is He who creates or makes; on other occasions still He commands the elements to form the creatures).

(3). The distribution of the acts of creation over six days is not balanced, for the works of the first three days do not properly correspond to those of the last three days. Thus we have:

1. Light	2. Heavens	3. Earth (including vegetation) and sea
4. Luminaries	5. Fish and birds	6. Living creatures on land, and man

(4). The use of antiquated words and concepts.

Not one of these contentions, however, is tenable in the face of critical examination. On the problem of the existence of day and night and plant-life before the formation of the luminaries, see below on i 14. With reference to the variations in phrasing and formulation, I have shown (in *Tarbiz,* xiii, pp. 205–206, sec. 2, [Hebrew], and subsequently in *Keneseth,* dedicated to the memory of H. N. Bialik, viii, pp. 126–127, sec. 15 [Hebrew]) that, in contrast to the style of epic poetry, which is prone to word-for-word repetition, it is a basic principle of Biblical narrative prose not to repeat a statement in identical terms; with fine artistic sense, the narrator likes to alter the wording or to shorten it or to change the order of the words when reverting to any subject (except when dealing with technical matters like the work of the Tabernacle, the sacrifices of the princes, or the genealogies). Concerning the expressions *and it was so* and *that it was good,* see below the detailed annotations on the verses where they occur or are omitted.

As for the three different ways of describing the acts of creation, it should be noted, firstly, that, quite apart from the point made previously regarding the characteristics of narrative prose style, these linguistic variations could serve to prove the existence of different versions only if it had been possible to employ each type of wording in all instances; in such circumstances the choice of one mode of expression in preference to the other two could be construed as typical of a given recension. Actually, this is not the case.

In regard to the light, which was but an immaterial phenomenon so long as it was independent of the luminaries, neither the second nor the third form of wording was applicable, and so the Bible had necessarily to use the first form. Similarly, in respect of the gathering of the water into one place, which represents only movement and not the creation of a new element, the first mode of expression had, perforce, to be chosen. Furthermore, the three ways of portraying the creative process cannot be considered of equal value. On the contrary, that which God creates or makes is of a higher order than what is formed by the elemental forces of nature. Bearing all this in mind, we cannot but conclude that throughout the section the three different modes of expression are used according to a systematic plan. When referring to non-material things, such as the creation of light or the gathering of the waters, the first mode, as stated, is inevitably chosen. In depicting the fashioning of new material entities, the second or third type of phrasing, according to the category of creation, is employed. Thus the second type — to wit, the creation or making by God — serves for the highest forms of being, namely, the firmament, the luminaries and man (there is a difference of degree even between making and creating, as we shall see later on verses 2–3); the combined second and third forms of expression are used for living creatures (fifth and sixth days); the third by itself is applied to plant-life.

As to the distribution of the acts of creation over six days and the culmination of the process on the seventh day, reference to the ancient examples of similar schemes in the literatures of the East, to which I alluded above (at the beginning of § 3), will suffice to convince us at once that there are no grounds whatsoever for attributing the division adopted in our text to a later redaction. Regarding the parallelism between the first three days and the last three days, it will be clear from my commentary that only the version before us provides a completely harmonious balance, *viz*:

1. Light	2. Sea and Heaven	3. Earth (with its plants)
4. Luminaries	5. Fish and Fowl	6. Land creatures and Man

In so far as the archaic expressions and concepts are concerned, they are fully explained by our hypothesis regarding the Israelite tradition of epic poetry that antedated the Torah account.

§ 7. On the relationship of our section to the next — the story of the Garden of Eden — see the introduction to the latter, where the use of the Divine name אֱלֹהִים *'Elōhīm* ['God'] in this section, and of ה׳ אֱלֹהִים *YHWH 'Elōhīm* ['Lord God'] in the following section, is also discussed.

§ 8. *Special bibliography for this section.* Detailed lists of relevant literature up to 1934 (including part of that year) the reader will find in those portions of my book, *La Questione della Genesi* (Florence, 1934), that deal with our section (see pp. 36, 151–152, 257–276), and in my aforementioned essay in *Annuario di studi ebraici,* I (1934), pp. 9–47. Of subsequent publications the following may be noted:

Torczyner, *Lĕšonēnu,* vi (1934–5), pp. 6–10 [Hebrew]; Bertholet, 'Zum Schöpfungsbericht in Genesis I', *JBL,* liii (1934), pp. 237–240; Rost, 'Der Schöpfungsbericht der Priesterschrift', *Christentum und Wissenschaft,* x (1934), pp. 172–178; Sutcliffe, 'Primeval Chaos not Scriptural', *Miscellanea Biblica,* ii, Romae, 1934, pp. 203–215; Deimel, *'Enuma eliš' und Hexaëmeron,* Rom, 1934; Humbert, 'La rélation de Génèse 1 et du Psaume 104 avec la liturgie du Nouvel-An israëlite', *RHPhR,* xv (1935), pp. 1–27; Krappe, 'The Birth of Eve', *Occident and Orient* (Gaster Anniversary Volume), London, 1936, pp. 312–322; Dumaine, 'L'Heptaméron biblique', *RB,* xlvi (1937), pp. 161–181; Feigin, '*Yeṣīrath hā'iššā bammiqrā*'', SEPHER TUROV, Boston, 1938, pp. 213-222 [Hebrew]; May, 'The Creation of Light in Gen. 1, 3–5', *JBL,* lviii (1939), pp. 203–211; Schulz, 'Bemerkungen zu Gen. 2, 3', *BZ,* xxiv (1939), pp. 233–235; Eissfeldt, 'Das Chaos in der bibl. und in der phönizischen Kosmogonie', *Forschungen und Fortschritte,* xvi (1940), pp. 1–3; Jean, 'Les traditions suméro-babyloniennes sur la création d'après les découvertes et les études récentes', *NRTh,* lxvii (1940), pp. 169–186; Pfeiffer, *Introduction to the Old Testament,* New York–London, 1941, pp. 191–197; Heidel, *The Babylonian Genesis: the Story of the Creation,* Chicago, 1942.

On the various views advanced recently concerning the question of the *Sabbath,* see the survey of Kraeling, 'The Present Status of the Sabbath Question', *AJSL,* xlix (1932–3), pp. 218–228. For a detailed discussion of the sources relating to the Mesopotamian *Šabattu* or *Šapattu,* consult Landsberger, *Der kultische Kalender der Babylonier und Assyrer,* Erste Hälfte [Leipziger Semitistische Studien, vi. Band, Heft 1–2], Leipzig, 1917, pp. 92–100, 119–126, 131–136, and Langdon's work (which appeared after the above-mentioned article by Kraeling) entitled, *Babylonian Menologies and the Semitic Calendars,* London, 1935, pp. 73–96. Compare, further, the essay by Wolfe, which was likewise published after Kraeling's study, called 'New Moon and Sabbath', *JBL,* lix (1940), p. xiv. I do not know whether Wolfe's article was completed in subsequent numbers, as, on account of the war, the *JBL* was not received in Jerusalem during the last few years. See also Albright, *From Stone Age to Christianity,* Baltimore 1940, pp. 205, 329; Oppenheim, 'Assyriological Gleanings II', *BASOR,* 93 (February, 1944), pp. 16–17, No. vi; H. and J. Lewy, 'The Origin of the Week and the Oldest West Asiatic Calendar', *HUCA,* xvii (1943), pp. 1–152 c.

INTRODUCTORY VERSE

I. 1. *In the beginning God created / the heavens and the earth.*

RASHI [Rabbi Solomon son of Isaac] and Abraham ibn Ezra and many modern commentators are of the opinion that this verse is not an independent sentence but is subordinate to what follows and should be rendered either (1) 'At the beginning of the creation of the heavens and the earth, the earth was without form and void', or (2) 'At the beginning of the creation of the heavens and the earth, when the earth was without form and void . . . God said "Let there be light"', etc. The verb בָּרָא *bārā'* is used here, according to Rashi, as though it were the infinitive, בְּרֹא *b^{e}rō',* and so, in fact, the modern commentators referred to above vocalize the word. The arguments that have hitherto been advanced against both these interpretations are not conclusive; but a decisive objection can be raised on the basis of the syntactical construction of *v.* 2. If the first rendering were correct, the predicate in the second verse would precede the subject, *viz* וַתְּהִי הָאָרֶץ *watt^{e}hī hā'āreṣ* ['and was the earth'], or הָיְתָה הָאָרֶץ *hāy^{e}thā hā'āreṣ* ['was the earth']; cf. Jer. xxvi 1, *In the beginning of the reign of Jehoiakim . . .* CAME THIS WORD, etc.; so, too, *ibid.* xxvii 1, xxviii 1, and Hos. i 2: *When the Lord first spoke through Hosea,* SAID THE LORD *to Hosea.* Had the second translation been correct, the wording would have been:

וְהָאָרֶץ תֹּהוּ וָבֹהוּ *wehā'āreṣ tōhū wābhōhū* ['and the earth without form and void'], omitting הָיְתָה *hāyethā* ['was']; cf. i Sam. iii 2–4, where שֹׁכֵב *šōkhēbh* ['lying down'] occurs twice, but not הָיָה שֹׁכֵב *hāyā šōkhēbh* ['was lying down']. The construction וְהָאָרֶץ הָיְתָה תֹהוּ וָבֹהוּ *wehā'āreṣ hāyethā thōhū wābhōhū* proves (see on this below) that *v.* 2 begins a new subject. It follows, therefore, that the first verse is an independent sentence that constitutes a formal introduction to the entire section, and expresses at the outset, with majestic brevity, the main thought of the section: that in the beginning, that is, at the commencement of time, in the remotest past that the human mind can conceive, God created the heavens and the earth. How He created them will be related in detail further on. Following the principle that one should 'first state the general proposition and then specify the particulars', the Bible will now pass in review before us all the component parts of the universe, one by one, and tell us, concerning each one, that it was created by the word of God.

The heavens and the earth] It has been widely held that Scripture used this phrase because classical Hebrew had no special word for what we call today 'the universe'; hence it was necessary to employ a circumlocution of this kind. But this view is incorrect. The concept of the unity of the world was unknown among the Israelites till a late period, and then the appropriate term for it was immediately coined. The ancient Hebrew conceived God alone as a unity; what we designate 'the universe', they regarded as two separate entities: *the* HEAVENS *are the Lord's heavens, but the* EARTH *He has given to the sons of men* (Psa. cxv 16). By earth is to be understood here everything under the heavens, including the sea; cf. Psa. cxlviii 7: *Praise the Lord from the earth, you sea monsters and all deeps.*

FIRST PARAGRAPH

THE STORY OF THE FIRST DAY

2. *As for the earth, it was without form or life, / and darkness was upon the face of the Deep;*
but the Spirit of God / was hovering over the face of the waters.

3. *And God said,*
'Let there be light'; / and there was light.

4. *And God saw / that the light was good;*
and God separated / the light from the darkness.

5. *And God called the light Day, / and the darkness He called Night.*
And there was evening and there was morning, / one day.

2. *As for the earth, it was,* etc.] Whenever the subject comes before the predicate, as here, the intention of the Bible is to give emphasis to the subject and to tell us something new about it; see, for instance, iii 1: *Now the serpent was cunning,* etc. (the serpent had not previously been mentioned by name, but was merely implied in the general term *beast of the field* — ii 19, 20). But in most cases, including our own, the subject has already been mentioned earlier, and the verse comes to focus the reader's attention on it; *e.g.* iv 1, 18 (four times); vii 16, 19; x 8, 9, 13, 15, 24, 26; xi 12, 14; xiii 14; xviii 17, 18; xx 4; xxi 1; xxii 23; etc., etc. It is as though Scripture said: 'As for this subject, I have to tell you that this is what happened, or what he did, or what befel him'. Here, too, the meaning is: 'As for the earth alluded to in the first verse, I must tell you that at the beginning of its creation, it was without form or life,' etc. In *v.* 1 the heavens come first, because in referring to the two parts of the universe together, the more important part must be given precedence; but when the Bible proceeds to describe the work of creation in detail, the earth, which was created first, is mentioned first, whereas the heavens are dealt with in the second paragraph.

Without form or life [תֹהוּ וָבֹהוּ *tōhū wābhōhū*] / This poetic expression seems to have been used already in the ancient Hebrew epos, which I discussed in the Introduction, § 3; possibly it was to be found even in the still earlier poems of the Canaanites (Philo of Byblus mentions Βάαυ as a goddess of the primal night, the mother of the first mortals; but there is no connection apparently with the Mesopotamian goddess *Ba-u*). To ascertain the precise meaning of the phrase תֹהוּ וָבֹהוּ *tōhū wābhōhū,* one cannot rely, as the commentators usually do, only on the etymological signification of its two component words: תֹהוּ *tōhū,* 'wilderness'; בֹהוּ *bōhū,* 'emptiness'. In language, as in chemistry, a compound may be found to possess qualities absent from its constituent elements. For example, any one who does not know what 'broadcast' denotes, will not be able to guess the connotation of the word from its separate elements 'broad' and 'cast'. * For the same reason it is profitless to compare other passages in which either of the words תֹהוּ *tōhū* or בֹהוּ *bōhū* occurs; and even Jer. iv 23, where the complete phrase in the identical form is found (*I looked on the earth, and lo, it was* תֹהוּ *tōhū* [E.V. *waste*] *and* בֹהוּ *bōhū* [E.V. *void*], throws no light on the meaning, since it is only an allusion, without further explanation, to our own passage. The same applies to Isa. xxxiv 11: *And He shall stretch over it the line of* תֹהוּ *tōhū* [E.V. *confusion*] *and the plummet of* בֹהוּ *bōhū* [E.V. *chaos*].

The sense of the idiom can be determined only from the context, that is, from the continuation of the verse, which reads, *and darkness was upon the face of the deep,* as though the reader already knew that a 'deep' [תְּהוֹם *tehōm*] existed in the world, despite the fact that it had not yet been mentioned in our section. From this we may infer that the notion of the *deep* was subsumed, according to the conception of the ancient Israelites, in that of תֹהוּ וָבֹהוּ *tōhū wābhōhū.* Now the Deep is to be identified with the World-Ocean, as we shall see later, and hence it was possible for the sentence to conclude with the words, *upon the face of the waters,* although no mention had yet been made of the waters.

There is something else, too, that we learn from the phrasing of the verse. Since we are told that the darkness, which was spread over everything, was *upon the face of the deep,* it follows that the

* In the original Hebrew the example is קוֹלְנוֹעַ *qōlnōaʿ* ['a sound film']; the etymological sense of the stems, קוֹל *qōl* ['voice'] and נוֹעַ *nōaʿ* [moving'], would not convey to the uninitiated the meaning of the compound word.

water of the deep formed the uppermost layer, which was in direct contact with the surrounding darkness; this agrees with the specific statement in Psa. civ 6: *Thou didst cover it* [mas.] *with the deep as with a garment* (the Targum and other ancient versions read, *Thou didst cover her,* that is, Thou didst cover the earth with the waters of the deep); *the waters stood above the mountains.* Just as the potter, when he wishes to fashion a beautiful vessel, takes first of all a lump of clay, and places it upon his wheel in order to mould it according to his wish, so the Creator first prepared for Himself the raw material of the universe with a view to giving it afterwards order and life. In this chaos of unformed matter, the heaviest materials were naturally at the bottom, and the waters, which were the lightest, floated on top. This apart, the whole material was an undifferentiated, unorganized, confused and lifeless agglomeration. It is this terrestrial state that is called תֹהוּ וָבֹהוּ *tōhū* and *bōhū.*

As for the earth, it was tōhū and bōhū, that is to say, the unformed material from which the earth was to be fashioned was at the beginning of its creation in a state of *tōhū* and *bōhū,* to wit, water above and solid matter beneath, and the whole a chaotic mass, without order or life.

And darkness was upon the face of the deep] Until the light was created, the unformed matter was enveloped in utter darkness.

The word תְּהוֹם *tehōm,* rendered 'deep', undoubtedly belonged to the poetic tradition of antiquity, and consequently it is used without the definite article, which is rarely found in Biblical verse and is entirely wanting in Canaanite poetry. Linguistically, the word corresponds precisely to the Arabic word *Tihāmat,* تهامة which denotes the low-lying Arabian littoral (the Arabic تهم *tahmun* generally signifies, 'land sloping towards the sea' [see G. W. Freytag, *Lexicon Arabico-Latinum,* s.v.]), and to the Akkadian word *Tiamat,* the name of the goddess of the primeval World-Ocean, who had existed from time immemorial and was the mighty foe of the Creative God. Although the equivalent noun in Hebrew lacks the feminine termination ־ת *-t,* it is nevertheless treated as a feminine substantive.

In the Bible, the word occurs a number of times as a synonym for the *sea.* But in the ancient Israelite poetry, to which the prophets and the Biblical poets allude on occasion (see above, Introduction,

§ 3), the Deep was still depicted as a creature endowed with its own volition, which rebelled against God and was ultimately subdued by the Divine might (see, for instance, Isa. li 9–10: *Awake, awake, put on strength, O arm of the Lord; awake, as in days of old, the generations of long ago. Was it not Thou that didst cut Rahab in pieces, that didst pierce the dragon? Was it not Thou that didst dry up the sea, the waters of the great* DEEP . . .?).

The Torah, however, refrained from accepting any part of this tradition. In the Pentateuch, תְּהוֹם *tehōm* denotes simply the primeval World-Ocean — a purely physical concept. It is matter and has no personality or autonomy; it had not existed from time immemorial but was created by the will of God, and was ready to receive whatever form its Maker would be pleased to fashion for it.

BUT THE SPIRIT [וְרוּחַ *werūaḥ*] *of God was* HOVERING [מְרַחֶפֶת *meraḥepheth*] *over the face of the waters*]. The *Wāw* [literally, 'and'] of וְרוּחַ *werūaḥ* ['wind, spirit'] has an adversative sense: 'Although the earth was without form or life, and all was steeped in darkness, yet above the unformed matter hovered the רוּחַ *rūaḥ* of God, the source of light and life'. According to the Talmudic interpretation (Ḥagiga 12a), the word רוּחַ *rūaḥ* denotes here an actual wind, moving air — an entity created by God on the first day. The majority of present-day commentators likewise understand the word to signify a powerful wind that came to separate the upper waters from the lower waters, or the lower waters from the dry land. But this does not appear to accord with the real meaning of the verse. These tasks of separation were to be executed only on the second and the third day, and they were to be performed solely by the word of God not with the help of any additional agency. Furthermore, neither the verb מְרַחֶפֶת *meraḥepheth* nor the expression *over the face of the waters* fits this explanation. The meaning of רוּחַ אֱלֹהִים *rūaḥ 'Elōhīm* in our verse is the same as that of רוּחַ אֵל *rūaḥ 'El* ['Spirit of God'] in Job xxxiii 4: *The spirit of God has made me, and the breath of the Almighty gives me life.*

מְרַחֶפֶת *meraḥepheth.* Many modern exegetes render the word, on the basis of one of the senses of the root in Syriac, 'brooding' (like a bird brooding over its eggs) and see here a reference to the idea of the World-Egg, which is found in the cosmogonies of several peoples, including the Canaanites. The myth tells of an egg that existed since the days of creation, and a power from on high came and brooded over it, and from it the world was hatched. But the expression used in the Bible is *over the face of the waters,* and the waters of the deep are not an egg or anything resembling one.

It should also be noted that the verb רחף *rāḥaph* never has the connotation of 'brooding' in Hebrew, and that even in Syriac this is only a secondary meaning of the word, flowing from its primary signification, 'to fly to and fro, flutter', the sense in which it is used in Deut. xxxii 11: *Like an eagle that stirs up its nest, that* FLUTTERS *over its young.* Likewise in the Ugaritic writings, the meaning of the stem *rḫp* is 'to flutter' ('The Epic of Dan'el', Tablet I, line 32; *ibid.,* Tablet III, col. i, lines 20–21, 31–32). Other mythological explanations that have recently been suggested are also incompatible with the wording of our verse, the sense of which, it seems, corresponds exactly to the meaning of the root רחף *rāḥaph* in Deut. xxxii 11, to wit, that just as the young eaglets, which are not yet capable of fending for themselves, are unable by their own efforts to subsist and grow strong and become fully-grown eagles, and only the care of their parents, who hover over them, enables them to survive and develop, so, too, in the case of the earth, which was still an unformed, lifeless mass, the paternal care of the Divine Spirit, which hovered over it, assured its future evolution and life.

Over the face of the waters — that is, the waters of the deep, which, as stated, covered everything. The phrase *over the face of the waters* at the end of the second half of the verse corresponds to the concluding words of the first half, *upon the face of the deep.* Both of these expressions recur in Biblical poetry and precisely in those passages that reflect the poetic tradition concerning the waters of the primordial deep (see below, on *v.* 9); cf. Prov. viii 27, Job xxvi 10.

3. *And God said, 'Let there be light'*] 'It is like the case of a king who wishes to build a palace, but the site was in darkness. What did he do? He kindled lamps and torches to see where to lay the foundations' (Bereshith Rabba iii 1; for the variant readings consult Theodor's edition). Adapting the parable to our interpretation of *v.* 2, we might say: It is like the case of a man who came to arrange various articles that were lying in confusion in a dark room. What does he do first of all? He kindles lamps in the room and so illumines the chamber and everything in it.

And there was light] It is a basic rule of style in ancient epic poetry that after citing the words of the command or charge given by any one, the poet *repeats* the *ipsissima verba* of the directive when relating that it had been fulfilled. In the Introduction to this section (§ 6, p. 16), I have indicated how this literary convention, subject to certain modifications, continues in the prose style of Bible narrative. In the present verse, this formal repetition assumes its tersest form (fiat: *'Let there be light';* execution: *and there was light*) to show the precision and celerity with which the injunction was carried out: as He commanded, and as soon as He commanded.

The rabbinic statement that this light was hidden away for the benefit of the saints in the world to come and the views expressed in recent publications on the bearing of our verse on eschatological speculation (see especially the study by May mentioned in the bibliography) do not accord with the actual meaning of the verse.

The existence of light even before the creation of the luminaries does not, of course, present any difficulty, for we are all familiar with light that does not emanate from the heavenly bodies, e.g. lightning. The real problem is how there could be a *day* when there was no *sun.* On this question see the notes to verses 14–15.

4. *And God saw that the light was good*] An optimistic formula that occurs, as we have noted, seven times in the section: all that God has made is good. This verse, unlike the corresponding verses, specifies the thing that is good — the *light* — to prevent the misconception that the darkness is also good. It is the light that God created; the darkness is only the absence of light, and therefore is not good (the declaration, *I form light and create darkness,* in Isa. xlv 7, is directed against the dualistic doctrine of the Persians).

And God separated the light from the darkness] It was not the Creator's intention that there should be perpetual light and no darkness at all, but that the light and the darkness should operate consecutively for given periods and in unchanging order. Consequently, God divided the one from the other, that is, He separated their respective spheres of activity.

5. *And God called the light Day,* etc.] According to the conception current in the ancient East, the name of a thing was to be identified with its essential nature and existence; hence to name a thing meant to bring it into being. The Babylonian account of

creation begins as follows: 'Ere the heavens above were named, or the foundation below was given an appellation', that is, before the creation of heaven and earth (I shall explain elsewhere my reason for translating the word *ammatu* in the original by 'foundation'). Many commentators detect a similar concept in our verse. But this interpretation is difficult, since it has already been stated earlier that the darkness and the light were in existence before they were given names. It is more correct to suppose that the intention here, in conformity with the general thought of the section (see the beginning of my Introduction), is to explain that the two divisions of time known to us as Day and Night are precisely the same as those that God established at the time of creation, the *light* being the Day, and the *darkness* the Night. The same applies to the naming of the *heavens* and the *earth* and the *seas* referred to in *v.* 8 and *v.* 10. The three parts of the universe that we designate by these names are precisely those that God organized in the period of creation: the firmament that He made is none other than the *heavens* that we know; the pool into which the waters were gathered is our *sea;* and the dry land that appeared then is our *earth.*

And the darkness He called Night] It is a fundamental rule of Biblical narrative style that verbs describing acts that took place in sequence should head their respective clauses, and take the form of the *imperfect* with consecutive *Wāw,* thus: וַיֹּאמֶר *wayyō'mer* ['and... said'], וַיְהִי *way^{e}hī* ['and there was'], וַיִּקְרָא *wayyiqrā'* ['and...called'] and so forth. But when the same verb occurs twice in two consecutive clauses, then the second verb usually occupies the second or third place in the sentence and is in the *perfect,* as in the present case (see my remarks on this subject in my book *The Documentary Hypothesis,* English translation, pp. 91–92, where many instances are cited). Three consecutive examples are found in the story of Cain and Abel (iv 2–5): וַיְהִי *way^{e}hī* ['and (Abel) was'] . . . הָיָה *hāyā* ['(Cain) was']; וַיָּבֵא *wayyābhē'* ['and (Cain) brought'] . . . הֵבִיא *hēbhī'* ['(Abel) brought']; וַיִּשַׁע *wayyiša',* ['and (God) turned'] . . . שָׁעָה *šā'ā* ['He turned']. At the end of our verse, the brevity of the clauses and the tendency to stress the parallelism resulted in the verbs appearing twice in the form required by the general rule [to wit, that the past tense be expressed by the imperfect with consecutive *Wāw*], וַיְהִי *way^{e}hī* ['and there was'] . . . וַיְהִי *way^{e}hī.*

And there was evening and there was morning, one day] When day-time had passed, the period allotted to darkness returned (and there was evening), and when night-time came to an end, the light held sway a second time (and there was morning), and this completed the first calendar day (one day), which had begun *with the creation of light.*

This method of reckoning the day [i.e. a day and a night] from sunrise appears to be at variance with the accepted Israelite practice of connecting the day-time with the preceding night, that is, the custom of regarding sunset as the starting-point of the day. In order to remove this inconsistency, Jewish exegetes, both medieval and modern (among the latter, Hoffman and Jacob), sought to place forced and improbable interpretations on the words, *and there was evening and there was morning.* Only a few, like Rashbam [Rabbi Samuel son of Meir], gave the correct explanation of the verse, which Ibn Ezra, nevertheless, endeavoured to refute by composing his *Sabbath Letter.*

Present-day scholars are of the opinion either that our section reflects an old usage that subsequently fell into desuetude (so, for instance, Dillmann and Holzinger), or that the two methods of reckoning the day were used concurrently in different circles (so, for example, Gunkel and, among Jewish exegetes, Bornstein, see הַתְּקוּפָה *Hatkufa,* vi, pp. 302–311). But the verse remains difficult, even for those who accept the documentary hypothesis, since the account of creation and the laws of the Pentateuch are attributed by them to P [Priestly Code], and it is unthinkable that this source should mention at the beginning a detail that conflicts with the statutes recorded in subsequent sections of the document.

It would appear, therefore, that the solution to the problem must be sought in another direction. An examination of the narrative passages of the Bible makes it evident that whenever clear reference is made to the relationship between a given day and the next, it is precisely sunrise that is accounted the beginning of the second day. For example: *They made their father drink wine that night . . . and* ON THE NEXT DAY, etc. (xix 33–34). Similarly: *When he arose early* NEXT MORNING (Jud. vi 38); *and* ON THE MORROW *the people rose early* (ibid. xxi 4); *If you do not save your life tonight,* TOMORROW *you will be killed.* (I Sam. xix 11); *and* TOMORROW *you and your sons shall be with me* (ibid. xxviii 19). Consonant with this tradition is the use of the expressions: הַיּוֹם *hayyōm* ['the day' = *today*], הַלַּיְלָה *hallaylā* ['the night' = *tonight*], אֶמֶשׁ *'emeš* ['yesterday' = *last night*].

Nor is this all. If we consider the Scriptural sections dealing with the ritual laws, particularly those that prescribe that the observance of Israel's holy days must begin in the evening, we see clearly that these passages corroborate, in their method of reckoning the dates, the evidence of the narrative portions. In Exod. xii 18, it is stated: *In the first month, on the* FOURTEENTH *day of the month at evening, you shall eat unleavened bread.* It is on the evening preceding the fifteenth day that the obligation of eating unleavened bread comes into force, yet that evening is referred to as the *fourteenth.* So, too, in Lev. xxiii 32, with regard to the Day of Atonement, it is enjoined: *and you shall afflict yourselves on the* NINTH *day of the month beginning at evening, from evening to evening shall you keep your Sabbath;* thus the evening before the tenth is called *the ninth of the month.*

It will thus be seen that throughout the Bible there obtains only one system of *computing time*: the day is considered to begin in the morning; but in regard to the festivals and appointed times, the Torah ordains that they shall be observed also on the night of the *preceding day.* This point is explicitly emphasized whenever a certain precept has to be observed particularly at *night,* like the eating of unleavened bread on the night of Passover and fasting on the evening of the Day of Atonement. In the case of the Sabbath and the other festival days, however, there was no need to *stress* that work was prohibited on the night preceding, since agricultural tasks (and it is specifically these that the Torah has in mind) are performed only by day. There is no discrepancy, therefore, in our verse at all.

The underlying reason of the particular rule applying to the incidence of festivals and appointed times may be explained thus: the method of counting the day from the evening, which is customary among nomads, was the older usage; but when in civil life a new system came into force, which regarded sunrise as the commencement of the day in accordance with the conditions prevailing in the Land of Canaan, the change did not affect the religious tradition, which is by nature conservative, and just as of old the holy days began at evening, so the custom remained and was embodied in the laws of the Bible. The sacrificial regulations, which connect the night with the preceding day, offer no difficulty to our hypothesis. On the contrary, they tally with our explanation, for all the laws relating to the sacrifices were framed to accord specifically with the conditions obtaining in the Land of Canaan.

At a later period, when the whole of Jewish life was concentrated in the sphere of religion, the mode of reckoning appertaining to the Sabbath and festivals once again became norm for civil affairs, too. Nevertheless, traces of the former civil practice are still to be discerned in such Talmudic expressions as 'the night after the thirteenth which is the evening preceding the fourteenth' (B. Berakhoth 4a), and in some penitential hymns for the evening of the Day of Atonement, which refer to the Day of Atonement as *tomorrow* (e.g. the hymn יִרְצֶה עַם אֶבְיוֹן *Yirṣe ʿam ʾebhyōn* — 'May He regard the needy people with favour' by Isaac ibn Giʾat).

One Day] The use here of the *cardinal* instead of the *ordinal* number, as for the other days, is to be explained, with Naḥmanides [Rabbi Moses son of Naḥman], as follows: '*First* implies precedence over another in number or grading, when both are in existence', but in our case there was only *one day,* for the second had not yet been created. In the same way we may explain expressions like בְּאֶחָד לַחֹדֶשׁ *beʾeḥādh laḥōdheš* [literally, 'on one of the month', that is, on the first of the month] and בְּאֶחָד בְּשַׁבָּת *beʾeḥādh bešabbāth* ['on one of the week', that is, on the first day of the week]; see Gesenius — Buhl, *Hebr. und aram. Handwörterbuch über das A T,* s.v. אֶחָד *ʾeḥādh.* But verses like ii 11, *The name of the first* [literally, 'one'] *is Pishon,* compel us to extend the rule of Naḥmanides and to state that even when all the objects enumerated together exist at the same time, we are able, momentarily, to pay attention only to the first of them, and must therefore designate it *one.*

SECOND PARAGRAPH

THE STORY OF THE SECOND DAY

6. *And God said,*
'Let there be a firmament / in the midst of the waters,
and let it serve as a means of separating / the waters from the waters.'

7. *And God made the firmament / and separated*
the waters / which were under the firmament
from the waters / which were above the firmament.
And it was so.

8. *And God called / the firmament Heaven.*
And there was evening and there was morning, / a second day.

6. *Let there be a firmament in the midst of the waters*] In the midst of the waters of the deep, which constituted the upper stratum of the original amorphous matter, there was to be formed a *firmament* [רָקִיעַ *rāqīaʿ*]. The root of the word is the same as that of וַיְרַקְּעוּ *wayeraqqeʿū* ['and they did hammer out'] in Exod. xxxix 3: *And they did hammer out gold leaf;* the term signifies a kind of horizontal area, extending through the very heart of the mass of water and cleaving it into two layers, one above the other — the upper and lower layers of water.

How the space between heaven and earth was formed we are not told here explicitly; nor are the attempts of the commentators to elucidate the matter satisfactory (see my remarks on this subject in my aforementioned article in *Annuario,* p. 24, note 1). To me it seems that the sense of the passage is to be explained in the light of the statement in *v.* 8: *And God called the firmament Heaven,* that is, this firmament is none other than what we designate *heaven.* From this we may infer that immediately after its formation, the firmament occupied of its own accord the place appointed for it by the will of God, which is the site of the heavens as we know it. Thus as soon as the firmament was established in the midst of the layer of water, it began to rise in the middle, arching like a vault, and in the course of its upward expansion it lifted at the same time the upper waters resting on top of it. This marked a considerable advance in the marshalling of the components of the universe.

Above now stands the vault of heaven surmounted by the upper waters; beneath stretches the expanse of lower waters, that is, the waters of the vast sea, which still covers all the heavy, solid matter below. The universe is beginning to take shape.

When we consider how the Mesopotamian mythology portrays the making of heaven and earth, we cannot but realize the enormous difference, despite a few points of resemblance, between this creation story and that of the Bible, nor can we fail to appreciate the originality of the Torah account. The former relates that after the god Marduk (or a different deity according to other versions) had vanquished Tiamat, the goddess of the world-ocean, depicted as a great and mighty sea-monster, as well as the other monsters and monstrosities that she had created to aid her in her combat, and after he had slain his chief enemy with his weapons, he cut her carcass horizontally, dividing it into two halves, which lay one on top of the other, and out of the upper half he formed the heavens and of the lower half he made the earth (which includes, of course, the sea, the 'Deep'). Here is a quotation from the Babylonian account of creation (Tablet iv, 137–140):

He split her like a fish into two parts;
The one half of her he set up and laid therewith the beams of the heavens (cf. Psa. civ 3 WHO HAST LAID THE BEAMS *of Thy chambers on the waters*).
He pulled down a bar and stationed a watch,
He enjoined them not to let her waters go forth.

The last two lines ('He pulled down a bar', etc.) do not refer to the heavens, as they are usually understood, but apply to the earth and the sea. In the Greek summary of the myth by the Babylonian priest Berossus, it is clearly stated that the god Bel, that is, Marduk, sliced the body of Thamte (Tiamat, Tâmtu) into two, and of the one half he formed the *earth* and of the other half the *heavens*. With the parallel traditions in the Canaanite and the ancient Israelite poetry, I shall deal in my annotations below, on *v.* 9. Here it will suffice to note the opposition of the Torah to the entire mythological account. It is true that in the Pentateuch, too, reference is made to the division of the primeval world-ocean into two halves, situated one above the other, but the entire mythological picture is completely erased. Here we have neither war nor weapons; a body is not carved up, nor are its segments used for construction; a simple process of physical unfoldment takes the place of the mythical train of events described in the pagan legends.

7. *And God made the firmament,* etc.] Here, too, as in verse 3, the words of the Divine fiat are repeated in the announcement that it had been executed. But in the present case, since the theme is much more comprehensive than that of the two short words [יְהִי אוֹר *yᵉhī 'ōr,* 'Let there be light'] in *v.* 3, modifications have been introduced in accordance with the principle described above in the Introduction § 6, p. 16f., and the verbal changes serve to explain the subject more clearly. The phrase, *separating the waters from the waters,* of the preceding verse is here elucidated thus: *separated the waters which were under the firmament from the waters which were above the firmament.*

On the use of the verb *made,* see below on ii 3.

And separated] The subject is God and not, as some interpret, the firmament; compare *v.* 4: *and* GOD *separated the light from the darkness.* Furthermore, in *v.* 6 it is not written: Let there be a firmament in the midst of the waters, and *let it separate* [וְיַבְדֵּל *wᵉyabhdēl*] the waters from the waters; the text is: וִיהִי מַבְדִּיל *wīhī mabhdīl* . . . — 'and let it be a *separator',* etc., that is, and let it be the means that I shall use for the purpose of separating the waters from the waters.

And it was so] At first sight this clause seems redundant, for we have already been told that *God made the firmament,* etc. Hence some modern commentators transfer the words, in agreement with the Septuagint, to the end of *v.* 6. Others, on the contrary, are of the opinion that the sentence, *And God made,* etc., is a later interpolation and that originally the text had only: *And it was so.*

But if we examine the two verses carefully, we shall see that both are necessary. The reiteration of the words of the Divine utterance is required, as previously stated, by the rules of Biblical narrative style; moreover, the separation mentioned here as a work of God provides a fitting parallel to the separation described in *v.* 3 — also as a work of God. As for the expression *and it was so,* it is needed here, but not in *v.* 3, because the two separations differed from each other: the first was *temporal* and was due to recur at regular intervals; the second was *spatial* and was destined to remain unchanged for ever (see Naḥmanides *ad loc.*). This then is the meaning of the expression *and it was* SO [כֵּן *kēn*] throughout the section: *and it was* FIRM [which is the root signification of כֵּן *kēn*], like an established thing; so it came to pass, and so it has remained for all time.

8. *And God called the firmament Heaven*] See the notes to *vv.* 5-6. After the word *Heaven,* the Septuagint reads: *And God saw that it was good,* and many modern scholars consider this reading to be correct, since this formula is found in the account of each of the other days. But, as we have explained earlier, the repetitions that occur in Biblical narrative prose are characterised, as a rule, by verbal changes, and we must not expect the word-for-word reiteration of an unvarying formula on every occasion. In so far as our verse is concerned, the Rabbinic Sages already (Bereshith Rabba iv 8, according to one of the opinions cited) noted correctly — and their view is shared by some modern exegetes (e.g. Gunkel and Budde) — that the words *it was good* were not appropriate at this stage, in as much as the work of the water had not yet been completed. The situation was not yet *good;* for had it been good, there would have been no necessity for another separation on the third day. For the same reason, it is not stated here that God gave a name to the sea just as He had named the heavens. For the lower waters had not yet reached their final distribution, and were still covering everything beneath the heavens. The Greek translator has added at this point the usual formula ['that it is good'] for the sake of mechanical uniformity; this is typical of his method throughout the section.

And there was evening and there was morning, a second day] A fitting parallel to the concluding sentence of the preceding paragraph and of the subsequent paragraphs.

THIRD PARAGRAPH

THE STORY OF THE THIRD DAY

9. *And God said,*
'Let the waters be gathered together / under the heavens
into one place, / and let the dry land appear.'
And it was so.

10. *And God called the dry land Earth, / and the waters that were gathered together He called Seas.*
And God saw that it was good.

11. *And God said,*
'Let the earth put forth vegetation, / plants yielding seed,
[and] fruit trees bearing fruit each according to its kind, / in which is their seed, upon the earth.'
And it was so.

12. *And the earth brought forth vegetation, / plants yielding seed according to their own kinds,*
and trees bearing fruit / in which is their seed, each according to its kind.
And God saw that it was good.

13. *And there was evening and there was morning, / a third day.*

9. *Let the waters be gathered together,* etc.] The waters, which were still covering everything under the heavens, were to be concentrated in one place, and, as a result, the solid matter hidden beneath them would be revealed in the remaining areas.

Into one PLACE [מָקוֹם *māqōm*] / The Septuagint reads: *into one* POOL [συναγωγή = מִקְוֶה *mikwe,* literally, 'gathering'], and the vast majority of modern commentators prefer this reading. But it is hard to accept it as correct, for two reasons: (a) there was no pool of water till the waters had been gathered together; (b) the number *one* can readily be understood in connection with *place* — that is, *one place* in contradistinction to *every place,* which the waters had previously occupied — but it is not appropriate to *pool,* for there were no other pools in existence. Possibly Scripture intended a play on the words מָקוֹם *māqōm,* 'place' [in this verse] and מִקְוֶה *miqwe,* 'pool' (in *v.* 10), that is, the *place* became a *pool.*

And it was so] As we have explained in our note on *v.* 7, the meaning is: according to the word of God so it was, and so the situation remained for ever.

Also this verse, which speaks of the assignment of a fixed place for the waters of the sea, should be studied against the background of the myths current in the Orient, as well as, needless to say, the ancient epic poems of the Israelites. The peoples of the East used to tell many stories about the battle waged by one of the great gods against the deity of the sea. It was indicated above, on *v.* 6, that the Mesopotamian mythology described in detail the combat of the creative god against Tiamat and his ultimate victory over her; we quoted there the verses from the Babylonian account of creation that relate how Marduk, after his victory,

> '. . . pulled down a bar and stationed a watch;
> He enjoined them not to let the waters (of Tiamat) go forth.'

and we stated that these lines refer only to the lower waters.

Similar myths were known to the Canaanites. In one of the Ugaritic texts — Tablet III AB (Baal V in Ginsberg's Hebrew edition) — the story of Baal's fight with the lord of the sea is narrated. But it is impossible to say with certainty whether it also made mention of the limitation of the area to be occupied by the sea, because the tablet is damaged and only a fragment of it remains. But if we may assume the word *l'ašṣ'i,* found in one of the incomplete lines of the tablet (line 2), to be composed of the negative *l–* and of some form of the verb *yṣ'* in the *Šaph'ēl* conjugation (which would make it an exact parallel to the expression *la šu–ṣa–a* in the stanza of the Babylonian creation-story quoted above), the term may be presumed to refer to the confinement of the sea.

As for the Israelites, it is clear from many allusions in the Bible, as well as from a number of legends in rabbinic literature, that there had existed among them an ancient poetic tradition that told of *Rahab,* the lord of the sea, who opposed the will of God and would not confine his waters within given limits, until the Holy One, blessed be He, subdued him and slew him, and fixed a boundary for the waters of the sea that they should never be able to pass. Here there is no trace of war between the gods as related by the gentile myths, but only the revolt of one of the creatures against his Creator; the tradition has acquired an aspect more in keeping with the ethos of the people of Israel.

The question of the existence of Israelite epic poetry in general and of this poem on the revolt of the sea in particular, I have discussed at length in my aforementioned Hebrew essay in K^{e}*neseth*. I do not propose to repeat here the proofs that I advanced in the article, or the detailed reconstruction of the poem from the sources at our disposal that I attempted there; I shall merely cite a few examples from the Bible and from rabbinic dicta in which the rebellion of the sea is reflected, quoting particularly those passages that allude to the setting of bounds for the waters of the sea.

(1) Examples from the Bible:

Isa. li 9–10: *Awake, awake, put on strength, O arm of the Lord; awake as in days of old, the generations of long ago. Was it not Thou that didst cut Rahab in pieces, that didst pierce the dragon? Was it not Thou that didst dry up the sea, the waters of the great deep . . . ?*

Jer. v 22: . . . *I placed the sand as the bound for the sea, a perpetual barrier which it cannot pass; though the waves toss, they cannot prevail, though they roar, they cannot pass over it.*

Psa. lxxiv 13: *Thou didst divide the sea by Thy might; Thou didst break the heads of the dragons on the waters,* etc..

Ibid. lxxxix 10 (Hebrew, *v.* 11): *Thou didst crush Rahab like a carcass, Thou didst scatter Thy enemies with Thy mighty arm.*

Ibid. civ 7–9: *At Thy rebuke they* (the waters of the Deep) *fled: at the sound of Thy thunder they took to flight. The mountains rose, the valleys sank down to the place which Thou didst appoint for them. Thou didst set a bound which they should not pass, so that they might not again cover the earth.*

Prov. viii 27–29: *When He established the Heavens, I was there, when He drew a circle on the face of the deep . . . when He assigned to the sea its limit, so that the waters might not transgress His command.*

Job vii 12: *Am I the sea, or a sea monster, that Thou settest a guard over me?* (cf. *He stationed a watch* in the Babylonian epic quoted above).

Ibid. ix 13: *God will not turn back His anger; beneath Him bowed the helpers of Rahab.*

Ibid. xxvi 10–12: *He described a circle upon the face of the waters at the boundary between light and darkness . . . By His power He stilled the sea; by His understanding He smote Rahab.*

Ibid. xxxviii 8–10: *Or who shut in the sea with doors, when it burst forth from the womb; when I made clouds its garment, and thick darkness its swaddling band, and prescribed bounds for it, and set bars and doors* (cf. *He pulled down a bar* in the Babylonian epic cited above), *and said, 'Thus far shall you come, and no farther, and here shall your proud waves be stayed'?*

Similar references to the subjugation of the sea are to be found in many other verses, which need not be quoted here.

(2) Examples from rabbinic literature:

B. Ḥagiga 12a. 'Resh Lakish said: When the Holy One, blessed be He, created the sea it continued to expand until the Holy One, blessed be He, rebuked it and caused it to dry up.'

B. Baba Bathra 74b: 'R. Judah said in the name of Rab: When the Holy One, blessed be He, desired to create the world, He said to the lord of the sea: "Open thy mouth and swallow up all the waters of the world". The latter answered: "Sovereign of the universe, I have enough with my own!" Thereupon God instantly trod him down and slew him, as it is said: *By this power He stamped down* [E. V. 'stilled'] *the sea; by His understanding He smote Rahab.* R. Isaac said: From this you may infer that the lord of the sea is called Rahab.'

Pirke Rabbi Eliezer, V: 'Thereupon the waters immediately became turbulent and rose up to cover the earth as in the beginning, until the Holy One, blessed be He, rebuked them and subdued them, placing them under the soles of his feet; and He measured them with His palm so as not to augment or diminish them, and He made the sand the boundary of the sea, like a man who makes a fence for his vineyard; and when they [the waters] rise up and see the sand before them, they turn back, as it is said: *Do you not fear Me? says the Lord; do you not tremble before Me? I placed the sand as the bound for the sea,* etc. (Jer. v 22).

Many more rabbinic dicta of the same *genre* occur in Talmudic and Midrashic literature and also in the works of the Cabbala, but there is no deed to prolong the series of quotations. Any one who wishes to study the whole of the relevant material in Hebrew literature will find the passages listed in Ginzberg's work, *The Legends of the Jews,* v, pp. 17–18, 26–27, notes 50–53, 71–73.

From our investigations so far we may draw the following conclusions: (a) that the prophets and Biblical poets were accustomed to employ allusions to the ancient epic concerning the revolt of the sea as poetic similes and figures of speech (compare above, Introduction, § 3); (b) that the Rabbis included in their tradition the myth of the sea's rebellion, which the memory of the people continued to keep alive even after the ancient epic had, in the course of time, become lost; and they did not feel any misgivings about those elements in it that resembled the heathen mythology, since in their day paganism was no longer a danger to Judaism. But the Torah, which uses a simple prose style as the vehicle of its teachings, without undue embellishment of poetic metaphors and figures of speech, not only meticulously avoided making any use whatsoever of this legendary poetic material, which, if embodied in a book of prose, might have been understood literally by the reader, but it even voiced a kind of *protest* against these myths whose pagan origin was still discernible, and more particularly against the concepts of the heathens themselves (Introduction, § 4). In the verse, *And God said, 'Let the waters be gathered together',* etc., the underlying thought of the Torah is: Far be it from you to think, as do the Gentiles, that the sea is endowed with an autonomous divine power that fought, as it were, against the Creator of the universe; and far be it also from you to imagine, as the Israelite poets relate, that the sea refused to do the will of its Maker, and that He was compelled to subdue it and force it to obey. It is true that the Torah, too, records that God assigned a fixed place for the waters of the sea, but this was not done by suppressing the will of the sea, which sought to rebel against God, Heaven forfend. God said: *'Let the waters be gathered together',* and forthwith *it was so.*

10. *And God called the dry land Earth*] Since the earth then received the form that it has retained to this day, it became entitled to the name by which it is still called today. See above, on *v.* 5.

And the waters that were gathered together He called Seas] The sea likewise acquired at that time the aspect with which we are familiar; hence God gave it the name appropriate to it. *And He called* [וַיִּקְרָא *wayyiqrā'*, imperfect with *Wāw* consecutive] — *He called* [קָרָא *qārā'*, perfect]; see above, on *v.* 5.

Seas. Poetic plural; cf. xlix 13: *Zebulun shall dwell at the shore of the* SEAS [E.V. *sea*]; Jud. v 17: *Asher sat still at the coast of the* SEAS [E.V. *sea*]. It may be that a play upon words is also intended here, *viz* מַיִם *mayim* ['waters'] — יַמִּים *yammīm* ['seas'].

And God saw that it was good] Now that the work of the water was completed and the world had assumed its proper tripartite form of Heaven, Earth and Sea, it is possible to declare, *that it was good.*

11. *And God said, 'Let the earth put forth vegetation',* etc.] On the selfsame day, as soon as the inanimate matter, which serves as a foundation for plant-life, had been set in order, there were created, without delay, the various kinds of vegetation. Similarly on the sixth day: immediately after the formation of vegetable and animal life, which, in turn, are the basis of human life — on the same day — man was created.

Let the earth put forth VEGETATION [דֶּשֶׁא *deše'*], PLANTS [עֵשֶׂב *'ēśebh*] *yielding seed, fruit trees,* etc.] The exact nature of this classification of the various species of plants has proved a difficult exegetical problem, and many different explanations have been offered (I have discussed them in detail in *Questione,* pp. 261–262). The most likely interpretation appears to be that the classification here is not threefold — דֶּשֶׁא *deše'* [=grass], עֵשֶׂב *'ēśebh* [=herbs] and עֵץ *'ēṣ* [=trees] — but only twofold. The noun דֶּשֶׁא *deše'* and the verb תַּדְשֵׁא *tadhšē',* derived from it, refer to vegetation generally, and the clause תַּדְשֵׁא הָאָרֶץ דֶּשֶׁא *tadhšē' hā'āreṣ deše'* ['Let the earth put forth vegetation'] means: Let the earth be covered with a fresh green mantle of verdure. Thereafter two categories of vegetation are distinguished: עֵשֶׂב *'ēśebh* ['plants'] and עֵץ *'ēṣ* ['trees']. The correctness of this interpretation is attested by the fact that in *vv.* 29–30 only the two categories, *plants* and *trees,* are mentioned.

Fruit trees include shade-trees, for these, too, bear fruit, although it is not edible.

Each according to its kind [לְמִינוֹ *lemīnō*] / Here the expression refers to the trees alone, but in *v.* 12 (there the form is לְמִינֵהוּ *lemīnēhū*) it is applied to *the plants* as well; see Rashi *ad loc.*

Yielding seed ... in which is their seed, upon the earth] The

Torah emphasizes and re-emphasizes, both here and in the next verse, and again in *v.* 29, the matter of the seed and the producing of seed (in these three verses the stem זרע *zr'* ['seed, to yield seed'] occurs no less than ten times), as though it wished to draw the reader's attention to the fact that the plants that were created on the third day were capable of reproducing themselves after their likeness by means of the seed. Undoubtedly there is a definite purpose in all this; what this purpose is we shall see further on (on ii 5).

Upon the earth — to continue existing on the earth.

And it was so] It was so instantly, in accordance with God's fiat; and thus were different species of plants perpetuated through the seed. This is a general statement; the details follow in *v.* 12.

12. *And the earth brought forth,* etc.] In accordance with the rule explained above, the fulfilment of the Divine command is related in terms similar to, but not identical with, those of the command itself. Characteristically, the Septuagint has harmonized the two verses completely.

The verbal changes that appear in the announcement made here of the execution of the Divine fiat are partly a matter of outward form only: for example *and trees* is substituted for *trees* (but it must be noted that most of the ancient versions and a few Hebrew MSS read *and trees* also in *v.* 11); so, too, לְמִינֵהוּ *lemīnēhū* ['according to its kind'] *with the termination* ֵהוּ *-ēhū,* on the analogy of nouns derived from stems whose third radical is a *Hē'*, takes the place of לְמִינוֹ *lemīnō.* But some of the modifications are introduced for the purpose of clarification: the use of the word וַתּוֹצֵא *wattōṣē'* ['and (the earth) brought forth'] instead of תַּדְשֵׁא *tadhšē'* ['Let (the earth) be covered with verdure'] indicates that the intention of the command was that the vegetation should be produced by germination from the ground. So, too, from the repetition of the word לְמִינֵהוּ *lemīnēhū,* which is used to qualify עֵשֶׂב *'ēśebh* as well, we infer that it was the Divine intention that the latter should connote all kinds of plants.

And God saw that it was good] He saw that also the vegetation was good. Two works were performed on the third day, the separation of the sea from the dry land and the creation of plants; hence the formula *that it was good* is uttered twice on this day.

FOURTH PARAGRAPH

THE STORY OF THE FOURTH DAY

14. *And God said,*
'Let there be lights in the firmament of the heavens / to separate the day from the night;
and let them be for signs and for seasons / and for days and years;

15. *and let them be lights in the firmament of the heavens / to give light upon the earth.'*
And it was so.

16. *And God made / the two great lights,*
the greater light / to rule the day,
and the lesser light / to rule the night;
He made the stars also.

17. *And God set them in the firmament of the heavens / to give light upon the earth,*

18. *to rule over* [or *during*] *the day and over* [or *during*] *the night, / and to separate the light from the darkness.*
And God saw that it was good.

19. *And there was evening and there was morning, / a fourth day.*

Now begins the second phase of the six days of creation. In the first stage were created the three sections of the inanimate world, followed by vegetation, that is, all the created entities that cannot move by themselves. In the second there were made, in precisely parallel order to that of the first, the mobile beings, to wit, on the fourth day the luminaries, the moving bodies in which the light formed on the first day is crystallized; and on the fifth and sixth days, in like manner, the creatures that correspond to the works of the second and third days (see the Introduction, § 6 end).

14–15. *And God said, 'Let there be lights',* etc.] It would appear, at first sight, that there is a redundancy in the Divine fiat; hence present-day commentators delete, as a rule, some words from the text. But if we analyse the content of the two verses carefully we shall find that every detail fits into its place. The luminaries were given three functions by the Divine command: (a) to separate day from night; (b) to be for signs and for seasons and for days and years; (c) to serve as luminaries and to give light upon the earth. In verses 17–18, all these functions are mentioned again, according to the recognized rule, in similar, but not completely identical, terms.

In connection with this paragraph, too, we must pay attention to the concepts prevailing among the peoples of the ancient East. Also in the Babylonian creation epic these three functions of the luminaries are to be found; an additional example is thus provided of the common traditional approach in apprehending physical phenomena. The verses relating to the sun in this epic have been lost; but concerning the moon and its god, Nannaru, we read (Tablet V, lines 12–13):

He caused Nannaru to shine (that is, Marduk gave brightness to the moon; this is the third task in our paragraph); *He set it over the night* (the first duty in our account); *He made it the adornment of the night for the fixing of the days* (the second function in our narrative).

But there is a vast difference in the interpretation of the phenomena: the Babylonian poem presents the luminaries and stars to us as the "likeness" (*tamšilšunu,* line 2) of the gods, and to a certain extent identifies them with the gods, endowing them with personality and mind and will. The Torah, on the contrary, depicts them as material entities, created by the word of the One God, and wholly devoid of personality, mind or will. The fact that in the rabbinic legends the heavenly bodies appear again as personalities, who hold intercourse with the Creator, is to be explained in the same way as the similar attitude adopted by the Rabbis towards the myths about the revolt of the sea. In the age of the Talmudic sages idolatry had long ceased to be a source of danger to Israel, and consequently they saw no further necessity for undue caution in regard to mythological themes, nor the need to obliterate all references to them.

The first function: *to separate the day from the night.* This expression enables us to comprehend the existence of the first three days, when there was as yet no sun in the world. To separate one thing from another means to mark the distinction between two things *already in existence.* It is manifest that the night exists even without the presence of moon and stars. Similarly, according to the view reflected here, the sun is not the *cause* of daytime, for the latter is to be found without the former. This is an empirical concept based on the observation that light pervades the atmosphere even before sunrise and also after sundown. Although we know that this light emanates from the sun only, nevertheless it is a fact that there is daylight even when the sun is not visible in the sky. This then is the meaning of the verse: that just as at the beginning and at the end of every day there is light without sun, so throughout those first three days God caused light to shine upon the earth from some other source without recourse to the sun; but when He created the luminaries He handed over to them the task of separation, that is, He commanded that the one should serve by day and the others should serve at night, and thus they would all become signs for distinguishing the two periods of time. In addition, the sun's light would naturally augment the already-existing daylight, but this would form its third function, as we shall see later. Note also verse 18: *and to separate the light from the darkness,* and my annotation thereon.

The question has also been raised: how could the plants grow on the third day without sun? This is not a difficult problem. Seeing that light was there already, and where there is light there must be heat, the requisite conditions for plant-life were already in existence.

The second function: *and let them be for signs and for seasons and for days and years.* Various interpretations of the clause, and particularly of the word *signs* (eclipses, portents, moments, and so forth) have been suggested. The correct explanation appears to be this: the verb וְהָיוּ *wehāyū* ['and let them be'] signifies 'to serve', and אתת *'ōthōth* is used in its normal connotation of 'signs', that is, let them serve as signs unto the inhabitants of the world (Gunkel), to wit, as signs for the determination of the seasons (the *Wāw* ['and'] of וּלְמוֹעֲדִים *ūlemō'ădhīm* ['and for seasons'] is explanatory) and for the division of time (*and for days and years*).

The third function: *and let them be lights in the firmament of the heavens.* At first the clause appears difficult; seeing that it speaks of lights [מְאוֹרֹת *me'ōrōth*] how can it say that the *lights* should be for *lights?* Hence the Peshiṭta [Syriac version] and the Vulgate translate, 'that they may shine' (possibly they read: לְמְאִירוֹת

lime'irōth [*Hiph'il* participle fem. pl.] = 'for light-givers'), and some moderns have suggested that the word לִמְאוֹרֹת *lime'ōrōth* ['for lights'] should be deleted as superfluous, or that it should be amended to הַמְּאוֹרֹת *hamme'ōrōth* ['the lights'; the sentence would then read: 'and let the lights in the firmament of the heavens be for giving light upon the earth']. But there is another expression similar to it in the Bible (Num. xv 38–39): *to make* TASSELS . . . *and it shall be to you a* TASSEL, the meaning being that the tassels that they would make would actually serve as *tassels*. Likewise here, the *lights*, just because they were lights — that is, sources of light — would serve as lights in the firmament, to *give light* upon the earth; the sun would augment the light of the day, as I have explained above, and the moon and stars would illumine the darkness of the night.

And it was so] As God had enjoined so it was, and so it remained for ever. After this general statement follows the usual detailed account.

16. *And God made*, etc.] In the narration, in this verse and in the two succeeding verses, of the fulfilment of God's purpose, the words of the Divine fiat are, as usual, repeated with certain modifications. Some of the changes serve to elucidate God's intention; in particular is the identity of the different lights made clear.

The two great lights, etc.] Some consider the word הַגְּדוֹלִים *haggedhōlīm* ['great'] redundant, since הַגָּדוֹל *haggadhōl* ['greater'] occurs soon afterwards; but the phrase in Psa. cxxxvi 7, *to Him who made the great lights*, corroborates the Massoretic reading here. The intention is to divide the heavenly host into two groups: the one consisting of the two great lights, that is, those that seem the biggest to us and that exert the greatest and most important influence on terrestrial life, and the other comprising a multitude of small lights, or those that appear small. Of the two great luminaries one is greater than the other; it is great in the group of great lights. It excels its companion particularly in its power and in its action.

To rule [לְמֶמְשֶׁלֶת *lememšeleth* literally, 'for the rule of'] *the day... to rule the night*] In verse 18 the wording is: וְלִמְשֹׁל בַּיּוֹם וּבַלַּיְלָה *welimšōl bayyōm ūbhallaylā* [E.V. *to rule over the day and over the night*]; the preposition–ב *b*– can be understood either in a temporal sense ['during'], or in the sense of עַל *'al* ['over'] as in xxxvii 8: *are you indeed to reign* OVER *us* [בָּנוּ *bānū*]; and in Psa. cxxxvi 8–9 the text is: לְמֶמְשֶׁלֶת בַּיּוֹם... לְמֶמְשְׁלוֹת בַּלָּיְלָה *l^e^memšeleth bayyōm . . . l^e^-memš^e^lōth ballaylā* [*to rule over* (or *during*) *the day . . . to rule over* (or *during*) *the night*], with a noun [לְמֶמְשֶׁלֶת *l^e^memšeleth*] as in our verse (16), and with the preposition –בּ *b*– as in verse 18.

Apparently the expression was used in the ancient poetic tradition concerning the creation of the world. We need not assume that the Psalmist took it necessarily from our section, for he employs other phrases belonging to the poetic tradition that do not occur in our section. Thus in verse 5 [Psa. cxxxvi] he writes: *to Him who by* UNDERSTANDING *made the heavens,* recalling the words of Job xxvi 12: *by His* UNDERSTANDING *He smote Rahab* (on the connection between the two verses see above, on *v.* 6), and similar passages in Akkadian. In verse 6 (Psa. *ibid.*) we read: *to Him who* SPREAD OUT THE EARTH *upon the waters,* with which should be compared Isa. xlii 5: WHO SPREAD FORTH THE EARTH *and what comes from it,* and *ibid.* xliv 24: *who* SPREAD OUT THE EARTH — *Who was with Me?*

The primary source of the expressions derived from the stem מָשַׁל *māšal* ['to rule'] is certainly to be found in the literary tradition of the Gentiles, who regarded the lights as actual *rulers.* Generally speaking, the original connotation of traditional phrases in literature tends to become obscured and even to be forgottten; here, in our verse, the meaning is simply this: since the luminaries are situated *above the earth,* they appear to be ruling over it, as well as over its days and nights.

17–18. *And God set them,* etc.] After God had *made* the lights (*v.* 16), He set them (וַיִּתֵּן *wayyittēn* [literally, 'and He gave'] = 'and He set') in the place appointed for them, in order that they should discharge the three functions, mentioned above, that had been assigned to them. The functions are enumerated here in reverse order to that given at first (chiastic order): (1) *to give light upon the earth* — the third function in the Divine fiat; (2) *to rule over* [or *during*] *the day and over* [or *during*] *the night* — the second task; (3) *and to separate the light from the darkness* — the first duty in the injunction.

And to rule over [or *during*] *the day and over* [or *during*] *the night*] See above, at the end of the commentary to *v.* 16.

To separate the light from the darkness] Ostensibly this presents a difficulty: how is it possible for the luminaries, which by their nature shed light, to separate the light from the *darkness?* The meaning, however, is *to separate the day from the night,* as it is phrased in the Divine command in *v.* 14. The day and night are here called *light and darkness* in accordance with *v.* 5, which parallels this verse. If we now take into account my annotations above, on *vv.* 14–15, in relation to the first function of the luminaries, the sense of our text becomes clear: the sun serves during daylight, and the moon and the stars serve during the darkness of the night.

And God saw that it was good] Some commentators consider that a clause stating that God called the greater light *sun* and the lesser light *moon* is missing; but this is unlikely. I have already stated above (on *v.* 5) that the purpose of naming the light, the darkness, the heavens, the earth and the seas was to inform us that what God created was precisely what we know today by the same names; otherwise the identification would not have been obvious. But in the present instance, we know perfectly well, without any need for further explanation, what is meant by the greater light and the lesser light. Had it been intended to assign names here, too, the stars would not have been specified by *their name* in *v.* 16.

FIFTH PARAGRAPH

THE STORY OF THE FIFTH DAY

20. *And God said,*
'Let the waters swarm / with swarming things, living creatures,
and let flying creatures fly above the earth / in front of the firmament of the heavens.'

21. *So God created / the great sea monsters*
and every living creature that moves, / with which the waters swarm, according to their kinds,
and every winged creature according to its kind.
And God saw that it was good.

22. *And God blessed them, saying,*
'Be fruitful and multiply / and fill the waters in the seas,
and let the flying creatures multiply on earth.'

23. *And there was evening and there was morning, / a fifth day.*

20. *And God said, 'Let the waters* SWARM [יִשְׁרְצוּ *yišreṣū*] *with* SWARMING THINGS [שֶׁרֶץ *šereṣ*]', etc.] On the fifth day, which parallels the second, were created the living creatures existing in the two parts of the universe that were created on the second day, namely, the heavens and the sea. Although the sea attained its final form only on the third day, it had already been created on the second; indeed, it was at that stage more extensive than it was later. יִשְׁרְצוּ ... שֶׁרֶץ *yišreṣū . . . šereṣ* — paronomasia, as in *v.* 11: תַּדְשֵׁא ... דֶּשֶׁא *tadhšē' . . . deše'* [literally, 'let (the earth) vegetate vegetation']. The primary signification of the stem שרץ *šāraṣ* is 'movement', with specific reference to the abundant, swift movement of many creatures who jostle one another as they proceed criss-cross in all possible directions. God willed that into the midst of the waste and inanimate waters, from one end of the sea to the other, there should now enter a living spirit, and that there should be born in their midst moving, animate beings, subject to no limitation of numbers or intermission of movement.

As a rule, the stem שרץ *šāraṣ* is used of small or tiny creatures, but here, in the command of God, who is communing with Himself, it refers also to large creatures, for vis-à-vis the Creator, they are all equally small. But when, in *v.* 21, the Torah tells its readers of the implementation of the fiat, it uses human phraseology and distinguishes between the big and the small creatures. A similar instance is found in the preceding paragraph: the Divine utterance refers to lights in general, but in the account of their creation, which is addressed to the reader, their sizes are differentiated.

And let flying creatures fly about above the earth, etc.] This is another example of paronomasia [עוֹף יְעוֹפֵף *'ōph ye'ōphēph,* 'and let flying creatures fly about'], and the root in this case, too, connotes movement resembling, and corresponding to, *swarming,* the term used of living creatures inhabiting the water. The text has not יָעוּף *yā'ūph* [*Qal,* 'flies'] but יְעוֹפֵף *ye'ōphēph* [*Pō'lēl,* 'fly about']: the flying creatures fly about hither and thither, in all directions.

The collective noun עוֹף *'ōph* [E.V. 'fowl, birds'] does not refer to birds only, but signifies all creatures that fly about in the air (cf. Lev. xi 19f).

עַל הָאָרֶץ *'al hā'āreṣ* — [literally, 'upon the earth'] means here: *above the earth.*

In front of [literally, 'on the face of'] *the firmament of the heavens.* The attempts that have been made to explain this phrase are not satisfactory. It seems to reflect the impression that a person receives on looking upward: the creatures that fly about above one's head appear then to be set against the background of the sky — *in front of the firmament of the heavens.*

At the end of this verse the Septuagint reads, *And it was so,* and many consider this reading to be correct, since this clause is found in the parallel verses. But this tendency of the Greek translator, as well as of several modern exegetes, to achieve complete correspondence between the paragraphs is not justified. Having regard to the explanation we gave above of the meaning of the expression *and it was so,* it could not be used here, because the sea monsters, the first kind of creation to be formed on the fifth day, have not survived in our time (Naḥmanides).

21. *So God created the great sea monsters*] Throughout the whole section only the general categories of plants and animals are mentioned, but not the separate species, save the sea monsters. This exception has not been made, we may be sure, without a specific motive. Here, too, it would seem, the Torah intended to sound a protest, as it were, against concepts that were current among the Gentiles, and to a certain extent even among the Israelites, but which were not in accord with its own spirit. In Egypt, in Mesopotamia, in the land of Canaan and in the countries of the East generally, all sorts of legends used to be recounted about the battles of the great gods against the sea dragon and similar monsters. In particular are the sagas of the people nearest to Israel, the people of Canaan, of importance to our subject. The Ugaritic epics mention among the enemies of Baal, along with the god Môt — his chief foe — and the lord of the sea, a number of different monsters like the Dragon, Leviathan the Fleeing Serpent, the Twisting Serpent, and similar creatures (see *Tarbiz,* xiii, pp. 7–5, 170, 172 [Hebrew]). In Israelite circles, the tradition concerning the sea monsters

and their confederates assumed an aspect in keeping with the spirit of Israel. No longer do divine forces oppose the supreme godhead, but, following the same principle as in the case of the lord of the sea, Scripture depicts them as creatures in revolt against their Maker. This Israelite tradition, which apparently assumed its literary form as part of the epic of the rebellion of the sea (see above, on *v.* 9), is alluded to in a number of Biblical verses and in various dicta in Talmudic, Midrashic and Cabbalisitic literature. In Isa. xxvii 1, these monsters, bearing the very same names as occur in Canaanite poetry, are mentioned as symbols of the principle of evil, which God will ultimately uproot from the world: *In that day the Lord with His hard and great and strong sword will punish* LEVIATHAN THE FLEEING SERPENT, LEVIATHAN THE TWISTING SERPENT, *and He will slay the* DRAGON *that is in the sea.* A number of verses also refer to Leviathan and the sea monsters in connection with the revolt of the sea against God, implying that they joined forces with the rebellious lord of the sea and rose up against their Creator, but were compelled in the end to submit to Him. Above I have already quoted Isa. li 9–10 (*that* DIDST PIERCE THE DRAGON in combination with *that didst* CUT RAHAB IN PIECES and *that didst* DRY UP THE SEA); see also Psa. lxxiv 13–14: *Thou didst divide the* SEA *by Thy might; Thou didst break the heads of the* DRAGONS *on the* WATERS. *Thou didst crush the heads of* LEVIATHAN, *Thou didst give him as food to the folk inhabiting the wilderness;* Job vii 12: *Am I the* SEA, *or a* SEA MONSTER, *that Thou settest a guard over me?;* ibid. xxvi 13: *His hand pierced the* FLEEING SERPENT. In my aforementioned essay in *Keneseth* (Hebrew), I cite a number of additional verses. I likewise quote there passages from rabbinic literature that tell of the slaying of Leviathan by the hand of God, and of matters related thereto. I have already explained earlier how we have to interpret the attitude of the spiritual leaders of Israel — an attitude that varied with the different epochs — towards legends of this nature; here, too, in accordance with what I have stated previously, the Torah is entirely opposed to these myths. It voices its protest in its own quiet manner, relating: *So God created the great sea monsters.* It is as though the Torah said, in effect: Far be it from any one to suppose that the sea monsters were mythological beings opposed to God or in revolt against Him; they were as natural as the rest of the creatures, and were formed in their proper time and in their proper place by the word of the Creator, in order that they might fulfil His will like the other created beings. Similarly it is stated in Psa. cxlviii 7: *Praise the Lord from the earth,* YOU SEA MONSTERS AND ALL DEEPS. The poet invites all created forms of life to praise the Lord, and among the terrestrial creatures, beneath the heavens, he invites, first and foremost, the sea monsters and the deeps specifically.

And every living creature that moves] — that is, in other words, the *swarms* mentioned in *v.* 20.

With which the waters swarmed] The meaning of this expression in the past tense is: with which they swarmed from that moment onward in obedience to the command in *v.* 20.

According to their kinds [לְמִינֵהֶם *l^emīnēhem*]/The Hebrew form, which is the equivalent of לְמִינָם *l^emīnām* [the regular form], is constructed on the analogy of nouns derived from *Lāmedh-Hē'* stems. It nevertheless appears strange at first, since the pronominal suffix refers to נֶפֶשׁ חַיָּה *nepheš ḥayyā* [sing. fem., 'living creature'], and therefore we should have expected לְמִינָהּ *l^emīnāh* ['her kind']. But possibly the suffix is in agreement, by attraction, with the number and gender of the preceding word מַיִם *mayīm* ['waters']; cf. i Sam. ii 4: קֶשֶׁת גִּבֹּרִים חַתִּים *qesheth gibbōrīm ḥattīm* ['the bow of the mighty men is broken'; חַתִּים *ḥattīm,* rendered 'broken', agrees in number and gender not with קֶשֶׁת *qešeth* (fem. sing., 'bow') but with גִּבֹּרִים *gibbōrīm* (mas. pl., 'mighty men').

And God saw that it was good] Another allusion to the subject of the sea-monsters; of them, too, it is possible to say: *that it was good.*

22. *And God blessed them*] The reference is to the fish; this is shown by the continuation of the sentence: *and fill* THE WATERS IN THE SEA. The fecundity of the fish, which is so great as to have become proverbial, is indicative of the special blessing that was bestowed on them at the time of their creation. The blessing mentioned in this verse is purely one of fertility and increase: BE FRUITFUL AND MULTIPLY *and fill,* etc. Also the blessing bestowed upon man on the sixth day (*v.* 28) is couched in similar terms, as though to say: Be fruitful and multiply like the fish. Many more expressions of benison, linked with the idea of fecundity, occur in

the book of Genesis, *viz* ix 1; xvii 16, 20; xxii 17; xxiv 60; xxvi 3–4, 24; xxviii 3; xxxv 9–11; xlviii 3–4; xlix 25. Compare also xlviii 15–16: 'AND HE BLESSED *Joseph, and said . . .* BLESS *the lads . . .* AND LET THEM GROW [וְיִדְגּוּ *weyidhgū;* cf. דָּג *dagh,* 'a fish'] *in multitude in the midst of the earth.*

In the seas] The reason for the omission of any reference to the rivers and pools is that the exact appellations used in *v.* 10 (*seas — earth*) are repeated in this verse. Apparently, the intention here is to inform us that one of these two portions of the world, to wit, the one containing the seas, would be the special domain of the fish and of other aquatic creatures, and that the air of the second portion, the air above the *earth,* would be the exclusive sphere of the flying creatures. The aerial creatures flying about in the air over the seas, and the fish in the rivers and in the pools, beneath the atmosphere appointed for the flying creatures, are mere details that do not materially affect the main partition, described in its general outline by our verse.

And let the flying creatures multiply upon the earth] The aerial creatures were not blessed with the same exceeding fertility as the fish, hence in their case only the term *multiply* is used.

Upon the earth] Although the winged creatures fly about *in front of the heavens,* their nests are made, and their young are hatched, upon the ground, or upon the trees, which are planted in the ground.

SIXTH PARAGRAPH
THE STORY OF THE SIXTH DAY

24\. *And God said,*
'Let the earth bring forth / living creatures according to their kinds;
cattle and creeping things / and beasts of the earth according to their kinds.'
And it was so.

25\. *And God made / the beasts of the earth according to their kinds and the cattle according to their kinds, / and everything that creeps upon the ground according to its kind.*
And God saw that it was good.

26. *Then God said,*
'Let us make man / in our image, after our likeness;
and let them have dominion over the fish of the sea, / and over the flying creatures of the air,
and over the cattle, / and over all the earth,
and over every creeping thing / that creeps upon the earth.'

27. *So God created / man in His own image,*
in the image of God / He created him;
male and female / He created them.

28. *And God blessed them, / and God said to them,*
'Be fruitful and multiply, / and fill the earth and subdue it;
and have dominion over the fish of the sea / and over the flying creatures of the air
and over every living thing / that moves upon the earth.'

29. *And God said,*
'Behold, I have given you / every plant yielding seed
which is upon the face of all the earth,
and every tree / with seed in its fruit;
You shall have them for food.

30. *And to every beast of the earth, / and to every flying creature of the air,*
and to everything that moves on the earth, / wherein there is the breath of life,
[I have given] every green plant for food.'
And it was so.

31. *And God saw everything that He had made, / and behold, it was very good.*
And there was evening and there was morning, / the sixth day.

24. *And God said, 'Let the earth bring forth'*, etc.] The sixth day corresponds to the third: on the third day the earth was created, and on the sixth the living creatures of the earth were made; on the third day, immediately after the organization of inanimate nature had been completed, the plants, whose dominion extends throughout the earth, were brought into being; so, too, on the sixth day,

when vegetation and animal life had been fully established, man, who bears rule over all created life upon earth, was formed forthwith.

Living creatures according to their kinds] — a general statement followed by detailed specification, enumerating the three kinds of living creatures. These are: *cattle,* that is, living creatures whom man can domesticate or tame; *creeping things,* to wit, small creatures that creep about on the ground, or even big animals that have no legs, or have very short legs, so that they appear to be walking on their bellies; *beasts of the earth*: four-legged creatures that can never be domesticated or tamed.

Beasts of the earth [חַיְתוֹ אֶרֶץ *ḥayethō-'ereṣ*] / The expression is poetic. The view, it may be noted, that regards the termination וֹ- *-ō* as a substitute for the definite article is erroneous. It is particularly in poetic style that the definite article is most frequently omitted, and its omission is in no way connected with the presence of the suffix וֹ- *-ō* (Torczyner). Furthermore, in so far as our verse is concerned, there is no need here for the definite article; nor is it found with the other nouns occurring here, namely, נֶפֶשׁ חַיָּה *nephes̀ ḥayyā* ['living creatures'], בְּהֵמָה *behēmā* ['cattle'], רֶמֶשׂ *remeś* ['creeping things']. In view of this, we may explain the reason for the difference that we find in our section between חַיְתוֹ־אֶרֶץ *ḥayethō-'ereṣ* in this verse and חַיַּת הָאָרֶץ *ḥayyath hā'āreṣ* in *vv.* 25, 30, as follows: when there is need for the definite article חַיַּת הָאָרֶץ *ḥayyath hā'āreṣ* is used, and when the phrase is required without definition, it is written חַיְתוֹ־אֶרֶץ *ḥayethō-'ereṣ.*

לְמִינָהּ *lemīnāh* [literally, 'according to her kind'; rendered: *according to their kinds*] / The pronominal suffix [הּ *-āh,* third person fem. sing.] refers also to the cattle and the creeping things; thus the word should, properly, have been written לְמִינֵהֶם *lemīnēhem* [pronominal suffix mas. pl.]. The existing termination [fem. sing.] must be due either to the attraction of the preceding word אֶרֶץ *'ereṣ* [fem. sing.] or to that of the combined phrase חַיְתוֹ־אֶרֶץ *ḥayethō-'ereṣ;* cf. the word לְמִינֵהֶם *lemīnēhem* in *v.* 21.

And it was so] — a general statement to be followed, in *v.* 25, by a detailed account.

25. *The beasts of the earth,* etc.] The verse enumerates again the three categories of the living creatures of the earth, changing to

some extent the phrasing and the word-order, as is usual in recapitulations.

26. *Then God said, 'Let us make man'*, etc.] Only in the case of man, because of his special importance, does Scripture allude to the Divine thought preceding the act of creation.

Let us make man, etc.] Many interpretations have been offered regarding the use of the plural in this verse. According to the rabbinic explanation, it connotes that God took counsel with someone or something. As to whom or what He consulted, there are divergent opinions (*see* Bereshith Rabba viii 3–7, and the parallel passages). The view that God took counsel with the ministering angels has been regarded by some commentators, both medieval and modern, as the actual meaning of the verse. But against this interpretation it can be contended: (1) that it conflicts with the central thought of the section that God *alone* created the entire world; (2) that the expression *Let us make* is not one of consultation; (3) that if the intention was to tell us that God took counsel, the Bible would have explicitly stated whom He consulted, as we are told in the other passages that are usually cited in support of this theory (i Kings xxii 19; Isa. vi 2–8; Job i–ii). The same objections, or some of them, or different arguments can be submitted in refutation of other interpretations (e.g. that God took counsel with Himself, or that the verse uses the language of kings who are accustomed to speak of themselves in the plural, or that there is a reference here to various elements within the Godhead, or that there is to be heard in the words of the Torah an echo, as it were, of the pagan myths, which relate that the decision to create man was taken in the assembly of the gods, and so forth). The best explanation, although rejected by the majority of contemporary commentators, is that we have here the plural of exhortation. When a person exhorts himself to do a given task he uses the plural: 'Let us go!' 'Let us rise up!' 'Let us sit!' and the like. Thus we find in ii Sam. xxiv 14: LET US FALL [נִפְּלָה *nippelā*] *into the hand of the Lord . . . but into the hand of man* LET ME *not* FALL [אֶפֹּלָה *'eppōlā*]'; at the end of the verse, since a negation is expressed, the self-exhortation no longer obtains, and consequently the singular form appears again (it is not to be supposed, as Yalon has suggested in *Kirjath Sepher,* xiii, p. 302 [Hebrew], that נִפְּלָה *nippelā* ['let us fall'], too, is singular, *Nūn* taking the place of *'Āleph,* in accordance with the linguistic rules of Palestinian Aramaic, for in that case *Nūn* should appear also in the last word of the verse). In the same way we must explain xi 7: *Come,* LET US GO DOWN [נֵרְדָה *nēr^e^dhā*], *and there* LET US CONFUSE [נָבְלָה *nābh^e^lā*] *their language.*

In our image, after our likeness] The Jewish exegetes have endeavoured to soften the corporeality implicit in the statement by means of forced interpretations (on these interpretations see Geiger, *Nachgel. Schriften,* V part i, Hebrew Section, pp. 102–105). On the other hand, many modern commentators take the view that in fact we have here an unquestionably corporeal concept. This view is also difficult, since corporeality of this kind is not in keeping with the general idea informing our section. The correct interpretation is to be sought elsewhere. There is no doubt that the original signification of this expression in the Canaanite tongue was, judging by Babylonian usage, corporeal, in accordance with the anthropomorphic conception of the godhead among the peoples of the ancient East. Nevertheless, when we use it in modern Hebrew, and say, for instance, 'all that has been created in the Divine image', we certainly do not associate any material idea with it, but give it a purely spiritual connotation, to wit, that man, although he resembles the creatures in his physical structure, approaches God in his thought and in his conscience. It is clear, therefore, that the meaning of the phrase changed in the course of time; it was corporeal to begin with but subsequently it became spiritual. The question then arises: when did this change come about? before or after our verse was written? Generally speaking, it is an error of perspective to regard all ancient texts as forming a single group. Although they are all far removed from us, they may also be distant from one another in time or in their degree of maturity. Reverting to our own subject, when we consider the lofty conception of God that is reflected in our section, we are compelled to conclude that the change referred to antedated its composition, and that the expression is used here in a sense similar to (if not actually identical with) that which it has in Hebrew today.

And let them (the plural is used because man is a collective noun) *have dominion over the fish of the sea,* etc.] The fish of the sea are mentioned first either because the different categories of animal life are enumerated here in the order of their creation, or in order to emphasize that man would hold sway even over those creatures that were blessed with special fertility, or for both these reasons together.

And over the cattle, and over all the earth] Here and in *vv.* 28, 30, the categories of creatures mentioned previously in *vv.* 24, 25, are repeated; but not only do the terms undergo a change of form and order, in accordance with the usual practice in these recapitulations, but they are also shortened, and not all the categories are explicitly named, so as to avoid the monotony of their being listed five times in succession. However, Scripture has succeeded in finding in each verse a generic expression that includes also that which is not specifically named. In our verse we have the phrase, *and over all the earth,* which implies both the creeping things and the beasts. In *v.* 28 the words, *and over every living thing that moves upon the earth,* clearly do not refer to חַיָּה *ḥayyā* in the restricted sense of the term ['beast'], but to all living beings that move on the earth (הָרֹמֶשֶׂת *hārōmeśeth* here means *moves*). The same applies to *v.* 30, which mentions *every beast of the earth* [חַיַּת הָאָרֶץ *ḥayyath hā'āreṣ*] first, and *everything that moves* [רֹמֵשׂ *rōmēś*] *on the earth, wherein there is a breath of life* later. Some amend the text, inserting in every verse what appears to be missing, but they only destroy the charm of the style.

27. *So God created man in His own image,* etc.] At this point the text assumes a more exalted tone and becomes poetic. The verse consists of three lines, each of which has four stresses and contains the verb בָּרָא *bārā'* ['create'], the repetition being for emphasis. The first line speaks, in general terms, of man's *creation;* the second draws attention to the fact that he was created in the *Divine image;* the third notes the creation of *two sexes.* The poetic structure of the sentence, its stately diction and its particular emotional quality attest the special importance that the Torah attributes to the making of man — the noblest of the creatures.

Male and female He created them] According to the rabbinic interpretation (B. Berakhoth 61a; B. 'Erubin 18a; Bereshith Rabba viii 1 and the parallel passages) man was created with two faces, that is, a hermaphrodite. This, too, is how many commentators of our own day, basing their view on similar legends that were current in the ancient world (see especially the essay of Krappe mentioned above) understand the passage. But this is not the true sense of the verse, for it distinctly states: *He created* THEM — in the plural.

Schwally has proposed that we read *him* [אתו *'ōthō*] instead of *them* [אֹתָם *'ōthām*]. But the suggestion is unacceptable for three reasons: (1) it would make the second and third parts of the verse have identical endings, which is not possible; (2) the emendation is based on a hypothetical interpretation, which, in turn, assumes the emendation; (3) the plural is found again later (v 2): *Male and female He created* THEM, *and He blessed* THEM *and named* THEM *Man when* THEY *were created.*

28. *And God blessed them,* etc.] On the use of an expression of blessing in connection with fecundity, see above on *v.* 22. Here the benison contains also another concept, namely, that of dominion over the living creatures and over the earth as a whole (including the plants), since man alone was created in the Divine image and likeness.

Be fruitful and multiply, and fill the earth and subdue it] Although you are only two, yet, through your fruitfulness and increase, your descendants will fill the land and subdue it. For similar expressions used of Noah and Abraham and the children of Israel, see my book, *The Documentary Hypothesis,* English translation, p. 39.

29–30. *Behold, I have given you,* etc.] You are permitted to make use of the living creatures and their service, you are allowed to exercise power over them so that they may promote your subsistence; but you may not treat the life-force within them contemptuously and slay them in order to eat their flesh; your proper diet shall be vegetable food. It is true that the eating of flesh is not specifically forbidden here, but the prohibition is clearly to be inferred. No contradiction in this regard is presented by iii 21 (*garments of skin*), iv 2 (*Abel was a keeper of sheep*), or by the sacrifices of Abel and Noah (iv 4; viii 20), as we shall show in our notes to these verses. Apparently, the Torah seeks to convey that in principle man should refrain from eating meat, and that when Noah and his sons were granted permission to eat flesh (ix 3) this was only a concession subject to the condition that the blood was not to be consumed. This prohibition implies respect for the principle of life (*for the blood is the life*), and it serves also, in a sense, to remind us that rightly all parts of the flesh should have been forbidden; it behoves us, therefore, to eschew eating at least one element thereof in order to remember the earlier prohibition.

The Torah presents here a kind of idealized picture of the primeval world situation. Not only man but even the animals were expected to show reverence for the principle of life (see *v.* 30, which, too, is governed by the verb *I have given* of *v.* 29). In full accord with this standpoint is the prophetic view that the prohibition was never annulled, and that in the Messianic era it would be operative again and even the carnivorous beasts would then feed only on vegetation (Isa. xi 7; lxv 25: *the lion shall eat straw like the ox*).

With regard to the gentile legends connected with the doctrine of vegetarianism in ancient times — in the 'Golden Age' — see the texts listed by Dillmann, *op. cit.* p. 36. The originality of the Israelite contribution consisted in the belief that in the millenial period the prohibition would come into force once more.

Concerning the classification of the living creatures in these two verses, see notes on *v.* 26.

And it was so] The explanation we have given of this expression (above, on *v.* 7) is not invalidated by its use here; despite the fact that a change came about later, when permission was given to Noah and his sons to eat meat, the prohibition was not, as we have explained, abrogated, but was only temporarily suspended.

31. *And God saw,* etc.] Instead of the usual simple formula, we have here, at the conclusion of the story of creation, a more elaborate and imposing statement that points to the general harmony prevailing in the world of the Almighty. On the previous days the words *that it was good* were applied to a specific detail; now *God saw* EVERYTHING *that He had made,* the creation in its totality, and He perceived that not only were the details, taken separately, good, but that each one harmonized with the rest; hence the whole was not just *good,* but *very good.* An analogy might be found in an artist who, having completed his masterpiece, steps back a little and surveys his handiwork with delight, for both in detail and in its entirety it had emerged perfect from his hand.

Since on the sixth day the whole work of creation was described as *very good,* it was superfluous to state specifically of the last work, which was performed on this day, *that it was good.* Indeed it had to be omitted in order to avoid a seeming contradiction of what is subsequently written of man: *and that every imagination of the thoughts of his heart was only* EVIL *continually* (vi 5); and afterwards: *for the imagination of man's heart is* EVIL *from his youth* (viii 21). In our commentary below we shall consider the meaning of these verses in relation to the statement here.

The sixth day [יוֹם הַשִּׁשִּׁי *yōm haššiššī*]/The use of יוֹם *yōm* ['day'] without the definite article followed by an ordinal number with the definite article is not rare in the Bible; compare, for example, ii 3; Exod. xii 15; xx 10, etc. The meaning in all these cases is the same as though the definite article were attached to the noun. This construction is found in our section only here, but not in connection with the other days, for the reason, apparently, that each of the preceding days was merely *one of the days* in the series of days of creation, whereas this was *the last day* in the sequence, the day *appointed* for the completion of the task, in accordance with the system described in the introduction to this section, in the first two paragraphs of § 5.

SEVENTH PARAGRAPH

THE SEVENTH DAY; END OF THE SECTION

CHAPTER II

1. *Thus the heavens and the earth were finished, / and all the host of them.*

2. *And since God was finished on the seventh day / with His work which He had done,*
He abstained on the seventh day / from all His work which He had done.

3. *So God blessed the seventh day / and hallowed it,*
because on it God abstained from all His work / which He had creatively made.

1. *Thus the heavens and the earth were finished, and all the host of them*] The story of God's work in the six days of creation has come to an end, and there now stands before us the complete picture of the heavens and the earth and all that they contain in their harmonious perfection.

And all the host of them] — with the heavens the host of the heavens, and with the earth the fullness thereof. The phrase 'the host of the heavens' usually indicates the sun, the moon and the stars (sometimes, but certainly not in this instance, it refers to the angels). As a rule the word 'host' is not associated with the 'earth', but here, since the verse employs the term 'host' in connection with the heavens, it is used also in relation to the earth — a figure of speech that the Greeks called *zeugma.*

2. וַיְכַל אֱלֹהִים בַּיּוֹם הַשְּׁבִיעִי *wayᵉkhal ʾElōhīm bayyōm haššᵉbhīʿī* [E.V. *And on the seventh day God finished*] / Ostensibly this is difficult; for God did not finish His work on the *seventh* day but on the *sixth!* Hence the present-day tendency is to amend the text and to read the *sixth* instead of the *seventh* on the basis of the Samaritan Version, the Septuagint, the Peshiṭta and the Book of Jubilees ii 1, 16 (Talmudic sources also mention this reading as one of the textual changes introduced into the Greek translation of the Torah made for Ptolemy Philadelphus). But careful study of the passage will convince us that the correct reading is *on the seventh day.* Our verse consists of three consecutive, parallel lines, each of which contains *seven* words and is divided into two parts, the first part ending in every case, like a threefold refrain, with the words — *the seventh day.* Only one who is insensitive to the beauty and majesty of these lines could conceive the possibility of omitting the first mention of *the seventh day* and of substituting for it *on the sixth day.*

Other attempts that have been made to solve the problem by textual emendations have been equally unsuccessful. This is not surprising, because the problem does not inhere in the text, but stems from the erroneous interpretation put upon it. To understand the verse correctly we must examine similar sentences, such as 'And He finished talking with him, and God went up from Abraham' *

* This is the literal rendering of the Hebrew.

(xvii 22); 'And she finished giving him a drink, and she said' * etc. (xxiv 19); 'And Jacob finished charging his sons, and he drew up his feet into the bed' * (xlix 33), and other instances of this kind. The clause 'And He finished talking with him' does not connote 'And He spoke His concluding words to him', for God's final words were cited in the preceding verse; the meaning is: 'Having finished talking with him, He went up from Abraham'. The same applies to the verse 'And she finished giving him a drink'; in the previous sentence it is stated 'and she gave him a drink', thus the completion of the giving of the drink has already been described; hence the meaning of the verse (xxiv 19) is: 'Having finished giving him a drink, she said' etc. In the same way we have to understand the words, 'And Jacob finished charging his sons'; since the whole of Jacob's charge to his sons was already given in the preceding verses, the sense of this sentence is: 'Having finished charging his sons, he drew up his feet into the bed'. An example that is still closer to our text, because the passage speaks specifically of *work,* we find in Exod. xl 33–34: 'And he erected the court round the tabernacle and the altar, and set up the screen of the gate of the court. *And Moses finished the work,* and the cloud covered the tent of meeting' * etc. It is perfectly clear that the clause 'And Moses finished the work' does not refer to the completion of the work, since the preceding clauses have already spoken of the completion of the final tasks; but the meaning is: 'Moses being in the position of one who had already finished the work, the cloud thereupon covered the tent of meeting'. Other verses commencing with the expression, 'And it came to pass when he finished' or 'And it came to pass when they finished' * (xxvii 30; xliii 2), could be cited; but there is no need to prolong the list of quotations, and the examples of verses beginning, like our verse, with the words 'And he finished' or 'And she finished' will suffice. They clearly establish that the meaning of our verse is: 'Since God was on the seventh day in the position of one who had already finished His work, consequently He abstained from work on the seventh day' etc.

His work which He had done] The expression *His work* also occurs three times in this paragraph; likewise we find thrice: *which*

* This is the literal rendering of the Hebrew.

He had done — which He had done — which He had created [the full text is rendered: *creatively made*]. They all come to emphasize the principal ideas involved.

וַיִּשְׁבֹּת *wayyišbōth* ['and He abstained from work']/This verb has been translated or interpreted by many as if it signified 'to rest' or 'to cease work'; but this is incorrect. It has a negative connotation: 'not to do work'. Verses like Exod. xxiii 12: *Six days you shall* DO YOUR WORK, *but on the seventh day* תִּשְׁבֹּת *tišbōth;* ibid. xxxiv 21: *Six days* YOU SHALL WORK, *but on the seventh day* תִּשְׁבֹּת *tišbōth; in plowing time and in harvest* תִּשְׁבֹּת *tišbōth,* make it clear that תִּשְׁבֹּת *tišbōth* is simply the opposite of *you shall do your work* or *you shall work.* At times *you shall not do any work* actually takes the place of תִּשְׁבֹּת *tišbōth,* which is found in the parallel verses: e.g. *Six days you shall labour and* DO ALL YOUR WORK; *but the seventh day . . .* YOU SHALL NOT DO ANY WORK (*ibid.* xx 9–10). Furthermore, the passages, *but on the seventh day* תִּשְׁבֹּת *tišbōth; that your ox and your ass may have* REST, *and the son of your bondmaid, and the alien, may be* REFRESHED (*ibid.* xxiii 12), and שָׁבַת *šābhath* [3rd pers. masc. sing. Perfect] *and was refreshed* (*ibid.* xxxi 17), clearly establish that the rest and refreshment are only the *outcome* of תִּשְׁבֹּת *tišbōth* and שָׁבַת *šābhath.* In our section there is no mention of either rest or refreshment. Although elsewhere the Bible does employ such concepts in reference to God (*ibid.* xx 11: *and He* RESTED *on the seventh day;* ibid. xxxi 17: *He abstained from work and was* REFRESHED), nevertheless in this section, which avoids all possible use of anthropomorphic expressions in order to teach us, particularly in the account of creation, how great is the gulf between the Creator and the created, such notions would have been incongruous; hence the Bible uses only a term that signifies 'abstention from work'.

The verb שָׁבַת *šābhath* also contains an allusion to the name יוֹם הַשַּׁבָּת *yōm haššabbāth* ['the Sabbath day']. This name does not occur here, and is subsequently mentioned in other books of the Pentateuch only in connection with the commandment to keep the Sabbath, which was given to Israel. Here the hallowed day is called only *the seventh day* (the reason for this we shall see later). The Torah laid here the foundation for the precept of the Sabbath; this day was already sanctified by God at the beginning of the world's history, and its greatness is not dependent on any other factor, not even on calendary determination by Israel, like the festivals, *which* [it is enjoined] *you shall proclaim.* Every seventh day, without intermission since the days of creation, serves as a memorial to the idea of the creation of the world by the word of God, and we must refrain from work thereon so that we may follow the Creator's example and cleave to His ways. Scripture wishes to emphasize that the sanctity of the Sabbath is older than Israel, and rests upon all mankind. The fact that the name אֱלֹהִים *'Elōhīm* ['God'], which was current also among the Gentile nations, and not the name יהוה *YHWH* [E.V. 'Lord'], which was used by the Israelites only, occurs here is not without significance; the latter designation will be found in connection with the commandments concerning the proper *observance* of the Sabbath, which devolves only upon Israel. Thus in the Ten Commandments it is said, REMEMBER *the Sabbath day to keep it holy,* not, 'know that there is a Sabbath in the world'; that was already known. Possibly, in agreement with what I have stated above, at the beginning of § 5 of the Introduction, Scripture perceives a kind of dim recollection of the sanctity of the Sabbath in the day *šabattu* or *šapattu* of the Mesopotamian peoples. I shall deal with the day *šabattu–šapattu,* and with the problem connected with it, later in my annotations on *v.* 3.

It may be asked: In what way is the seventh day different from the succeeding days, since on them, too, God did no additional work? In answer to the question it may be said: (1) that the difference consists in the *novel character* of the seventh day; after a series of six days on each of which some work of creation was wrought, came a day on which God did not work or add anything to his creation; hence the remembrance of this abstinence from labour remained linked with the day on which this situation first arose; (2) that in accordance with what I have noted above in the Introduction § 5, seven days are considered a *period* [unit of time]; consequently, the seventh day, following on the six days of creation, completed the first period, and in every subsequent period the first day calls to mind the creation of the light, the second the creation of the heavens, and so forth, and the seventh reminds us of the day on which God did no work at all.

3. *So God blessed the seventh day*] This is the third time that an

expression of blessing occurs in our section. As previously stated, threefold repetition indicates emphasis, and the emphasis has again an optimistic significance: not only is the world *very good,* but it received from God a threefold blessing. The repeated blessings, it may be noted, are in a kind of ascending order: the fish are blessed with physical fertility: on man a twofold blessing is bestowed, comprising both physical fecundity and spiritual elevation; the benison of the Sabbath is wholly one of spiritual exaltation, a blessing imbued with sanctity (*and hallowed it;* cf. also Exod. xx 11: *therefore the Lord* BLESSED *the Sabbath day and* HALLOWED *it*).

And hallowed it] The real meaning of קְדוּשָׁה *qᵉdhūšā* ['holiness'] is elevation and exaltation above the usual level; the seventh day was lifted up above the plane of the other days.

It is not my intention to discuss here all the questions that some modern scholars have raised in regard to the origin of the Sabbath and its internal development among the Israelites. My aim is purely to explain the language and meaning of the text; whereas most of the views expressed on the former subjects are no more than hypotheses appertaining to the history of religion rather than to the field of exegesis. Those who wish to study these topics further are referred to the survey by Kraeling mentioned above. But the elucidation of the verse before us compels us to consider also here one of the questions alluded to. It is the question of *the relationship between the Israelite Sabbath and the days resembling it, in name or in order of their incidence, in the religious calendar of the Mesopotamian peoples* (for the sources and their interpretation see particularly the passages I have noted in the works of Landsberger and Langdon listed above in § 8 of the Introduction to this section). The Babylonians and the Assyrians used to call by the name of *šabattu* or *šapattu* the day of the full moon, the fifteenth of the month, which was specifically dedicated to the worship of the moon god, Sin-Nannaru, and of the gods related to it. The secondary meanings of this word, such as 'half the month, fourteen days', or that recently suggested by J. Lewy (*Archiv Orientální,* xi [1939] pp. 44–45), to wit, the intercalated days required to equalize the lunar with the solar year, do not come within our purview. Of importance to us is only the use of the word to denote the day of the full moon. This day used to be called also *ūm nūḫ libbi*, 'day of the rest of the heart', that is, according to the generally accepted explanation, the day of the appeasement of the heart of the gods by means of worship. Germane to our problem are also the seventh, fourteenth, twenty-first and twenty-eighth days of the month, which likewise have a special character in the Mesopotamian calendar. They are connected with the four phases of the moon, and are spaced *seven days* apart from one another, except for the seventh day of the month, which comes eight days after the twenty-eighth day of the preceding month if it is deficient, or nine days after it, if that month is full. These days, to which must be added the nineteenth of the month, which occurs seven weeks after the beginning of the preceding month, were regarded as unlucky days on which a man should afflict himself, eschew pleasures, and refrain from performing important works, for they would not prosper. This system was not just the product of a late development and sophistication, as was thought till a few years ago; nor is it reflected only in the arrangement of the Assyrian calendar, consisting of fifteen tablets, that was drawn up in the seventh century B.C.E. and called *inbu bēl arḫim* ('the fruit [moon] is lord of the month'), but it is also found in an edition of the calendar belonging to the beginning of the tenth century, which contains much older material. The recension of the seventh century sets down the laws of those days as follows: '"The shepherd of many people" (that is, the king, or possibly one of the high priests) shall not eat cooked meat or baked bread, nor may he change the garment on his body or put on a clean garment; the king shall not ride in a chariot nor shall he speak words of rulership; the seer shall not enquire of his god; the physician shall not attend to the sick; and in general the day is not propitious for doing any desired thing'. The version of the tenth century likewise states that the seer shall not enquire of his god, that the physician shall not attend to the sick, and generally that those days are not favourable for doing the thing desired. It adds that anyone doing work on the fourteenth day of the month will lose his money, and that on the twenty-eighth day no one should undertake a journey. There are also other days that it mentions as 'unpropitious for doing the thing desired' (*viz* the first, the fifteenth, the twenty-ninth and the thirtieth); but on the first, it rules, the king *may* speak words of rulership and clean his garment. In regard to the ninth, it declares that no one should appear thereon before the judge; and on the twenty-ninth and thirtieth, it prescribes that, just as on the twenty-eighth, no one should set out on a journey. So far the sources.

Many scholars have discussed the question of the relationship between these days and the Israelite Sabbath, and having regard to the highly complicated nature of the problem it is not surprising that their opinions differ; nor is it a matter for wonder that not all of them have been careful to express well-founded views. Some have supposed that the Israelite Sabbath, too, was originally the day of the full moon, but there is no basis for this theory (even the association of the words *new moon* and *Sabbath* does not prove anything); in the final analysis it is based only on the identification of the Israelite Sabbath with the Mesopotamian Sabbath, which itself requires proof, and thus begs the question. The same applies to the view that the 7th, 14th, 21st and 28th days of the month were also called by the Babylonians and Assyrians *šabattu–šapattu;* there is no evidence of this in the sources, and the hypothesis rests on the supposed connection between these days and the Israelite Sabbath: another instance of begging the question! Similarly, the surmise that the children of Israel derived the essential idea of the Sabbath and its detailed laws from the Mesopotamian system of 'rest days' on the 7th, 14th, 21st and 28th of the month, days 'on which work is forbidden', cannot be correct; it is clear from the regulations governing these days quoted above that they are not 'rest days' at all, and that this name was given to them only on the basis of the presumed connection with our Sabbath. Nor, for that matter, is 'work forbidden' on these days in the way that it is prohibited on the Sabbath; it is merely stated that important works should not be done on them lest they do not prosper. In truth, the Jewish people also observe days of a similar type and with comparable regulations, and in several respects the resemblance is quite *startling,* but they are not Sabbath days; they are the first nine days of the month of Ab, whose character, of course, is polarically different from that of the Sabbath.

An acceptable solution to the problem must be sought in a different direction. Undoubtedly, the Israelite Sabbath and what we find among the Babylonians and Assyrians have common elements.

The name *šabattu* or *šapattu* (be its etymology, on which opinion is divided, what it may), the expression synonymous with it, *ūm nūḫ libbi,* which brings to mind the concept of 'Sabbath *rest*' (most scholars have overlooked this point), the special days that occur every month once in seven days — all this is thought-provoking. On the other hand, there are many differences, and they are far more important than the resemblances; the former concern the inner content, whereas the points of correspondence are related to the external aspect. These divergences indicate that the solution to the problem is not to suppose that the children of Israel borrowed the idea of the Sabbath from the peoples of Mesopotamia, but, on the contrary, that the Israelite Sabbath was instituted in *opposition* to the Mesopotamian system. Since it is not my wish, as I have stated, to enter into the question of the internal development of the Sabbath among the Israelites, I shall base my argument only on the paragraph under consideration and on verses that are wholly parallel to it. The Torah, it seems to me, purports to say this: Israel's Sabbath day shall not be as the Sabbath of the heathen nations; it shall not be the day of the full moon, or any other day connected with the phases of the moon and linked, in consequence, with the worship of the moon, but it shall be the *seventh day* (this enables us to understand why this particular name, *the seventh day,* is emphasized here), the seventh in *perpetual* order, independent and free from any association with the signs of the heavens and any astrological concept. It shall not be a day appointed for the worship of the hosts of the heavens, but one sanctified to Him who created the heavenly hosts and the universe as a whole (cf. *but the seventh day is a sabbath to the Lord your God* in the Decalogue), as a memorial to the work of creation; not a day of self-affliction and misfortune, but one of *blessing* (*So God* BLESSED *the seventh day;* cf. also, in the Ten Commandments, Exod. xx 11: *therefore the Lord* BLESSED *the sabbath day and hallowed it*); not a day intended to *propitiate the angry godhead,* but one on which the Divine *work was not done,* thus a day that is worthy of serving as an example to humanity upon whom devolves the duty of imitating the ways of God, and that, consequently, is fitted to become a day of *rest for mankind,* who are weary and weighed down by the yoke of hard toil, and also for the brute creatures (cf. Deut. v 14: *that your manservant and your maidservant may* REST *as well as you;* Exod. xxiii 12: *that your ox and your ass* HAVE REST, *and the son of your handmaid, and the alien,* MAY BE REFRESHED); hence a day that will serve as a memorial to the liberation of the children of Israel from the house of bondage (Deut. v 15). See further my remarks above, in the penultimate paragraph of my commentary on *v.* 2, commencing 'the verb שָׁבַת *šābhath*'.

אֲשֶׁר בָּרָא אֱלֹהִים לַעֲשׂוֹת *'ăšer bārā' 'Elōhīm la'ăśōth* ['which God had creatively made'] / Many interpretations of this subordinate clause have been suggested, for example: that God created roots in all the species, endowing them with the power to reproduce their likeness (Ibn Ezra); that He created on the first day the elements with which to do all the works that are mentioned on the other days (Nahmanides); that He abstained thereon from doing any of the work that He had created (Naḥmanides, second explanation, supported among the moderns by Schill in *ZAW,* xxiii, pp. 147–148); in making which He created (Dillmann); which He created and made (Gunkel, Heinisch); which He created in order to make it (Jacob), and so on and so forth. All these interpretations are difficult; certain emendations have also been proposed, but these are even more forced than the explanations of the existing text.

In order to understand the verse properly, we must first determine the manner in which the two roots, בָּרָא *bārā'* ['create'] and עָשָׂה *'āśā* ['make'], are used. The verb בָּרָא *bārā'* signifies not only the making of the world in the six days of creation but connotes every act of God that transcends the bounds of normality (e.g. Exod. xxxiv 10: *Before all your people I will do marvels, such as have not been* WROUGHT [literally, 'created'] *in all the earth or in any nation;* Num. xvi 30: *But if the Lord* CREATES SOMETHING NEW [literally, 'creates a creation'] *and the ground opens its mouth,* etc.), and sometimes it refers to Divine acts that are quite normal (e.g. Isa. liv 16: *Behold, I have* CREATED *the smith . . . I have also* CREATED *the ravager to destroy;* ibid. lvii 19: *that* CREATETH *the fruit of the lips;* Ezek. xxi 35 [E.V. *v.* 30]; *In the place where you were* CREATED, *in the land of your origin;* Psa. li 12 [E.V. *v.* 10]: CREATE *in me a clean heart, O God*). In our section it is used only when Scripture wishes to sress the wonder of something, *viz* in the opening verse, in the concluding sentence, in connection with the sea-monsters — abnormal beings — and with regard to man, the highest of all the creatures.

The verb עָשָׂה *'āśā* betokens, among its other meanings (it is used as a synonym of בָּרָא *bārā'* in Exod. xxxiv 10 quoted above), the making of something that did not exist before (it will suffice to mention i 7, 16, 25, 26, 27 and ii 2 of our section). As regards the construction of our clause, which contains two synonymous verbs, the second being in the infinitive with the preposition *Lāmedh* ['to'], compare Psa. lxiii 3 [E.V. *v.* 2]: So I HAVE LOOKED UPON THEE *in the sanctuary,* TO BEHOLD [E.V. 'beholding'] *Thy power and glory.* The second verb comes to elucidate the particular sense in which the first is to be understood. Similarly in our verse: the word לַעֲשׂוֹת *la'ăśōth* ['to make'] comes after בָּרָא *bārā'* ['He created'] to specify the kind of creation of which the verse speaks, namely, an act of creation that is also a 'making', that is, a wondrous work implying the making of things that never existed before.

The closing verse corresponds to the introductory sentence of the section; in both it is written: *God created.* But whereas the word בָּרָא *bārā'* alludes to the first verse, לַעֲשׂוֹת *la'ăśōth* recalls all the 'makings' mentioned in the rest of the section. Just as the prologue announces at the outset the main subject-matter of the account that follows, so the epilogue looks back and epitomizes within the limits of one short sentence the content of the preceding narrative, re-awakening in the heart of the reader, by means of this synthesis inherent in its words, the sentiments that were aroused within him in the course of his reading. A truly majestic conclusion to the section.

SECTION TWO

THE STORY OF THE GARDEN OF EDEN

CHAPTER II, VERSE 4 — CHAPTER III, VERSE 24

INTRODUCTION

§ 1. In this section we are told how the first man was formed of dust from the ground, how he dwelt in the garden of Eden, of the creation of woman, of the sin that they both committed, and of the punishment meted out to them. The primary purpose of the Torah in these chapters is to explain how it is that in the Lord's world, the world of the good and beneficent God, evil should exist and man should endure pain and troubles and calamities. The answer given here to the burning question of the origin of evil in the world is this: although the world that issued from the hand of the Creator is, according to the testimony of the previous section, good — yea, very good — yet man corrupts it by his conduct and brings evil into the world as a result of his corruption. Apart from this primary teaching, it is also possible to draw, incidentally, other lessons from this section: we learn of the necessity of discipline founded on God's statutes; of man's innate conscience; of the law of Divine reward and punishment; of the bonds of brotherhood uniting the inhabitants of the world, who are all descended from one human pair, are all kin and all equal to one another; of the humane treatment that we should accord to animals, for like ourselves they were formed of the earth; of the value of marriage; of the importance of monogamy; of the humility with which it behoves us to conduct ourselves, seeing that we are dust and unto dust we return, and similar ideas.

§ 2. These teachings, like the truth that the Torah sought to convey in the preceding section, could not be imparted in abstract terms, for the reasons that I have indicated above, in the Introduction to the story of creation (p. 12, end of § 4). In this instance, too, Scripture had to inculcate its doctrines through the medium of concrete description, that is, by telling a story from which the reader could draw a moral. As I shall show further on, there existed among the Israelites, before ever the Torah was written, a poetic tradition concerning the garden of Eden, even as there was a poetic tradition relating to the work of creation, and an epic poem, or possibly several epics, had already been composed on the theme of the garden of Eden and what took place there. The two traditions, the one dealing with the story of creation and the other with that of the garden of Eden, were of different types. The former, which treats of a more speculative subject, passed apparently through the circles of the 'wise men' (see above, p. 12, end of § 4), the philosophical groups who delved into the mystery of the world's existence. The latter, which is concerned with a simpler and more popular topic, remained nearer to the broad masses of the people and assumed a form more suited to them in its colourful and vivid portrayals. It would have been natural to suppose that, when the Torah came to instruct us concerning the creation of the world and man, it would not overlook the existing traditions, whether they emanated from the schools of the sages or from popular folklore. We should have expected Scripture to adopt a given attitude towards them, and to teach us how to extract from them the kernel of real worth and to reject the husk, how to refine and purify them in order, on the one hand, to remove from them whatever was incompatible with its ethos, and, on the other hand, to harmonize them with its own doctrines and views, so that they could be of value to the people of Israel for the future. Now this is precisely what the Torah did. It took material for its construction from the creation saga as well as from the traditional story about the garden of Eden, in accordance with the method with which we have already become familiar. It selected from the traditional material what accorded with its spirit and purpose, it rejected and nullified, by silence or some critical remark, whatever appeared to it objectionable, and it gave the entire account a new complexion patterned to fit its outlook and the educational aim that it had set itself.

My hypothesis that the Israelites had an epic tradition concerning the story of the Garden of Eden before the Torah was written, and that this tradition had already received a definite literary form in one or more epic poems, finds support in a number of Biblical verses some of which belong to our section and some to other sections or other books. It is worth while examining these passages in detail, paying attention, at the same time, to what the literary works of the peoples of the ancient East tell us on cognate subjects. I deal fully with the whole matter in a special article in the volume published in memory of the late Professor Moses Schorr; here, then, I can be brief (see also my Hebrew essay on 'The Epic Poetry of Israel' published in *Keneseth,* viii, pp. 139–141).

§ 3. It is stated in our section (iii 24): *and at the east of the garden of Eden He placed the cherubim and the sword-flame which turned every way.* Now it is obvious that *the cherubim and the sword-flame which turned every way,* which are mentioned here with the definite article, although there is no previous reference to them in our section, were not new to the children of Israel. We must therefore conclude that their story was recorded in some ancient literary work that enjoyed general currency among the people. Since, moreover, a phrase like *the sword-flame which turned every way* is certainly poetic, we learn that the ancient text in question was a poem and not a prose composition. Undoubtedly it was an Israelite epic, for it is not conceivable that the Torah would allude to a pagan epic of gentile origin. Also in the book of Ezekiel, which makes repeated reference to Eden, especially in two sections that we shall discuss later, mention is made of the *cherub* in connection with the garden of Eden (xxviii 14f); but the cherub there is not necessarily *outside* Paradise, as it is depicted here, but actually *inside* it. This indicates that the passage in Ezekiel is independent of our section (further on we shall see that there are several other details there that are absent here) and that the prophet had a different source before him, with which his listeners as well as he were familiar, that told of a cherub or cherubim in the garden of Eden; this source was doubtless poetic, as is evidenced by the prophet's colourful description.

There are also other indications of a poetic tradition to be found in our section: the poetic rhythm of a number of the utterances that it contains (ii 18, 23; iii 14–19); the examples of parallelism that we meet here and there apart from the utterances (e.g. ii 5; iii 3, 6, etc.); poetic words like the noun אֵד *'ēdh* [see below on ii 6], which occurs also in Job (xxxvi 27); the verb בָּנָה *bānā* [literally, 'build'] used in the sense of 'create' or 'form' (ii 22), which is the connotation it has in Akkadian and Ugaritic poetry; likewise the sentences commencing with the word טֶרֶם *ṭerem* (ii 5), which are characteristic of the style, both among the Israelites and the Gentiles, of the poems that portray the earliest period of creation. Noteworthy also are the trees of the garden of Eden (ii 9; cf. iii 6). Similar phrases occur in the Gilgameš Epic in the description of the garden of the goddess Siduri; there, too, we find the very words 'pleasant to the sight' [literally, 'to behold'] and in the parallel clause 'good to look upon' (Assyrian recension, Tablet IX, v, end). This definitely points to an established poetic tradition in the ancient East, in which Israel shared. There are other expressions in our section, too, that can serve, although not definitely attributable to a poetic source, as additional proof that the story told here is not the first Israelite account of the subject. It is written, for example: THE TREE OF LIFE *also in the midst of the garden* (ii 9). The fact that the definite article occurs in the phrase '*the* tree of life' on its very first appearance in this section, indicates, as I have stated in connection with *the cherubim and the sword-flame which turned every way,* that it was something with which the Israelites were already familiar, and that consequently the reader was instantly able to understand the reference. Later on, when we deal with the parallels to the concept to the tree of life, it will be seen that although no clear and exact analogies have been found so far among the neighbouring peoples, the idea was certainly widespread among the Israelites, as is evidenced by the fact that in Proverbs the expression 'tree of life' occurs several times as a common metaphor for things from which life-giving power emanates (Prov. iii 18; xi 30; xiii 12; xv 4).

The same applies to *the tree of the knowledge of good and evil.* The name of this tree likewise has the definite article even when first mentioned (ii 9); and although no parallels to it have been discovered either in Israelite or pagan literature, this tree, also, was undoubtedly known to Scripture readers from another source. Hence there was no need to give here a detailed explanation of its nature.

Apart from our section and those verses in which the *garden of Eden* or *the garden of the Lord* is introduced as a simile (Gen. xiii 10; Isa. li 3; Ezek. xxxvi 35; Joel ii 3), the garden of Eden is referred to at length, as I have mentioned earlier, in two passages in Ezekiel: xxviii 11–19; xxxi 8–9, 16–18. Beside the reference to *the cherub* cited above, these passages contain a number of details that point to an ancient epic tradition to which the prophet alludes as a matter of common knowledge to his audience. Some of the details found in the prophecies correspond to those of our section, others do not. The points of agreement are as follows: (a) The garden is in *Eden;* (b) it contains *miraculous trees;* (c) the *cherub,* as stated previously, is mentioned in association with the garden; (d) the creature that dwelt in the garden (man in Genesis, the cherub in Ezekiel) sinned and was, in consequence, expelled from it; (e) particular phrases like, *on the day when you were created* (Ezek. xxviii 13), *from the day you were created* (ibid. 15), which resemble the expression in our section (Gen. ii 4): *when they were created,* which is parallel to, *In the day that the Lord God made* (and further on, v 2: *in the day when they were created*); or like, *in the midst of the stones of fire* (of the garden of Eden) *you walked* (Ezek. xxviii 14), which recalls the words in Genesis (iii 8), *walking in the garden;* or like, *and I turned you to* ASHES [אֵפֶר *'ēpher*] *upon the earth* (Ezek. xxviii 18), which reminds us of the verse, *For you are* DUST [עָפָר *'āphār*] *and to dust you shall return* (Gen. iii 19). These parallels are indicative of the existence of an established Israelite tradition, marked even by a distinctive phraseology.

The points of difference from our section are by no means few, and they must be considered in detail. In order to understand the cause of these divergencies between the prophetic and our own version, we should bear in mind what was stated above in regard to other discrepancies of this kind (in the Introduction to the story of Creation, p. 11, § 4, and in the commentary on i 6, 9), namely: (a) that in the ancient Israelite epics, despite the fact that the traditional material of the Orient acquired in them a new aspect in keeping on the whole with the national spirit and conscience, there remained, notwithstanding, certain elements in which can be heard a faint echo of their origin in a foreign environment; (b) that the prophets and Bible poets, who are accustomed to use the rhetorical methods commonly applied in poetry and to express their thoughts in poetic form, did not refrain from alluding to these epics or even from utilizing the aforementioned elements as similes and poetic figures of speech; (c) that the Torah, which is written in prose, not poetry, and uses, as a rule, simple language, was not only careful to avoid making the slightest use of the pagan elements, for fear that the reader might understand them literally, but even voiced, whenever necessary, its protest against them.

The first difference between the passages in Ezekiel and our section is this: in the former, both in ch. xxviii and ch. xxxi, the garden is called גַּן אֱלֹהִים *gan 'Elōhīm* ['garden of God'] or גַּן הָאֱלֹהִים *gan hā'Elōhīm* ['the garden of God'], whereas in the latter it is said that the Lord planted the garden for the sake of *man*. It thus appears that the ancient epic tradition made mention of a garden that belonged specifically to God, a concept akin to that current among the peoples of the ancient East, who used to tell many legends about the gardens of the gods. The prophet, characteristically, did not hesitate to allude to the poetic figure 'the garden of God'; the Torah, however, not only excluded from its account all reference to this concept, but expressed its disapproval of it. It is written in Genesis ii 8: *And the Lord planted a garden in Eden, in the east; and there He put* THE MAN *whom He had formed,* and later we read (*ibid.* 15): *The Lord God took* THE MAN *and put him in the garden of Eden to serve and to guard.* It is as though the Torah purports to say: Do not imagine that the garden of Eden was the garden of the Lord God, as the poets relate; you must understand that the Lord God planted the garden only for man's benefit; God Himself has no need of a garden. The simile *like the garden of the Lord,* which occurs not only in Isa. li 3 but also in Gen. xiii 10, is a stereotyped comparison in Hebrew that was coined in an ancient period on the basis of the tradition referred to, and the Torah also used it as a common, idiomatic phrase, for, having become stereotyped, the etymological signification of the words of which it is composed could be disregarded. Concerning iii 8, see below, the annotations to the verse.

The second difference. According to Ezekiel the garden is situated on A MOUNTAIN SACRED UNTO GOD: *and I placed you on the holy mountain of God* (ch. xxviii 14); *so I cast you as a profane thing from the mountain of God* (ibid. 16). In the Torah there is no reference at all to a holy mountain (although even the pentateuchal description implies that the garden was on high ground, for we are told that a river flowed out of Eden to water the garden, and thereafter it divided into four big rivers, but there is no mention whatever of a ***mountain,*** much less of ***a holy mountain***). Unquestionably, Ezekiel did not invent the idea of the mountain, but found it in the poetic tradition. There this feature must have played an important role, corresponding to the belief current in the ancient Orient concerning a Divine garden planted on a hallowed mountain, the seat of the gods, in the recesses of the north. The Torah, as usual, refrained from mentioning this detail and, by its silence, negatives it. It writes simply: *a garden in Eden, in the east,* nothing more.

The third difference. Ezekiel alludes to *the precious stones* and *the gold* that were to be found in the garden of Eden and formed the covering of the cherub (xxviii 13). But the Torah contains no reference to such things in the garden of Eden. It is evident that here, too, the prophet refers to something recounted in the ancient poem that was known to his listeners. The precise subject spoken of there and alluded to in the words of Ezekiel, it is impossible to tell from the allusions alone, but we may draw certain inferences from the parallel account in the epic of Gilgameš, which depicts the garden of the goddess Siduri (in the tablet mentioned above, end of col. v and the fragment of col. vi). In this passage we are told of the trees in the garden, which bear precious stones instead of fruit, and, first and foremost, mention is made of the *sându* [Hebrew: שֹׁהַם *šōham*]* and the *uqnû* [Hebrew: סַפִּיר *sappīr*] **. Thereafter the text is defective, and from the fragmentary lines remaining it is certain that the poem went on to speak of other trees, among them *cedars,* and of other gems (for the identification of *sându* or *sâmtu* with the Hebrew שֹׁהַם *šōham,* see Albright's remarks in *AJSL,* xxxiv, 1917–1918, p. 230). Both the *šōham* and the *sappīr* are listed among the precious stones mentioned in Ezekiel xxviii; likewise are cedars included among the trees enumerated in Ezekiel xxxi. It seems that the Israelite poem available to the prophet contained a story about miraculous trees in the garden of Eden that bore jewels instead of fruit, and with their boughs formed a covering for the head of the cherub (*your covering,* in Ezekiel

* שֹׁהַם *šōham* is variously identified as: *onyx, beryl, chrysoprasus* or *malachite.*

** סַפִּיר *Sappir* is *sapphire* or *lapis lazuli.*

xxviii 13). We may also presume that the poem spoke of trees that bore fruit of gold, a concept that one frequently meets in pagan myths, including those of Europe. Whether the Gilgameš epic also referred to golden fruit in the garden of Siduri or not, it is no longer possible to determine on account of the defect in the text.

It is noteworthy, however, that in Job xxviii 16, in the eulogy of *wisdom,* not only the *šōham* and *sappīr,* which head the list of gems in the garden of Siduri, the *goddess of wisdom,* but also *gold,* called *gold* [כֶּתֶם *kethem*] *of Ophir,* are mentioned together. Earlier in the same chapter of Job (*vv.* 5–6), we read of *sappīr* and *gold,* to which is juxtaposed לָחֶם *lāḥem* [E.V. 'bread'], a word whose authenticity is in doubt, and for which Torczyner in his commentary suggests, without reference to our subject, that we should read the name of some precious stone, possibly יַהֲלֹם *yahălōm* [diamond, jasper or onyx], or לֶשֶׁם *lešem* [jacinth, ligure or amber], or שֹׁהַם *šōham.* All this points to the existence of an established poetic tradition among the Israelites, and it is to this poetic tradition that Ezekiel alludes in his prophecies. We may also add that immediately after the *gold* Ezekiel mentions מְלֶאכֶת תֻּפֶּיךָ וּנְקָבֶיךָ *meleʼkheth tuppekhā ūneqābhekhā* [E.V. 'the workmanship of thy tabrets and thy pipes']; the obscure word at the end — נְקָבֶיךָ *neqābhekhā* [E.V. 'pipes'] — may also be explained, on the basis of the literary tradition of the East, as the name of *gold* and silver ornaments that belonged, according to the heathen myths, to the gods and demi-gods; I adduced the evidence for this some years ago from a Ugaritic text (*Orientalia,* New Series, Vol. vii [1939], p. 282).

In our section there is nothing of all this. So strange a mythological notion as trees bearing precious stones or golden bowls instead of fruit was not consonant with the spirit of the Torah, which accordingly rejected it emphatically. In the Torah narrative, the fruits of the garden of Eden are quite natural, like any other fruit in the world, and even though the fruits of two of the trees were capable of producing unique effects (this could not be avoided since it was bound up with the essential teaching that the Torah wished to inculcate in this section), they are, notwithstanding, depicted as possessing the qualities of ordinary fruit (iii 6): *that the tree was good for food and that it was a delight to the eyes.*

Nor is this all; on this occasion the Torah is not content with silent negation, but expresses its opposition explicitly. It attributes the source of the שֹׁהַם *šōham,* בְּדֹלַח *beḏhōlaḥ* [see commentary on ii 12, p. 119] and *gold* to the land of Havilah, one of the countries of our world (ii 11–12). Only in the light of the present exposition can we understand why these substances are mentioned in our section; otherwise the reference to them would appear out of place. We shall deal with the subject in detail in the commentary on ii 11–12; but it is worth noting even at this stage that in these verses the Torah intends to say, as it were: 'It does not behove you, O children of Israel, to believe that precious stones and gold grow, as the poets tell, on trees like fruit, and that they originate in the garden of Eden. They are natural, created substances of the earth that come to us from one of the countries that you know; and if they are connected with the garden of Eden, it is not a direct connection — they come from the land of Havilah, which is encompassed by one of the rivers branching off from the stream that flows from Eden. That is all'.

The fourth difference. Ezekiel speaks of *stones of fire* that were in the garden of Eden (xxviii 14: *You were on the holy mountain of God, in the midst of the stones of fire you walked;* ibid. *v.* 16: *I cast you as a profane thing from the mountain of God, and the guardian cherub drove you out from the midst of the* STONES OF FIRE); but the Torah makes no mention of them. Without doubt these stones, to which the prophet alludes as something well-known, were referred to in the ancient epic as one of the characteristic features of the garden of Eden. The commentators usually identify them with the gems listed above, but this is unlikely — firstly, because the prophet had no need to speak of them again; secondly, the precious stones constituted the *covering* of the cherub, that is to say, they formed a protection for his head among the high branches of the trees, whereas the stones of fire, *in the midst of which* the cherub *walked,* were apparently lying on the ground of the garden. If I am not mistaken, the *fire* is none other than the fire of heaven that we see in the form of *lightning,* which issues from above the towering *mountains of God,* whose summits reach the sky and on which the garden of Eden is situated. This view finds support in Ezekiel, where, in the description of the fire of the

Divine chariot, it is written (i 13): *and out of the fire went forth* LIGHTNING. Hence we must regard the 'stones of fire' of Ezekiel as analogous to the 'stones of lightning' mentioned in Ugaritic poetry in connection with the dialogue between Baʿal, the god of the heavens, and ʿAnath his sister (Tablet V AB, part iii, line 23, and part iv, line 61, according to the suggested restoration of the text) and also to the 'stones of lightning' that occur in the Akkadian prayer to Ramman, the god of the storm-wind (King, *Babylonian Magic and Sorcery,* London, 1896, p. 78, line 2 [No. 21, line 17]; further information on this subject is contained in my aforementioned essay in *Studies in Memory of Moses Schorr*). The theme of the 'stones of fire' in the ancient Israelite poetry was one of the elements in which is still to be discerned the link with gentile religious concepts; consequently the Torah wished to nullify it, and, in accordance with its usual practice, passed it over in silence.

The fifth difference. In our section the trees of the garden are referred to in general terms only — *every tree that is pleasant to the sight and good for food* (ii 9); but in the book of Ezekiel they are specified in detail. When the prophet describes the majestic beauty of his cedar of Lebanon, symbol of Pharaoh king of Egypt, he declares that *the* CEDARS *in the garden of God could not dim it* — that is, were not its peers — *and the* FIR *trees* (which were in the same garden, needless to say) *could not equal its boughs;* that *the* PLANE TREES (which stood there) *were as nothing compared with its branches,* and that generally *no tree in the garden of God was like it in beauty, and all the trees of Eden that were in the garden of God envied it* (xxxi 8–9). Thereafter Ezekiel asks (*v.* 18): *Whom are you thus like in glory and in greatness among the trees of Eden?* The names of these trees — *cedars, fir trees, plane trees* — as well as their characteristics — their beauty, their size and their majesty (*glory*) — must certainly have been known to the prophet's listeners, for otherwise his allusions would not have created the effect that he intended. We have already noted that the Gilgameš epic gave a detailed and colourful description of the divine garden and the trees therein, and that this description, although only fragments of it have come down to us, mentioned at least the *cedars* by name. So, too, without doubt the Israelite poetry must have depicted in detail and with poetic colouring the garden and its graceful, majestic trees. The prophet, characteristically, alludes to this description, but the Torah, no less typically, passes over it in silence.

The sixth and fundamental difference. In Ezekiel ch. xxviii, as stated earlier, the being who inhabited the garden of Eden, and sinned there and was banished from it, was the cherub and not man, as in our section. In the prophetic passage, the references to the parable, namely, the story of the cherub, are intermingled with references to the subject that it illustrates, to wit, the fate of the king of Tyre, and it is not always easy to disentangle the former from the latter. But we may reasonably attribute to the cherub at least the following clauses: *You were blameless in your ways... till iniquity was found in you* (*v.* 15)... *and you sinned; I cast you as a profane thing from the mountain of God, and the guardian cherub drove you out from the midst of the stones of fire* (*v.* 16); *Your heart was proud because of your beauty; you corrupted your wisdom for the sake of your splendour, I cast you to the ground...* (*v.* 17); *By the multitude of your iniquities... you profaned your sanctuaries; so I brought forth fire from the midst of you; it consumed you, and I turned you to ashes upon the earth in the sight of all who saw you* (*v.* 18); possibly we should also include: *you have come to a dreadful end and you shall be no more for ever* (*v.* 19). All this testifies to the fact that in a remote period of antiquity there was an Israelite saga that related how the cherub — or one of the cherubs — who dwelt in the garden of Eden, upon the top of the mountain of God, which was as high as the heavens, sinned in his pride against God, and as a punishment for his transgression he was driven out from the garden of Eden and cast down to the earth. It may be that the word *earth* occurs here in the sense of *Sheol* [abode of the dead], in which sense it is also found in Akkadian. This saga, therefore, belongs to the cycle of legends concerning the angels who were hurled down from Heaven; we shall deal with this subject in detail when we come to the episode of the sons of God and the daughters of man (vi 1–4). The prophet alludes to this tradition and uses it as a poetic parable for the downfall of the king of Tyre. The Torah, on the other hand, seeks to refine and purify the tradition. The story of the angels who sinned and were punished is not consonant with the spirit of the Pentateuch and is deprecated by it, just as at a subsequent period the sages of the Talmud expressed opposition to the later legends of a similar character. The angels are all beloved, pure and holy, and the one who sinned in the garden of Eden and was expelled therefrom was not a cherub nor an angel, but a man. The cherubs are devoted ministers of the Most High, who faithfully fulfil the task entrusted to them, namely, to guard the way leading to the tree of life (iii 24).

§ 4. Apart from the affinities that we have already noted in the description of the garden of the goddess in the Gilgameš epic, it is possible to find in the literary records of the ancient East other points of correspondence to the story related in our section. But in this case, as in other Pentateuchal passages, the divergences and the originality of the Torah's ideas compared with the gentile tradition and viewpoints are of greater interest than the resemblances. Thus, for example, the pagan peoples likewise used to tell stories about the creation of mankind by the gods, and they mentioned, among the materials used for the purpose, also the clay of the earth. But there is a vast gulf between these accounts and the Biblical story. Sumerian and Akkadian literature contains numerous works on this subject, which differ from one another in their details (see further on these texts below, in my annotations on ii 7). The various recensions describe the work of creation in different forms and attribute it to different deities or types of deities, namely, to the goddess Aruru (which has other designations, too), to Marduk, to both of them together, to Enki, to Enlil, to the four great gods, or to the Anunnaki. Sometimes the accounts speak of the gods giving *birth* to human beings, sometimes of birth in connection with *creation* from the clay of the earth, and at other times they refer to creation alone, either from the clay by itself or from clay mingled with the blood of a god slaughtered for the purpose, or mixed with his blood and flesh, and so forth. Similarly, the Egyptians held the belief that the god Khnum fashioned with his hands the bodies of men and women, and they used to depict him performing this work on the potter's wheel. But the Torah came and opposed all this. It does not portray a deity linked to nature, begetting human beings or contributing its blood or a part of its body for their creation, or actually moulding them with its hands on the potter's wheel. Nor does our section relate a mythological tale about what befell a divinity or what it suffered. Here we are told simply that man was formed from *dust* from the ground (not *clay;* on this point see my comments *ad loc.*), and that consequently it is incumbent on him always to remember that he is dust and that unto dust he shall return. The Creator remains in Genesis above nature, and His work is not described in detailed material terms; it is stated that He created man, but it is not recorded *how* He did this. In another respect, too, the Pentateuchal account differs from those given in the aforementioned texts, namely, in that it speaks of the creation of only one human pair, a fact that implies the brotherhood and equality of man, whereas the pagan texts refer to the mass creation of mankind as a whole.

In the eastern environment it is possible to find analogies also to other features of our section, for example, to the tree of life, the serpent, the cherubs, and so forth. I shall deal with these matters in detail in my annotations.

But to the heart of the story, that is, man's transgression and punishment, there appears, according to our present knowledge, to be no parallel among the other oriental peoples. It is true that several scholars have held that affinities were to be found in certain inscriptions, especially in (1) the myth of Adapa; (2) the Sumerian inscription that was first published by Langdon in *Publications of the University of Pennsylvania, Babylonian Section,* vol. x, part 1, 1915; (3) the Sumerian text first published by Barton in his book, *Miscellaneous Babylonian Inscriptions,* New Haven, 1918, pp. 52–56; (4) the Sumerian inscription first investigated by Chiera in AJSL, xxxix (1922–1923), pp. 40–51. But conflicting opinions have been expressed on these matters, which have been discussed at great length from different viewpoints and with varying results. Vriezen has recently (1937) given us a full bibliography and a careful study of the whole subject in his basic work on the concepts of the ancient Semitic peoples relative to the garden of Eden (cited below, in § 11), pp. 22–48, 69–73, 235–236. The conclusion of the author is that it is possible to discover in these texts only a few points of similarity to the Biblical narrative, but not a parallel to the leading motif of the story (see also the essay of Witzel mentioned below, in § 11).

The writer is likewise doubtful if an analogy is provided by the famous Babylonian seal on which are depicted a man and woman sitting on opposite sides of a tree, and a serpent behind the man (*op. cit.*, pp. 67– 69); he is equally sceptical about other representations of this kind.

We may add that latterly Speiser discovered in the excavations at Tepe-Gawra the imprint of a seal showing a man and a woman in a bent position as though bowed down by the burden of a terrible calamity, and behind them a serpent. Speiser, however, pointed out, when he drew the attention of scholars to the seal, that in his opinion it is difficult to see any affinity between it and the Scriptural narrative concerning the garden of Eden, particularly in view of the antiquity of the seal, which belongs to the first half of the fourth millenium B.C.E. (*BASOR*, 47 [1932], p. 23). In his report on the excavations at Tepe-Gawra, he left the interpretation of the seal unsolved (*Excavations at Tepe-Gawra*, Philadelphia, 1935, pp. 124–125, No. 41).

§ 5. The question of the relationship between this and the preceding section presents a formidable problem and merits special attention.

At the very first glance it becomes apparent that the two passages differ in their use of the Divine appellations. In the story of creation only the name אֱלֹהִים *'Elōhīm* ['God'] occurs, and ה' *YHWH* [E.V. 'Lord'] does not appear once; in this — the second — section we almost always find the compound name *YHWH 'Elōhīm*, and only in the conversation between the serpent and the woman (iii 1–5) does *'Elōhīm* occur by itself. This difference aroused long ago the suspicions of Bible students, and has served as the starting-point for all the learned writings and the protracted discussions ensuing through the years (since Witter's volume, which appeared in 1711, and Astruc's work, which was published in 1753) on the question of the sources of Genesis and the succeeding books, and on the combination of the elements emanating from those sources. A detailed survey of the history of these researches and discussions will be given in the Introduction * to this commentary (for the time being, however, the reader is referred to

* This introductory volume remained unwritten.

my book *The Documentary Hypothesis,* English translation, pp. 9–12). Here it will suffice to note that according to the documentary theory, which the majority of scholars have accepted, the difference in regard to the Divine names employed and a number of other divergences between the two sections prove that they belonged originally to two separate works: the first, which uses the appellation *'Elōhīm* exclusively, formed the beginning of document P, according to which the name *YHWH* was not revealed until the time of Moses; the second was the opening passage of document J, which mentioned *YHWH* from the very commencement of the world's history. Each of these narratives told the story of creation from its respective viewpoint and in a different manner, and a later editor took over the two sections verbatim from their source-works and joined them together without paying heed to the fact that, as a result, in the composite narrative the creation account appears twice (it is customary to call the first part of our section 'the second account of creation'). Nor was the redactor concerned that the two narratives differ from each other in character, style and the choice of God's names, and on a number of points even contradict one another. According to this view (the recent discussions among the adherents of the documentary hypothesis affect only particular details of the theory, not its general propositions) we have here not two adjoining sections of a single unified work that follow each other in one connected sequence, but two excerpts from two separate compositions, which a later editor arranged consecutively by pure chance.

§ 6. Is this view justified? I have dealt with this question at length in my book, *La Questione della Genesi,* pp. 257–276. Here I shall give a brief resumé of my investigations; but since scholarship is never at a standstill, I shall take the opportunity to buttress my standpoint with new arguments.

The fact that the two sections differ from each other not only in the use of the Divine names but also in other respects is not in doubt. In the first section we have before us a sublime picture of the totality of creation, depicted with great synthetic power and absolute simplicity of expression; the Godhead is revealed therein as a wholly transcendental Being, who abides in His own high sphere without contact with the creatures. The second section, on the other hand, gives us a graphic and dramatic story embellished with the marvels of the colourful oriental imagination, which is addressed to the feelings rather than the intellect of the reader; and there we see God in definite communion with man and the other creatures of His world.

But these divergences still do not prove the theory referred to. They are easily explicable on the basis of my hypothesis concerning the existence of various epic poems, whose contents served as material for the structure of the Pentateuchal narrative in these two passages — an epic poem emanating from the circle of the 'wise men' being used for the story of creation, and a more popular epic for the story of the garden of Eden. Needless to say, the character of the two poems differed considerably; the first was suited to the intellectuals and philosophers, whilst the second was intended more for the broad masses of the people, and consequently made use of picturesque and vivid descriptions, which were apt to capture the heart of the simple person. And it is self-understood that although the Torah gave the two sections a literary form of its own, some residual elements of the original character of the two ancient poems were bound to remain discernible in both of these passages.

§ 7. In this way we can also explain the change in the Divine names. I shall not deal at this stage with the general question of the use of these names; the Introductory Volume * will provide the proper place for this discussion. Here I shall touch only on matters necessary for the understanding of the specific problem relating to the first two sections. I have already shown, as a result of a study of the occurrence of the names of God throughout the Bible and Hebrew literature generally, combined with an investigation into the use of the personal designation of the deities and the generic names for God in the writings of the peoples of the ancient East (*La Questione della Genesi,* pp. 1–92; *The Documentary Hypothesis,* English translation, pp. 15–41), that the variation in the employment of the two names, *YHWH* and *'Elōhīm* in the book of Genesis is subject to certain rules, which I have been able to determine and formulate with precision (the reader will find them in *The Documentary Hypothesis,* English translation, pp. 31–32).

* This introductory volume remained unwritten.

These rules are based on the difference in the nature of the two names, for they are not of the same type; the name *YHWH* is a proper noun that denotes specifically the God of Israel, whereas *'Elōhīm* was originally a generic term and became a proper noun among the Israelites through the realisation that there is only One God and that *YHWH* alone is *'Elōhīm* ['God']. Following are some of the rules governing the use of the two Names in the book of Genesis that emerged from my investigations:

(a) The Tetragrammaton occurs when Scripture reflects the concept of God, especially in His *ethical* aspect, that belongs *specifically to the people of Israel; 'Elōhīm* appears when the Bible refers to the abstract conception of God that was current in the international circles of the Sages, the idea of God conceived in a general sense as the Creator of the *material* world, as the Ruler of nature, and as the Source of life.

(b) The name *YHWH* is used when Scripture wishes to express that direct and intuitive notion of God that is characteristic of the unsophisticated faith of the multitude; but *'Elōhīm* is employed when it is intended to convey the concept of the philosophically minded who study the abstruse problems connected with the existence of the world and humanity.

(c) *YHWH* appears when the Bible presents the Deity to us in His personal character, and in direct relationship to human beings or to nature; whereas *'Elōhīm* occurs when Holy Writ speaks of God as a Transcendental Being, who stands entirely outside nature, and above it.

According to these rules, the name *'Elōhīm* had necessarily to be used in the story of creation, for there God appears as the Creator of the *material* universe, and as the Master of the world who has dominion over everything and forms everything by His word alone, without there being any direct relationship between Himself and nature; and generally the description of creation given in that account is related to the tradition of the 'wise men' as stated above (regarding the name *'Elōhīm* in the last paragraph of the section, see my annotations above, on ii 2, p. 64).

In the narrative of the garden of Eden, on the other hand, God appears as the ruler of the *moral* world, for He enjoins a given precept on man, and demands an account of his actions; that apart, stress is laid here on His personal aspect, manifested in His direct relationship with man and the other creatures. For these reasons the name *YHWH* was required in this section, and this is the name that we actually find. Its association, however, with the appellation *'Elōhīm,* which is restricted to this one section of the entire book, is easily explained by Scripture's desire to teach us that *YHWH,* which occurs here for the *first time,* is to be wholly identified with *'Elōhīm* mentioned in the preceding section; in other words, that the God of the moral world is none other than the God of the material world, that the God of Israel is in fact the God of the entire universe, and that the names *YHWH* and *'Elōhīm* merely indicate two different facets of His activity or two different ways in which He reveals Himself to mankind. Once this truth has been inculcated here, there is no need to repeat it later; hence in the subsequent sections the Torah employs either the Tetragrammaton or *'Elōhīm* only, according to the context.

As for the exclusive use of *'Elōhīm* in the duologue between the serpent and the woman (iii 1–5), the explanation is very simple: it was unfitting (a point already made by other critics) that the personal name of God, which is supremely holy, should be used by the creature that counsels evil, or by the woman holding converse with it.

§ 8. The two remaining reasons for regarding the two passages as separate accounts, namely, the existence of contradictions between them and the repetition of the creation story, are interconnected; hence it will be best to consider both of them together.

The discrepancies that the exponents of the documentary hypothesis have found between the first section and the second (see the commentaries; for instance, that of König, pp. 224–225) are as follows:

(a) Instead of *six days,* as in the first section, the second section speaks of the creation of heaven and earth in *one day* (ii 4: IN THE DAY *that the Lord God made the earth and the heavens*);

(b) According to the first section, the world to begin with was a mass of water (i 1), but according to the second the land came first (ii 5–6);

(c) Ch. i 27 informs us that the two sexes were created simultaneously (*male and female He created them*), but the second section relates that first the man was formed (ii 7) and afterwards the woman (ii 21–22);

(d) In i 11–12 we are told that the plants came into being on the third day, that is, prior to man who was created on the sixth day, whereas in section two it is said that before the creation of man *no plant of the field was yet in the earth and no herb of the field had yet sprung up* (ii 5), and thereafter it is further stated that, after man had been formed, *the Lord God made to grow out of the ground every tree that is pleasant to the sight and good for food* etc. (ii 9);

(e) Likewise the living creatures, which the first section declares were created before man (i 20–21, 24–25), were, according to the second section, created after, and for the sake of, man (ii 19).

As far as the first point is concerned, the Scriptural use of the expression *in the day* (see the proofs adduced below, in the notes to ii 4) indicates that in cases such as this it does not mean in a day of twelve hours or in one of twenty-four hours, but generally *at the time, at the period.*

The third point (we shall deal with the second later) represents no incongruity at all. In the story of creation man is referred to as one of many creatures (see further on this subject below), and his creation is mentioned only as a link in the long chain of created beings; hence it was not possible to enter into details there without impairing the symmetry of the narrative. By stating, *male and female He created them,* the Bible merely records the fact that both sexes were created, without indicating the order of their formation; we are not told whether they were brought into being simultaneously or successively. In the second section, where the Bible speaks of the creation of man at greater length, the details are explained, and we are informed that first the man was made out of dust from the ground and afterwards the woman was formed from the rib. In accordance with the prevailing method, a general statement is followed here by a detailed description.

Concerning the fourth and fifth divergencies, see further my exposition of ii 5, 9, 19, where I demonstrate, by careful analysis of the text, that the reference is not to the first creation of plants and animals, but to something else.

There still remains the second inconsistency. If we examine our section closely, we shall see clearly that in its present form it does not contain a cosmogony. Although it is possible that the ancient epos relating the story of the garden of Eden linked the beginning of its narrative with a reference to the creation of the world (it was actually our method of interpretation that revealed that both here and in Ezekiel there are expressions belonging to the literary tradition concerning the beginning of creation), nevertheless in the passage before us there is no cosmogonic account at all. Not only is there no mention in it of the *hosts of the heavens,* or the *sea* and the *fishes* — other scholars have already drawn attention to this fact — but there is no reference even to the creation of the *cattle;* and of the entire *vegetable world* there appear here only the trees good for food of the garden of Eden and the particular species that are referred to in ii 5 and iii 18. And even in relation to these plants, and so, too, in regard to the *beasts* and the *flying creatures* (ii 19), Scripture does not necessarily speak of their original creation.

There is also another point. The creation of *heaven and earth* is likewise mentioned only incidentally (see below, my commentary on ii 4), as something already known, which is alluded to as a background to the scene to be described and as a prelude to the work to be accomplished. From all this it clearly emerges that there is no cosmogony here. When we read the Torah as we have it, as a continuous narrative, we find no discrepancy between the earlier statement that at first the world was a mass of water, and what we are told about the dry land at the beginning of the present section. Relying on the account of the first stages of creation given above, our section does not recapitulate the story; it depicts simply the position as it was at the *closing phase* of creation when man alone was wanting. An incongruity presents itself only if we separate the conjoined passages and treat our section as an independent narrative; then, of course, we need to find in it the beginning of the creation story. The contradiction appears, therefore, only when we regard as proven what the contradiction is supposed to prove; a clear example of begging the question! The theory that the two sections are not a unity does not help us to resolve the inherent problem of the text but creates instead an otherwise non-existent problem.

As for the repetition of the story of man's creation, which is told both in the preceding and in the present section, it should be noted that such duplications, although they may seem strange to those who are accustomed to the Hellenic process of thought, are not at all incongruous to the Semitic way of thinking. When the Torah made use of the two ancient poetic sagas, both of which described man's creation — the one in brief, general outline, as an account of the making of *one of the creatures* of the material world, and the second at length and in detail, as the story of the creation of the *central being* of the moral world — it had no reason to refrain from duplicating the theme, since such a repetition was consonant with the stylistic principle of presenting first a general statement and thereafter the detailed elaboration, which is commonly found not only in Biblical literature but also in the literary works of the rest of the ancient East. In the Babylonian creation epos, for instance, it is related at the end of Tablet III (line 138), in terse, general terms, that the gods determined the destiny of Marduk; yet Table IV reverts to the subject and describes the preparations made by the gods for the purpose of making this decision (lines 1–2), and thereafter it tells, in full detail, the manner in which the determination of Marduk's fate was carried out (lines 3–34). Ugaritic poetry provides further examples of this literary method (see, for example, my Hebrew article in the *Bulletin of the Jewish Palestine Exploration Society*, x, 1943, pp. 48–49). An interesting example in the Pentateuch occurs in Gen. xxviii. In verse 5 of that chapter we are told: *Thus Isaac sent Jacob away;* AND HE WENT TO PADDAN-ARAM TO LABAN, *the son of Bethuel the Aramean* etc., and in the following verses (6–9) Esau's reaction to the incident is described; when this matter has been disposed of, the narrative returns to the subject of Jacob's journey, which is of especial importance, and describes it in detail (*vv.* 10f.): *Jacob left Beer-sheba, and went toward Haran. And he lighted upon the place,* etc.. The same principle applies in the case of the creation of man: after recounting the whole story of the birth of the world to the end, Scripture returns to the theme of man's genesis, which is of particular significance, and gives us a detailed description thereof. At a later period, when the Jewish people had grown used to the Greek ways of thinking, the rabbinic sages became conscious of this duplication and expressed their surprise at it, but since they were not yet far removed from the ancient Semitic thought-processes, they found the correct answer to their query. In *The Mishnah of R. Eliezer b. R. José the Galilean,* Enelow's edition, p. 24 (cf. Rashi on ii 8), we read: 'The listener may think that this is another narrative, whereas it is only the elaboration of the first'.

§ 9. There is still another point, to consider. There are indications in the text of a *connection* between the two sections, and of a clear intention to harmonize the two narratives. We shall deal with this evidence in our commentary, especially in our notes on ii 5. Other pointers to this effect are:

(a) Emphasis is given to the creation both of man in the first section, and of woman in the second section, by stating the Divine *intention* before describing the *work* (i 26: *Let us make man in our image, after our likeness;* ii 18: *I will make* [the Septuagint and Vulgate read here, too: *Let us make*] *him a helper fit for him*);

(b) The verb עָשָׂה *ʿāśā* ['make'] and its synonyms are used in an identical manner in the aforementioned verses, that is, the verb עָשָׂה *ʿāśā,* which has the most general signification, is employed in stating God's intention, whilst a special verb describes the corresponding act in the narration of the work performed (i 27: *created,* ii 22: *built*);

(c) In the same way as God in the story of creation gave names, as a token of His sovereignty, to the created entities that are higher than man (i 5, 8, 10), so man in the story of the garden of Eden (ii 19–20) determined the names of those creatures over which, according to *the preceding section* (i 26, 28), he has dominion.

It would be possible to prolong this list further (see also the end of § 10, below); but it will suffice to bring only one additional example that appertains to the two narratives as a whole. It is this: the answer that the Torah seeks to give, as stated above (§ 1, p. 71), to the question of the existence of evil in the world, flows from the continuity of the two sections, which implies that although the world that emerged from the hands of the Creator was very good (i 31), man's transgressions were the cause of all manner of evils and troubles (iii 16–19). We receive this answer only when we study the two sections as a single sequence; but once we separate them, we obtain from each one of them only half the answer.

§ 10. Many of the critics who attribute our section to document

J consider that this document is itself not unitary, but is composed of fragments culled from two different sources (two strata of J or the like), which they specify by the symbols J[1] and J[2], or by similar devices. I have provided a comprehensive bibliography on this subject up to the year 1934 in my book, *La Questione della Genesi,* p. 257, note 2; to this must now be added the views of Mowinckel and Humbert, which I outline in the next paragraph.

Mowinckel expressed the opinion that the later of the two sources is not a special stratum of J but the Elohist source, E. Humbert has a different theory. He examined minutely the reasons advanced for assuming the existence of the two sources (mainly the repetition of certain particulars), and came to the conclusion that almost all these arguments are unsound, and that only two duplications are in fact to be found in the section: the one, which he considers to contain, in effect, an actual incongruity, appears in the first part of ii 8 (*the garden* is planted in a given place) and ii 9 (the trees are made to grow *out of the ground* generally, that is, out of the whole earth); and the second, in the latter half of ii 8 (*and there He put the man whom He had formed*) and ii 15 (*The Lord God took the man* etc.). Consequently he does not accept the thesis of two complete narratives belonging to two parallel sources, but takes the view, on the ground of the two repetitions mentioned and certain additional reasons, that we have here a composite work of J, who interpolated into his main narrative about the garden of Eden several elements derived from the tradition concerning the creation of the world. The verses dealing with the rivers (ii 10–14) he regards, in common with the majority of present-day scholars, as a later addition.

In my opinion, too, there is no doubt that many of the matters related in our section are linked with *various* schools of tradition, and not necessarily with two only. This was already apparent from our discussions in the preceding paragraphs, and the conclusion will be reinforced by detailed study of the text. But this is true only from the viewpoint of the *content,* but not from the *literary* aspect. Literary dissection in the divergent ways proposed by the different critics is impossible; for the variegated material deriving from the ancient sagas that the Torah utilized consists not of verses or fragments of verses, but of themes, ideas, narratives. This material, and also its own original contribution, the Torah cast, as it were, into a crucible and fused the whole together, and out of the integrated matter it created a unitary product.

Concerning the cosmogonic elements, it will suffice to refer to my previous observations on this subject; and as regards the above-mentioned two repetitions and other duplications and recapitulations in the section, as well as the sub-section about the rivers, I shall take the opportunity of dealing with them in detail in the course of my commentary, where the reader will find convincing proof that there is no justification for the literary analysis of the section into separate elements, and that, on the contrary, there is a firm and indissoluble link between the verses.

I shall add only this one point here, that a clear indication of the unity of the section (and at the same time of the connection between it and the preceding section) is to be seen in the numerical symmetry based on the number *seven* that we find in this section just as we encountered it in the story of creation. Here, too, the words that express the fundamental concepts of the passage recur a given number of times — *seven* times, or a multiple of *seven.* The name Eden occurs, together with קֶדֶם *qedhem* ['east'], seven times; the names אָדָם *'ādhām* and אִישׁ *'īš* [both mean 'man'] appear altogether twenty-eight times, that is, four times *seven;* the word אִשָּׁה *'iššā* and its synonyms עֵזֶר *'ēzer* ['helper'] and צֵלָע *ṣēlā'* ['rib'] are used twenty-one times, that is, three times *seven;* so, too, we find twenty-one examples of words derived from the root אָכַל *'ākhal* ['eat'] (*seven* in the very paragraph describing the sin, iii 1–7). Likewise, the verb לָקַח *lāqaḥ* ['take'], which is given special emphasis in a number of verses — e.g., *because she was taken out of man; for out of it you were taken; from whence he was taken* (ii 23; iii 19, 23) — occurs, all told, *seven* times in the course of the section. And when I sought to break up the section into paragraphs according to the logical division of the contents, there naturally emerged *seven* paragraphs.

§ 11. *Special bibliography for this section.* Detailed bibliographical information up to 1934 is contained in my book, *La Questione della Genesi,* in the passages dealing with this section (pp. 37–39, 151–152, 184–190, 257–276). Of the subsequent literature, the following works should be noted (additional articles referring to particular verses will be cited in my annotations; it should also be borne in mind that part of the bibliography given above, pp. 18f., on the creation story, pertains also to the present section):

Fischer, 'טוֹב וָרָע' in der Erzählung von Paradies und Sündenfall', *BZ,* xxii (1934), pp. 323–331; Brock-Utne, *Der Gottesgarten: eine vergleichende religionsgeschichtliche Studie,* Oslo 1935 (this work I have not been able to consult); Böhmer, 'Die geschlechtliche Stellung des Weibes in Gen. 2 und 3', *MGWJ,* lxxix (1935), pp. 281–302; Gordis, 'The significance of the Paradise Myth', *AJSL,* lii (1935–36), pp. 86–94; Staerk, 'Hat sich der Paradiesesmythos Gen. 2 f. in parsistischer Tradition erhalten?' *Werden u. Wesen des A.T.* (=*BZAW,* lxvi), Berlin 1936, pp. 225–232; Humbert, 'Mythe de création et mythe paradisiaque dans le second chapitre de la Genèse' *RHPhR,* xvi (1936), p. 445–461; Torczyner, *,Kᵉrūbh mimšaḥ hassōkhēkh' Studies in Memory of Alexander Kohut,* New York 1935, Heb. Sect., pp. 41–45; Vriezen, *Onderzoek naar de Paradijsvoorstelling bij de oude semietische Volken,* Wageningen 1937; Weiser, 'Die biblische Geschichte von Paradies und Sündenfall', *Deutsche Theol.,* 1937, pp. 9–37; Witzel, 'Eine weitere angebliche sumerische Parallele zum biblischen Sündenfall-Bericht', *Antonianum,* xii (1937), pp. 237–250; Reisner, *Der Baum des Lebens: eine Ausdeutung von Gen. 2,8–3,24,* Berlin 1937; Mowinckel, *The two Sources of the Predeuteronomic Primeval History (JE) in Gen. i–ii,* Oslo 1937; *idem,* 'De fire Paradiselvene (Gen. 2, 10–14), *Norsk Theol. Tidsskr.,* xxxix (1938), pp. 47–64; Robertson, 'The Paradise Narrative in Gen. 2–3, *Journ. Manchester Univ. Egypt Or. Soc.,* xxii (1938), pp. 21–35; De Groot, 'Un Paradis Palestinien?' *Mélanges Dussaud,* I, Paris 1939, pp. 67–72; Miklik, 'Der Fall des Menschen', *Biblica,* xx (1939), pp. 387–396; Renz, 'Die kluge Schlange', *BZ,* xxiv (1939), pp. 236–241; Schulz, 'Nachlese zu Gen. 3, 15', *ibid.,* pp. 343–356; Humbert, *Études sur le récit du Paradis et de la chute dans la Genèse,* Neuchâtel 1940.

See also, in connection with the trees of Eden, the following studies on the representations of holy trees in the ancient East: Perrot, 'Les représentations de l'arbre sacré sur les monuments de Mésopotamie et d'Élam', *Babyloniaca,* xvii (1937), pp. 1–144, pl. 1–32; Danthine, *Le palmier-dattier et les arbres sacrés dans l'iconographie de l'Asie occidentale ancienne,* Paris 1937; May, 'The Sacred Tree on Palestine Painted Pottery', *JAOS,* lix (1939), pp. 251–259; Marcus, 'The Tree of Life in Proverbs', *JBL,* lxii (1943), pp. 117–120.

INTRODUCTORY VERSE
TRANSITION FROM PREVIOUS SECTION

4. *This is the history of the heavens and the earth / when they were created,*
in the day that the Lord God made / the earth and the heavens.

4. Various suggestions have been submitted by modern commentators in regard to this verse. I have discussed them at length in my treatise, *La Questione della Genesi,* pp. 268–272; there is no need, therefore, for me to deal with the whole subject again in full. It will suffice if I summarize the gist of it here; those who are interested in the detailed aspects of the problem are referred to my aforementioned work, which also contains the requisite bibliography (for literature that has appeared after the publication of my book see above, pp. 95 f.).

The general tendency is to divide the verse into two unrelated parts: the first half is attributed, like the preceding section, to source P, and the second is ascribed to source J, and is regarded as the beginning of our section. The main reason for this division is that the second portion of the sentence contains the name *YHWH,* which is peculiar to J, whereas the first comprises expressions that are considered to be typical of P, namely: אֵלֶּה תוֹלְדוֹת *'ēlle thōl^edhōth* [literally, 'These are the generations', rendered here — ***This is the history***]; the phrase *the heavens and the earth,* which has the identical word-order that we find at the beginning of the previous section; and the verb בָּרָא *bārā'* ['created'], which also occurs in that section a number of times. Other reasons given for this dichotomy are that the second half of the verse seems redundant after the first, and that the changed order of the words *the earth and the heavens* and the use of the verb עָשָׂה *'āśā* ['made'] instead of

בָּרָא *bārā'* appear to point to a different origin from that of the first part of the sentence.

This analysis, however, creates a number of difficulties in respect of both parts of the verse. The first half does not connect properly with the continuation of P, namely: *This is the book of the history* [תּוֹלְדוֹת *tōl^edhōth*] *of Adam* (v 1); nor does it link up well with the preceding text, for according to the accepted view the expression אֵלֶּה תּוֹלְדוֹת *'ēlle thōl^edhōth* always refers to what follows, not to what was stated before. Hence some are of the opinion that originally the sentence *This is the history of the heavens and the earth when they were created* came before *In the beginning God created* (i 1); others consider that it was added by the editor at the end of P's section, couched in the latter's style, in order to connect the first section with ours; and others, again, suggest further variations of these views.

So far as the second half of the verse is concerned, a difficulty arises in regard to its syntactical relation to the succeeding verses, since it is not by itself a complete sentence. To solve the problem various interpretations have been proposed, for instance: *In the day that the Lord God made the heavens and the earth, when no plant of the field was yet . . . for the Lord God had not caused it to rain . . . and there was no man . . . but a mist went up . . . then the Lord God formed man,* etc., and other explanations of this kind, all of which are improbable and contrary — as I have demonstrated in detail in my above-mentioned work — to the spirit of the Hebrew tongue, as well as to eastern diction generally and Biblical style in particular. Further differentiation of sources in the following verses has also been suggested, resulting, as I have shown in my book, in a syntactic construction that defies the rules of Hebrew grammar and composition. We are thus confronted here with a concatenation of difficulties emanating from the assumption of a plurality of sources — a veritable tangle of problems from which, once caught, one can never extricate oneself.

On the other hand, a careful and unbiased examination of the verse will convince us that not only is there no justification for resolving it into two separate parts but that, on the contrary, there are definite indications that it is a unity, and also that the first half belongs to the story of the garden of Eden.

The reasons for regarding the verse as composite are all based on the general assumption of the existence of different sources distinguished by particular characteristics; for any one not accepting this postulate *a priori* as proven and unchallengeable these reasons have no force. Furthermore, even if we concede for a moment that J and P did exist, we must still point out:

(a) that the formula אֵלֶּה תוֹלְדוֹת *'ēlle thōl^edhōth* in a verse containing the name *YHWH* should indicate that this phrase is not restricted to P;

(b) that the fact that a given writer once uses the word-sequence *the heavens and the earth* does not exclude the possibility that another writer may also employ this order of words, which is assuredly not of a unique character; nor does it imply that the former is never permitted to reverse the word-order and say, *the earth and the heavens;*

(c) that in the preceding section we find not only the verb בָּרָא *bārā'* but also the verb עָשָׂה *'āśā,* and some expositors think that it is the latter verb that is characteristic of P's account of creation (for example, Böhl in the *Kittel Jubilee Volume,* pp. 55–60; see also Schwally in *ARW,* ix, pp. 159 f);

(d) that the verb בָּרָא *bārā'* occurs also in connection with the Tetragrammaton, e.g. vi 7: *So the Lord* [*YHWH*] *said, 'I will blot out man whom I have* CREATED [בָּרָאתִי *bārā'thī*]' (it is true that those who hold that the verb בָּרָא *bārā'* is characteristic of P omit the words *whom I have created,* which contradict their contention, as a later addition, and adopt a similar procedure in other passages; but it is obvious that an exegetic method that forces the verses to fit in with preconceived theories cannot be regarded as scientific criticism);

(e) that even the expression אֵלֶּה תוֹלְדוֹת *'ēlle thōl^edhōth,* although it occurs in a number of passages that are attributed to P on other grounds, is so simple that its use cannot possibly be held to be forbidden to any author apart from P.

The structure of the verse follows the precise rules of sentence-building and parallelism that normally govern exalted prose as well as poetry. It is composed of two parallel half-sentences, each of which consists of two parts arranged in chiastic order, that is, like the Greek *chi* (χ): *when they were created* corresponds to *in the day that the Lord God made;* similarly, the phrase *the heavens and the earth* is parallel to *the earth and the heavens* in the second half of the verse — again an example of chiasmus.

Furthermore, we have seen above (p. 75) that the word בְּהִבָּרְאָם *behibbāre'ām* ['when they were created'] and likewise the parallel phrase בְּיוֹם עֲשׂוֹת *beyōm 'ăśōth* ['in the day . . . made'] — which resemble the expressions in the passage in Ezekiel dealing with the garden of Eden, בְּיוֹם הִבָּרַאֲךָ *beyōm hibbāra'ăkhā* ['on the day that you were created'] (xxviii 13) and וּמִיּוֹם הִבָּרַאֲךָ *ūmiyyōm hibbāra'ăkhā* ['from the day you were created'] (*ibid.* 15) — are rooted in the ancient poetic tradition concerning Paradise. Hence the word בְּהִבָּרְאָם *behibbāre'ām* clearly indicates that the first half of the verse belongs to the section of the *garden of Eden.*

As for the formula אֵלֶּה תוֹלְדוֹת *'ēlle thōledhōth,* although it refers in many instances to the succeeding text, we may nevertheless not conclude therefrom that it cannot in any circumstances relate to the preceding verses (cf. Rashi on this verse: '*these* — the things mentioned above'). It will suffice to point to the similar expression *these are the children of so-and-so,* which alludes sometimes to what was stated earlier (e.g. xxxvi 13, 17, 18) and sometimes to what comes after (*v.* 19, for example, in the very same section).

Our verse is, therefore, an organic whole and belongs entirely to the section of the garden of Eden. It serves to connect the narrative of the first section to that of the second; and its meaning is: *These* — the events described in the previous portion — constituted *the history of the heavens and the earth,* when they were created, that is, when the Lord God made them; and now I shall tell you in detail what happened at the conclusion of this Divine work (see above, pp. 91–93).

In the day] This phrase does not signify specifically a day of twelve or of twenty-four hours, just as the idiom בְּשָׁעָה שֶׁ- *beśā'ā še-* [literally, 'in the hour that'] does not connote an hour of sixty minutes; the meaning, in each case, is — 'at the time when'. Compare, for instance, Num. iii 1: IN THE DAY *that the Lord spoke with Moses on Mount Sinai* (actually, Moses remained on Mount Sinai forty days and forty nights); *ibid.* vii 84: *This was the dedication-offering of the altar,* IN THE DAY *when it was anointed, at the hands of the princes of Israel,* etc. (the offering of the sacrifices of the princes lasted twelve days); ii Sam. xxii 1 = Psa. xviii 1: IN THE DAY *that the Lord delivered him out of the hand of all his enemies,* etc. (obviously it was not *in one day* that the Lord delivered David from *all* his enemies); and so forth.

The Lord God] On the use of these names in this section see above, pp. 84 ff.

FIRST PARAGRAPH

CREATION OF MAN

5. *Now no thorns of the field / were yet in the earth*
and no grain of the field / had yet sprung up,
for the Lord God had not caused it to rain / upon the earth,
and there was no man / to till the ground;

6. *but the waters of the deep went up from the earth / and watered the whole face of the ground.*

7. *Then the Lord God formed / man / of dust from the ground,*
and breathed into his nostrils the breath of life; / and man became a living being.

Following my usual method, I have arranged the text in such a form as to make its structure and the parallelism of the verses clear. Three times consecutively (three for emphasis, as I have stated earlier) the word אֲדָמָה *ʾădhāmā* ['ground'] occurs at the end of the second hemistich of its line. We also observe parallels between different hemistichs, (verse 5: וְכֹל — וְכָל *wᵉkhōl — wᵉkhol* [literally, 'and all — and all'; rendered here: *now no — and no*] הַשָּׂדֶה — הַשָּׂדֶה *haśśādhe — haśśādhe* ['the field']; טֶרֶם — טֶרֶם *ṭerem — ṭerem* [literally, 'not yet'; rendered: (*no*) ... *was yet* — (*no*) *had yet*]; verse 7: חַיִּים — חַיָּה *ḥayyīm — ḥayyā* ['life—living']). Certain assonances may also be noted (אָדָם *ʾādhām* ['man'], אֲדָמָה *ʾădhāmā,* אֵד *ʾēdh* ['waters of the deep']; possibly also וַיִּפַּח *way-yippaḥ* — בְּאַפָּיו *beʾappāw* ['and breathed — into his nostrils']).

5. *Now no thorns* [שִׂיחַ *śīaḥ*] *of the field were yet* [טֶרֶם *ṭerem*] *in the earth and no grain* [עֵשֶׂב *ʿēśebh*], etc.] The narrative begins with a description of the conditions existing prior to the creation

of man. There was no שִׂיחַ *śīaḥ* of the field yet, and the עֵשֶׂב *'ēśebh* of the field had not yet sprung up; the word טֶרֶם *ṭerem* means: 'not yet'. The verse is an independent sentence and is not, as many have supposed, subordinate to what follows (*viz* 'BEFORE there were any thorns of the field etc., then the Lord God created man', or some similar construction). If the sentence were joined to the succeeding verses, not טֶרֶם *ṭerem* but בְּטֶרֶם *b^eṭerem*—that is, the conjunction not the adverb — would have been used here, as in Psa. xc 2: BEFORE (בְּטֶרֶם *b^eṭerem*) *the mountains were brought forth, or ever Thou hadst formed the earth and the world, from everlasting to everlasting Thou art God* (the difference between טֶרֶם *ṭerem* and בְּטֶרֶם *b^eṭerem* I have discussed at length in my Italian work cited above, pp. 121–122, and briefly in *The Documentary Hypothesis,* English translation, p. 51; cf. Rashi on the present verse, and Rashi, Ibn Ezra and Naḥmanides on Exod. ix 30).

On the customary use of טֶרֶם *ṭerem* or בְּטֶרֶם *b^eṭerem,* in conformity with the general literary tradition of the ancient East, in passages referring to the creation of the world, see above, p. 74, § 3 of the Introduction.

What is meant by *the* שִׂיחַ śīaḥ *of the field* and *the* עֵשֶׂב 'ēśebh *of the field* mentioned here? Modern commentators usually consider the terms to connote the *vegetable kingdom as a whole;* thence it follows that our section contradicts the preceding chapter, according to which vegetation came into being on the third day. Dillmann, for example, states that שִׂיחַ *śīaḥ* and עֵשֶׂב *'ēśebh,* the most important categories of the vegetable world, represent the latter in its entirety. But it is difficult to concur in the view that שִׂיחַ *śīaḥ* and עֵשֶׂב *'ēśebh* are the most important plants and worthy to be mentioned as representative of all vegetation. Others, like Proksch, suggest the opposite interpretation, namely, that *even* the שִׂיחַ *śīaḥ* of the field and the עֵשֶׂב *'ēśebh* of the field were lacking — *a fortiori* the other species. But there is nothing in the text corresponding to the all-important word *even.* All interpretations of this kind introduce something into the text that is not there, in order to create the inconsistency. When the verse declares that these species were missing, the meaning is simply that *these* kinds were wanting, but ***no*** *others.* If we wish to understand the significance of the שִׂיחַ śīaḥ *of the field* and the עֵשֶׂב 'ēśebh *of the field* in the context of our narrative, we must take a glance at the end of the story. It is stated there, in the words addressed by the Lord God to Adam after he had sinned: THORNS AND THISTLES *it shall bring forth to you; and you shall eat the* עֵשֶׂב ʿēśebh *of the field* (iii 18). The words עֵשֶׂב ʿēśebh *of the field* are identical with the expression in our verse; whilst *thorns and thistles,* which are synonymous with the שִׂיחַ śīaḥ *of the field,* are a particularization of the general concept conveyed by the latter (cf. *one of the* שִׂיחִים śīḥīm, in Gen. xxi 15). These species did not exist, or were not found in the form known to us, until after Adam's transgression, and it was in consequence of his fall that they came into the world or received their present form. Man, who was no longer able to enjoy the fruits of the garden of Eden, was compelled *to till the ground* (iii 23 — the same phrase as in our verse here) in order to *eat bread;* and the clause quoted above, *and you shall eat the* עֵשֶׂב ʿēśebh *of the field* (iii 18), corresponds to the words immediately following: *In the sweat of your face* YOU SHALL EAT BREAD (iii 19). Thus the term עֵשֶׂב ʿēśebh *of the field* comprises wheat and barley and the other kinds of grain from which *bread* is made; and it is obvious that fields of wheat and barley and the like did not exist in the world until man began *to till the ground.* In the areas, however, that were not tilled, the earth brought forth of its own accord, as a punishment to man, *thorns and thistles* — that שִׂיחַ śīaḥ *of the field* that we see growing profusely to this day in the Land of Israel *after the rains.* How the rain was related to man's punishment and how the ground was irrigated by the waters of the deep before he sinned, we shall see immediately below. Here we must point out that the two reasons given in our verse [for the absence of thorns and grain] follow the same order as the two preceding clauses that they come to explain: no thorns of the field were yet in the earth, because the Lord God *had not caused it to rain* upon the earth, and the grain of the field had not yet sprung up, because *there was no man to till the ground.*

Now we are able to understand why the Torah emphasized in the previous section *the seed* and the *yielding of seed* in connection with the plants. The purpose was to remove the discrepancy that might have been felt to exist between the account of creation given by the ancient poetic tradition and the story of the garden of Eden as recorded by the same tradition. To this end Scripture stressed again and again that the world of vegetation, as it was formed on the third day, was composed of those trees and herbs that naturally reproduce themselves by *seed* alone. Those plants that needed something else, in addition to seed, were excluded: to this category belonged, on the one hand, all species of corn, which, even though isolated specimens might have existed here and there from the very beginning, were not found in the form of fields of grain until man began to till the ground; and on the other hand, thorns and thistles, or שִׂיחַ *śīaḥ* of the field, whose seeds are unable to propagate and grow fresh plants until it rains. After man's fall and expulsion from the garden of Eden, when he was compelled to till the ground and the rains began to come down, there spread through the earth thorns and thistles and fields of wheat — the שִׂיחַ śīaḥ *of the field* and the עֵשֶׂב ʿēśebh *of the field*.

6. *But the waters of the deep* [אֵד *'ēdh*] *went up from the earth*, etc.] The commentators have found the interpretation of this verse most difficult, particularly on account of the word אֵד *'ēdh*, whose meaning is uncertain; nor does the expression in Job xxxvi 27 — *which* (*they*) *distil* (*in*) *rain from His* אֵד 'ēdh — give us any assistance, since it is equally obscure. According to the usual rendering of the word, *vapour*, the reference is to the water that vaporizes in the air and forms clouds (cf. Targum Onkelos, Targum Jonathan *ad loc.*, B. Taʿanith 9b, Bereshith Rabba xiii 9, and parallel passages; see also the medieval commentaries). But there is the objection that it is not *from the earth* but from the water that vapour rises; furthermore, vapour waters the ground (in our verse: *and watered the whole face of the ground*) only through *rain*, but in the preceding verse we are told that the *Lord God had* NOT CAUSED IT TO RAIN *upon the earth*.

Other expositors (Rabbi Saadia Gaon and also some moderns) hold that the negative at the end of the previous sentence applies also to our verse, *viz, and* אֵד 'ēdh *did not go up from the earth;* but this is a very forced explanation.

In the Septuagint, the Vulgate and the Peshiṭta, the word אד *'ēdh* is translated *spring* (similarly in Aquila: *fountain*), that is, water *gushing* UP from the ground (cf. Num. xxi 17: SPRING UP, *O well! — Sing to it!*). On the whole this rendering is acceptable, but it is hard to imagine that Scripture refers to only *one* spring, since it says: *and watered the* WHOLE FACE OF THE GROUND.

The best explanation is the one based on the Mesopotamian name *Id,* which is the designation of the guardian deity of the waters of the deep (see Albright, *JBL,* lviii [1939], pp. 102–103). Accordingly the word אֵד *'ēdh* refers here to the waters of the deep generally and to all the springs issuing therefrom. This accords with the statement below (*v.* 10): *A river flowed out of Eden to water the garden,* that is, the garden was watered by a river emanating from a spring, and not by rain. It is also in keeping with the general tenor of the section: at first the ground did not *absorb water from above* (Bereshith Rabba xiii 9–10, Theodor's edition, pp. 118–119, and parallel passages), in other words, its fructification was not dependent on rain, which sometimes comes down in due time and sometimes is withheld, but it *drew water from below,* that is, it was constantly irrigated by the waters of the deep. This blissful state of affairs prevailing in the garden of Eden and the similar circumstances obtaining in Egypt served as classic examples of a land blessed with fertility: *like the garden of the Lord, like the land of Egypt* (xiii 10). Man would have continued to enjoy these conditions had he remained free from sin, but when he transgressed the Lord punished him by decreeing that the soil should obtain its moisture from above, so that He might requite man according to his deeds, giving him rain in its season if he was worthy and withholding it if he was unworthy.

7. *The Lord God formed man*] Regarding the duplication of the story of man's creation, which has already been narrated in the previous sections, see above, pp. 90 ff., end of § 8. The explanation, given by some commentators, of וַיִּיצֶר *wayyīṣer* as a pluperfect (*Now the Lord God had already formed*) is simply an unsuccessful attempt at harmonization.

Of dust from the ground] We have seen above (pp. 82 f.) that, according to the notions of the peoples of the ancient East, among the materials used by the gods for the creation of man the clay of the earth (טִיט *ṭīṭ* [B D B: 'mud, mire, clay'], or חֹמֶר *ḥōmer* [B D B: 'cement, mortar, clay'] in the restricted sense of the term) occupies an important place. In the poetic and prophetic literature of the Bible there are also allusions to a tradition according to which God formed mankind specifically from *clay* (חֹמֶר *ḥōmer*).

We read, for example, in Job xxxiii 6: *I too was formed* [קֹרַצְתִּי *qōraṣtī,* literally, 'nipped off']. The verb קָרַץ *qāraṣ* is used in this sense also in Akkadian: in the Gilgameš Epic (the Assyrian version, Tablet I, ii, lines 34–35) we are told that the goddess Aruru 'washed her hands, *nipped off* CLAY [*ṭīṭu*], cast it upon the ground, the hero Enkidu she built'. We further find in Scripture: *those who dwell in* HOUSES OF CLAY (Job iv 19), that is, human beings; *Thou hast made me of* [literally, 'as'] CLAY (*ibid.* x 9); *shall the* POTTER *be regarded as the* CLAY (Isa. xxix 16); *Woe to him who strives with his* MAKER! *a potsherd among the potsherds of the earth! Shall the* CLAY *say to* HIM WHO FASHIONS IT, *'What are you making'?* (*ibid.* xlv 9); *we are* THE CLAY, *and Thou art* OUR POTTER; *we are all* THE WORK OF THY HAND (*ibid.* lxiv 8 [Heb., 7]). Compare also the section in Jer. xviii 1–14, which is entirely based on the aforementioned tradition, and other verses such as: THY HANDS HAVE MADE AND FASHIONED ME (Psa. cxix 73), or THY HANDS FASHIONED ME AND MADE ME (Job x 8), and phrases like THE WORK OF THY HANDS, and so forth. The prophets and poets, following their usual practice, did not refrain from accepting in their original form expressions derived from the storehouse of the ancient tradition and using them as poetic figures of speech; but the Torah, according to its wont, is more cautious. The latter declares only that the Lord God *formed* man of the *dust* from the ground, but it does not describe the details of the creation, nor does it mention the *hands* of the Lord God, and in place of the word *clay,* which is connected with the idea of the potter's work on his wheel, it prefers the synonym *dust* [עָפָר *ʿāphār*] (this word is frequently found parallel to *clay* in Job: iv 19; x 9 [an expression borrowed from Gen. iii 19]; xxvii 16; xxx 19; so, too, *ashes* [אֵפֶר *'ēpher*] occurs as a parallel to *clay,* ibid. xiii 12). The Torah did not dispense with the detail DUST FROM THE GROUND, since it intended making use of the fact in the continuation of the section for its didactic purpose (iii 19: *till you return to the* GROUND, *for out of it you were taken; for you are* DUST *and to* DUST *you shall return;* and *ibid. v.* 23: THE GROUND *from which he was taken*).

It has been suggested that the word *dust* here is a later addition, but this view is incorrect, as is clearly shown by the parallels in the continuation of the section (iii 19), and in the verses quoted from the Book of Job. Syntactically, *dust* is the accusative of material (cf. *all its utensils he made of* BRONZE — Exod. xxxviii 3); the addition of *from the* GROUND indicates the source whence the dust was taken.

And breathed into his nostrils the breath of life, etc.] After fashioning the inanimate figure, God enabled it to *breathe* the air — a clear indication of *life* — and thereby the lifeless body became a *living soul,* a living being. Apparently, this is also a traditional concept. Berossus the Babylonian relates that human beings and animals capable of *breathing* air were formed of divine blood mixed with the clay of the ground; and the Egyptians, according to their custom, used to depict the god *Khnum* sitting before the potter's wheel and making human beings, and next to him his consort *Ḥeḳet* putting to the noses of the created people the sign of life (*ʿnḫ*). In Isa. xlii 5 it is written in connection with *the creation of the world*: *who gives* BREATH *to the people upon it* (upon the earth); and in Job xxxiii 4: *The spirit of God* HAS MADE ME, *and the* BREATH *of the Almighty* GIVES ME LIFE.

SECOND PARAGRAPH

THE PLANTING OF THE GARDEN OF EDEN

8. *And the Lord God planted / a garden in Eden, in the east;*
and there He put / the man whom He had formed.

9. *And the Lord God made to grow / out of the ground*
every tree that is pleasant to the sight / and good for food,
the tree of life also in the midst of the garden / and the tree of the knowledge of good and evil.

10. *A river flowed out of Eden / to water the garden,*
and from there it divided / and became four branch-streams.

11. *The name of the first is Pishon / it is the one which flows around*
the whole land of Ḥavilah / where there is gold;

12. *and the gold of that land / is good;*
bdellium is there / and the šōham stone.

13. *The name of the second river / is Gihon;*
it [הוא *hū'*] *is the one which flows around / the whole land of Cush.*
And the name of the third river / is Ḥiddekel
which [הוא *hu'*] *flows / east of Ašur.*
And the fourth river / is [הוא *hū'*] *the Euphrates.*

In this paragraph, too, it may be noted that a number of words occur thrice for the sake of emphasis or parallelism (*garden, tree, name, river,* and, at the end of the paragraph, הוא *hū'*).

8. *And . . . planted*] This is not to be explained, with the harmonizers, as signifying: *and He had already previously planted.* The meaning is that immediately after fashioning man the Lord God planted the garden.

Garden] On the subject of the garden and the traditions connected therewith, see my remarks above, in the introduction to this section, § 2–3.

In Eden] — in the place called *Eden.* The suggested explanations of the name that connect it either with the Sumero-Akkadian word *edinu* ('steppe-land, wilderness') or with the expression הָאֹכְלִים לְמַעֲדַנִּים *hā'ōkhᵉlīm lemaʿădhannīm* ['those who feasted on dainties'] (Lam. iv 5), are unacceptable: the first, because it does not fit the context; the second, because the stem עָדַן *ʿādhan* in question corresponds to the Arabic غدن *ghadana* spelt with a *ghayin* غ, whereas in Ugaritic we find the stem *ʿdn,* with an ordinary *ʿayin,* whose signification is well-suited to our theme. In the Epic of Baal, for example, it is stated (Tablet II AB, V, lines 68–69): *wn 'p ʿdn mṭrh bʿl yʿdn ʿdn* [to be rendered according to some authorities: 'and now also the moisture of his rain/Baal shall surely make moist'; *yʿdn ʿdn* are derived from the root *ʿdn*] in connection with the watering of the ground. In this connotation it is possible to find the root עָדַן *ʿādhan* also in Hebrew: *and Thou givest them to drink from the river of Thy watering* [עֲדָנֶיךָ *ʿădhānékha;* E.V. *Thy delights*] (Psa. xxxvi 9); and in rabbinic language: 'rain waters, saturates, fertilizes and *refreshes* [מְעַדֵּן *meʿaddēn*] (B. Kethuboth 10 b); 'Just as the showers come down upon the herbs and *refresh* [מְעַדְּנִין *me'add^enīn*] them', etc. (Sifrê Deut. 32: 2). The etymological meaning of the name Eden will, accordingly, be: *a place that is well watered throughout;* and thus we read further on: *that it was well watered everywhere like the garden of the Lord* (xiii 10). Compare also my notes to verses 6 and 10.

Regarding the attempts to identify the site of the garden of Eden with an existing geographical place, see below, on *vv.* 11–14, pp. 115 ff.

In the east] — on the eastern side, that is, east of the land of Israel. A parallel to this phrase, but with the order of the words changed, is provided by the expression, *at the east of the garden of Eden,* which occurs at the end of the section (iii 24).

And there He put the man whom He had formed] See the Introduction, § 3. p. 76.

9. *And the Lord God made to grow,* etc.] After the *general statement,* AND THE LORD GOD PLANTED A GARDEN IN EDEN IN THE EAST (*v.* 8), there now follows a *detailed account,* describing *how* God planted the garden. The object of this verse is not to inform us of the original creation of the different *kinds* of trees, but to tell us of the growth of those trees that were in the garden. Hence there is no contradiction between this verse and i 12. The species were already in existence — in other places — but now, in order to form the garden, the Lord God caused to grow, from the ground that He had chosen, particularly beautiful examples of these varieties, just as a human gardener, when he makes a garden in a given place, grows from its soil, by planting or sowing, new trees and vegetation of the kinds already in existence, but he does not create new genera. Proof that our text does not speak of the creation of plant-life as a whole but only of the making of the garden of Eden, is to be found in two facts:

(a) only the trees appropriate to, and found in, the garden are mentioned here, and there is no reference whatsoever to the rest of the flora, or to a single tree or plant in any other part of the world;

(b) the expressions *pleasant to the sight and good for food* belong, as we have seen above (p. 74) from the parallel passages in the Gilgameš Epic, to the general eastern tradition concerning *the trees of the gardens of the gods.*

According to our interpretation, verses 8 and 9 neither duplicate nor contradict each other, as Humbert thought (see above, p. 93): there is no duplication, because *v.* 9, as stated, is a *detailed amplification* of the preceding *general statement* about the planting of the garden; and there is no contradiction, because not the *whole* earth is referred to here, but only that region in which the Lord God chose to make the garden. Humbert, it is true, makes the point that if the reference was specifically to the site of the garden, the text should have read *out of* ITS *ground* and not *out of* THE *ground;* but this is incorrect, for before the trees had grown the garden was non-existent, and hence that ground was not *the ground of the garden.*

The tree of life also] Further on (iii 22) it is written: *and now, lest he put forth his hand and take also of the tree of life, and eat, and live for ever.* This indicates that the reference is to a *miraculous tree,* which endows man, when he eats of its fruit, with eternal life. The Torah mentions this tree with the definite article, as something well known to the reader. Apparently, the concept was widely current among the Israelites, as may be deduced also from the fact that the expression *tree of life* serves as a common simile for things from which the power of life flows (Prov. iii 18: *She is a tree of life to those who lay hold of her;* ibid. xi 30: *The fruit of the righteous is a tree of life;* ibid. xiii 12: *but a desire fulfilled is a tree of life;* ibid. xv 4: *A gentle tongue is a tree of life*). On the parallels to be found among the other Semitic peoples, see Vriezen, *op. cit.,* pp. 51–56, 79–84, 121, 236, 237, and the subsequent publications on sacred trees, which I have cited above, in the Introduction, § 11. Vriezen, who is very cautious in his conclusions, arrives at the view that an actual tree of life has not yet been discovered among these nations, although many pictorial designs have been interpreted as representations of this tree, and there did exist among them very similar notions, for instance, the *plant of life* (in Akkadian, *šammu balāṭi*), which is found in many texts, and the plant called in the Gilgameš Epos, 'in his hoary age man shall become young again'. Vriezen may be considered over-cautious. The argument 'I have not seen' is no proof, and the fact that the idea of the tree of life was *wide-spread* among the Israelites and is alluded to frequently in the Book of Proverbs, which belongs to the international type of Wisdom Literature, inclines one to the belief that this concept was also international. In the final analysis, there is no great difference between a *plant of life* and a *tree of life*. It should also be noted that in post-Biblical Hebrew the expression סַם חַיִּים *sam ḥayyīm* ['medicine of life'] — likewise in Aramaic סַמָּא דְחַיֵּי *sammā' dᵉḥayyē* —, which corresponds exactly to the Akkadian *šammu balāṭi* (perhaps it would be preferable at times to translate this term 'medicine of life' rather than 'plant of life'), is used as a familiar simile in the very sense in which *tree of life* occurs in the Bible; thus a certain relationship between the two concepts is indicated. See, for example, B. Yoma 72 b: 'Rabbi Joshua the son of Levi said: What is the meaning of the verse [Deut. iv 44]: *This is the law which Moses set [before the children of Israel]?* — If a man is worthy it proves a *medicine of life* for him; if he is not worthy, it becomes a deadly poison. This accords with Raba's statement: For one who is skilled therein [in the Torah] it is a *medicine of life;* for one who is not skilled it is a deadly poison'. In B. Qiddushin 30 b: 'The Torah is compared to a *medicine of life';* and similar dicta.

Be this as it may, the Torah makes only brief mention of the tree of life and declares, in the end, that the Lord God set the cherubim *to guard the way to the tree of life* (iii 24), as though to tell us that now there is no connection between the tree and our world, and we need pay no further heed to it. Incidentally, this recapitulation at the close of the section is interesting also from the aspect of style, like the one we noted earlier in the same verse: *at the east of the garden of Eden.* Indeed, there are many echoes from the opening of the narrative audible in the conclusion.

On the connection between the tree of life and the central theme of our story, see below, the exposition of *v.* 17.

In the midst of the garden] Two interpretations are possible:

(a) *in the garden* generally; compare, *in the midst of the trees of the garden* (iii 8), which means: among the trees of the garden;

(b) in the *middle* of the garden.

Against the first explanation it may be urged that *all the trees* were in the garden; furthermore, in regard to the tree of knowledge the phrase, *in the midst of the garden* (below, iii 3), serves to define the position of the tree. An objection to the second explanation is the fact that both these trees are said to be *in the midst* of the garden, and it is impossible for both of them to occupy exactly the same spot. But there is no need to understand the expression with mathematical exactitude; the second interpretation, which is that of Targum Onkelos and Rashi, is therefore to be preferred.

And the tree of the knowledge of good and evil] The meaning is: likewise *there, in the midst of the garden,* was the tree of the knowledge of good and evil. The word-order has been dictated by the rhythmic requirements of the verse; it would have been unthinkable to write: also the tree of life and the tree of the knowledge of good and evil in the midst of the garden!

Numerous interpretations of the *tree of knowledge* have been suggested. Almost all the commentators are agreed that it is an allegory, but when they come to elucidate its significance their views are divided. Many are of the opinion that the moral has a bearing on *sexual life* (the Catholics interpret it thus; so, too, Ibn Ezra and a great number of moderns, like Gunkel, and in recent years Dornseiff and Gordis in their previously mentioned articles). But this explanation is, from many viewpoints, open to objection, especially since the woman had not yet been created at the time when the prohibition [not to eat of the fruit] was imposed upon the man; and also because, as Naḥmanides has noted, the knowledge of good and evil is later on (iii 5, 22) attributed to God. Others, like Dillmann, think that the reference is to the distinction between good and evil in the *ethical sense.* But this interpretation is even more difficult of acceptance, for it would assuredly have been wrong to forbid man to distinguish between the two, and all Dillmann's casuistical attempts to clarify the matter (pp. 45–46, 64) are unconvincing. According to others again, like Wellhausen, the allusion is to the knowledge of what is *beneficial* and *injurious,* that is, of mundane matters, which, according to their nature, bring benefit or harm to man, and of the possibility of using them for the advancement of the practical civilisation of mankind. This explanation is also open to criticism, because, as Dillmann (p. 65) has pointed out, the significance of this knowledge when attributed to God would be incomprehensible. Numerous other suggestions, too, have been put forward, each commentator reading into the verses before us some of his own thoughts and musings. But there is no need to detail here all the different views that have been advanced (see the lengthy discussion in Humbert, *op. cit.*, pp. 82–116). If we wish to understand the allegory employed by the Torah here, although, unlike the Biblical prophets and poets, it does not, as a rule, make use of allegorical devices to any great extent, we must set aside preconceived ideas and endeavour to arrive at the meaning by examining *the words of the text* themselves, and comparing them with other Biblical passages that can help us to understand the expressions involved. So far as the subject-matter is concerned, we can receive no aid from parallels, because as far as is known today, there is no analogue to this tree to be found either among the Israelites or among the neighbouring peoples.

Let us first consider what happened to the man and his wife after they had eaten of the fruit of the tree. It is written (iii 7), *and they knew that they were naked*: this was the first *knowledge* that they had gained as a result of eating of the tree of *knowledge*. The verse does not say that they knew that it was not good to stand naked, or words to that effect, but simply that they knew the *fact* that they were naked; that means to say that previously they were not conscious of this fact (cf. also iii 11: *Who told you that you were naked? Have you eaten of the tree of which I commanded you not to eat?*). This interpretation fits the name of the tree precisely: *the tree of the knowledge of* GOOD AND EVIL. This is not an expression implying any discrimination *between good and evil,* such as we find in other verses, e.g., ii Sam. xix 35 [Hebrew, 36]: *I am this day eighty years old;* CAN I DISCERN WHAT IS GOOD [i.e., pleasant] AND WHAT IS NOT?; or Isa. vii 15–16: WHEN HE KNOWS HOW TO REJECT THE BAD AND CHOOSE THE GOOD . . . *before the child* KNOWS HOW TO REJECT THE BAD AND CHOOSE THE GOOD. Hence there is no suggestion here of discernment, judgment or choice between good and evil, but of the objective awareness of all things, both good and bad. Before they ate of the tree of knowledge, the man and his wife were like small children, who know nought of what exists around them; and it is precisely in connection with small children that we find a similar expression in Deut. i 39: *and your children, who this day* HAVE NO KNOW-

LEDGE OF GOOD OR EVIL, that is, they know nothing (only after the objective knowledge of things good and bad does the ability of the child develop *to reject the bad and choose the good*).

We find further corroboration of this interpretation in the continuation of the passage; thus we read later on (iii 5): *and you will be* LIKE GOD, *knowing good and evil;* and thereafter (iii 22): *Behold, the man has become* LIKE ONE OF US, *knowing good and evil.* In the first of these verses it is possible, and in the second it is certain, that the reference is to angels of God (see below, the annotations to these verses). Elsewhere it is stated, specifically in relation to an angel (ii Sam. xiv 17): *for my lord the king is like the angel of God to discern* GOOD AND EVIL; and later (in the parallel verse, *ibid.* 20): *But my lord has wisdom like the wisdom of the angel of God* TO KNOW ALL THINGS THAT ARE ON EARTH. The expression *good and evil* is thus synonymous with the phrase *all things that are on earth.* See also Gen. xxiv 50; xxxi 24, 29.

On the basis of this exposition, we are enabled to understand the reason for the prohibition and the purport of the entire parable of Adam's sin and punishment. When man was created he was simple as a new-born child; and like a babe of a day, who receives his food without any toil, he was happy in the garden that his God had prepared for him beyond the confines of the world in which we live today — a garden that furnished him with all his life's needs, without trouble or anxiety for the future. Out of fatherly love the Lord God forbade him to eat of the fruit, which would have opened before him the gateway to the knowledge of the world, the source of care and pain, and would have brought both his simplicity and his bliss to an end, *for in much wisdom is much vexation, and he who increases knowledge increases sorrow* (Eccles. i 18). But man transgressed the prohibition, like a child that disobeys his father, who warns him for his own good, and thereby does harm to himself. He was not content with what was given to him, and desired to obtain more. He did not wish to remain in the position of a child who is under the supervision of his father and is constantly dependent on him; he wanted to learn by himself of the world around him, and to act independently on the basis of this knowledge; he aspired to become in *knowledge,* too, like God — a likeness that has, it is true, its glory (Psa. viii 6: *Yet Thou has made him little less than God*), but also its danger, since man has insufficient means with which to overcome the difficulties and obstacles with which the external world confronts him. Having transgressed the commands of his Creator, he was deserving of punishment. This retribution, according to the established rule of the Bible, came upon him in a manner befitting his crime, and found expression in the direct consequences of his disobedience. He was not content with the blissful life that he enjoyed in the garden of Eden, therefore, he was banished from it; he wished to enlarge the boundaries set for him in the *very good* world that had emerged from the hands of his Father in heaven, hence he fell a prey to all the travails, perils and misfortunes that lurk outside these boundaries; he wanted to know both the good and the evil, consequently he brought about the existence of evil in the world.

10. *A river flowed out of Eden,* etc.] The ancient peoples of the East, and not of the East alone, used to tell many stories about the primeval rivers (sometimes they even mention *four* specifically) in connection with the creation of the world or the dwelling places of the gods. Of the literature dealing with these parallels, particularly worthy of mention are the articles by Albright in *AJSL,* xxxv (1918–19), pp. 161–195, xxxix (1922–23), pp. 15–31; Vriezen, *op. cit.,* pp. 138–153; and also the essays that appeared subsequently, which I have listed above, pp. 94–95, in the bibliography of more recent publications. Here there is no need to enter into details; it will suffice to indicate the fact that the tradition relating to such rivers was widely known in the ancient East. What is of importance to us at this stage is to determine the purpose of verses 10–14 in introducing the subject of the rivers, and to enquire whether they are integrally connected with the essential narrative or whether they are foreign to it, which is the view of most modern commentators, who tend to regard them as an interpolation, the work of a later author or a part of some ancient text that was inserted here by a later redactor.

Regarding *v.* 10 it should be noted that it resembles *v.* 6 both in its phrasing and in its external construction, and also — which is most important — in its connotation. What is stated in the earlier verse concerning the waters of the deep [אֵד *'ēdh*] — that is, the waters of the springs and the rivers — is repeated here with reference to this specific river. In *v.* 6 it is written, *went up from the earth,* and in our verse, *went out* [יֹצֵא *yōṣē'*] *of Eden,* that is, flowed out of the land of Eden; in the former passage we find, *and watered the whole face of the ground,* and here, *to water the garden;* and stress is given in our verse to the subject *river* by its position before the predicate, in the same way as in the other verse, it will be recalled, the subject *waters of the deep* is emphasized. We are thus told here about the garden what we are told there about the earth in general, namely, that irrigation was effected by water flowing from the earth, rain being unnecessary. That was the happy position enjoyed by man in the garden of Eden. The connection between this verse and what precedes is therefore clear; concerning the succeeding verses, see below.

Flow [literally, 'come forth'] . . . *water*] Compare Joel iv 18: *In that day . . . and a fountain shall* COME FORTH *from the house of the Lord and* WATER *the valley of Shittim.* In this verse of Joel and in other passages expression is given to the idea of the Divine river which is destined to bring blessing in the days of the Messiah; see Ezek. xlvii 1–12: *and behold, water* WAS ISSUING [literally, 'coming forth'] *from below the threshold of the temple,* etc.; Zech. xiv 8: *On that day living waters shall flow out from Jerusalem;* Psa. xlvi 4 [Hebrew, 5]: *There is a river whose streams make glad the city of God.* Possibly this promise contains an allusion to the restoration of the situation that obtained in the garden of Eden.

And from there] — on flowing out of there, out of the garden of Eden. Compare xxv 23: *and two peoples* SHALL BE DIVIDED FROM YOUR BOWELS.

רָאשִׁים *rā'šīm*] Various interpretations have been suggested: *beginnings, chief rivers, branches;* the last rendering is to be preferred. The main river divided and branched off into a number of sub-streams, each of which became a great river on its own (in the continuation of the passage three of them are actually called 'river').

11–14] The four rivers are divisible into two groups: two of the rivers, *Ḥiddekel* and *Euphrates,* are well known (see below), and are mentioned here by the names given to them in the language of their country: the remaining two, *Pishon* and *Giḥon,* are not known to us by these designations from any other source and are therefore difficult to identify. The latter names are patently Hebrew appellations and have the same grammatical structure: *Pīshōn* [פִּישׁוֹן] is derived from the root פוש *pūš*, 'to jump and run to and fro' (Jer. l 11: *though you* GAMBOL [תָּפוּשִׁי *tāphūšī;* E.V. *are wanton*] *as a heifer at grass;* Mal. iv 2 [Hebrew, iii 20]: *you shall* GO FORTH LEAPING [וּפִשְׁתֶּם *ūphištem*] *like calves from the stall;* Hab. i 8: *their horsemen* PRESS PROUDLY ON [וּפָשׁוּ *ūphāšū;* literally, 'prance']; cf. also Nah. iii 18). Similarly *Gīḥōn* [גִּיחוֹן] is formed, with the help of the termination ־וֹן *-ōn* and the vowel *ḥīreq* [ī] in the first syllable, from the root גוח *gūaḥ* or גִּיח *gīaḥ,* 'to flow' (Ezek. xxxii 2: *you* BURST FORTH [וַתָּגַח *wattāghaḥ*] *in your rivers;* Job xxxviii 8: *Or who shut in the sea with doors, when it* BURST FORTH [בְּגִיחוֹ ... יֵצֵא *beghīḥō . . . yāṣā';* literally, 'burst out . . . went forth'] *from the womb;* ibid. xl 23: *though Jordan* RUSHES [יָגִיחַ *yāghīaḥ*] *against his mouth;* cf. also Jud. xx 33; Mic. iv 10, and the name of the spring *Giḥon* in the vicinity of Jerusalem). It is clear that these Hebrew names are not the names used in the countries through which the rivers run, but are descriptive terms or translations. We shall not mention here all the suggestions put forward to identify these two rivers, from the time of the Talmudic sages and Josephus Flavius down to the scholars of our own day; those who are interested will find them recorded in the new commentaries. I shall draw attention only to this, that just as the Ḥiddekel and Euphrates constitute a pair of rivers that are close to each other and conjoin at the end of their course, so it seems probable that Pishon and Giḥon, which resemble each other even in the formation of their names, and are depicted in similar terms (*it is the one which flows around,* etc.), also form a pair of rivers that are in close proximity to each other and are interconnected. Bearing this in mind, and also that the names of the countries around which the rivers flow point to districts south of Egypt (see below), it appears that the most satisfactory explanation is the one that identifies them with two of the streams that jointly form the Nile (see on this especially the aforementioned article of Albright in *AJSL,* xxxix [1922–23], pp. 15–31). At the first blush it would seem that a strong objection can be raised against this identification, namely, that the sources of the Ḥiddekel and the

Euphrates are situated in the north-east, whereas those of the Nile are in the south-west. To overcome this difficulty the theory has been advanced that possibly the text had in mind a confluence of the two pairs of rivers beneath the ground or as the result of a circuit round the earth — a very far-fetched hypothesis! However, in the light of the interpretation that we have adopted, the problem solves itself. We remarked earlier that the conditions envisaged here are different from those prevailing in our present world; before the first man's fall, the ground absorbed moisture from below and the waters of the springs and streams sufficed to irrigate the whole face of the earth (see above, on *v.* 6); but after man's sin, when it was decreed as his punishment that the subterranean waters should be insufficient for his needs, and he was compelled to depend on rain water, the world-order, including the rivers mentioned in our passage, suffered a change. At first they had all issued from one place, but now they became separated and far-removed from one another, two flowing in one direction and two in other. Nevertheless, they are all still in existence, serving to remind us of the former state of bliss. The Nile in particular recalls the ancient character of the river that issued from Eden, for it irrigates the whole land of Egypt, obviating the need for rain water. Thus it is not without reason that the *land of Egypt* is mentioned, together with the *garden of the Lord,* as a classic example of a country that is *well watered everyhere* (xiii 10). Also the Ḥiddekel and Euphrates on their part make a valuable contribution to the irrigation of the land of Assyria and Babylonia.

We have seen above that the prophecies concernnig the Divine river, which is destined to become a source of blessing in the Messianic era, may refer to the renewal of the bliss of the garden of Eden by means of the stream that will flow from the site of the Temple.

Thus the prophetic utterances alluding to the importance of the waters issuing from Jerusalem — an importance transcending that of the water of the great rivers — now become perfectly clear to us. Their purport is this: although the fertility and prosperity of the two mighty countries, Egypt in the south and Assyria and Babylonia in the north, which are irrigated by the waters of the great rivers that flowed originally from the region of Eden, reflect to some extent the happiness enjoyed of old by the first man, nevertheless it is only a distant and pale reflection. That happiness, however, will be restored in all its fulness in the future thanks to the waters of the modest spring in the land of Israel, the country that lies in between the two mighty states. So Isaiah (viii 6–7), for instance, speaks of the *waters of Shiloaḥ that flow gently,* that is, the waters of *Giḥon* in Jerusalem, in contradistinction to the Euphrates, *the waters of the River, mighty and many.* In the same book, again in the prophecy about the days of the Messiah, reference is made to the diminution of the great rivers in the future (xi 15): *And the Lord will utterly destroy the tongue of the* SEA OF EGYPT [i.e. the Nile; Arabic: بحر النّيل *baḥru an-nīli*]*; and will wave His hand over the* RIVER (i.e. the Euphrates) *with His scorching wind, and smite it into seven channels that men* MAY CROSS DRYSHOD. In contrast thereto, mention is immediately made after this (the passage must be read as an integrated whole, despite the prevailing views of contemporary exegesis) of the wells of salvation in the land of Israel (xii 3): *With joy you will draw water from the* WELLS OF SALVATION.

On the basis of the various identifications of Pishon and Giḥon that have been suggested, numerous attempts have been made to ascertain the site of the garden of Eden according to Scripture. Many hypotheses have been put forward and a number of different opinions have been expressed. But in the light of our exposition all these theorizings are valueless. Our text, as stated, describes a state of affairs that no longer exists, and it is impossible to determine the details on the premiss of present-day geographical data. The garden of Eden according to the Torah was not situated in our world.

It is the one which flows around the whole land of Ḥavilah] The meaning is that it is to be identified with the river that now encompasses the entire land of Ḥavilah. The name Ḥavilah occurs below (x 7) and in i Chr. i 9 as the name of one of the sons of Cush, that is, as the designation of one of the regions of the land of Cush, which is referred to as a whole in verse 13 in connection with the second river. The fact that Ḥavilah is also mentioned among the sons of Joktan (Gen. x 29, i Chr. i 23; cf. Gen. xxv 18, i Sam. xv 7) is to be explained as reflecting the ethnic relations between the peoples dwelling on both sides of the Red Sea.

Where there is gold] Gold was brought both to the land of Egypt and to the land of Israel from the countries of the south, *Put* or *Ophir*. Now *Put* is mentioned as the brother of *Cush*, the father of *Havilah*, in Gen. x 6 and in i Chr. i 8, whilst *Ophir* occurs beside the second reference to *Ḥavilah* in Gen. x 29, and in i Chr. i 23.

And the gold of that land is good; bdellium is there and the שֹּׁהַם šōham *stone*] We have seen above, in the introduction, what the tradition of the people of the ancient Orient related regarding the precious stones to be found on the branches of the trees in the gardens of the gods, and we noted that among the Israelites, too, the poets used to tell of similar gems. The Torah is opposed to these legends, and specifically as a protest against them mentions here the *good* gold and the bdellium and the *šōham* in connection with the *land of Ḥavilah*. As we have already stated, its purpose is to teach us that we must not believe that precious stones and gold grow on trees like fruit, or that they originate from the garden of Eden. The very *best* gold is simply a natural substance, a metal like any of the other metals, which are found in the ground in one of the countries of our own world. Likewise, with regard to the precious stones (*bdellium* also, as we shall see later, belongs to the category of gems): they, too, are to be found in the ground of our world and not on the trees of the garden of Eden. If gold and gems are in any way connected with the garden of Eden, it is only an indirect connection: the land of Havilah, in which they are found, is near to Pishon, which was originally one of the rivers formed from the river that watered the garden of Eden.

At all events, this indirect association alluded to here by the Torah, which at the same time rejects the direct relationship that the poets held to exist, suffices to give the gold and the *bdellium* and the *šōham*, and generally all precious stones, the character of tokens and memorials of the garden of Eden. In regard to the *manna*, the *bread from heaven* (Psa. cv 40) or the *grain of heaven* (*ibid.* lxxviii 24), which was given by God and required no human toil, just as in the case of Adam's food in the garden of Eden, it is said (Num. xi 7): *and its appearance was like that of* BDELLIUM. This comparison is assuredly not accidental. Similarly the *šōham* stones, enclosed in setting of *gold* filigree, were set on the shoulder-pieces of the ephod of the priest (Exod. xxviii 9, 12; xxxix 6–7), who made atonement for the sins of the children of Israel, as a memorial to the time when man had not yet fallen into sin. So, too, the *šōham* and the other stones for setting affixed to the breastpiece (Exod. xxviii 17–20; xxxix 10–13), which provide a remarkable parallel to those listed in Ezek. xxviii 13, in connection with the *garden of Eden,* serve as a reminder of the time when man was still free from transgression. Likewise the midrashic tradition connects the *šōham* stones and the stones for setting with the river Pishon and the garden of Eden (Targum Pseudo-Jonathan on Exod. xxxv 27–28: 'and the clouds of heaven go to Pishon and draw from there the sand-coloured berylls and the stones for setting to fit them into the ephod and the breastpiece . . . and the clouds of heaven return and go to the garden of Eden', etc.; cf. B. Yoma 75a).

הַבְּדֹלַח *habbᵉdhōlaḥ* [E.V. *bdellium*] / There are two interpretations of the word: (a) that it is a kind of precious stone (the Septuagint renders it in this verse, ἄνθραξ ['carbuncle, ruby'], and in Num. xi 7, κρύσταλλος ['crystal']: (b) that it is the apothecary's **בְּדֹלַח** *bᵉdhōlaḥ,* that is, an aromatic resin exuded from a tree that grows in many countries of the East (βδέλλιον in Aquila and other Greek translations). Apparently the word was used in the language in both meanings, possibly because the resin looked like a gem in colour and in its transparency. The question is: which sense does the word bear here? At present the commentators are inclined to prefer the second interpretation, but from the context it appears more probable that the **בְּדֹלַח** *bᵉdhōlaḥ,* like the **שֹׁהַם** *šōham,* is a precious stone (see Bereshith Rabba, xvi 2, and the variant readings in Theodor's edition, p. 163). The fact that the word *stone* is used with **שֹׁהַם** *šōham* but not with **בְּדֹלַח** *bᵉdhōlaḥ* presents no difficulty, for this difference may be due to idiomatic usage. The precise nature of the stone we are unable to determine.

And the **שֹׁהַם** *šōham stone*] As explained above, in the introduction, the Biblical **שֹׁהַם** *šōham* stone is the same as the Babylonian *sāndu* or *sāmtu.* But the identity of the gem called by this name in the Babylonian language is itself in doubt.

Land of Cush] See x 6.

Hiddekel] — the Babylonian *Idiglat* (in Aramaic, and also in the Talmud, דיגלת *Dighlath*), the Greek Τίγρις or Τίγρης.

East of Aššur] — among the various explanations advanced, the most acceptable appears to be: east of the city of Aššur.

Euphrates [פְּרָת *Perāth*] / — in the language of the country, *Purattu;* in Greek, Εὐφράτης.

THIRD PARAGRAPH

ADAM'S TASK IN THE GARDEN OF EDEN

15. *The Lord God took / the man*
and put him in the garden of Eden / to serve and to guard.

16. *And the Lord God commanded / the man, saying,*
'Of every tree of the garden / you may freely eat;

17. *but of the tree of the knowledge of good and evil / you shall not eat,*
for in the day that you eat of it / you shall surely die.'

15. Having interrupted the narrative with the portrayal of the garden, its rivers and related matters, the Bible now reverts to the last point reached in the story prior to this description — the theme of the second half of *v.* 8. In doing so, Scripture adds certain details (*to serve and to guard*) in accordance with its usual practice of making first a general statement and setting forth the particulars thereafter. Incidentally, it is worth noting that we have here indirect confirmation of our view that verses 10–14 form an integral part of the section: it is difficult to believe that, if these verses had been introduced into the passage at a later period, the interpolator would have been concerned to integrate them with the original text by a recapitulation of this kind; and even if we assume that he did take the trouble to do this, it is hardly to be imagined that he would have succeeded so well. It is quite clear, therefore, that there is no unnecessary duplication here of what is stated in *v.* 8.

וַיַּנִּחֵהוּ *wayyannīḥēhū*] In Bereshith Rabba, xvi 8, the word is interpreted as though it were connected with מְנוּחָה *menūḥā*, 'rest' [i.e. 'and caused him to rest']; a similar explanation is given in modern times by Jacob. This is, however, a homiletical exposition; according to the natural meaning of the verse, the verb is synonymous with וַיָּשֶׂם *wayyāśem* ['and He put'] in *v.* 8, and signifies: *and He put him.*

לְעָבְדָהּ וּלְשָׁמְרָהּ *le'obhdhā(h) ūleśomrā(h)* [E.V. *to dress it and to keep it*] / In most texts the final *Hē'* has a *Mappīq,* which creates a difficulty, because the word גַּן *gan* ['garden'] is invariably masculine. Nor is the suggestion, put forward by some commentators, that the pronominal suffix refers to אֲדָמָה *'ădhāmā* [a feminine word, meaning 'ground'] acceptable, since this noun [in *v.* 9] is too far away from our verse. Furthermore, the task of tilling the earth, as we are subsequently informed, was not imposed upon man till after his banishment from the garden of Eden (iii 23: *therefore the Lord God sent him forth from the garden of Eden to till the ground from which he was taken*). In several texts, however, the *Hē'* has no *Mappīq,* and the form, in that case, is that of the infinitive [with added *Hē'*], like לְאָכְלָה *le'okhlā* [literally, 'to eat'; rendered, *for food*] (i 29, 30), לְמָשְׁחָה *lemošḥā* ['to be anointed'] (Exod. xxix 29), לְרָחְצָה *lerohṣā* ['for washing'] (*ibid.* xxx 18). This is apparently the correct spelling; and it forms the basis of the following rabbinic teaching (Bereshith Rabba, xvi 5): לְעָבְדָה וּלְשָׁמְרָה *le'obhdhā ūleśomrā*—these denote the sacrifices, as it is said: *You shall serve God* [Exod. iii 12], and it is written: *you shall take heed* [literally, 'keep'] *to offer to Me in its due seasons* [Num. xxviii 2]. There is no need, therefore, to emend the vocalisation and to read, as some scholars have suggested, לְעָבְדוֹ וּלְשָׁמְרוֹ *le'obhdhō ūleśomrō* [masc. for fem. accusative pronominal suffix].

Regarding the meaning of the word לְעָבְדָה *le'obhdhā,* it should be noted that the rabbinic interpretation just quoted, which explains the term to refer to the sacrificial service, corresponds to an ancient tradition of the Orient, often mentioned in Mesopotamian inscriptions, according to which man was created for the express purpose of *serving God.* Particular attention should be paid to the new fragment of the Babylonian Epic of Creation, which was recently published by Weidner in *AfO,* xi (1936–37) pp. 72–74, since it mentions, in juxtaposition, both the *serving* and the *guarding.* This fragment completes the account, which suffered from lacunae in the texts previously known. It is related there *inter alia* that mankind was created with the blood of Kingu in order to serve the Gods, and in consequence the Anunnaki, deities of the second rank, on whom the *service* of the supreme gods had hitherto devolved, were released from this duty, and instead they were given the task of *guarding,* half of them being appointed guards of heaven and half guards of Sheol. In the light of this tradition, the rabbinic interpretation of the word לְעָבְדָה *leʿobhdhā* is seen to be not just a homiletical exposition, but the actual meaning of the text. As for the work of *guarding,* which according to the Babylonians was handed over to a specific group of deities, Israel's ancient poetic traditions entrusted it to a given category of angels, the *cherubim.* I believe we shall not err if we assume that Ezekiel alludes to this tradition when he calls the cherub in the garden of Eden *guardian cherub* or *measuring* [E.V. *anointed*] *guardian cherub* (Ezek. xxviii 14, 16). The word סוֹכֵךְ *sōkhēkh* is to be explained in the sense of הֲגַנָּה *hăghannā* ['defence'], which is synonymous with שְׁמִירָה *šemīrā* ['guarding'] (this traditional association of the cherubim with the stem סָכַךְ *sākhakh* enables us to understand the customary use of this stem in connection with the cherubim on the Ark of the Testament), whilst the word מִמְשַׁח *mimšaḥ* may be understood in the sense of 'measuring' (the cherub *measures* the areas assigned to him to guard). All this accords with the ancient poetic tradition; but the Torah, which, as we have explained (Introduction, § 3, pp. 73–82), amended and purified this tradition and substituted man for the cherubs, attributed to the former not only the duty of *serving* but also that of *guarding.* The function of the cherubim, on the other hand, the Torah reduced to a minimum; only after Adam's expulsion from the garden of Eden is mention made in our section of the cherubim, who were commanded TO GUARD *the way to the tree of life* (iii 24).

16. *And . . . commanded*] For the significance of this injunction and its reason, see above pp. 111–114, and below on *v.* 17.

Of every tree of the garden you may freely eat] This clause must be read in conjunction with the following verse: although you are permitted to eat of every tree of the garden, yet of the tree of knowledge of good and evil you may not eat.

It is not forbidden here to eat of the tree of life; nevertheless, it is stated later (iii 22): *and now, lest he put forth his hand and take also of the tree of life, and eat, and live forever,* as though the Lord God were unwilling that man should eat of that tree. Most modern exegetes have failed to deal with this problem, or have entirely eliminated it by expunging all reference to the tree of life from the section as being a later addition (so, for example, Budde, Holzinger and others). Obbink, in a special article published in *Expository Times,* xliv (1932–33), p. 475, has offered the following explanation of the difficulty: the tree of life bestowed the power of life if its fruit was constantly eaten, and in fact the man had already partaken thereof during his stay in the garden of Eden; but after he had sinned, the Lord God banished him from the garden of Eden, so that he might eat of the fruit no more. This is a forced interpretation, and the word *also* in iii 22, militates against it (see *ibid.* xlv, pp. 44, 236–237). The meaning of the verse is apparently this: had man remained in his state of simplicity, *he could have attained* even to immortality, but on account of his disobedience, the Lord God decreed that he should not be able to achieve this state; hence He forbade him then to eat of the tree of life, and expelled him from the garden of Eden, so that he should not transgress this second prohibition even as he had transgressed the first.

17. *You shall not eat (thereof)*] See above, the notes to ii 9, pp. 111–114. It may further be observed that incidentally the verse also teaches us that it is not good for man to acquire the habit of indulging all his desires without restraint, and that it is proper for him to discipline himself according to Heaven's precept, and thereby accustom himself to conquer his evil inclination and abstain, when necessary, from temptation. This is the first time that the verb to *command* appears in the Torah; the first commandment in connection with forbidden food is enjoined here, serving as a symbol of, and introduction to, similar injunctions that were to be given to Israel in the future.

In the day that you eat of it you shall die] *In the day* may be interpreted to mean *in the time,* as we have seen above (*v.* 4); nonetheless, the expression *you shall die* is difficult, for Adam did not die at that time, but reached the age of *nine hundred and thirty years.* Various explanations of the words *you shall die* have, therefore, been proposed: (a) there shall come upon you afflictions cruel as death, the beginning, as it were, of death; (b) you shall not attain the measure of life that was originally allotted to you, namely, a thousand years; (c) you will be deserving of death, which shall overtake you when I shall will it; (d) *you shall die* is here an exaggerated statement, the purpose of which was to restrain man from sinning; (e) *you shall die* was intended literally, only afterwards the Lord God tempered the severity of the judgement, because man had repented; (f) now you are immortal, but hereafter you shall become mortal. All those interpretations, and similar explanations, do not accord with the wording of the text. A simple expression like *you shall die* must be understood strictly; it is not possible to regard it merely as an allusion to severe afflictions or to a diminution (what a reduction!) of the span of life from one thousand to nine hundred and thirty years. Nor is it conceivable that the Bible attributed to the Lord God an extravagant utterance that did not correspond to His true intention. The fifth suggestion is improbable, because there is no mention of the punishment being reduced on account of repentance. Likewise, there is not the slightest indication that man was already immortal before his Fall; on the contrary, it is clear from iii 24 that he could not have achieved this condition save by an additional act on his part, to wit, by stretching forth his hand and eating of the fruit of the tree of life. The natural meaning of the words requires us to understand them in accordance with what I have stated above: when you eat of the tree of knowledge it shall be decreed against you never to be able to eat of the tree of life, that is, you will be unable to achieve eternal life and you will be compelled one day to succumb to death; *you shall die,* in actual fact. It was necessary to use simple words like *you shall die,* because prior to his eating of the tree of knowledge man was as unsophisticated as a child who knows nothing, and he could not have comprehended a more elaborate warning.

See further on the whole subject my notes to iii 17, 19. Concerning the phrase *in the day,* see below, on iii 8.

FOURTH PARAGRAPH

CREATION OF WOMAN

18. *Then the Lord God said,*
'It is not good / that the man should be alone;
I will make him a helper / corresponding to him.'

19. *So the Lord God formed / out of the ground*
every beast of the field / and every flying creature of the air,
and brought [them] to the man / to see what he would call each one,
and whatever name the man would give to each one / of the living creatures / that would be its name.

20. *The man gave names / to all cattle,*
and to the flying creatures of the air, / and to every beast of the field;
but as for man, / he did not find a helper corresponding to him.

21. *So the Lord God caused a deep sleep / to fall upon the man, / and he slept;*
then He took one of his ribs, / and He closed up its place with flesh.

22. *And the Lord God built up / the rib*
which He had taken from the man / into a woman
and brought her to the man.

23. *Then the man said,*
'This, at last, / is bone of my bones / and flesh of my flesh;
*she shall be called Woman [*אִשָּׁה *'Iššā], / because she was taken out of Man [*אִישׁ *'Iš].'*

24. *Therefore a man leaves / his father and his mother*
and cleaves to his wife, / and they become one flesh.

25. *And they were both naked, / the man and his wife,*
and were not ashamed.

18. *It is not* [לֹא *lō'*] *good* etc.] The word לֹא *lō'*, before an adjective, is a more emphatic negation than אֵין *'ēn* ['not']. If I say, for example, אֵין דָּבָר פְּלוֹנִי טוֹב *'ēn dābhār pelōnī ṭōbh* ['such and

such a thing is not good'], I deny that that thing can be considered good, but I do not yet assert that it is absolutely bad; it may be intermediate. On the other hand, when I say, דָּבָר זֶה לֹא טוֹב *dābhār ze lō' ṭōbh* ['This thing is not good'], I definitely declare that it is the opposite of good (see my remarks regarding the expression לֹא טוֹב *lō' ṭōbh* in my article on the Lachish Letters in *MGWJ*, 1939, p. 399).

Here it is stated, *It is not good* etc., and above it is said, at the end of the story of the sixth day (i 31), *and behold, it was very good.* The two verses do not contradict each other: before the woman was formed, the man's position was *not good;* but after we have been told, *male and female He created them* (i 27), it is possible to declare: *and behold, it was very good.*

אֶעֱשֶׂה *'e'ĕśe* ['I will make'] / Above (i 26) we find נַעֲשֶׂה *na'ăśe,* and this is the reading here, too, according to the Septuagint and the Vulgate. Although the form is similar (see the introduction, § 9), the sense is different: in the earlier passage, as we have explained, the plural expresses exhortation; here there is no need for exhortation, because the woman is not due to be created immediately after this statement. Hence, the singular is required in our verse. The future here merely signifies intention: *I will make,* that is, I desire to make.

עֵזֶר כְּנֶגְדּוֹ *'ēzer kᵉneghdō* [literally, 'a helper as in front of him'] / — a helper like him, suited to him, worthy of him, corresponding to him. In the previous section, which deals with the physical world, the Bible stressed the sexual aspect of the relationship between the man and his wife (*male and female,* i 27); in the present section, which is concerned with the moral world, Scripture gives special emphasis to the ethical aspect of this relationship.

19. Most modern commentators consider that this verse and the next imply that the Lord God made, as it were, a number of unsuccessful attempts, by creating various kinds of creatures and by passing them in review before Adam, to see if the man would find in one of them a helper corresponding to him; but it was all in vain, for not one of them satisfied man. This interpretation is unacceptable for the following reasons:

(a) that this exposition is, in general, not in keeping with the concept of God reflected in this section;

(b) that especially in regard to the acts of the Lord God, the section tells us how He immediately executed whatever He wished to do; and it would be strange if just in this particular instance He should have failed to accomplish what He intended;

(c) that it would be stranger still to declare that God did not understand, so to speak, what man understood, to wit, that among the animals there was none fit to become a helper corresponding to him;

(d) that it is inconceivable that the experiment was carried out with *all* the beasts of the field and *all* the flying creatures of the air without exception, that is, even with creatures that were most unlike man;

(e) that precisely the *cattle,* which should have been considered first and foremost, are not mentioned at all in *v.* 19;

(f) that later on it is stated (*vv.* 21–22) that when the Lord God wished to make the woman, He formed her immediately in accordance with His will; if so, He could have created her at the beginning;

(g) that it is explicitly written in *v.* 20 that the purpose of the Lord God in bringing the creatures before man, was only *to see what he would call each one.*

It would seem that the text intends to tell us only that the Lord God wished to engender in the heart of man a desire for a helper who should correspond to him exactly. When the man would inspect all the species of animals in turn, and would find that some of them were indeed suited to serve him and help him to some extent, but yet there was not one among them that was his *like* [כְּנֶגְדּוֹ *keneghdō*], he would become conscious of his loneliness and would yearn for one who could be his life-companion and a helper fit to be his soul-mate [עֵזֶר כְּנֶגְדּוֹ *'ēzer keneghdō*] in the full sense of the words, and, in consequence, he would be ready to appreciate and cherish the gift that the Lord God was to give him.

So [*the Lord God*] *formed* etc.] This presents a difficulty, for according to the preceding section all the creatures were formed *before man.* The harmonistic interpretation that explains the verb וַיִּצֶר *wayyīṣer* to mean, *now He had already created before,* cannot be considered seriously. But the usual explanation given in modern commentaries, to wit, that we have here two contradictory accounts — according to the one the creatures were created before man, and according to the other they were formed only after man — is not as simple as it appears at first glance. Not only must the redactor have noticed so glaring a contradiction, but there is also another problem, namely, that here in *v.* 19 only the *beasts of the field* and the *flying creatures of the air* are referred to, and no mention whatsoever is made of the *cattle*. If the term *beasts* only had been used here, or *beasts of the earth,* one might have assumed that it included the cattle as well; but the expression *beasts of the field* is actually an antonym of *cattle*. And another point: it is just the *cattle,* as we have noted earlier, that would in particular have had a claim to consideration. Had the meaning, therefore, been that the Lord God created them then, they should have been referred to in unmistakable terms. Now in *v.* 20, the first category of creatures to be named by man is precisely the *cattle*. From this it may be inferred that the cattle were already to be found with man in the garden of Eden, and there was no need to create them and bring them before him. This was not the case, however, with the *beasts of the field* and the *flying creatures of the air;* undoubtedly, they were not staying with man. Also in Lev. xvii 13, the kinds known as *beasts and flying creatures* are mentioned, in contradistinction to *cattle,* as two classes of creatures that man can catch only by hunting. Hence it seems that in the passage *before us* (in the ancient epic poem the position may have been different) we must understand the creation of the beasts and the flying creatures in a similar sense to that of the growing of the trees in *v.* 9, to wit, that of all the species of beasts and flying creatures that had already been created and had spread over the face of the earth and the firmament of the heavens, the Lord God now formed particular specimens for the purpose of presenting them all before man in the midst of the Garden. If we approach the text without preconceived ideas concerning the existence of two cosmogonic accounts, this exposition will appear simple and clear; and thus it seems to me the Torah intended the words to be understood.

Out of the ground] The Samaritan Pentateuch and the Septuagint read: *further* [עוֹד *ʿōdh*] *out of the ground.*

כָּל חַיַּת הַשָּׂדֶה *kol ḥayyath haśśadhe* ['every beast of the field'] /

— in the Samaritan Pentateuch: אֶת כָּל חַיַּת הַשָּׂדֶה *'eth kol ḥayyath haśśādhe.* Since we have אֶת *'eth* [sign of the definite accusative] before כָּל עוֹף הַשָּׁמַיִם *kol 'ōph haššāmayim* ['every flying creature of the air'], it would seem, on the face of it, that the Samaritan reading is the correct one. On the other hand, it is hard to imagine that the word אֶת *'eth* would be omitted by mistake from so accurate a text as the one before us. Hence it seems more likely that it was intentionally written thus, without אֶת *'eth,* in order to emphasize the parallelism with *v.* 9 [where, too, אֶת *'eth* is omitted]: *and out of the ground the Lord God made to grow* EVERY TREE THAT IS PLEASANT TO THE SIGHT etc. [כָּל עֵץ נֶחְמָד לְמַרְאֶה *kol 'ēṣ neḥmādh lᵉmar'e*].

To see what he would call each one] The exegetes who regard this as idle curiosity on the part of the Lord God have failed to understand the passage. It must be read as a continuous statement right to the end of the sentence: to see what he would call each one, and to establish the names that man would give the creatures as their permanent designations. The naming of something or someone is a token of lordship (cf. Num. xxxii 38; ii Kings xxiii 34; xxiv 17; ii Chr. xxxvi 4). The Lord of the universe named the parts of the universe and its time-divisions (i 5, 8, 10), and He left it to man to determine the names of those creatures over which He had given him dominion.

לוֹ *lō* [literally, 'unto it'; rendered: *each one*] / It is characteristic Hebrew usage to employ the singular in a distributive sense. We find, for example, in Isa. v 26: *He will raise a signal for the nations afar off, and whistle* FOR IT [לוֹ *lō*] *from the ends of the earth;* 'for it' signifies, 'for each one of them'. Similarly *ibid.* xxx 22: *you will fling them away as an unclean thing; you will say* TO HIM [לוֹ *lō*], *'Begone!'* Likewise here the meaning is: 'what he would call each one of them':

Living creature] The commentators have found great difficulty in determining the connection of these words with the other parts of the sentence [literally the verse reads: 'and all that the man would call unto it / a living creature / that is its name']:

Rashi: 'Recast the sentence and explain it thus: every living creature to which the man will give a name that shall be its name forever.'

Ibn Ezra: '*The Lāmedh* in the clause, *that the man would call it* [לוֹ *lō*], applies also to another word [in apposition to 'it'], as follows: That the man would call it, [namely], a living creature.'

Naḥmanides: 'And every species among them that the man would call after his own name (see *v.* 7), regarding it as a living creature like himself, by that name [i.e. 'living creature'] would it be known.'

Isaac Samuel Reggio: 'Every name given by the man, who is a living creature, to each one of the animals and birds, that is its name.'

Jacob: 'And every name that the man will coin for it, in recognizing it as a living creature, shall be its name.'

Not one of these explanations is satisfactory. The generally accepted view to-day is that the words *living creature* are superfluous, and are to be omitted as a later addition. But Alexander's method of undoing the Gordian knot is not the correct one for philology. It seems that the term *living creature* must be understood as the accusative of limitation and definition, like the expression *the throne* in the sentence, *only the throne* [E.V. *as regards the throne*] *will I be greater than you* (xli 40). The preceding clause in our verse reads [literally]: *and all* [כֹּל *kōl*] *that the man would call;* now the word *all* in this expression requires limitation and definition, for the man had not the right to name *everything* that had been created, but only (as I pointed out in my exposition of the words, *to see what he would call each one*), the living beings, over which he was granted dominion, that is, *every living creature*. Accordingly, the verse has to be construed as follows: and whatever name the man would call any created being, within the category of living creatures, that would be the name of that created being in future.

20. *The man gave names to all cattle,* etc.] — to the cattle, which were already with him in the garden of Eden, and to the beasts and the flying creatures that the Lord God passed in review before him. The word יִקְרָא *yiqrā'* ['call, name'] occurs three times consecutively, for emphasis.

And to the flying creatures of the air] In several ancient translations, as well as in a few Hebrew MSS., the reading is: *and to* ALL *the flying creatures of the air.* The version before us, without *all,* was possibly intended to ease the style a little.

וּלְאָדָם לֹא מָצָא עֵזֶר כְּנֶגְדּוֹ *ūleʾādhām lōʾ māṣāʾ ʿēzer keneghdō* [literally, 'and (= but) for the man he did not find a helper corresponding to him']. There are differences of opinion as to who is the subject of the verb מָצָא *māṣāʾ* ['he found']. Many consider that it is *the Lord God,* but the Divine Name is too far away. Others think it is *the man;* this, too, seems at the first blush difficult, since the verb is preceded by *but for the man,* and if *the man* were the subject, the correct wording would have been: *but for himself* [וְלוֹ *welō*] *he did not find a helper corresponding to him,* or some similar construction. To overcome the impasse, it has been suggested that we read *but the man* [וְהָאָדָם *wehāʾādhām*] instead of *but for the man* [וּלְאָדָם *ūleʾādhām*]. This, however, is also inadmissible, because the subject, *the man,* has already been mentioned at the beginning of the verse, and there was no need to repeat it. Possibly לֹא מָצָא *lōʾ māṣāʾ* [literally, 'he did not find'] should be understood in an impersonal sense [i.e. 'one did not find'] as the equivalent of *there was not found* [i.e. the passive]; cf. xi 9: *Therefore, one called its name* [i.e. its name was called] *Babel.* The meaning of our verse would then be: *for the man there was not found a helper corresponding to him* (there is a view that the text should be emended to read: לֹא נִמְצָא *lōʾ nimṣāʾ,* 'was not found'; but the emendation is unnecessary, since the existing text can be interpreted in this sense).

However, this explanation, too, is not free from objection. Even according to the interpretation suggested, it would still have been preferable to write וְלוֹ *welō* ['for him'] instead of וּלְאָדָם *ūleʾādhām* ['for the man']. It is better therefore to construe the verse thus: the subject of the verb מָצָא *māṣāʾ* is indeed *the man,* but the word וּלְאָדָם *ūleʾādhām* is not connected with this verb ('he did not find unto the man', or 'he did not find for the man'), but stands unrelated, the meaning being: *as for the man;* compare: *And as for Ishmael* [וּלְיִשְׁמָעֵאל *ūleyišmāʿēʾl*] *I have heard you* (xvii 20). Then, since the word is not an integral part of the sentence whose subject is *the man,* it was possible to say וּלְאָדָם *ūleʾādhām* and not וְלוֹ *welō.* Nay more, it was not merely possible, but correct to do so, in order to stress the antithesis that Scripture wished to express not only between [*the man*] *gave names* and *he did not find,* but also — and even more so — between *the man* and *the other species* of living creatures mentioned before him (*to all cattle, and to the flying creatures of the air, and to every beast of the field*). Thus the sense of the verse is: unto every kind of *living being* the man succeeded in giving a name befitting the character and qualities of that kind, *but* (antithetic *Wāw*) as far as *man* was concerned, he did not find a creature worthy to be his helper and to be deemed his *counterpart* [כְּנֶגְדּוֹ *keneghdō*], and hence to be called by a name corresponding to אָדָם *'ādhām,* or to the name of the male of the 'Adamic' species, as he found subsequently when the Lord God brought him the woman (ii 23: *she shall be called* WOMAN אִשָּׁה *'Iššā*], *because she was taken out of* MAN [אִישׁ *'Iš*]). Regarding the vocalisation of וּלְאָדָם *ūle'ādhām,* see below (iii 17).

After he has scrutinized all the living creatures and is convinced that there is not yet in the world a helper corresponding to him, man waits yearningly for what the Lord God will still do in his behalf. And we, the readers, also await with intense interest the outcome of the story. The phrase, *a helper corresponding to him,* at the conclusion of the verse, which reiterates the words of the Lord God at the end of *v.* 18, recalls the Divine intention, emphasizing that this has not yet been fulfilled, and we look forward to its realization. And lo! in the verses that follow we have before us the dramatic description of the creation of Woman.

21. *So the Lord God caused a deep sleep to fall upon the man and he slept*] The commentators who regard this as a symbolic expression of the idea that man is unable to apprehend the mystery of creation (so, for instance, Dillmann and Gunkel; also Jacob's exposition of *v.* 22 approximates to this view), introduce into the passage a philosophical concept that is completely foreign to it. The deep sleep is mentioned before the words *then He took* and not before *And* [*the Lord God*] *built up;* the process of 'building', the man may have witnessed, and at least he knew of it, since he said: *This at last is bone of my bones and flesh of my flesh* (*v.* 23). Actually, the matter is quite simple: we certainly could not picture to ourselves, in a beautiful and exalted narrative, an account of the removal of the rib from the body of a conscious person; his reaction to this operation would have destroyed the charm of the story, and would have introduced into it elements unsuited to its purpose. The act could not have been performed unless the man was

unconscious, and to this end a deep sleep was cast upon him.

Then He took one of his ribs] He did not take the bone alone, as the exegetes usually understand the verse; the hard bone would not have been suitable material for the fashioning of the tender and delicate body of the woman. The meaning of the text is that the Creator took together with the bone also the flesh attached to it, and from the flesh He formed the woman's flesh, and from the bone her bones (see also the commentary of Abravanel). Proof of this we find in the words of the man (*v.* 23): *This at last is bone of my bones* AND FLESH OF MY FLESH.

The story of the rib, as other commentators have rightly interpreted it, is an allegory of the relationship of the woman to her husband. Just as the rib is found at the side of the man and is attached to him, even so the good wife, the *rib* of her husband, stands at his side to be his helper-counterpart, and her soul is bound up with his. Regarding the hermaphrodite character of the first man, to which, according to some of the Talmudic sages and contemporary expositors, the Bible alludes, see my comments above, on i 27.

And He closed up its place with flesh] This detail is also emphasized for the sake of the beauty of the narrative, so that the reader should not picture to himself the body of Adam in a state of mutilation, with a bleeding wound. After the Creator had taken the rib, the flesh was immediately restored to health, and Adam's body became well and whole again as before. The subject of וַיִּסְגֹּר *wayyisgōr* ['closed up', third person masc. sing.] may be the Lord God (and He closed up in its stead, that is, the place where it was, *by means of* flesh), or it may be *flesh* (the flesh closed up in the place of the rib that had been removed, that is, flesh grew in its place; cf. Jud. iii 22: *and the fat closed* [וַיִּסְגֹּר *wayyisgōr*] *over the blade*).

22. *And* [*the Lord God*] *built up*] In the hands of the Lord God, the raw material taken from the man's body received the lovely form of the woman. The verb *bānû* ['to build'] is the regular term employed in Akkadian literature to describe the creation of human beings by the gods; so, too, in Ugaritic, one of the titles of the deity who is the father of the gods and of man (*'b 'dm*) is *bny bnwt,* that is, creator of creatures. We thus

hear in the word וַיִּבֶן *wayyibhen* in our verse an echo of the ancient literary tradition. At the same time, it should be noted that it was not without reason that the Bible chose the verb בָּנָה *bānā* in this particular instance. Owing to the normal signification of the verb in Hebrew, it arouses associations suited to the theme; just as a builder builds, with the raw materials of stones and dust, an edifice of grace and perfection, so from an ordinary piece of bone and flesh the Lord God fashioned the most comely of his creatures.

And brought her to the man] — not just *and brought,* as in *v.* 19. The pronominal suffix emphasizes the object. God was like a father who presents his son with a valuable gift that is bound to please him and be cherished by him. 'See [he says] what I have prepared for you!'

23. זֹאת הַפַּעַם *zō'th happa'am* [literally, 'This, the time'] / This does not mean, as some commentators have supposed, 'This time', for in the Biblical idiom the demonstrative pronoun does not precede the substantive when it is in apposition. Sforno's interpretation is correct: *This — this female.* The *Hē'* in the word הַפַּעַם *happa'am* serves as a demonstrative pronoun, as in the words הַיּוֹם *hayyōm* ['this day, today'], הַלַּיְלָה *hallaylā* ['this night, tonight'], and the like. The sense is: This creature, this time [that is, at last], is in truth a helper corresponding to me! Thus the man exclaims in his enthusiasm and heart's joy.

The verse is divisible into two parts. [In the Hebrew] the first part is composed of three segments, each containing two words, both accented, whilst the second part is composed of two segments, each comprising three words, all accented; thus each part has six accented words. The word זֹאת *zō'th* [rendered once, *this,* and twice, *she*], which refers to the woman, occurs three times in the man's utterance: he begins and ends therewith, and uses it also in the middle of his speech. The reiteration is for emphasis.

Bone of my bones and flesh of my flesh] In Hebrew such expressions are commonly used to indicate family propinquity: *Surely you are* MY BONE AND MY FLESH! (xxix 14); *I am* YOUR BONE AND YOUR FLESH (Jud. ix 2); *Behold, we are* YOUR BONE AND YOUR FLESH (ii Sam. v 1); *you are my kinsmen, you are* MY BONE AND MY FLESH (*ibid.* xix 12 [Hebrew, *v.* 13]); *Are you not* MY BONE AND MY FLESH? (*ibid. v.* 13 [Hebrew, *v.* 14]);

Behold, we are YOUR BONE AND YOUR FLESH (i Chr. xi 1).

The meaning is: formed from the same parents or from the same family; the source of the bones and the flesh is the same. Our verse is based on this metaphorical expression, as though to say: the first man could employ this phrase in the full sense of the words, in their literal connotation: actually, bone of his bones and flesh of his flesh!

She shall be called Woman [אִשָּׁה *'Iššā*] / She is worthy of being called by the same name as myself (Naḥmanides), that is to say: I have given names to all living beings, but I have not succeeded in finding one among them fit to be called by a name resembling mine, thus indicating its kinship with me. She, at last, deserves to be given a name corresponding to my own.

Because she was taken out of Man [אִישׁ *'Iš*] / Although the two names, אִישׁ *'īš* and אִשָּׁה *'iššā,* are known to have different roots (אִישׁ *'īš* from the root אוש *'wš,* and אִשָּׁה *'iššā* from אנת׳–אנש *'nth–'nš*), they have a similar sound in Hebrew, and therefore aptly mark the affinity between the man and his spouse.

Similar expressions occur twice at the end of the section: *till you return to the ground,* FOR OUT OF IT YOU WERE TAKEN (iii 19); and thereafter; *to till the ground* FROM WHICH HE WAS TAKEN (*v.* 23). The analogy of expression points to analogy of thought. The man who was taken from the ground must associate himself with it in his lifetime through his work, and return to it at his demise; similarly, the woman who was taken from the man and brought forth from his body must return to the man and associate with him constantly. Emphasis is given to the verb לָקַח *lāqaḥ* by its occurrence seven times in the section, as I have noted previously.

24. *Therefore a man leaves,* etc.] This is not the continuation of Adam's words, but a comment made by the Torah (see Rashi), in a kind of bracketed aside. A similar construction is found below (xxxii 32 [Hebrew, *v.* 33]): *Therefore, to this day, the Israelites do not eat the sinew of the hip,* etc.

Therefore] — that is, since 'the experiences of the fathers are an augury unto the children'.

יַעֲזָב *ya'ăzōbh* [imperfect Qal of stem meaning 'to leave'] / It does not denote the future, but constant and continuing action.

A man leaves his father and his mother and cleaves to his wife] Some commentators regard this verse as an echo of the system of matriarchy, in which the woman was the head of the family. But in the epoch of the Torah this system had long disappeared, and the words that occur later on in our section, *and he shall rule over you* (iii 16), suffice to show that, according to the narrative before us, it is the man who is deemed the family head. The meaning of the verse is simply this: whilst a man is single, he forms part of his father's family, but when he takes a wife, he founds a new family; so long as he is in his father's house, all his love is dedicated to his father and mother, but when he marries, his love for his wife transcends that for his parents.

And he cleaves to his wife] The reference is not solely to sexual relations, as many exegetes, from the rabbinic sages onward, understood it, but also — and more especially — to the spiritual relationship, as is shown by the antithesis between this and the preceding verse: *Therefore a man leaves his father and his mother.* See also above, on *v.* 18.

25. *And they were both naked*] This detail prepares us for what we shall be told later (iii 7): *and they knew that they were naked.*

And were not ashamed] According to some commentators this means that sexual desire had not yet been aroused in them, but there is no foundation for such an interpretation in the verse before us. It is preferable to explain it as follows: since they did not yet know good or evil, nor had they yet learned that sexual desire could also be directed towards *evil ends,* they had no cause to feel ashamed at the fact that they were naked; the feeling of shame in regard to anything is born only of the consciousness of the evil that may exist in that thing (R. Obadiah Sforno comments: they looked upon the sexual organs in the same way as we regard the mouth, the face and hands).

FIFTH PARAGRAPH

ADAM'S SIN

CHAPTER III

1. *Now the serpent was cunning / beyond any beast of the field that the Lord God / had made.*
He said to the woman, / 'Did God really say,
"You shall not eat / of any tree of the garden"?'

2. *And the woman said to the serpent,*
'Of the fruit of the trees of the garden / we may eat.

3. *But of the fruit of the tree / which is in the centre of the garden,*
God said, / "You shall not eat thereof,
neither shall you touch it, / lest you die."'

4. *Then the serpent said to the woman,*
'You shall by no means die.

5. *For God knows / that when you eat of it*
Your eyes will be opened / and you will be like 'Elōhīm [God or Divine beings], / knowing good and evil.'

6. *So when the woman saw / that the tree was good for food,*
and that it was a delight to the eyes / and that the tree was to be desired to make one wise,
she took of its fruit / and ate;
and she also gave [some] to her husband with her, / and he ate.

7. *Then the eyes of both were opened, / and they knew / that they were naked;*
and they sewed fig leaves together / and made themselves aprons.

On the general import of this and the following paragraphs we have spoken above, in the introduction to the section and in the annotations on *v.* 9. Before we come to the exposition of the details, we must consider the possibility of interpreting a number of them as aetiological notes, that is, as explanations of the *causes* of given phenomena, after the manner of the Greek αἴτια. Many incline to the view (see recent commentaries, and also, for example, Dornseiff's article in *ZAW*, lii [1934], p. 61) that many verses have to be understood in this way and regarded as explanations of the cause not only of the Fall, of evil and of death, but also of numerous other phenomena, like human speech (ii 19–20), the wearing of apparel (iii 7, 21), the fact that the serpent crawls on his belly (iii 14), his inclination to bite (iii 15), and the like. This expositional approach does not take into account the difference between the Semitic way of thinking and the Greek. The Hellene had a natural bent for abstract speculation, and consequently he was eager to know the causes of things; this knowledge, unrelated to any practical purpose—knowledge for its own sake—he deemed of great importance. To the Semite, on the other hand, the desire for knowledge that has no practical value was mere dilettantism. It will suffice to recall the well-known anecdote of the man who wished to annoy Hillel the Elder and asked him why the heads of the Babylonians were round, and then why the eyes of the Palmyreans were bleared, and thereafter why the feet of the Africans were broad (B. Shab. 30b–31a). Moreover, the central theme of our section does not aim to give a philosophical explanation of the origin of evil in the world, but has the practical purpose of providing moral instruction and of assuaging the feeling of perplexity in the heart of man, who finds a contradiction between the Creator's paternal love and the multitudinous troubles that throng his world; whereas the investigation of the causes of particular phenomena, like human speech, man's clothing and the characteristics of the serpent, are not, to the Semitic mind, matters of moment. Hence aetiological interpretations of the kind mentioned should be viewed with great caution.

1. *Now the serpent*] The commentators have found extreme difficulty in determining the nature of the serpent in our section. The interpretation reflected in the pseudepigraphical writings, the New Testament and in the later rabbinic literature, according to which the serpent is none other than Satan, or the beast on which Samael rode, introduces into the text concepts that are foreign to it. This applies also to the exposition that regards the serpent as a kind of symbol of the evil impulse in the human heart; the idea

of the evil impulse is likewise of later origin (Gen. vi 5 and viii 21 refer to a different matter). According to ancient Talmudic sources, the primeval serpent is just a species of animal, although differing in character from the serpent of to-day, and resembling man in his upright stature and in his manner of eating (see, for instance, B. Soṭa 9b). When we come to *v.* 14, we shall revert to the question whether, according to the plain sense of Scripture, the primordial serpent was in truth different from the kind that we know. At any rate, it is beyond doubt that the Bible refers to an ordinary, natural creature, for it is distinctly stated here: BEYOND ANY BEAST OF THE FIELD *that the Lord God had made.*

But this interpretation also encounters difficulties. First, if the serpent were only an ordinary animal, why woes Scripture tell us that he *spoke?* It is no answer to say, *Is anything too hard for the Lord?* For the serpent's speech is not comparable to that of Balaam's ass: the latter's mouth was opened by the Divine command, whereas the serpent here speaks solely for the purpose of inciting against the will of the Lord God. Nor is his speech like that of the creatures in fox fables or that of the plants in parables of the kind employed by Jotham and Jehoash, for it is not for his own benefit and good that he talks (according to the haggadic interpretation his intention was to destroy the man, because he [the serpent] had set his heart on Eve, but there is no hint of this in the plain meaning of the text).

Furthermore, how could a mere animal know all that the serpent here knows, including even the hidden purpose of the Lord God? This apart, there is the further question: if we are concerned here with an ordinary creature, why just a serpent and not another animal? And if we answer that the cunning of the serpent was the determining factor, then why just this and not another wily creature, like the fox?

The documents and pictures of the peoples of the ancient East do not assist us to solve the problem of the serpent in our section. We find there all kinds of snakes: sacred serpents, serpent-gods or serpents that symbolize the deities, serpents that are symbols of life or fertility, serpents that guard the sanctuaries or the boundaries, serpents used for 'divining' future events, and so forth; but so far no serpents have been found corresponding in character to the one in this section.

To solve the problem, we must consider the ideas that were associated with the concept of the serpent among the Israelites themselves. As I have already stated above (pp. 49 f.), there existed among them an ancient poetic tradition that told of the revolt of the prince of the sea against God — the Israelite version of the eastern legends concerning the battles between the great gods and the god of the sea in the era of creation. Both the Israelites and the Gentiles used to relate that the sea and its confederates, the rivers, had many helpers, like the dragon or dragons, Leviathan the fleeing *serpent,* Leviathan the twisting *serpent,* and other monsters and animals. I dealt in detail with this group of helpers of the sea and the rivers in *Tarbiz,* xii, pp. 6–9 [Hebrew], and subsequently in *Keneseth,* dedicated to the memory of H. N. Bialik, viii, pp. 130–134, 136 [Hebrew], in my attempt to reconstruct the ancient epic on the rebellion of the sea. There is no need, therefore, for me to discuss the subject here at length I shall mention only, as I showed in *Tarbiz, ibid.* pp. 7–8, and in *Keneseth, ibid.* p. 136, that once the tradition concerning the revolt of the sea and its allies against the Creator of the world became current among the Israelites, important innovations began to be made therein: not only were the pagan elements attaching to the original versions of the heathen nations blurred, but new ideas were associated with it, in conformity with the conscience and ethos of the Israelites. One of the innovations consisted in the fact that the sea and the rivers and their helpers, who rebelled against their Creator, became among the Israelites symbols of the forces of wickedness, whilst God's victory over them foreshadowed the final triumph of absolute good over the principle of evil in the end of days, as we read in Isa. xxvii 1: *In that day the Lord with His hard and great and strong sword will punish Leviathan the fleeing serpent, Leviathan the twisting serpent, and He will slay the dragon that is in the sea.* In our section, which deals with the origin of evil in the world, it was only to be expected that the theme should be linked with one of the usual and well-known symbols connected therewith, and particularly with the ordinary *serpent,* an animal that is found in the sea and the rivers and on land, for the *dragons* and big serpents called *Leviathan* exist only in the sea, and could not appear in the garden. However, the Torah as we have previously stated, rejects the entire poetic tradition relating to the revolt of the sea and the rivers and the monsters; the sea, it holds, is only a created entity, which was made according to the will of the Creator and forthwith received the form that He wished to give it (above, p. 39); the rivers are merely the means employed by God for the purpose of fructifying the earth (above, pp. 103 f., 114 f.); the dragons are but natural creatures, which were created by the word of God to do His will like the other created beings (above, pp. 49 ff.). But since in the popular thought and lan-guage the concept of *evil* was strongly associated with that of the *serpent,* it was possible for the Torah, without changing its attitude to the ancient poetic tradition, to use the accepted folk ideas and phraseology that were a *product* of that tradition, and hence to choose specifically the *serpent* out of the animal world as the symbol of evil. And in order to make it quite clear that we have here only a symbol, and that we must not regard the serpent as an independent entity in opposition, as it were, to the Creator of the world, as the ancient tradition of the poets narrated, the Torah stressed at the very outset that the serpent belonged to the category of the *beasts of the field that the Lord God had made.* The Torah's method here is similar to that followed in the previous chapter, where it is emphasized that the great sea monsters were created like the other creatures by the fiat of God.

The special characteristic that the Bible attributes to the serpent is *cunning,* and since it does not ascribe any other quality to him, it intends, apparently, to convey that the evil flowing from the serpent emanated only from his *cunning.* In the ultimate analysis, we have here an allegorical allusion to the craftiness to be found in *man himself.* The man and his wife were, it is true, still devoid of comprehensive knowledge, like children who know neither good nor bad; but even those who lack wisdom sometimes possess slyness. The duologue between the serpent and the woman is actually, in a manner of speaking, a duologue that took place in the woman's mind, between her wiliness and her innocence, clothed in the garb of a parable. Only in this way is it possible to understand the conversation clearly; otherwise it remains obscure (in regard to the details, see below). In her cunning the woman begins to think that possibly some inference can be drawn from the fact that the prohibition is restricted to a single tree. She asks herself: 'Has God then forbidden us all the trees of the garden?' 'Surely not', she answers herself in her simplicity; 'He forbade us only the tree in the middle of the garden'. 'In that case', she continues to argue in the manner of a sly person who considers herself extremely clever when she imputes cunning to other people and imagines that she has thereby discovered their secret intention, 'in that case, just as the prohibition is restricted to this tree, so must the reason for it inhere in the nature of this tree, which bestows the knowledge of good and evil; undoubtedly, the interdict was not imposed upon us in order to preserve us from death, but because God, who knows good and evil is jealous of us and does not wish us also to have knowledge of good and evil like Himself'. On the basis of this conclusion, she acted as she did.

By interpreting the text in this way, we can understand why the serpent is said to think and speak; in reality it is not he that thinks and speaks but the woman does so in her heart. Thus we need not wonder at the serpent's knowledge of the prohibition; it is the woman who is aware of it. Nor should we be surprised that he knows the purpose of the Lord God; it is the woman who imagines that she has plumbed the Divine intention — but is quite mistaken!

Now the serpent was cunning] The subject is placed before the predicate in order to emphasize the former and to mark the introduction of a new theme relative to it; see my note above, p. 21, on i 2.

Cunning] The play on the resemblance of the word עָרוּם *'ārūm* ['cunning'], in this verse, to עֲרוּמִּים *'ărūmmīm* ['naked'], at the end of the preceding paragraph, may be explained in the light of our interpretation as follows: It is true that the man and his wife were *naked* [עֲרוּמִּים *'ărūmmīm*], and that they remained *naked* because their ignorance of good and evil prevented them from feeling ashamed of their nakedness, yet, notwithstanding their lack of *knowledge,* they were not wanting in *cunning* [עָרְמָה *'ormā*]; the serpent within them was *cunning.* In order to make the word-play more apparent, Scripture uses in the previous verse the form עָרוֹם *'ārōm* and not עֵירוֹם *'ērōm,* which occurs subsequently in verses 7, 10, 11, and it prefers the full [that is, with a *Wāw*] to the defective mode of spelling. The only difference between עֲרוּמִּים *'ărūmmīm* ['naked'] and עֲרוּמִּים *'ărūmmīm* ['cunning'] is the *Dāghēš* [represented by an additional *m* in the transliteration].

That the Lord God had made] In the previous section (i 25) the word *made* is used specifically with regard to the *beasts.*

Did God really say, etc.] Modern commentators have found difficulty in determining the meaning of the expression אַף כִּי *'aph kī* [rendered: *did . . . really*]. Dillmann, for example, interpreted it thus: 'Is it so, that God' etc. (כִּי *kī* in the sense of -שֶׁ *še-* 'that'). He is followed by Gunkel, whilst others give a slightly different explanation. However, the word אַף *'aph* by itself, without the interrogative *Hē'* in front of it, does not express a question. It is כִּי *kī* that serves as the interrogative particle in this verse, in accordance with a usage that is found in post-Biblical Hebrew, and occasionally also in the Bible (e.g. Isa. liv 6: *but a wife of youth, how* [כִּי *kī*] *can she be cast off? says your God.*), and the word אַף *'aph* is employed for emphasis; cf. *Shall I* IN VERY TRUTH [אַף אֻמְנָם *'aph 'omnām*] *bear a child, now that I am old?* (xviii 13), which is a stronger expression than *Shall I* TRULY [אֻמְנָם *'omnām*] *bear a child* etc., or, *Will you* INDEED [אַף *'aph*] *destroy?* (*ibid.* 23, 24), which is more forceful than *Will you destroy?*

The general import of the serpent's words does not, at first, seem clear. The various attempts made to elucidate the meaning — for example the suggestion that we have here only the *conclusion* of the serpent's speech, and that his preceding remarks are not quoted (Ibn Ezra; a similar view is expressed by Dillmann); or that the verse represents an introductory observation intended to give the woman an opportunity to speak on the subject (Jacob; cf. Rashi), and other interpretations of this kind — are all forced. For a preferable explanation see above, at the end of the exposition of the words, *Now the serpent.*

2–3. These verses are connected in the same way as ii 16–17, the meaning being: *in general* we may eat of the fruit of the trees of the garden, only of the fruit of the tree that is in the centre of the garden we may not eat.

The tree which is in the centre of the garden] The woman emphasizes the site of the tree, since it is the most important place in the garden; and consequently she is particularly grieved that this tree, which is of outstanding significance, should be prohibited.

Although there was in the *centre* of the garden also the tree of life, and possibly there were other trees as well, her interest is focussed at the moment on the *forbidden tree,* and for her it is *the tree* — with the definite article — in the centre of the garden.

Neither shall you touch it] This is not stated in the instruction of the Lord God quoted above (ii 17). Most exegetes, whether of the middle ages or contemporary, consider that the woman added this point of her own accord, and they advance various reasons for this interpolation. Jacob, in his commentary, suggests that Scripture purports to tell us here something that was actually said by the Lord God but was not expressly mentioned above. But this hypothesis is improbable, for the exact nature of the prohibition should have been precisely formulated when the Lord God spoke to the man. A more correct approach is to pay attention to the fact that the verb נָגַע *nāghaʿ* often has a graver connotation than mere touching, as, for example, in the following verses: *therefore I did not let you touch her* (xx 6); *whoever touches this man or his wife shall be put to death* (xxvi 11). Hence, in the final analysis, the clause *neither shall you touch it* is simply synonymous with the preceding clause *you shall not eat thereof.*

4. *You shall by no means die* [לֹא מוֹת תְּמֻתוּן *lōʾ mōth temūthūn*] / The commentators and grammarians (see Gesenius — Kautsch § 113 v) usually assert that according to rule the negative particle [לֹא *lōʾ*] must come between the absolute infinitive and the conjugated verb, and that here we have an exceptional construction intended to rebut the statement *you shall surely die* [מוֹת תָּמוּת *mōth tāmūth*] contained in the Lord God's utterance (ii 17). But this expression is too far away; moreover, in the woman's speech the warning is worded differently (פֶּן תְּמֻתוּן *pen temūthūn* ['lest you die']), and there was thus no point in making the phrasing here correspond to that in ii 17. Furthermore, in the earlier passage it is written מוֹת תָּמוּת *mōth tāmūth* in the singular and not תְּמֻתוּן *temūthūn* [in the plural] as here.

The rule has to be formulated differently. The negative particle comes between the absolute infinitive and the conjugated verb when it is intended to express the antithesis of *another verb,* for example, Exod. xxxiv 7: FORGIVING *iniquity and transgression and sin,* BUT WHO WILL BY NO MEANS CLEAR THE GUILTY [וְנַקֵּה לֹא יְנַקֶּה *wenaqqē lō' yenaqqe*]; Jud. xv 13: *No;* WE WILL ONLY BIND YOU AND GIVE YOU *into their hands;* BUT WE WILL SURELY NOT KILL YOU [וְהָמֵת לֹא נְמִיתֶךָ *wehāmēth lō' nemīthekhā*]; Jer. xxx 11: I WILL CHASTEN YOU IN *just measure,* AND I WILL BY NO MEANS LEAVE YOU UNPUNISHED [וְנַקֵּה לֹא אֲנַקֶּךָּ *wenaqqē lō' 'ănaqqekkā*]. The rule applies also when there is no antithesis at all, e.g. Jer. xiii 12: DO WE NOT INDEED KNOW [הֲיָדֹעַ לֹא נֵדַע *hăyādhōa' lō' nēdha'*] *that every jar will be filled with wine?* But when the intention is to qualify adversatively a clause containing the *selfsame root,* then the negative particle *precedes* the absolute infinitive, for instance, Amos ix 8: AND I WILL DESTROY [וְהִשְׁמַדְתִּי *wehišmadhtī*] *it from the surface of the ground; except that* I WILL NOT UTTERLY DESTROY [לֹא הַשְׁמֵד אַשְׁמִיד *lō' hašmēdh 'ašmīdh*] the house of Jacob; Psa. xlix 8–9: TRULY NO *man* CAN RANSOM [לֹא־פָדֹה יִפְדֶּה *lō'-phādhō yiphde*] *a brother . . . for the* RANSOM [פִּדְיוֹן *pidhyōn*] *of their life is costly, and can never suffice* [the rendering of the last clause is in doubt]. So, too, in our case: the answer of the serpent לֹא מוֹת תְּמֻתוּן *lō' mōth temūthūn* ['you shall by no means die'] is opposed to the woman's words: פֶּן תְּמֻתוּן *pen temūthūn* ['lest you die'].

5. *For God knows,* etc.] The cunning creature — that is, the cunning within the woman — thinks that she has discovered herein the reason for the prohibition. Since the prohibition applies only to the tree that bestows the knowledge of good and evil, she concludes that the underlying cause must be none other than God's jealousy. He who *knows* everything (not without reason is it said here, *For God knows*) does not wish his creatures to possess the same knowledge as Himself. The concept of God's jealousy, which many modern expositors regard as a doctrine taught here by Scripture itself, is, in truth, only an inference drawn by the serpent or the woman. For the interpretation of verse 24, see the commentary *ibid.*

Like 'Elōhīm] Two interpretations are possible: (a) like Divine beings (Ibn Ezra: like angels); (b) like the Lord God. The first explanation, which agrees with what is stated later (*v.* 22): *Behold, the man has become* LIKE ONE OF US, would apparently seem the better; but, on the other hand, since it is hard to suppose that the word *God* would be used in two different senses in the same verse, and seeing, moreover, that here the greater expectation is more suited to the theme, the second view is perhaps to be preferred.

Knowing good and evil] If we accept the first interpretation of the preceding word *'Elōhīm,* the verse may be understood either as, *and you will be like Divine beings, who know good and evil,* or, *and you will know good and evil like Divine beings.* According to the second explanation of the word *'Elōhīm,* as a singular, the clause can only mean: *and you will know good and evil like God.*

6. *So when the woman saw*] *Saw* here means *gave heed,* perceived. Similarly, later on (xxx 1): *When Rachel* SAW *that she bore Jacob no children,* and subsequently (*ibid. v.* 9): *When Leah* SAW *that she had ceased bearing children.*

That the tree was good for food, and that it was a delight to the eyes and that the tree was to be desired to make one wise] In repeating here, in somewhat altered form, the expressions employed above (ii 9) in connection with the trees of the garden generally, the Bible appears to give these phrases meanings that are, to some extent, new and different. The woman noted *that the tree was good for food,* that is, that it was not only of a pleasant flavour (perhaps she was able to judge the taste by the fragrance), but also, and particularly, that it was *good to eat,* because the eating thereof raised one to an *'Elōhīm*-like plane. *And that it was a delight to the eyes*: not only by virtue of its beauty, which charmed the eye, but also, and more especially, because through eating it *the eyes were opened* (*your eyes will be opened,* we read in the previous verse). *And that the tree was to be desired to make one wise*: not just נֶחְמָד *neḥmādh* ['pleasant'] *to the sight,* as it is phrased above, but also, and in particular, *neḥmādh* ['to be desired'] in the sense that by eating of it one acquired *discernment and knowledge.* In imagination the woman magnifies the effects of the eating amazingly; possibly, for the very reason that a woman's imagination surpasses a man's, it was the woman who was enticed first.

And she took of its fruit and ate] Perception and flight of imagination were followed immediately by decision and action. The extreme brevity of this part of the sentence, in contrast to the length of the first section of the verse, indicates the swiftness of the action.

And she also gave some to her husband with her and he ate] Here, too, we have extreme brevity, and this terseness likewise betokens the celerity with which the deed was performed. In regard to the man, the Bible does not state his motives for eating, as in the case of the woman, since for him it suffices that *she* is the one who gives him the fruit. It is the way of the world for the man to be easily swayed by the woman.

It is doubtful whether Hos. vi 7 refers to our passage.

With her [עִמָּהּ *'immāh*] / Expressions of this kind (עִם *'im* or אֵת *'eth* ['with'] with the pronominal suffixes) occur as a rule when a person is said to associate himself in a given action with someone who leads him. Examples are: *you, your sons, your wife, and your sons' wives* WITH YOU (vi 18); *and his sons and his wife and his sons' wives* WITH HIM (vii 7); *So Abram went up from Egypt, he and his wife, and all that he had, and Lot* WITH HIM, *into the Negeb* (xiii 1).

Eating of the fruit of the tree means nothing more, according to the Bible, than the actual eating thereof, in the literal sense of the term. The text *in no way purports* to allude to any aspect of *sexual relationship;* and the multitude of allegorical interpretations with which a number of commentators have embroidered the passage, on the assumption of some such intention, are out of place.

7. *Then the eyes of both were opened,* etc.] The verse recalls the expression used above, *your eyes will be opened* (*v.* 5), as though to say: In truth their eyes were opened as they had expected, but the outcome was not what they had awaited. They had hoped that by eating of the fruit of the tree they would attain *Divine knowledge;* in point of fact, they did gain *knowledge,* but of what kind? *They knew that they were naked!* The cognition that had seemed so *desirable* to them as to warrant the transgression, for its sake, of the Creator's precept, appeared to them, once they had achieved it, vastly different from what they had originally imagined. The first knowledge they acquired was the wretched and grieving realization that they were naked. The significance of this consciousness in relation to their previous state, when they felt no shame, I have already explained above, in my note on *and were not ashamed* (ii 25).

The reference to *nakedness* here at the end of the paragraph forms a fitting parallel to the close of the preceding paragraph (ii 25), to the conclusion of the next paragraph (iii 21), and also to the beginning of this passage, which emphasizes the word עָרוּם *ʿārūm* ['cunning'], which is similar in sound to עָרוֹם *ʿārōm* and עֵירוֹם *ʿērōm* [both words mean: *naked*].

SIXTH PARAGRAPH

THE JUDGEMENT AND THE SENTENCE

8. *And they heard / the sound of the Lord God*
walking in the garden / in the afternoon,
and the man and his wife / hid themselves
from the presence of the Lord God / among the trees of the garden.

9. *But the Lord God called / to the man,*
and said to him, / 'Where are you?'

10. *He said,*
'I heard the sound of Thee in the garden, / and I was afraid,
because I was naked; / and I hid myself.'

11. *He said,*
'Who told you / that you were naked?
Have you eaten / of the tree
of which I commanded you / not to eat?'

12. *The man said,*
'The woman / whom Thou gavest to be with me,
she gave me fruit of the tree, / and I ate.'

13. *Then the Lord God said / to the woman,*
'What is this that you have done?'
The woman said,
'The serpent beguiled me / and I ate.'

14. *The Lord God said / to the serpent,*
'Because you have done this, / cursed are you
above all cattle, / and above all the beasts of the field;

upon your belly you shall go, / and dust you shall eat / all the days of your life.

15. *I will put enmity / between you and the woman*
and between your seed / and her seed;
he shall crush your head / and you shall crave his heel.'

16. *To the woman He said,*
'I will greatly multiply your suffering, especially of your child-bearing; / in pain you shall bring forth children,
yet your desire shall be for your husband, / and he shall rule over you.'

17. *And to Adam He said,*
'Because you have listened to the voice of your wife, / and have eaten of the tree
of which I commanded you, saying: / "You shall not eat of it",
cursed is the ground / because of you;
in suffering you shall eat of it / all the days of your life;

18. *thorns and thistles / it shall bring forth to you;*
and you shall eat / the grain of the field.

19. *In the sweat of your face / you shall eat bread*
till you return to the ground, / for out of it you were taken;
for you are dust / and to dust you shall return.'

20. *The man called / his wife's name Eve*
because she was / the mother of all living.

21. *And the Lord God made / for Adam and for his wife*
tunics of skins, / and clothed them.

8. *And they heard the sound of the Lord God walking in the garden in the afternoon*] The phrase *walking in the garden* is an example of Biblical anthropomorphism, and therefore constitutes one of the points of difference, as we stated above (pp. 85 f.), between the present and the preceding section, which avoids the use of anthropomorphic expressions in so far as ordinary human language permits. We have already seen how the divergences between the two sections are satisfactorily explained by our theory concerning the two ancient epic poems, whose contents furnished the material for the composition of these two sections. But the com-

mentators who extended the anthropomorphism still further by interpreting לְרוּחַ הַיּוֹם *lerūaḥ hayyōm* [literally, according to this explanation, 'to the wind of the day'] to mean, *at the time when the usual wind springs up towards evening* (or, according to others, *at dawn*) — that is, that God came into the garden to take a stroll and refresh Himself, as it were, in the coolness of the breeze — have failed to understand the verse correctly. See, in this connection, the rest of our exposition, and especially our remarks on לְרוּחַ הַיּוֹם *lerūaḥ hayyōm*.

And they heard [וַיִּשְׁמְעוּ *wayyišmeʿū*] / In Biblical narrative prose, when it is desired to state that after a given action had taken place another action was performed, the second action is expressed by the imperfect tense with *Wāw* consecutive, as in the present case, וַיִּשְׁמְעוּ *wayyišmeʿū*. Thus the new point is not that God *walked* in the garden, but that they *heard* the sound of Him. If it had been intended to convey, as most contemporary exegetes think, that it so chanced that the Lord God, who did not yet know what the man and his wife had done, entered the garden for His pleasure, and the sinners, on hearing the sound of Him, hid themselves and thereby aroused His suspicions that they had committed some wrong, then the wording would have been: 'And the Lord God walked in the garden . . . and they heard' etc., or words to that effect. In the text as we have it, emphasis is given to the verb וַיִּשְׁמְעוּ *wayyišmeʿū;* this represents the new act — before they had not heard, and now they did hear. It is possible that the Lord God had already been walking in the garden prior to this; Scripture tells us only that the man and his wife, now that their conscience was uneasy, became aware of One who could demand from them an account of their deeds.

The sound [הַקּוֹל *haqqōl*] *of the Lord God,* etc.] The meaning of הַקּוֹל *haqqōl* does not appear to be clear. It cannot signify קוֹל הַדִּבּוּר *qōl haddibbūr* ['the sound of the voice'], for it is only in *v.* 9 that the Lord God begins to speak to the man, and it is not to be supposed that previously he was holding converse with Himself or with someone else. The usual interpretation is, *the sound of His feet,* which is based on the sense of the word in other Biblical passages, for example: *when you hear the* SOUND OF MARCHING *in the tops of the balsam trees* (ii Sam. v 24); *when Aḥijah heard the* SOUND OF HER FEET (i Kings xiv 6); *Is not the* SOUND OF HIS MASTER'S FEET *behind him?* (ii Kings vi 32). But it is precisely these verses that rule out this interpretation here, since in all these instances the word קוֹל *qōl* ['sound'] is expressly followed by the word for *feet* or *marching,* that is, in verses of this kind קוֹל *qōl* is not used by itself without an accompanying explanation of the nature of the sound referred to in the passage. In our verse, however, there is no such explanatory note, the gloss being provided only by the participle of the verb (*walking*), as is usual in sentences where the word קוֹל *qōl* occurs as an interjection (e.g. iv 10: *Hark* [קוֹל *qōl*] *your brother's blood is crying to Me from the ground!* Cant. ii 8: *Hark, it is my beloved! Behold, he comes;* ibid. v 2: *Hark, my beloved is knocking!*); the meaning is: *the sound of His walking.* In so far as the sense of the passage is concerned, this interpretation does not differ very much from the customary explanation; but from the point of view of the form, it should be noted that the Torah refrained from using a wholly anthropomorphic expression like *the sound of the feet of the Lord God,* and chose instead a phrase whose anthropomorphism is not excessive by Biblical standards (the *Hithpaʻēl* of the verb הָלַךְ *hālakh* ['walk'] often occurs in connection with the Lord, e.g. Lev. xxvi 12; Deut. xxiii 14 [Hebrew, verse 15]). Our passage does not go into great detail, but leaves the matter shrouded, as it were, in reverent ambiguity. They heard the Lord walking; precisely what they heard is not stated.

The suggestion that the word מִתְהַלֵּךְ *mithhallēkh* ['walking'] refers to קוֹל *qōl* (Bereshith Rabba, xix 7, and several medieval commentators) is improbable, for although a sound is said *to go* [the *Qal* of הָלַךְ *hālakh;* see Jer. xlvi 22], it is not described as *walking about* [the *Hithpaʻel* of הָלַךְ *hālakh*]; whilst to connect the word with *the man* (Abravanel) is, on the basis of our text, absolutely impossible.

לְרוּחַ הַיּוֹם *lerūaḥ hayyōm* [E.V. 'in the cool of the day']/Numerous attempts have been made to explain this expression, which is found nowhere else in the Bible. The rabbinic expositions — for instance: *He* [*God*] *judged him* [*Adam*] *in the east side;* לְרוּחַ הַיּוֹם *lerūaḥ hayyōm* means: *in the side* [רוּחַ *rūaḥ*] *that rises with the day:* or, *He judged him in the west side;* לְרוּחַ הַיּוֹם *lerūaḥ hayyōm* signifies:

in the side that declines with the day (Bereshith Rabba, xix 8) — do not reflect the actual sense of the verse. The interpretation of Naḥmanides, and also of Jacob in modern times, that the man and his wife heard the voice of the Lord God in the wind [רוּחַ *rūaḥ*] blowing in the garden, does not accord with the text. Many other explanations have been advanced, but they are unsatisfactory; equally unacceptable are the emendations that have been proposed, for example, that of Budde; לִרְוֹחַ הַיּוֹם *lirwōaḥ hayyōm* ['when the day became breezy'].

The view commonly held to-day is the one previously mentioned, according to which the phrase signifies: at the time when the wind springs up towards evening (or, at dawn). This interpretation is open to a number of objections. In the first place, it is difficult to understand the prepositional *Lāmedh* as one of time, unless it is linked to an expression having a temporal meaning. It is possible, for instance, to say לַבֹּקֶר *labbōqer* ['at morning'], לָעֶרֶב *lāʿerebh* ['at evening'] לִפְנוֹת בֹּקֶר *liphnōth bōqer* ['at the approach of morning'], לְעֵת עֶרֶב *leʿēth ʿerebh* ['at the time of evening'], and so forth; but it is impossible, for example, to say לְצֵאת הַשֹּׁאֲבֹת *leṣē'th haššō'ăbhōth* [literally, 'at (or, to) women going out to draw water']; the Bible writes: לְעֵת צֵאת הַשֹּׁאֲבֹת *leʿēth ṣē'th haššō'ăbhōth* ['at the time when women go out to draw water'] (xxiv 11). In order, therefore, to express the thought 'at the time when the wind of the day blows', it would have been necessary to write לְעֵת רוּחַ הַיּוֹם *leʿēth rūaḥ hayyōm* or its equivalent. Furthermore, even if we concede that this difficulty can be explained by reference to such doubtful examples as, *when he knows* [לְדַעְתּוֹ *ledhaʿtō*] *how to refuse the evil and choose the good* (Isa. vii 15), we must surely realize that the expression רוּחַ הַיּוֹם *rūaḥ hayyōm* cannot possibly indicate a wind blowing *at a specific time of the day.* This apart, seeing that the verse expressly comes to fix the *time,* there must doubtless be a reason for this, and it is inconceivable that this time should have no relation to the actual narrative; but the usual interpretation fails to establish such a connection.

These problems compel us to search for another explanation. It seems to me that the word רוּחַ *rūaḥ* is not to be understood as a *substantive* but as a verb in the *infinitive,* like חֹם *ḥōm* ['become hot'] in the phrase כְּחֹם הַיּוֹם *keḥōm hayyōm* [literally, 'as the day grew hot' that is, at noon] (xviii 1), and that it signifies: *to be in the period after midday.* Not only in Arabic does this stem (راح يروح *rāḥa yarūḥu*) denote an action taking place in the *afternoon* — that is, from the time when the sun begins to decline from the meridian till evening — but it is also found in this sense in Ugaritic (I have thus explained the word *rḥ* in this sense in Tablet V AB, ii, line 2). Since the verb occurs in the ancient Canaanite language, we may surmise that we have here a Canaanite expression that survived also in the poetic idiom of the people of Israel. Apparently the ancient epic poem on the story of the garden of Eden contained the words לְרוּחַ הַיּוֹם *leruaḥ hayyōm,* that is, at the time when the day רָח *rāḥ* — is in its second stage, namely, the afternoon. The Torah uses this phrase just as it uses other poetic expressions that occurred in that poem, for example, אֵד *'ēdh* ['waters of the deep']; *pleasant to the sight and good for food; the flaming sword which turned every way;* and other phrases that I noted above, pp. 73 ff. The purpose of fixing the time in this verse is readily explicable in the light of the statement (ii 17): *for* IN THE DAY *that you eat of it you shall surely die.* Although it is possible, as I indicated earlier, to understand the words *in the day* in a general sense, that is, *at the time,* nevertheless Scripture wished to emphasize that the word of the Lord God was wholly fulfilled, even in its literal meaning. The man was told that *in the day that he ate* from the tree of life he would surely die, and lo! on the very day that he ate, in the afternoon of the selfsame day, the Lord God appeared and decreed that he should be banished from the garden of Eden, so that he might no longer be able to approach the tree of life and eat of it and be liberated thereby from the power of death (see above, on ii 17).

Among the trees of the garden [בְּתוֹךְ עֵץ הַגָּן *bethōkh 'ēṣ haggān*]/ Why just *among the trees of the garden* (עֵץ *'ēṣ* [literally, 'tree'] has, of course, a collective sense here), and not in some other place; for example, in a cave or the like? All three of these words — בְּתוֹךְ *bethōkh* ['in the midst of, among, in the centre of'], עֵץ *'ēṣ* ['tree, trees'], גַּן *gan* ['garden'] — have already appeared a number of times in our section, and they remind us of what we read earlier concerning the sin of Adam and his wife. Such repetitions do not occur without a definite purpose. It would seem that the words are intended to hint that though the sinner was trying to forget his sin and cause others to forget it, he is unable to silence the voice of his conscience and to obliterate the traces of his misdeeds; at every step he encounters objects that remind him and others of the transgression that he has committed. It was *in connection with the tree which is in the centre of* [בְּתוֹךְ $b^{e}th\bar{o}kh$] *the garden* that they sinned, and it is *among* [בְּתוֹךְ $b^{e}th\bar{o}kh$] *the trees of the garden* that they were forced to hide themselves.

On Job xxxi 33, see Torczyner's commentary.

9. *But the Lord God called to the man*] In vain he attempted to conceal himself, for it is impossible to hide from the eyes of the Lord. Forthwith the Judge of the whole earth calls the man, in order to demand from him an account of his conduct. Also in other parts of the Bible the verb to *call* is used in the sense of to *summon a person to give an account of his actions;* compare xii 18: *So Pharaoh* CALLED *Abram, and said,* 'WHAT IS THIS YOU HAVE DONE TO ME?' (this question, too, is not unlike the continuation in our section); xx 9: *Then Abimelech* CALLED *Abraham, and said to him,* 'WHAT HAVE YOU DONE TO US?' etc.; xxvi 9–10: *So Abimelech* CALLED *Isaac . . . Abimelech said,* 'WHAT IS THIS YOU HAVE DONE TO US?'; Deut. xxv 8: *Then the elders of his city* SHALL CALL HIM, *and speak to him.*

The man was the first to be tried, because the primary responsibility rested upon him, and he was the first to receive the Divine command.

And said to him, 'Where are you?'] The verse does not read, *and said, 'Where are you?'*, but *and said* TO HIM, *'Where are you?'*. The Lord God turns direct to the man wherever he is. The commentators who consider the question to be *aimed at discovering* where the man was hiding have overlooked the words *to him.* They have likewise disregarded the fact that the sequel relates that the Lord God determined the fate of the man and his wife and the serpent according to His will; since the subsequent narrative portrays God as omnipotent, it stands to reason that He is not depicted here as one who is unaware of what is around him. The query *Where are you?* in our verse resembles the question that the Lord God asks Cain (iv 9), *Where is Abel your brother?*, when Abel's body is lying on the ground beneath the open sky, and no attempt is made to conceal it; indeed, the matter is so well known to the Lord, that He immediately thereafter says: *Hark, your brother's blood is crying to Me from the ground* (*ibid., v.* 10). Similarly David asks (i Sam. xxvi 16): *Where is the king's spear, and the cruse of water?,* knowing full well where they are. In all these passages we have only rhetorical questions of varying meaning. The same obtains here. We may compare the case to that of a man who comes to chide his little son who misbehaved himself and then hid himself behind the door in order to avoid looking at his father's angry face; the father who is well aware of the child's hiding-place, calls out to him, 'Where are you?', meaning: Why are you there? Is that where you should be? Come out and face me!

The man's answer is in keeping with this interpretation; he does not reply, 'I am in such-and-such a place', but he explains why he is concealing himself.

And said, etc.] Although this is not stated explicitly, we must picture to ourselves that the man, when he realizes that he has been discovered, emerges from his hiding-place and, standing shamefaced before the Judge, mumbles his reply. His wife creeps out slowly after him.

10. *I heard the sound of Thee in the Garden,* etc.] He does not dare to lie before his Creator, but he is not yet willing to avow his sin; hence he strives to turn the conversation to another subject, the last thing that happened *after* his transgression. He offers an excuse for hiding himself, without perceiving that his very excuse provides evidence of his misdeed.

The language of *v.* 8 is repeated here with slight changes; similar repetitions occur again further on. In the course of the dialogue between the Judge and the accused the whole concatenation of events of which we read above is recapitulated, but in *reverse* order: first, reference is made to the concluding phase of the story, when the sound of the Lord God is heard and the transgressors conceal themselves; then, one by one retrogressively, the other incidents are recounted until the starting-point is reached — the enticement by the serpent.

And I was afraid] He confesses only to a feeling of *reverence,* which prompts him to hide himself; but unwittingly he betrays in the remark, *I was afraid,* also the sense of *fear and tre-*

pidation felt by the transgressor who is summoned before the court.

Because I was naked] These words recall the penultimate stage of the story, *and they knew that they were naked* (*v.* 7), and thus testify to it before the Judge. Now the questions of the Judge press harder and harder on the accused to force him to admit the preceding episode.

11. *Who told you . . . have you eaten of the tree,* etc.] It is clear that these are not the questions of one who is ignorant of what has happened. Once the accused had inadvertently uttered the words, *and I was afraid,* BECAUSE I WAS NAKED, even a person of ordinary intelligence could have safely concluded that the man had eaten from the tree of knowledge. The purpose of the interrogation is only to force him to make a complete confession; after what he has already said, the accused can no longer deny his guilt.

That you were naked] This is the third reference to the subject (see *vv.* 7, 10); thrice for emphasis.

The tree of which I commanded you, etc.] The tree is not mentioned here by name. The name is no longer important; only the prohibition attached to it is of consequence now.

12. *The woman whom Thou gavest to be with me, she gave me fruit of the tree and I ate*] He confesses. The confession takes us still further back in the reconstruction of the course of events; we reach the incident described at the end of *v.* 6:*and also she gave some to her husband, and he ate.* The words are repeated, and the parallelism between the two verses is clear.

The man endeavours to lessen the gravity of his offence by emphasizing in the preface to his confession that it was not on his own, but on the woman's, initiative that he committed the wrong. Thus we often find excuses for ourselves by throwing the blame on our companions, without realizing that our very failure to resist the will of others constitutes our sin. Possibly there is also to be noted an attempt on Adam's part to exculpate himself by alluding to the fact that it was the Lord God Himself who *gave* the woman to be with him, as though to say: *Thou didst give* the woman to be with me, and *she gave* me of the fruit of the tree. This, too, is characteristically human: people are inclined to justify their conduct by pointing to the circumstances and fate that God has allotted to them in life. To this implicit contention of Adam, the Lord God gives, of course, no answer, for it was not consonant with His dignity to reply thereto, but the Divine silence indicates the rejection of the plea.

13. *Then the Lord God said to the woman*] Since the man mentioned the woman, the Judge turns to her.

What is this that you have done?] Here it is clearer still that the question is merely rhetorical. The woman's deed is already known from the man's answer; there is no need, therefore, for further questioning in order to establish the facts. It is difficult to understand how a number of commentators could interpret the question as having the purpose of ascertaining what the woman had done. Cain was addressed in similar terms (iv 10), *What have you done?,* at the very moment when he was told: *Hark, your brother's blood is crying to Me from the ground!* In like manner the kings of Egypt and Gerar formulated their questions in the three verses quoted above (xii 18; xx 9; xxvi 10), although they knew full well what Abraham and Isaac had done. In all these instances the question resembles an ejaculation, the meaning being: How could you do so terrible a thing!

The serpent beguiled me, and I ate] The woman also endeavours to exonerate herself by putting the responsibility on the inciter, and she does not realise that her sin lies in the very fact that she did not resist temptation, but listened to the words of incitement, to the prompting of the cunning within her soul.

The woman's answer brings us to the second act of the drama, which is described at the end of the first half of *v.* 6 (*she took of its fruit* AND ATE). It also contains an allusion to the first act, which we shall discuss specifically in connection with the next verse.

14. *The Lord God said to the serpent*] Since the woman mentioned the serpent, the Judge now turns to the latter. But He asks him no questions, and does not await his reply. Why? Various explanations have been advanced in regard to this point, but they all lack an adequate basis in the text. Possibly the solution is to be found in the general attitude of the Torah towards the ancient mythologies. It seeks to reject and refute, as I have already stated (pp. 49 f., 141 f.), the popular beliefs concerning the serpent and the monsters as sovereign entities that rise in revolt against the Creator and oppose His will. Here, too, it is implied that the serpent

is only an ordinary creature, which is not even summoned to judgement and has no right to speak in God's presence. He receives the rebuke due to him; that is all. By God's fiat his fate is decided forever.

We now reach, in our recapitulation of the events in reverse, the opening scene; the words *and above all the beasts of the field,* spoken by the Lord God, remind us of the statement in *v.* 1: *Now the serpent was cunning* BEYOND ANY BEAST OF THE FIELD. This last point in our retelling of the story backwards, becomes the starting-point for the judgement, which proceeds to determine the punishment of the transgressors in the order in which each sinned: to begin with, the tempter; then the woman who was the first to eat; and last the man who ate after his wife. The whole drama is re-enacted before us; and the order of events changes once again, reverting now to the original sequence of the happenings.

Cursed are you above all cattle, and above all the beasts of the field] 'According to the greatness of the serpent so was his downfall: because he was *cunning* ABOVE ALL, he is *cursed* ABOVE ALL' (Bereshith Rabba, xix 1; see the note in Theodor's edition, pp. 170–171). Not only is the expression *above all* repeated here, but there is a play on the assonance between עָרוּם *'ārūm* ['cunning, shrewdness'] and אָרוּר *'ārūr* ['cursed']. The verbal correspondence points to parallelism of thought. Since the serpent transcended all the beasts in shrewdness, and used this shrewdness for evil purposes, he will also surpass in his curse all the beasts of the field, and even all the cattle, whose life as a rule is harder than the free existence of the wild animals. Similarly it is said (i Sam. xv 33): *so shall your mother be bereaved* ABOVE [that is, most bereaved of] WOMEN; and in a passage of blessing (Jud. v 24): *Blessed* ABOVE WOMEN *be Jael, the wife of Heber the Kenite,* ABOVE *tent-dwelling* WOMEN blessed.

Upon your belly you shall go, and dust you shall eat, all the days of your life] This shall be the curse of the serpent. The state of this creature, which symbolizes *evil,* shall be ever *evil,* and shall be a warning to men of the consequence of wickedness. *Whatever goes on its belly* is accounted an *abomination* (Lev. xi 42).

And dust you shall eat, etc.] — measure for measure: having sinned in the matter of eating, he was punished in the same respect.

The man's punishment, as we shall see further on, was to be based on the same principle. In the expression, *and dust you shall eat,* there is possibly to be heard an echo of the ancient tradition concerning the subjugation of the serpent and the monsters by God (it is a literary echo only, for the Torah, as we have explained, is opposed to the actual legend). The idea of *eating dust,* in a metaphorical sense of course, occurs several times in Scripture with reference to the plight of conquered foes. It is written, for example, in Psa. lxxii 9: *May those who dwell in the wilderness bow down before him, and his enemies lick the dust!;* in Isa. xlix 23: *and lick the dust of your feet;* in Mic. vii 17: *they shall lick the dust* LIKE A SERPENT. And just as in Isa. xxvii 1, it is said that in the days of the Messiah *the Lord with His hard and great and strong sword will punish Leviathan the fleeing serpent, Leviathan the twisting serpent,* etc. — that is, that God will eradicate the principle of evil from the world — so we are told, with regard to the very same subject, in Isa. lxv 25: AND DUST SHALL BE THE SERPENT'S FOOD. *They shall not hurt or destroy in all my holy mountain, says the Lord.*

All the days of your life] The boundary between the primeval serpent and his successors is somewhat blurred; here the pronoun *you* addressed to the former includes the latter too, whereas in the following verse the first serpent is distinguished from his issue. See also below, on *I will greatly multiply,* etc. in *v.* 16.

We are not given the slightest indication of what kind of form, according to our section, the original serpent had before his doom was decreed; whether the haggadic expositions of this subject accord with the actual meaning of the text, it is difficult to determine. The rabbinic legend that the serpent resembled a human being in shape and stature (see above, p. 140), corresponds to the figures that appear on some Mesopotamian seals, which depict a composite creature, half serpent and half man (see, for example, Ward, *The Seal Cylinders of Western Asia,* Washington, 1910, pp. 127–128). The Torah may purposely have remained silent on this subject in accordance with its systematic opposition to whatever is connected with mythological beliefs.

15. *I will put enmity,* etc.] The serpent is not, as the ancient tradition declares, the enemy of God; he is the foe of man. On the

principle that the deeds of the fathers are an omen unto the children, this hostility created between the primeval serpent and the woman whom he had enticed would continue between his and her seed through the generations. 'And of the two antagonists', the serpent is told, 'you shall not be the stronger. *He* (namely, the woman's offspring) will easily be able to crush your head, but you will not be able to injure him except by biting his heel; and if he will beware of you and will quickly shatter your head before you bite his heel, he will be delivered from you.' Possibly we have here also a parable concerning the principle of evil: it lies in wait for man and seeks to instil its venom by its bite, but if man takes heed of it and hastens to break its skull, he will be saved from it, even as it was said to Cain in regard to sin: *its desire is for you, but you will be able to master it* (iv 7).

יְשׁוּפְךָ *yᵉšūphᵉkhā* [usually rendered: (*he*) *will bruise you*] .. תְּשׁוּפֶנּוּ *tᵉšūphennū* [usually rendered: (*you*) *shall bruise him*] / It is difficult to determine the precise meaning of the two verbs, which form a word-play here; much discussion has been devoted to the problem by the commentators. The most likely explanation is that the first verb יְשׁוּפְךָ *yᵉšūphᵉkhā* is derived from a root שׁוּף *šūph* that is akin to שָׁאַף *šā'aph* in Amos ii 7: *they that trample* הַשֹּׁאֲפִים *haššō'ăphīm*] *the* HEAD OF THE POOR INTO THE DUST OF THE EARTH, and *ibid.*, viii 4: *You who trample* [הַשֹּׁאֲפִים *haššō'ăphīm*] *upon the needy,* where it has the meaning of *tread upon* or *crush;* and that the second verb, תְּשׁוּפֶנּוּ *tᵉšūphennū,* comes from a stem שׁוּף *šūph* that is cognate with שָׁאַף *šā'aph* in the normal sense of that root, namely, *to crave, desire* (compare the expression *its desire* in the aforementioned verse of the next chapter [iv 7]).

16. *To the woman He said*] The reference to *the woman* in the previous verse provides the transition to this verse, which cites the words of the Lord God to the woman.

In order to understand this Divine utterance as well as the subsequent address to the man, a few preliminary remarks are necessary. The decrees pronounced by the Lord God appear unduly severe: because Adam and his wife sinned was it right that their children and children's children should be punished for all time? There is also another difficulty, which arises from the interpretation that I suggested above of ii 17 (p. 125). I stated that the Torah's intention was to declare that if the man and his wife had hearkened to the voice of the Creator and had been content with what He had given them, they could have eaten from the tree of life and lived forever in the garden of delight prepared for them. In that eventuality, they would have had no need, of course, to propagate their species or to spread abroad through the earth and fill it. Accepting this premise, there is a serious discrepancy between the preceding section and the present, which constitutes a far graver contradiction than any of those that I discussed in the introduction (pp. 88–92), for it is distinctly stated in the story of creation (i 28): *And God blessed them, and God said to them,* 'BE FRUITFUL AND MULTIPLY, AND FILL THE EARTH'. However, I believe that this objection, which can apparently be raised against my exposition, can be clearly and convincingly answered, if we understand well the words addressed by the Lord God to the woman and to the man. This will enable us also to solve the first problem that we enunciated here, namely, the question of the doom imposed by the Lord God upon the entire human race in consequence of the actions of the first man and his wife.

We have already seen above (pp. 90 ff.) that the Torah adopts the following method in describing the creation of the man and the woman: in the first section it recounts very briefly, in conformity with the general plan of that section, the gist of the story in the final form that it assumed in the last stage of its unfoldment, to wit, *male and female He created them;* and in the second section, when reverting to the subject for the purpose of giving a full and detailed account, it portrays the course of events in all its successive phases to the very end. The same procedure is followed in the present instance: in the first section, whose general structure prevents it from devoting more than a few sentences to man, only the last phase of the story is mentioned, the phase that determines, by the Divine blessing, mankind's destiny for all generations; but when the Torah recapitulates the narrative in detail in this, the second section, it records each separate stage in the chain of events until the *dénouement.*

As far as the conclusion is concerned, the two sections accord well with one another. Since man chose the knowledge of good and evil, which involves mortality, preferring it to primitive simplicity, which is linked to eternal life, the Lord God acted towards him as a human father would to his dearly beloved little son, who did something contrary to his counsel, and thereby brought great harm upon himself. On the one hand, the father rebukes his son for not having followed his advice, and on the other hand, he endeavours to remedy the hurt that his son has done to himself by his action. The decrees pronounced by the Lord God mentioned here are not exclusively *punishments;* they are also, and chiefly, *measures taken for the good of the human species* in its new situation. Immediately after eating of the fruit of the tree, they realized that it was not good to stand naked, and, for the time being, they sought relief in aprons of fig leaves. Needless to say, this was only a temporary palliative and inadequate for the future. Furthermore, when man went forth into the wide world, he was compelled to cover himself not only for reasons of *modesty* but also on account of the *cold* and all the other natural phenomena that are injurious to human beings: and behold, *the Lord God made for Adam and his wife garments of skin and clothed them* (*v.* 21). Even more essential was another ameliorative measure. Having lost the opportunity of achieving immortality, it was vital, in order to assure the survival of the human race, that man should be enabled to be fruitful and multiply; and so, indeed, the Lord God decreed. This reproductive capacity entails, forsooth, pain and suffering for the woman, which would be her punishment for her transgression, as it is written: *I will greatly multiply your suffering, especially of your child-bearing: in pain you shall bring forth children. In pain,* it is true, but *you shall bring forth children,* and that, ultimately, is what matters most. This is at once the benison of fertility and the assurance of the continued existence of the species, a promise that begins to be realized immediately, as it is said (iv 1): *Now Adam knew Eve his wife, and she conceived and bore Cain,* etc.

There was still a third measure necessary: the provision of sustenance. In the garden of Eden man maintained himself without difficulty; the soil of the garden was irrigated by the water of the river, without any need for rain, and he had only to stretch forth his hand and gather fruit from the trees, according to his requirements. When he was banished from the garden and went forth into the wide world, which could not be sufficiently fructified by well-water and rivers, the blessing of rain, which gives to the earth its fertility, came into force. It is true that the bringing forth of bread from the ground demands intensive toil on the part of man, which would be his punishment for his sin; it is true that rain cannot always be depended upon — a factor that is to be employed by God for requiting man according to the good or evil of his deeds. However, the possibility of obtaining sustenance was afforded him. *In toil you shall eat of it*: verily *in toil,* yet you will at least *eat of it. And you shall eat of the grain of the field*: granted it is only *the grain of the field,* but at all events *you will eat. In the sweat of your face you shall eat bread*: truly *in the sweat of your face;* nevertheless, *you shall eat bread.* In this case, too, in the final analysis, it is the positive outcome that is of primary importance.

According to this interpretation, it would appear that the rabbinic comment that all that is here related concerning the man took place on the very day that he was created, agrees with the actual meaning of the text, for it is stated above (i 28–29) that the blessings of fertility and sustenance were bestowed on the sixth day. There is not a single word in the passage that contradicts this hypothesis: on the contrary, it is possible that the expression לְרוּחַ הַיּוֹם *l^erūaḥ hayyōm* ['in the afternoon'] contains, as we have explained, an allusion to the fact that the whole drama was enacted on the same day.

I will greatly multiply, etc.] The woman is briefly told here what specifically concerns her and her female offspring. In addition, they are included in the sentence passed on the man (hence אָדָם *'ādhām* [i.e. man as species] is used instead of אִישׁ *'īš* [i.e. the male]). This particular penalty was not imposed on the woman because her transgression had any sexual implications, as many exegetes have thought; but since the punishment was specifically intended for the woman and her female descendants, and was not a penalty shared with the men, it had inevitably to be of a nature restricted to the female sex. The woman's female heirs are not explicitly mentioned here, although above (*v.* 15) the Bible distinguishes between her and her seed. In the case of the woman, as in the case of the serpent, there is a blurring of the boundary-line between the prototype of the species as an individual and as a symbol of the succeeding generations of kindred creatures.

Your suffering [עִצְּבוֹנֵךְ *ʿiṣṣᵉbhōnēkh*] . . . *in pain* [בְּעֶצֶב *bᵉʿeṣebh*] / The stem עָצַב *ʿāṣabh* ['to pain'] occurs three times: twice here and once in *v.* 17, in the words spoken by the Lord God to the man. Such repetition implies emphasis, and the emphasis has a reason. Apparently, we have here a play upon words with reference to עֵץ *ʿēṣ* ['tree']: it was with respect to עֵץ *ʿēṣ* that the man and woman sinned, and it was with עֶצֶב *ʿeṣebh* ['pain'] and עִצָּבוֹן *ʿiṣṣābhōn* ['toil, suffering'] that they were punished. The woman ate from the tree that seemed to her *good* for food, and a *delight* to the eyes, and was to be *desired* to make one wise; and she was punished with something that was not *good,* and no source of *delight,* and not *to be desired,* but a great *suffering,* a severe *pain,* which would become proverbial (such sayings as [to suffer] *pangs like a woman in travail* are familiar). The very fact that Scripture does not employ here the usual phrases found in connection with the suffering of childbirth, like חֵבֶל *ḥēbhel* ['pain'], חִיל *ḥīl* ['writhing, anguish'], צִיר *ṣīr* ['writhing, pang'], צָרָה *ṣārā* ['distress'], but chose expressions derived from the root עָצַב *ʿāṣabh,* proves that it was with some specific intention — for instance, to allude to the word עֵץ *ʿēṣ* — that these words were selected.

עִצְּבוֹנֵךְ וְהֵרֹנֵךְ *ʿiṣṣᵉbhōnēkh wᵉhērōnēkh* [literally, 'Your suffering and your childbearing'] / The phrase is usually understood to mean עִצְּבוֹן הֵרוֹנֵךְ *ʿiṣṣᵉbhōn hērōnēkh* ['the suffering of your childbearing'] (hendiadys), but a better interpretation is: *your suffering* in general, and more particularly that of *your childbearing;* cf., *from the hand of all enemies, and* [i.e. especially] *from the hand of Saul* (ii Sam. xxii 1); so, too, Psa. xviii 1: *and from the hand of Saul. Your suffering,* that is, 'the pains and maladies of women would exceed those of men because of their natural adynamia' (Abravanel); *and your childbearing,* that is, particularly during the period of childbearing women would suffer from increasing weakness and would need special attention, and when the time of parturition arrived, they would inevitably endure the most fearful pangs: *in pain you shall bring forth children.*

Yet your desire shall be for your husband, and he shall rule over you] Measure for measure: you influenced your husband and caused him to do what you wished; henceforth, you and your female descendants will be subservient to your husbands. You will yearn for them, but they will be the heads of the families, and will rule over you. See above, on ii 24.

The reading of the Septuagint, the Peshiṭta and the Old Latin version, תְּשׁוּבָתֵךְ *t*ᵉ*šûbhāthēkh* ['your turning'] instead of תְּשׁוּקָתֵךְ *t*ᵉ*šûqāthēkh,* ['your desire'] is unconvincing.

17. ***And to Adam He said***] The mention of the woman's husband in the previous verse provides the point of transition to the Lord God's pronouncement to the man, just as the reference to the woman in *v.* 15 served the same purpose for His address to the woman in *v.* 16.

On the general purport and significance of this utterance directed to the man, see my remarks above, in my annotations to *v.* 16. Similarly, with regard to the inclusion of all mankind in the sentence decreed on the first man, see my explanation *ibid.*

וּלְאָדָם *ûl*ᵉ*'ādhām* ['and to Adam'] / So the word is pointed [with *Š*ᵉ*wā'* under the *Lāmedh*], and not לָאָדָם *lā'ādhām* [with *Qāmeṣ* under the *Lāmedh*], also above, in ii 20, and further on, in iii 21. If ii 20 provided the sole example, we might have thought that it was intentionally vocalized thus, in order to embrace the whole of humanity and not the first man alone; but here, and again in *v.* 21, this interpretation is not possible. It is accepted to-day by almost all Biblical scholars that since throughout the section it is invariably written הָאָדָם *hā'ādhām,* with the definite article, it is to be inferred that in these three verses the Masoretes erred, and that we must emend their vocalization and read לָאָדָם *lā'ādhām.* On the other hand, Jacob in his commentary attempts to find a reason for this vocalization on homiletical lines. It appears to me that the exegetical approach of the latter, as well as of the former, is wrong, and that before we come to a conclusion on the question of the vocalization, we must first enquire whether it is not based on a linguistic rule. There is in Hebrew a substantive whose usage is similar to that of אָדָם *'ādhām,* namely, אֱלֹהִים *'Elōhîm.* It was also originally a *common* noun, and it is likewise used as a *proper* noun, because there is, in its category, only a single example, just as in the narrative before us there is but one man. Since the word אֱלֹהִים *'Elōhîm* occurs so often in the books of the Bible, it is particularly suited to serve as the basis for the determination of the grammatical rules pertaining to nouns that share its characteristics (the word אֵל *'ēl* has no

bearing on our subject, since its usage is governed by exceptional rules; see my article on this word in *SMSR,* viii [1932], pp. 125–145, and my aforementioned book, *La Questione della Genesi,* pp. 60–78). With regard to the use of the word אֱלֹהִים *'Elōhīm* as *a proper noun* — that is, as a *name of the God of Israel* — a study of the relevant passages enables us to establish the following rules:
(1) It can be used without the definite article, like any other proper name; so, for example, in the story of creation, (*In the beginning* GOD [אֱלֹהִים *'Elōhīm*] *created,* etc.); innumerable other instances — hundreds, in fact — may be quoted from Scripture.
(2) It can also take the definite article, since it had a *general* connotation to begin with, and was consequently capable of receiving the sign of determination; e.g. xxii 1: GOD [הָאֱלֹהִים *Hā'ĕlōhīm*] *tested Abraham;* hundreds of similar examples can be found in the Bible.
(3) Whenever the prefixes ל ,כ ,ב *Bēth, Kaph, Lāmedh* ['in, like, to'] are added to אֱלֹהִים *'Elōhīm,* they *never* receive the vocalization of the definite article (-לָ ,-כָּ ,-בָּ *bā–, kā–, lā–*), but always take, without exception, the form -לֵ ,-כֵּ ,-בֵּ *bē–, kē–, lē–.* Twice the Bible points the prepositional prefix before אֱלֹהִים *'Elōhīm* with *Qāmeṣ,* and in each of these verses the word is used as a *common noun* and not as a *proper noun,* that is, the reference is to the different pagan deities, in contradistinction to the God of Israel (Exod. xxii 20 [Hebrew, *v.* 19]: *Whosoever sacrifices* TO ANY GOD [לָאֱלֹהִים *lā'ĕlōhīm*], *save to the Lord only, shall be utterly destroyed,* Psa. lxxxvi 8: *There is none like Thee* AMONG THE GODS [בָאֱלֹהִים *bhā'ĕlōhīm*], *O Lord*). Precisely the same rules apply to the word אָדָם *'ādhām.* When it is used as a *proper name,* it may occur without the definite article (so, for example, iv 25, and several times in ch. v), or the definite article may be prefixed to it (as in our section and below, iv 1); but when it has a prepositional prefix, the latter is not pointed with *Qāmeṣ* but with *Šewā'* (ii 20; iii 17, 21) — the identical rules, in fact. It is clear therefore, that the pointing לְאָדָם *le'ādhām* is not due to an error, nor has it an esoteric significance, but is based on a general rule of the Hebrew tongue.

Because you have listened to the voice of your wife, and have eaten of the tree of which I commanded you, etc.] Since you listened to her voice, although by so doing you disobeyed My commands, and *you ate* what I forbade you *to eat,* your punishment will also be connected with *eating.* The stem אָכַל *'ākhal* occurs no less than five times in the Lord God's address to the man.

Cursed is the ground because of you] In order to understand the nature of the earth's curse, we must determine what is meant by its blessing. From a number of passages (e.g. Deut. xxxiii 13–15) we learn that a blessed land is one that is amply watered and fertile. It follows that a land is cursed when it lacks water and fertility. In the garden of Eden, which was well watered and produced abundant fruit, man ate to his satisfaction without any anxiety or undue exertion; from now on, the earth would yield its harvest to him only with difficulty and in meagre measure.

In toil [עִצָּבוֹן *'iṣṣābhōn*] *you shall eat it*] Only through your own hard work will you be able to obtain and eat the fruit of the earth. On עִצָּבוֹן *'iṣṣābhōn* see my remarks above, on *v.* 16. Here it may be added that the stem עָצַב *'āṣabh* is used in a number of passages in connection with human labour (sometimes, perhaps, not without allusion to our verse); for example, Psa. cxxvii 2: *eating the bread of* ANXIOUS TOIL [הָעֲצָבִים *hā'ăṣābhīm*]*;* Prov. x 22: *The blessing of the Lord makes rich, and* TOIL [עֶצֶב *'eṣebh*] *adds nothing to it;* ibid. xiv 23: *In all* TOIL [עֶצֶב *'eṣebh*] *there is profit, but mere talk tends only to want.* Possibly the word עַצְּבֵיכֶם *'aṣṣebhēkhem* in Isa. lviii 3 means 'Your labourers', who work for you in the house and in the field. The word עֶצֶב *'eṣebh* denotes also the *fruit* of toil; e.g. Prov. v 10: *Lest strangers take their fill of your strength, and* YOUR LABOURS [עֲצָבֶיךָ *'ăṣābhekhā*] *go to the house of an alien.*

All the days of your life] This corresponds to the closing words of *v.* 14 above. See my comment there.

After the general statement here, *in toil you shall eat of it all the days of your life,* a detailed elaboration is given in *vv.* 18, 19.

18. *Thorns and thistles* [וְקוֹץ וְדַרְדַּר *weqōṣ wedhardar*] *it shall bring forth to you*] Of its own accord, without your labour, the ground will produce for you only thorns and thistles, plants that do not provide you with sustenance. These are to be identified with שִׂיחַ הַשָּׂדֶה *śīaḥ haśśādhe* ['thorns of the field'] mentioned earlier (see my annotations to ii 5, pp. 101 ff.). Then — before man had been created — there were no thorns of the field yet upon

earth; now, on account of man's sin, the thorns of the field would be found there in abundance. Also in Hos. x 8, there is mention of *thorns and thistles* [קוֹץ וְדַרְדַּר *qōṣ wᵉdhardar*] in connection with the *sin* of Israel.

And you shall eat the grain of the field] Even when you succeed in eating of the fruit of your land, it will no longer be the desirable fruit of the garden of Eden but the *grain of the field,* that is, the bread that you will produce from grasses like wheat and barley and other kinds of cereals. This, too, recalls what is stated in ii 5: *and no grain of the field* had yet sprung up; see my comments thereon. At that time there were no cornfields yet; from now on, by dint of man's labour, cornfields would multiply upon the earth.

19. *In the sweat of your face you shall eat bread*] Although the word *bread* may connote food in general, the preceding declaration, *and you shall eat the* GRAIN OF THE FIELD, makes it clear that the reference here is to *bread proper,* in the restricted meaning of the term. The phrase *in the sweat of your face* — that is, through toil, which will bathe your face in sweat — provides an additional explanation of בְּעִצָּבוֹן *beʿiṣṣābhōn* ['in toil'] in *v.* 17.

Till you return to the ground, etc.] After making the general statement, *all the days of your life,* the Bible defines the expression more closely, and links it up with what has been said earlier (ii 7): *Then the Lord God formed man of* DUST FROM THE GROUND. We are approaching the end of the section, and the symmetry of the narrative requires that we should hear at this point echoes of the beginning of the narrative.

For out of it you were taken] You wished to be like God and to transcend the status of the earthly creatures, but you must not forget that although you were created in the Divine image, your body was derived from the ground, and everything in nature must return in the end to its original source.

For you are dust and to dust you shall return] A repetition of the thought in different words. Earlier (ii 7) it is stated, *of dust from the ground;* and here, after referring again to *the ground,* further mention is made of *the dust.* See, on the subject, my notes above, on ii 7, pp. 104 ff.

The idea that man is only *dust,* and that in the end he must return to *dust,* finds expression in various passages of the Bible, all of which are dependent apparently on our verse. Examples are: Psa. ciii 14: *For He knows our frame; He remembers that* WE ARE DUST; *ibid.* civ 29: *when Thou takest away their breath, they die,* AND RETURN TO THEIR DUST; Job iv 19: *how much more those who dwell in houses of clay,* WHOSE FOUNDATION IS IN THE DUST; *ibid.* x 9: *Remember that Thou hast made me of clay,* AND WILT THOU TURN ME TO DUST AGAIN?; *ibid.* xxxiv 15: *all flesh would perish together,* AND MAN WOULD RETURN TO DUST; Eccles. iii 20: *all are* FROM THE DUST AND ALL TURN TO DUST AGAIN; *ibid.* xii 7: AND THE DUST RETURNS TO THE EARTH *as it was.*

The words of the Lord God to the man explain to him in detail the meaning of the warning, *you shall surely die,* which had been addressed to him in the beginning (ii 17). Then he had not been able to comprehend the detailed implications (see my comments *ibid.*); but now, having eaten of the tree of knowledge, he is able to understand, and a comprehensive explanation is given him.

20. *The man called his wife's name Eve,* etc.] It may at first seem strange that this verse comes just here. Several expositors consider it misplaced; whilst the attempts of others to explain its present position are forced. To me it seems that the elucidation is to be sought in the fact that the giving of a name, as I have stated above (p. 92), was considered an indication of lordship. Since the Lord God decreed that *he* [the husband] *should rule over her* he assigns a name to her as a token of his rulership.

Because she was the mother of all living] These words have been added by the Bible; it is not Adam's own reason, for in that case he should have said: 'because she *shall be* the mother of all living'. Furthermore, how could Adam have known that she would be the mother of all living? This apart, how is it possible to find in the name חַוָּה *Ḥawwā* [Eve], even if we assume that it signifies חַיָּה *ḥayyā* ['living'] (fem. sing.), the idea of *the mother of all living?* The meaning of the verse is this: the man called his wife חַוָּה *Ḥawwā,* and this name was well suited to her, since she eventually became the mother of all living. But why did her husband call her חַוָּה *Ḥawwā?* It would seem that the correct view, anticipated already by the rabbinic sages, is that of the scholars who consider that this name is related to the Aramaic word חִוְיָא *ḥiwyā'* and the Arabic حيّة *ḥayyatun* ('serpent'; cf. Bereshith Rabba, xx 11: 'She was given to him for an adviser, but she played the eavesdropper like the serpent [חִיוְיָה *ḥiwyā*] . . . R. Aḥa said: The serpent was your [Eve's] serpent [i.e. seducer] and you are Adam's serpent'; see the variant readings in Theodor's commentary, p. 195; cf. also *ibid.* xx 2, where the dictum of R. Aḥa recurs). On account of what happened in the garden of Eden, the man named his wife חַוָּה *Ḥawwā,* that is, *Female Serpent,* and the Torah notes, as I observed, that the name was appropriate to her from another aspect, to wit, because of the *living* who were to issue from her. Thus, there is another reason for giving the verse its particular position here.

It is doubtful whether a parallel can be found to the name חַוָּה *Ḥawwā* in Phoenician inscriptions.

21. *And the Lord God made for Adam and for his wife tunics of skins, and clothed them*] The main significance of this verse has been explained above, in connection with *v.* 16; see *ibid.* Concerning the vocalization of לְאָדָם *le'ādhām,* see on *v.* 17.

Tunics of skins] Various fanciful interpretations have been advanced regarding the *tunics of skin,* but the term simply denotes tunics made of the skins of domestic or wild animals, enduring tunics in contrast to aprons of leaves (*v.* 7), which do not last a long time. There is no contradiction here to the principle of vegetarianism implied both in the previous section (i 29) and the present (iii 17–19), for there is no necessity to suppose that the verse refers specifically to skins of cattle that had been slaughtered for the purpose of eating their flesh.

And clothed them] The meaning is not, as Jacob thinks, that the Lord Himself clothed them, but that He enabled them to clothe themselves. So, too, it is written (ii Sam. i 24): *Ye daughters of Israel, weep over Saul, who* CLOTHED YOU *daintily in scarlet.*

The expression, *and He clothed them,* concludes the paragraph with a fitting parallel to the endings of the two preceding paragraphs (ii 25: *And they were both naked, the man and his wife, and were not ashamed;* iii 7: *and they knew that they were naked; and they sewed fig leaves together and made themselves aprons*).

SEVENTH PARAGRAPH

THE EXPULSION FROM THE GARDEN OF EDEN

22. *Then the Lord God said,*
'Behold, the man
has become like one of us, / knowing good and evil;
and now, lest he put forth his hand / and take also of the tree of life,
and eat, / and live for ever' —

23. *therefore the Lord God sent him forth / from the garden of Eden,*
to till the ground / from which he was taken.

24. *He drove out the man; / and at the east of the garden of Eden* [מִקֶּדֶם לְגַן עֵדֶן *miqqedhem leghan ʿēdhen*] *He placed the cherubim, / and the sword-flame which turned every way,*
to guard / the way to the tree of life.

22. *Like one of us*] — like one of my entourage, like one of the Divine entities, which are of a higher order than man, for example, the cherubim and their kind. We have already seen above (p. 113) that the idea prevailed among the Israelites that the knowledge of good and evil, that is, of everything in the world, was one of the specific attributes of the angels (ii Sam. xiv 17: *for my lord the king is like the angel of God* TO DISCERN GOOD AND EVIL; *ibid., v.* 20: *But my lord has wisdom like the wisdom of* THE ANGEL OF GOD TO KNOW ALL THINGS THAT ARE ON THE EARTH).

Knowing good and evil] This serves to qualify and define the preceding comparison, *like one of us.* The man has become like one of us in the sense that he also knows good and evil.

And now, lest he put forth his hand, etc.] The word וְעַתָּה *weʿattā* ['and now'] is usually, as here, the correlative of הֵן *hēn* (or הִנֵּה *hinnē*) ['behold'], which heads the previous clause. The clause beginning with הֵן *hēn* or הִנֵּה *hinnē* sets out the premise, whilst the clause commencing with וְעַתָּה *weʿattā* conveys the inference to be drawn from it. The man had been given permission to eat of the tree of life on condition, as we noted earlier (p. 124), that he would eschew the fruit of the tree of knowledge; since this condition had not been fulfilled, it was necessary to take heed lest (פֶּן *pen*) he eat also of the tree of life.

23. *Sent him forth* [וַיְשַׁלְּחֵהוּ *wayešallehēhū*] / There is a play here on the word יִשְׁלַח *yišlaḥ* ['he put forth'] in *v.* 22. So that he should not *put forth* his hand, *I shall send him forth.*

To till the ground] — in order to produce therefrom his food, as he had been told (*vv.* 17–19): *in toil* YOU SHALL EAT OF IT . . . AND YOU SHALL EAT *the grain of the field. In the sweat of your face* YOU SHALL EAT *bread.* The Bible repeats here the expression used in the first paragraph (ii 5): *and there was no man* TO TILL THE GROUND. Formerly, there was no man to till the ground; now there is a man to do this. The repetition of phrases occurring at the beginning of the section becomes increasingly frequent as we reach the close.

From which he was taken] This recalls what was stated in *v.* 19: *for out of it* YOU WERE TAKEN, and also in the first paragraph (ii 7): *Then the Lord God formed man of dust* FROM THE GROUND.

24. *He drove out the man*] Apparently a superfluous repetition, for we have already been told in the preceding verse: *therefore the Lord God sent him forth from the garden of Eden.* It is impossible, however, to regard this as a variant reading, because a vital point is missing here — mention of the *place* from which the man was expelled. If we examine the text carefully we shall clearly see that the Torah has a definite purpose in reverting to the subject again in different words. In the first place, the verb גֵּרַשׁ *gēraš* ['drive out'] has a stronger connotation than the verb שִׁלַּח *šillaḥ* ['send forth']. It is written in Exod. xi 1: WHEN HE LETS YOU GO [כְּשַׁלְּחוֹ *kešallehō*] HE WILL SURELY DRIVE [גָּרֵשׁ יְגָרֵשׁ *gārēš yeghārēš*] *you away completely* (cf. also Exod. vi 1: *for with a strong hand* HE SHALL SEND THEM OUT [יְשַׁלְּחֵם *yešallehēm*], *yea, with a strong hand* HE WILL DRIVE THEM OUT [יְגָרְשֵׁם *yeghārešēm*] *of his land*). A twofold expression is used here, as there, with the identical aim of achieving a climax: God did not just *send him forth,* an act that would not have precluded all possibility of his returning, but *He drove him out* — completely.

Furthermore, here the object — *the man* — is emphasized, and not without reason. The severance of man's association with the garden of Eden may be viewed from two aspects: from the standpoint of the man, who was compelled to leave the garden; and from the angle of the garden, which was left without man. The preceding verse speaks of the transformed situation of the man: the Lord God sent him forth from the garden in order that he should be forced to till the ground and bring forth from it his sustenance; and here, in *v.* 24, the new circumstances affecting the garden are referred to: although the Lord God had driven *the man* out of the garden, yet the garden was not left unprotected. The task of guarding it, which originally had been given to the man, was not annulled, but was handed over to someone else, to the *cherubim*.

And He placed [וַיַּשְׁכֵּן *wayyaškēn*] / Also in Psa. lxxviii 55, וַיַּשְׁכֵּן *wayyaškēn* [E.V. *made to dwell, settled*] occurs after וַיְגָרֶשׁ *wayeghāreš* ['and He drove out'] to tell us who was introduced in place of those expelled: HE DROVE OUT *nations before them* . . . AND SETTLED *the tribes of Israel in their tents*. This parallel makes it clear that the text is not to be emended to וַיָּשֶׂם *wayyāśem* ['and He put'] instead of וַיַּשְׁכֵּן *wayyaškēn,* as several expositors, on the basis of ii 8, suggest.

The Septuagint reads: 'And He placed him opposite the garden of Eden, and He put the cherubim' etc. In so far as the sense is concerned, there is no significant difference between the two versions, but the aforementioned verse of Psa. lxxviii shows that the Masoretic text is preferable.

מִקֶּדֶם לְגַן עֵדֶן *miqqedhem leghan ʿēdhen* [literally, 'from front (east) to garden of Eden'] / — *at the east of the garden of Eden* (Rashi). This agrees with what is stated further on (iv 16): *and dwelt in the land of Nod,* EAST OF EDEN. From the latter verse it is evident that the man was banished towards the east, and hence it was precisely on the east side of the garden that the guards who were to prevent him from returning to the garden had to be stationed. There, apparently, was the entrance and the exit. The phrase *at the east of the garden of Eden* reminds us, as I have indicated, of the earlier expression in the section (ii 8): *a garden in Eden, in the east.*

The cherubim] The definite article here does not connote the same as that in the clause, *Then the fugitive* [E.V. *one who had escaped*] *came* (xiv 13) — that is, *whichever fugitive came,* but points to something previously known to the reader. So, too, the bare mention of the cherubim in the sections dealing with the work of the Tabernacle and the building of the Temple, without the addition of any explanation of their character and form, proves that the cherubim were not new to the Israelites. On the ancient narrative tradition current among the people in regard to the cherubim in the garden of Eden, see what I have written earlier, pp. 81 f., and on the relationship between the Paradise sagas and the symbols in the Tabernacle and the Temple, note my remarks on p. 120. From what we are told in the Book of Ezekiel concerning the cherubim or the living creatures, as well as from archaeological discoveries, we can gain an idea of how the children of Israel and the other nations of the ancient East pictured the cherubim to themselves. Ezekiel's description is well-known. The neighbouring peoples also envisaged the cherubim as creatures of composite form, mostly as winged lions (or oxen) with a human head. See on the subject the essays of Dhorme and Vincent in *RB,* xxxv (1926), pp. 328–358, 481–495; the summary of data given by Vriezen in his aforementioned book, pp. 113–115, 198–200, 238; and the article by Albright in *Biblical Archaeologist,* i (1938), pp. 1–3. Additional archaeological material has been revealed in recent years.

The function of the cherubim is not always the same. There are, both in the Israelite and the Gentile tradition, *watchmen* cherubim, which 'keep guard' [סוֹכְכִים *sōkhᵉkhīm*] (see above, p. 123, on ii 15), and there are cherubim that appear as the embodiment of the strong winds, which drive the clouds of the sky, the chariots of the Holy One blessed be He. The latter aspect of the cherubim, namely, their symbolization of the winds, has already been dealt with by several scholars on the basis of the description of the Divine Chariot given in the Book of Ezekiel, and the statement in Psa. xviii 10 [Hebrew, *v.* 11]: HE RODE ON A CHERUB, *and flew; He came swiftly* UPON THE WINGS OF THE WIND (similarly in ii Sam. xxii 11, where *He was seen* [וַיֵּרָא *wayyērā'*] replaces *He came swiftly* [וַיֵּדֶא *wayyēdhe'*]); *upon the wings of the wind* is synonymous with *on a cherub.* We further find (Psa. civ 3–4): *who makest* THE CLOUDS THY CHARIOT, *who ridest on* THE WINGS

OF THE WIND, *who makest* THE WINDS *Thy* MESSENGERS; without doubt Thy *messengers* in this passage are to be identified with the cherubim.

It would seem that in our verse the two concepts are combined: the cherubim are referred to here both as guardians and as a symbol of the winds, as is shown by the words that immediately follow.

And the sword-flame which turned every way] Also in this instance we have the definite article, and doubtless on this subject, too, the ancient tradition provided detailed information (see above, p. 73). Apparently, this tradition concerning *the sword-flame which turned every way* is reflected also in Psa. civ 4. Immediately after the allusion to the chariot and the cherubs, which I have just quoted (*who makest* THE CLOUDS THY CHARIOT, WHO RIDEST ON THE WINGS OF THE WIND, *who makest* THY MESSENGERS THE WINDS), the continuation of the verse reads: *the flaming fire Thy ministers.* לֹהֵט *lōhēṭ* ['flaming'] is of the very same root as the word לַהַט *lahaṭ* ['flame'] in our verse, and likewise occurs in association with the cherubim. If the cherubim are actually the winds blowing in the skies, then the *flaming fire* and the *sword-flame* are none other than the lightning flashes, which appear in the clouds like a sharp sword, drawn by the hand of the cherubim, and *turning* [מִתְהַפֶּכֶת *mithhappekheth,* rendered: (*which*) *turned every way*], that is, revolving hither and thither. On the slopes of the mountain, on whose summit is situated the garden of Eden, violent storms constantly burst forth, fierce winds blow there, and fearful lightning-streaks flame round about. It is impossible for man to climb the mountain and reach the top of it.

To guard the way to the tree of life] Thus, by means of the terrible storms that they stir up, and the lightning-bolts that they wield, the cherubim guard the way to the tree of life, and bar it to the man. In its closing words, the section recalls what it stated at the beginning: *the tree of life also in the midst of the garden;* the repetition serves to point an antithesis, to emphasize the contrast between the original state of Adam and the situation created as a result of his sin. At first the man dwelt in the midst of the garden, in the vicinity of the tree of life, and he could at any moment approach it and eat of its fruit; now he is far from there, and the cherubim and the sword-flame guard the way and prevent him from again drawing near to the garden and to the tree of life. The bliss that he was privileged to enjoy in the garden of Eden passed away irretrievably, like a vanished dream. From now on, the human race will live only amidst the hardships and afflictions of the world below.

SECTION THREE

THE STORY OF CAIN AND ABEL

CHAPTER IV, 1–26

INTRODUCTION

§ 1. This section comprises a number of different themes. Although in the rubric I have entitled it *The Story of Cain and Abel,* after its central topic, nevertheless the verses directly connected with this story constitute, as we shall see later, only two of its paragraphs (*vv.* 3–16). Probably this focal episode and the other subjects grouped with it, which are intrinsically unrelated to one another, were separate narratives in the pre-Torah tradition, until they were interwoven in the present text, forming a unified narrative.

§ 2. If we attempt to determine in detail what themes are contained in the section, what their respective limits are, and how the section is to be divided into paragraphs, examining for this purpose both the content and form of the passages, the following analysis naturally presents itself:

(a) *The birth of Cain and Abel, and the nature of their occupations* (first paragraph, *vv.* 1–2).

(b) *The story of Cain and Abel,* which is separable into two subsections: *the murder of Abel by Cain* (second paragraph, *vv.* 3–8), and *the sentencing of Cain* to perpetual exile (third paragraph, *vv.* 9–16). The expression *In the course of time* at the beginning of *v.* 3 marks a new paragraph; furthermore, the word יָדַעְתִּי *yādha*ʿ*tī* ['I know'] in *v.* 9 constitutes a point of resemblance with the opening sentences of the first, fourth and sixth paragraphs, in each of which וַיֵּדַע *wayyēdha*ʿ or יָדַע *yādha*ʿ ['he knew'] occurs, and this parallelism also indicates the commencement of a new paragraph (on the parallelism formed by the verb יָדַע *yādha*ʿ between this and the preceding section, see below).

(c) *The genealogy of Cain* (fourth paragraph, *vv.* 17–22). The first sentence provides a striking parallel to the beginning of the first paragraph: *Cain knew his wife, and she conceived and bore Enoch* — *Now Adam knew Eve his wife, and she conceived and bore Cain.* Compare also, as I have mentioned previously, the opening verse of paragraph three and of paragraph six.

(d) *The Song of Lamech* (fifth paragraph, *vv.* 23–24). The poetic character of this paragraph clearly distinguishes it from the others.

(e) *The birth of Seth and Enosh* (sixth paragraph, *vv.* 25–26). The first verse (*v.* 25: *And Adam* KNEW *his wife again, and she bore a son*) corresponds, as stated, to the opening of the first, third and fourth paragraphs (for other parallels, see my commentary below).

It will thus be seen that the number of subjects dealt with in this section is five. We shall examine each one of them separately.

§ 3. Let us begin with the central theme, *the murder of Abel and the sentence of Cain.* Whereas many interesting parallels have been found to the account of Creation and the story of the Garden of Eden, both in Israelite literature and in the writings of the other peoples of the East, we possess so far nothing corresponding to the narrative of Cain and Abel. The motif of fratricide does, it is true, occur in pagan mythology. There is an Egyptian legend, for instance, about Seth who slew Osiris; there is, likewise, a Canaanite story, to quote another example, concerning Môt, who murdered Baal. But these parallels are remote and, apart from the motif mentioned, they have nothing else in common with our section. It follows that since we have no other material, save what we find in the Book of Genesis, any one seeking to trace the details, characteristics and intentions of the pre-Torah tradition regarding Cain and Abel necessarily leaves the *terra firma* of fact and ventures on the high seas of conjecture.

Many different theories have been advanced on the subject in our time. The hypothesis that has gained the widest acceptance among scholars is the one that connects the narrative with the tribe of the Kenites, and asserts that the original purpose of the story was to explain the causes underlying the destiny and mode of life of this tribe. Stade worked this theory out in full detail (after other savants had hinted at somewhat similar ideas) in a comprehensive essay, which he first published in *ZAW,* xiv (1894), pp.

250–318, and the exposition was widely accepted either in the exact form in which Stade submitted it or with some change of detail. Even Gunkel, who at first was opposed to it, accepted the interpretation in the third edition of his commentary. A similar view is adopted by Mowinckel in the detailed study that he recently devoted to our subject in his work on the sources of the early chapters of the Book of Genesis, which I have cited in the bibliography above (p. 95).

In broad outline the hypothesis may be summarized thus: Cain is not an individual but represents the tribe designated by the name *Cain* [קַיִן *Qayin*], or by the appellative *Kenite* [קֵינִי *Qēnī*] which is mentioned several times in Scripture; it was a nomadic tribe, which dwelt in the land of the Negeb, and from there part of it spread to other places in the Land of Israel. The name of the tribe indicates that it engaged in metal work (قَيْن *qaynun* means *a smith;* similarly קֵינָיָא *qēnāyā'* [otherwise: קֵינָיָא *qayenāyā'*] or קֵינָאָה *qēnā'ā* [otherwise: קֵינָאָה *qayenā'ā*] in Aramaic; cf. also *v.* 22). Hence, the tribe of the Kenites was utterly despised in the eyes of the neighbouring tribes, just as in Arabia today the wandering tribes of smiths are held in the utmost disdain by the Arabs. The fact, too, that the tribe of the Kenites is sometimes associated with Israel and at other times with Amalek or Midian shows that it was a weak and insignificant clan, incapable of maintaining its independence. The story of Cain and Abel reflects the contempt of the cultivators of the soil, or of the aristocratic cattle-owners, for this tribe of herdsmen-smiths, who ceaselessly wander from place to place without having a fixed abode, and its aim is to explain the lowly status of the Kenites by the curse put upon their progenitor because of a great and terrible crime that he had committed. The *sign* mentioned in *v.* 15 refers to the special mark of the tribe, the incision that distinguishes all the members of the tribe and obligates all of them to avenge the blood of any of their brethren who may be slain.

Other scholars have proposed different explanations; for example, Ehrenzweig, in an article published in *ZAW,* xxxv (1915), pp. 1–11 (see also Vol. xxxviii [1919–20], pp. 65–86, and Vol. xxxix [1921], pp. 67–76, 80–82). On the basis of *v.* 17, where it is stated, *and he built a city,* the writer developed the theory (which had also been anticipated by several suggestions along similar lines) that originally the narrative had some connection with the story of Romulus, the founder of the city of Rome, who killed his brother Remus, and that the two tales flow from an ancient ritual legend that has the aetiological purpose of seeking to explain the origin of the custom of offering human sacrifices at the laying of the foundation of a city or of some notable edifice; the recension before us changed, he contends, the original form of the myth out of deference to the Israelite view, which regards human sacrifice as an abomination.

It is not my intention to mention here all the theories that have been propounded on the subject, because there would be no end to the matter. I shall not detail the views of those who attempt to determine the original meaning of the narrative in the light of ethnology; nor the interpretations grounded in Israel's history, like the one, for instance, that identifies Cain with Edom on the basis of Amos i 11; nor yet the various other hypotheses that have been submitted. I shall not, *a fortiori,* dwell on bizarre conjectures like the suggestion that Cain was one of the moon gods, who, after slaying the serpent, discovered that it was his brother; and so forth. I shall only mention, as another example, the theory advanced recently by Brock-Utne in an essay that he published in *ZAW,* liv (1936), pp. 202–239. According to his view, our narrative reflects the course of certain events in the religious life of primitive man: in a period of dearth, the farmers desired to restore the fertility of the soil by the sacrifice of a man, whom the members of the Kenite clan, a tribe of inferior temple ministers, offered up. But the higher order of priests, who opposed human sacrifices, banished these Kenites from the vicinity of the shrines and sentenced them to exile.

§ 4. All the theories enumerated encounter difficulties. Against Stade's view, it is possible, in the first instance, to raise the following objections:

(a) It is true that in a number of passages in the Book of Genesis certain individuals represent whole tribes, the clans of their children and children's children; but in the present instance Cain's descendants are mentioned, and they are not vagrants and wanderers like him (see below, § 8); it follows that this characteristic is peculiar to him and not to his offspring.

(b) There is nothing to indicate that the *sign* belongs also to his children after him; apparently this, too, appertains only to him.
(c) Even if we assume that this sign was a tribal emblem, we must realise that many clans had a distinctive mark, and it would be unreasonable to regard the possession of a sign by the tribe of Cain as a feature unique to this clan.
(d) The Kenite tribe was treated with esteem and friendship by the Israelites, and it is impossible to suppose that the Torah accepted a story designed to denigrate it.
(e) *Smith* is only one of the secondary and incidental connotations of words derived from the root קין *qyn* (see the note on this below, in my commentary to iv 1). Although recent archaeological investigation has shown that in the Land of Midian, near the earliest sites occupied by the Kenites, there existed very valuable copper mines, which were undoubtedly exploited already in antiquity, this fact is insufficient to make Stade's theory more plausible. On other objections that can be raised against this hypothesis (see, for example, the aforementioned essay by Brock-Utne, pp. 204–207), there is no need to dwell here.

As for the further conjectures referred to, it is difficult to find manifest support for them in the text. Two general observations may be made in regard to them, which, in part, are applicable also to Stade's thesis.

The first is that these theories are based on the assumption that our present text has given the story, be it from a definite motive (so, for example, Ehrenzweig, *op. cit.*, p. 2) or through misunderstanding (thus, for instance, Gunkel, *op. cit.*, p. 49), *a different form and significance* from those of the ancient tradition; now this premise weakens considerably the validity of the hypotheses, since the feasible reconstructions of a narrative that *differs from the existing text* can, of course, be endless, and the degree of probability attaching to each of them is in inverse proportion to the number of possibilities. For the time being, pending the discovery of some ancient Eastern text dealing with the subject, we must admit that, in our present state of knowledge, we are not in a position to determine the original form and significance of the pre-Torah tradition relative to the story under discussion.

The second point to be noted is that the above-mentioned scholars, whose investigations aim to establish the original meaning of the *ancient narrative,* have given only casual and limited consideration to the *Pentateuchal account,* thus confusing primary and secondary tasks. For the Bible student, the elucidation of the Scriptural text is of paramount concern. Although to reach back, wherever possible, to an older stage of tradition and to determine what was known to the Israelites and their neighbours before the Biblical books were written, is of undoubted value for the understanding of the Scriptural text, yet in cases such as the one under consideration, where there is no clear evidence bearing on the oldest phase of the tradition, we must forgo this exegetical method, and we cannot accept fanciful conjectures as a substitute for it. In such instances, the Bible scholar has to rely solely on exact and profound study of the text itself.

§ 5. In the first place, an examination of the passage reveals that there is a noteworthy difference between the verses describing events (*vv.* 3–5, 8, the second half of *v.* 14, and *v.* 16) and those that comprise speeches and dialogues (*vv.* 6–7, 9–15 as far as the word יֻקָּם *yuqqām* ['vengeance shall be taken on him']). The account of the episodes is presented in summary form, the main points only being mentioned; no details are given, and even interesting and important particulars are passed over in silence. We are not given the slightest inkling, for example, how the two brothers discerned that the Lord had regard for Abel and his offering but not for Cain and his offering, or what occurred between the brothers before the murder, or what kind of sign was given to Cain. On the other hand, the speeches and dialogues are reported in detail and at length, constituting about two thirds of the whole of the two paragraphs under discussion. Their style is exalted and solemn, and in part is even marked by poetic rhythm; whilst the style of the narrative verses, though beautiful and distinguished, is nevertheless quite light and simple. From all this we must conclude that the focal point is to be sought in the spoken and not in the narrative portion. The latter gives the impression of being an epitome; as if it were summarizing a tale that had been told at length elsewhere. There seems to have existed an ancient tradition, setting forth fully the story of Cain and Abel, whose details — and even its purpose — can no longer be determined. The Torah recounts this saga briefly, in general outline only, since it regards the story as intrinsically of no great importance and not worth relating in detail, but yet one that can appropriately serve as a factual basis for valuable instruction. We have seen earlier (p. 12) that the Torah is accustomed to clothe its thoughts in concrete description and to impart its teachings through the narration of events from which it is possible to draw, or to which it is possible to append, the lessons in question. This is the method it has used in the present instance, too. Irrespective of the details of the original story, and of its primary object, the doctrines that the Torah wished to inculcate here are not comprised in the *episodes* it relates, but in *the words of the Lord* that it connects therewith.

These teachings, which are divisible into two categories (some of them are obvious, and are easily discernible even by the superficial reader; there is no need, therefore, to consider them in detail), are as follows: (a) emphasis of the principle that human life is sacred and may not be violated, and that the crime of murder is inexpressibly terrible, having no atonement; (b) the general moral, inculcated also by a number of other sections, that no deed of man — be it even performed secretly, even out of human sight, as, for example, in the *field* far from human habitation — is hidden from the eyes of God, and that God calls man to account, awakening within him the voice of conscience, and requiting him according to his works.

There are also other lessons, forming the second category, that, upon careful examination, can be discovered in the text, to wit: (a) the conclusions to be drawn from the Lord's utterance in *v.* 7 (we shall discuss these fully later on when we come to explain the verse, since the moral depends on the meaning attached to the words in their context); (b) the specific teaching of these passages, which constitutes the main new concept that they come to expound, namely, *the protest against the practice of blood-revenge.* It would be out of place to unfold here the whole complex chapter of the history of this custom among the Israelites and the relationship of the Torah statutes thereto. It will suffice to indicate that there is a noticeable trend in the Pentateuchal legislation to restrict the practice and reduce it to a minimum. The blood-avenger becomes little more than the executor of the community's sentence, whilst for unintentional homicide the penalty of *exile* to a city of refuge is substituted for blood-revenge. Now this trend finds expression in our section in connection with the first case of murder in the annals of mankind. Cain, who took his brother's life, is the prototype of the murderer, for all human beings are brothers, and whoever sheds the blood of man sheds his brother's blood. Hence, Cain's punishment is the primary precedent for murder sentences. Cain was afraid of blood-revenge (*v.* 14: *and whoever finds me will slay me*), because all mankind, both those already in existence and those still to be born, were relatives and avengers of the murdered man. But the Lord delivered him from their hand and sentenced him to *exile;* blood-revenge is not pleasing in the sight of the Lord.

For detailed annotation see the commentary below.

§ 6. Let us proceed now to the other subjects of our section. If we are to understand them thoroughly, we must not only consider each topic separately but also its relationship to the other parts of the section, and particularly its connection with the central theme. Although Brock-Utne stated in his aforementioned essay that in order to comprehend the story of Cain and Abel it is necessary to isolate it completely from its textual environment, this is true only if we wish to investigate the meaning of the oldest tradition, which is anterior to the Torah; but if we desire to understand the text before us in its present form, it is only by studying the connection between the several paragraphs that we can achieve our purpose and determine the significance of each part of our section.

§7. First paragraph (*vv.* 1–2). The main object of this paragraph is, of course, to serve as an introduction to the central theme of the section: to present to us the *dramatis personae,* and to acquaint us with those particulars concerning each one of them that are basic to the episode to be described subsequently. To the difference between the occupations of the two brothers is due the divergence between their sacrifices; and the oblations, in turn, give rise to the relationship between them that finally results in the murder.

At the same time, this paragraph forms a link between our section and the one preceding. At the end of the story of the garden of Eden reference is made to the birth of children, to the propagation of the human species as a means for the survival of the race in the great world after the expulsion from Paradise (see above, pp. 161–162); and behold, we see here the immediate realization of the Divine promise. Even the expressions in this paragraph, beginning with the word יָדַע *yādha'* ['knew'], correspond to those used in the previous section (as we shall note in detail further on), and serve to remind us of them, thus establishing a connection between the two sections.

§8. After the central theme, which comprises the SECOND and THIRD PARAGRAPHS, we are given in the FOURTH PARAGRAPH (*vv.* 17–22) *the genealogy of Cain's descendants.* The beginning of this paragraph, as we observed earlier, is analogous to those of the first, third and last paragraphs; also the mention of the occupations finds a parallel in the narrative of the first paragraph. Primarily this fourth paragraph continues the story of Cain's banishment, and tells us of the offspring that he begat in the land of his wandering, and how his descendants settled in definite localities *in contrast to his own bitter fate,* which compelled him to wander as an exile from place to place. His son Enoch already *built a city* (the builder referred to in *v.* 17 is not Cain, as is usually thought, but Enoch; see the commentary on this verse), and all the occupations mentioned in *vv.* 20–22 are associated with a mode of life that is more or less settled; *even those who dwell in tents and have cattle* are not constantly *vagrants and wanderers in the land* like Cain. At the close of this paragraph there is a link with the following paragraph, similar to the one that exists between the first and second paragraphs: the characters that are to figure in the next paragraph are introduced, their names appearing in the two passages in clear parallelism.

The material used by the Torah for composing the principal part of this paragraph differs in character and origin from that which is employed in the previous paragraphs. In the latter we have narratives — or, as we explained, allusions to such — and for this purpose the Bible chose its structural material from the rich storehouse of tradition current among the broad masses of the people, which took the form either of epic poetry or of tales handed down by word of mouth in simple prose; here we are presented with a genealogical tree. This subject belongs intrinsically to the learned circles, and it is precisely in their tradition that it appears to have originated. In the composition of our section the two kinds of material have been harmoniously blended together. It should also be noted that even in this paragraph there is to be found an element that derives from the epic tradition, as we shall see further on, at the end of § 10.

§ 9. The names of the heads of the generations in this genealogy bear a surprising resemblance to those of the genealogy of the children of Seth in chapter 5 (Cain — Kenan; Enoch, Irad, Mehujael — Mahalalel, Jared, Enoch; Methushael — Methuselah; Lamech — Lamech). This raises the question of the relationship between the two genealogies. We shall deal with this problem fully later on, in the introduction to the next section. There we shall also discuss the interesting parallels between these genealogies of the Torah and the Mesopotamian lists of ancient kings.

Here we would only note that there is no indication in the text of a difference in principle between the descendants of Cain and those of Seth, as though the former comprised the wicked and the latter the righteous. This distinction is customarily made in the exegesis of the Christian church (possibly it is not unrelated to some allusion in rabbinic literature), and traces of it are discernible even in the scientific commentaries of our time; but there is no foundation for it in the simple meaning of the Scriptural passage. According to the Bible, the generation of the Flood was wholly wicked, including the offspring of both Cain and Seth, as well as the descendants of their brothers who were born after them, save Noah and his family.

§ 10. In presenting this genealogy, the Torah was not content to furnish us with a dry and monotonous list of names, but characteristically it gave to its statements a beautiful and elegant form, vitalizing them by means of parallels, variations in the choice of expressions, the harmonious arrangement of words, and the insertion of details concerning the deeds and occupations of some of the personalities mentioned in the pedigree. Such details are given — thus providing a parallel to the first paragraph — at the beginning of our paragraph (*v.* 17: *and he built a city*), and with greater elaboration, at the close (*vv.* 20–22), in connection with the three sons of Lamech. When the genealogy reaches Lamech, the *seventh* generation from Adam. it broadens and ramifies into three branches, becoming more detailed. This is done not only for the sake of literary grace, but also with a specific view to the subject-matter, as we shall see forthwith.

The incorporation of the aforementioned biographical details in the genealogical data finds a parallel in the literary works of the neighbouring peoples. Thus, for example, in the Sumerian list of kings, next to the names of the kings and their kingdoms and the length of their reigns, there occur here and there notes on their activities and occupations before they ascended the throne (see Jacobsen, *The Sumerian King List,* Chicago, 1939, pp. 142–143), and mostly these notes are very similar to those in our passage. It will suffice to cite a few examples: col. ii, lines 16–18: *Etana, a shepherd, who to heaven ascended, the one who consolidated all lands;* col. iii, lines 8–9: *King of Uruk, the one who built Uruk* (or, according to another recension, *the one under whom Uruk was built*); ibid., line 12: *the shepherd;* ibid., line 31: the *smith;* col. iv, line 24: *the navigator;* and so on. Similarly, in the theogony of the Canaanites, as presented to us by Philo Byblius, there are incorporated notes on the gods or demigods, who invented all kinds of valuable devices for the benefit of human life, such as the use of fire, hunting and fishing, agriculture, the building of houses, the rearing of sheep, the art of government, and so forth. Irrespective of the meaning of the terms אֲבִי *'ăbhī* [E.V. *the father of*] and לֹטֵשׁ *lōṭēš* [E.V. *the forger of*] in our section, *vv.* 20–22 (see the commentary on this passage), there is undoubtedly some similarity between what is written here and what we are told by Philo Byblius. On the other hand, there is also a vital difference between them; indeed, the divergence is more important than the resemblance. In Philo's account the inventors are gods or half-gods; likewise several of the ancient kings in the Sumerian roll are designated as deities or semi-deities; and both in Philo's account and in the King List the themes are related to mythological legends. But in the Torah, we find only ordinary human beings and there is no mythological element whatsoever. This is a great innovation introduced by the Torah: it discards the mythological tradition and opposes the blurring of the boundaries between the Godhead and mankind. It seeks to emphasize that human civilisation was of human origin.

Apparently, these notes on the building of the city in *v.* 17 and the occupations of Lamech's sons in *vv.* 20–22 are only brief allusions to subjects treated at length in the ancient tradition — an epic tradition in this case (also in regard to the similar notes in the Sumerian King List, Jacobsen, *op. cit.,* pp. 144–147, conjectures that they are derived from epic literature). Naturally, when the Torah took this material over from the epic tradition, it gave the themes a new form, as I have explained, in accordance with its spirit and aesthetic standards.

§ 11. We shall now pass on to the FIFTH PARAGRAPH (*vv.* 23–24). Again our section provides here a harmonious combination of variegated elements. The material of this paragraph differs from that of the fourth, as well as from that of the first three paragraphs; it belongs to the category of *lyric poetry.* Without doubt many such poems must have been circulating among the people, and they were renowned as the compositions of poets and famous men of old. The Torah took this poem from the poetic treasury of antiquity and fitted it into its prose narrative, just as the medieval Jewish writers, following the example of Arabic literature, incorporated poems and poetic fragments in their prose works.

This poem is linked to the story of Cain and Abel both in outward form and in content. The formal link is found in the expression, *If Cain is avenged sevenfold* (*v.* 24), which recalls — although, perhaps, with a somewhat different meaning — the words of *v.* 15 above. The thematic connection consists in the fact that Lamech follows in the steps of his forefather and also slays a person, boasting of his cruel deed with a brazenness reminiscent of Cain, who did not hesitate to say to the Lord's face: *Am I my brother's keeper?*

Why did the Torah incorporate this poem in its text? Its aim appears to have been to introduce at this early stage a subject that could serve as a preparatory proof of what was to be stated later (vi 5): *that the wickedness of man was great in the earth, and that every imagination of the thoughts of his heart was only evil continually,* and thereafter (vi 11): *and the earth was filled with violence,* and again (vi 13): *for the earth is filled with violence through them.* The poem provides evidence of this. See how far the wickedness reached, and in what people gloried at that period! Lamech boasts to his wives of the murder that he committed, which shows that the women also found satisfaction in such deeds, and honoured and cherished their husbands just because of their barbaric and cruel valour. In very truth, *the earth was filled with violence.*

Although no dates are given in this section, it is clear that *Lamech the son of Methushael,* the seventh generation from Adam through Cain, corresponds to *Lamech the son of Methuselah,* the ninth generation after Adam through Seth, the father of Noah. Undoubtedly, Lamech the son of Methushael was also, according to Scripture, one of the important people of the generation of the Flood.

§ 12. The LAST PARAGRAPH (*vv.* 25–26). Modern scholars are accustomed to regard this paragraph as simply a part of the genealogy of mankind descended from Seth, according to source J, corresponding to P's version of the same genealogy in chapter v. In their view, this pedigree is in no way connected with the story of Cain and Abel, nor with the line of the children of Cain, but is an independent list, according to which Seth was the first son of Adam. There are, it is true, a number of explicit expressions in *v.* 25, which link it to what precedes: first, *Adam knew his wife* AGAIN; thereafter, *for God has appointed for me* ANOTHER *child;* and subsequently, INSTEAD OF ABEL, FOR CAIN SLEW HIM. But the scholars referred to delete the word *again* and the word *other,* as well as the entire phrase, *instead of Abel, for Cain slew him,* as additions made by the last redactor. This method, which establishes a given principle *a priori,* without taking into consideration what is expressly stated in the text, and then, placing the passage upon the procrustean bed of that principle, hacks off the textual limbs that do not fit into the bed, can hardly be accepted as valid.

It is particularly invalid in the present case, because if we bear in mind the normal structure of Biblical narratives, we shall see that here, at the end of the section, it is precisely a paragraph of this nature that was necessary. Firstly, it is a golden rule of the Torah that the conclusion of a narrative should reflect the opening, and therefore it was to be expected that our passage should contain something corresponding to the birth of Cain and Abel, which is recorded in the first paragraph. Furthermore, another rule requires that the stories should have *happy endings;* it was fitting, therefore, that we should be told how Adam and Eve found solace after losing their first two sons in one day, and how they saw, despite the terrible calamity that befell them in the death of Abel and the banishment of Cain, the realization of the Divine promise concerning procreation. The section would not have ended appropriately, if it had left in the reader's mind the grievous picture of two parents in mourning, bereaved and forlorn. Not only is this paragraph not an alien element in our section, but, on the contrary, if it did not come at this point, we should have had to surmise that something like it was missing from our text.

Just as our paragraph harmonizes in its general character with the other parts of our section, so it corresponds to them in its details and particular phraseology. In regard to the first of its two verses (*v.* 25), it not only forms a parallel, as we have noted, to the opening formula of the first paragraph, as well as to that of the third and fourth paragraphs, by means of the clause, *And Adam knew* etc., and it not only establishes a link with what precedes through the words *again* and *other,* but it also provides another parallel to verse 1 in the naming of the son by the mother and in the specification of her reason for the choice of the name. The words, *instead of Abel, for Cain slew him,* sum up, as it were, the whole section, and bring the entire episode before our eyes again, so that we may measure the full magnitude of the terrible tragedy that embittered the life of the parents, until compensation and consolation were granted them by Heaven.

The same applies to the concluding verse. The reference to the birth of Enosh adds a detail that fits in well with the general theme, and tells us that Adam and Eve were enabled to find twofold consolation by the continuance of the life of the family in the third generation. With this is also linked, as we shall see later in our commentary, the last sentence: *At that time men began to call upon the name of the Lord.*

§ 13. In this section, as in those that preceded, there is discernible the intention to apply to the text a system of numerical symmetry. The number *seven,* which is emphasized in *v.* 15 *(vengeance shall be taken on him sevenfold),* and even more in *v.* 24 *(If Cain is avenged sevenfold, truly Lamech seventy-sevenfold)* prevails throughout the section. The reference to Lamech, the *seventh* generation from Adam, is exceptionally elaborate. The names listed in Cain's family, counting from Adam and Eve to Naamah, total 14 — twice times *seven.* Apart from the reminiscences occurring in the utterances of Lamech and Eve at the end of the section, Cain's name is mentioned 14 times — twice *seven* — and Abel's name *seven* times, in the actual narration of events; so, too, the word אָח *'āḥ* ['brother'], in relation to Cain and Abel, is used *seven* times in the section, and likewise the word שֵׁם *šēm* ['name'] is found there *seven* times. Also the nouns אֶרֶץ *'ereṣ* ['earth'] שָׂדֶה *śādhe* ['field'] and אֲדָמָה *'ădhāmā* ['ground'] appear, severally, in the combined compass of the two sections comprising the stories of the Garden of Eden and Cain and Abel (chapters 2–4), a given number of times conforming to the same pattern: אֶרֶץ *'ereṣ—seven* times; שָׂדֶה *śādhe—seven* times; אֲדָמָה *'ădhāmā*—14 times, that is, twice *seven.* Likewise the words גַּן *gan* ['garden'], עֵדֶן *'ēdhen* ['Eden'] and קֶדֶם *qedhem* ['east'] occur collectively in the two sections 21 times — thrice *seven.* The Divine name (*YHWH* ['Lord'], *'Elōhīm* ['God'] and *YHWH 'Elōhīm* ['Lord God']) are found, in the two sections taken together, 35 times — five times *seven,* the exact number of times that אֱלֹהִים *'Elōhīm* occurs in the story of Creation. Altogether the Divine names in the three sections number *seventy*: אֱלֹהִים *'Elōhīm* alone appears 40 times; ה׳ אֱלֹהִים *YHWH 'Elōhīm* twenty times; ה׳ *YHWH* by itself ten times (regarding the number of times that the Divine names are mentioned separately—ה׳ *YHWH* alone and אֱלֹהִים *'Elōhīm* alone — see below in the continuation of this subsection [§ 13]). And precisely at the *seventieth* reference it is solemnly announced: *At that time men began to call upon the name of the Lord;* with these words the section comes to an end. It is inconceivable that all this should be pure coincidence.

Nor is it possible to regard as fortuitous the use, which also finds a place in our section, of numbers belonging to the *sexagesimal system,* the Sumerian method of numeration, which has left its mark to this day on the habits of our life (the division of the circle into three hundred and sixty degrees, of the hour into sixty minutes and of the minute into sixty seconds etc., counting by the dozen and multiples of twelve, and so forth), and on which are based many round figures in Biblical as well as in Talmudic and Midrashic literature. The male descendants of Adam mentioned in the section number *twelve;* and the stem ילד *yld* (the verb יָלַד *yāladh* ['to bear (a child)'] and the noun יֶלֶד *yeledh* ['child']) occur *twelve* times in the section. The paragraphs of the section, which are naturally separable by their content and the parallels between them, total *six.* The name אֱלֹהִים *'Elōhīm,* by itself or in conjunction with ה' *YHWH,* occurs *sixty* times, counting from the beginning of the book to the end of this section; whilst the name ה' *YHWH,* alone or in combination with אֱלֹהִים *'Elōhīm,* appears half that number of times, that is, *thirty* times, or five times *six.*

The *threefold repetition* of specific terms for the sake of emphasis is also exemplified frequently in our section, just as in the earlier sections (for instance: מִנְחָה *minḥā* ['offering'] in *vv.* 3–5; הָרַג *hāragh* ['slay'] in *vv.* 8, 14–15; so, too, *Cain made an appointment with* [E.V. spoke, said, to] *Abel his brother* — *Cain rose up against his brother Abel* — *Then the Lord said to Cain, Where is Abel your brother?, vv.* 8–9; likewise, *vengeance shall be taken on him* SEVENFOLD — *If Cain is avenged* SEVENFOLD — *truly Lamech* SEVENTY SEVENFOLD, *vv.* 15, 24).

§ 14. The parallels and similarities that we discovered between the various paragraphs and the numerical symmetry that was revealed throughout the section provide decisive proof of the unity of the section and the completeness of its structure, contrary to the opinion of the majority of modern scholars, who hold that our section was compiled by a complicated process of culling unconnected extracts from various sources, and of editing that failed to achieve the harmonization of the segments. According to this view, there are three main fragments, namely: (a) the story of Cain and Abel (this includes *v.* 2, or part of it; others add *v.* 1); (b) the genealogy of the descendants of Cain (including the song of Lamech, and also, according to some, *v.* 1); (c) part of the genealogy of the descendants of Seth, which is found in *vv.* 25–26. As regards the details, opinions differ: what exactly belongs to each fragment, from which sources the extracts derive (two strata of J, according to Budde and Gunkel; S and S^2 in Pfeiffer's view; Mowinckel suggests J and E, etc., etc.), how much is due to the labours of the redactors, and how the different elements were combined and fitted together — these are all matters of controversy. The reasons for regarding the text as composite are principally based on inconsistencies found between various verses. The most important are:

(a) An explanation is offered for giving Cain his name, but Abel's name remains unexplained.

(b) Cain was afraid lest any who came upon him should kill him. This proves that there were many inhabitants in the world already; hence it is not possible that Cain should have been the son of the first man.

(c) The picture drawn of Cain, the cursed, in *vv.* 10–12 does not agree with that of Cain who finds refuge and protection in the Lord according to *v.* 15, and who becomes the father of mankind according to *vv.* 17–22.

(d) On the one hand we are told that Cain was a vagrant and wanderer on the earth (*vv.* 12, 14), and on the other hand it is stated that he built a city (*v.* 17).

(e) According to *v.* 20 Jabal was the first to keep cattle, but according to *v.* 2 Abel already had been a shepherd.

(f) After the text has traced the line of Cain through a number of generations, coming as far as the eighth generation from Adam, it begins afresh and tells us of a new branch of Adam's family, headed by Seth.

(g) Verse 26 states that in the days of Enosh *men began to call upon the name of the Lord* [*YHWH*], whereas this name has already been mentioned many times in the preceding verses.

On account of these incongruities (to which may be added others that are not so important and need not be detailed here) the scholars referred to suspect the unity of our section and conclude that 'such a jumble' (this is Gunkel's phrase, p. 35) cannot be attributed to one hand, nor even to the hand of a single compiler.

However, the results that we have thus far achieved from the careful study of each individual paragraph in our section, as well as the further conclusions that we shall draw in the continuation of our commentary, not only prove that there is no confusion here whatsoever, but that even the inconsistencies enumerated are not, in fact, actual contradictions. On the difference between the naming of Cain and Abel see the commentary on *v.* 2. Cain was afraid lest anyone finding him would slay him for the very reason that his murdered brother was the son of the first man, and therefore all mankind were his blood-avengers; nay more, it is only in this way that we can understand Cain's words, for if the majority of people were strangers to the family of the murdered man, why should *all of them* wish to kill the murderer? (see the note on *v.* 14). Cain does not find refuge and protection in the Lord; the Lord fully implements the punishment and curse imposed upon him in the beginning, and saves him only from *blood-revenge,* which is displeasing to Him. That Cain is the father of mankind follows only from the view of those who decide *a priori* that the genealogy of the children of Seth must be regarded as distinct from the pedigree of the children of Cain, which is thus left isolated. It is not Cain who builds a city, but Enoch, his son. Concerning the first herdsman, see the commentary on *v.* 20. As for the fact that the genealogy of Seth appears after Cain's has reached the generation of the children of Lamech, it must be noted that this is the usual method adopted in the Book of Genesis when dealing with two brothers, one of whom is more important in relation to the primary aim of the book: first the Torah completes, in summary form, the list of the offspring of the lesser brother, then it reverts to the line of the more notable brother, and deals with it at length. This obtains in the case of Ishmael and Isaac, and again in the instance of Esau and Jacob. Regarding the use of the Tetragrammaton and the significance of the last clause of *v.* 26, see the commentary on that verse.

§ 15. On the links between our section and the preceding section, as well as the one that follows, see below, the exposition of *vv.* 1, 2, 7, 9, 10, 11, 12, 14, 16, 25, 26. Note also my remarks in § 13 on the words that occur a specific number of times in this section and in earlier parts of the book, and compare the commentary on iii 9 (pp. 154 f.) and iii 13 (p. 158).

§ 16. *Special bibliography for this section.* As in the case of the introductions to the previous sections, I give here a bibliography of the most important works on this section, or on parts thereof, that were published after 1934, in so far as these are known to me, having regard to wartime conditions (additional essays I have cited above in the introduction or I shall quote later in the commentary):

Closen, 'Der "Dämon Sünde": ein Deutungsversuch des massoretischen Textes von Gen. 4, 7', *Biblica,* xvi (1935), pp. 431–442; Gordon, 'Fratriarchy in the Old Testament', *JBL,* liv (1935), pp. 223–231; Brock-Utne, 'Die religionshistorischen Voraussetzungen der Kain-Abel-Geschichte', *ZAW,* liv (1936), pp. 202–239; Mowinckel, *The two Sources of the Predeuteronomic Primeval History (JE) in Gen. i–ii,* Oslo 1937 (cited above, p. 95); Albright–Mowinckel, discussion on this work, *JBL,* lvii (1938), pp. 230–231, lviii (1939), pp. 87–103; Albright, *From the Stone Age to Christianity,* Baltimore 1940, pp. 195–196; idem, *Archaeology and the Religion of Israel,* Baltimore 1942, pp. 98–99.

Hooke's article on the story of Cain and Abel, published in *Folk-Lore,* l (1939), pp. 58–65, which gives an exposition of the subject similar to that of Brock-Utne, I was unable to peruse, since that volume did not reach Jerusalem on account of the war; its general content is known to me from Hornblower's essay, 'Cain and Abel: The Choice of Kind of Sacrifice', which appeared in *Man,* xliv (1944), pp. 45–46. I would also mention here two lectures that were summarized in recent volumes of *JBL,* but I cannot ascertain whether they were subsequently published in full or not. They are: Cross, 'An Answer to J. G. Frazer Anent Cain and Abel', *JBL,* liv (1935), p. xii; McClellan, 'The original Text of Gen. 4, 8a', *JBL,* lvi (1937), p. xii.

FIRST PARAGRAPH

THE BIRTH AND OCCUPATIONS OF CAIN AND ABEL

CHAPTER IV

1. *Now Adam / knew Eve his wife,*
and she conceived / and bore Cain,
saying, / I have created a man equally with the Lord.

2. *And again, she bore / his brother Abel.*
Now Abel was / a keeper of sheep,
and Cain was / a tiller of the ground.

1. *Now Adam knew,* etc.] On the construction of the sentence, which puts the subject before the predicate, and its signification, see my comment on i 2, and compare iii 1. It should be particularly noted that this word-order, as stated there, points to a connection between what the text begins to recount now and what was narrated earlier. At the end of the preceding section the Torah focussed our attention on the cherubim and the revolving sword-flame, which barred the way to the tree of life, and momentarily, as it were, we were made to forget the man. At this stage, Scripture reverts to the man: *Now Adam,* so far as he is concerned, what happened to him? This happened to him: he knew Eve his wife; and she bore, etc.

Knew] This word also contains a link with the previous section, whose essential theme is centred on the tree of *knowledge.*

Eve his wife] This expression reminds us of what was stated above (iii 20): *his wife's name Eve.*

And she conceived and bore] These words not only constitute a formal link with the previous section, where also the two stems הָרָה *hārā* ['to conceive'] and יָלַד *yāladh* ['to bear'] occur together (iii 16), but they provide, in addition, a point of contact with the subject-matter: we are told here that the promise given to Eve that she would bear children in order that the human species might survive even after their expulsion from the garden of Eden and removal from the vicinity of the tree of life (see on this above, pp. 161–166) was actually fulfilled.

Cain [קַיִן *Qayin*] / The name is usually explained to mean *smith,* on the basis of the Arabic قين *qaynun* and the Aramaic קֵינָיָא *qēnāyā'* [otherwise: קַיְנָיָא *qaynāyā'*] or קֵינָאָה *qēnā'ā* [otherwise: קַיְנָאָה *qaynā'ā*] (see above, p. 180); but this is only a secondary sense of the word. The primary signification of the stem קין *qyn* in Arabic, too, is *to fashion, to shape, to give form* to something; and the noun قين *qaynun* denotes not only 'a smith, a worker in bronze and iron', but in general any 'artificer' who makes articles by giving form to the raw material before him. The Aramaic word cited is recognizable, even by its form, as a denominative noun, and in any case connotes also a *refiner,* who works in *silver* and *gold.* In Biblical Hebrew, קַיִן *qayin* signifies a 'weapon', which has been given *form* by the craftsman (ii Sam. xxi 16). The conclusion to be drawn from all this is that the name of Adam's first son means: *a creature* [literally, 'a formed being']. Compare *Kenan* [קֵינָן *Qēnān*] in the genealogy of Seth (v 10–14). It is not possible to determine the meaning of the designation of the well-known tribe of the Kenites [קֵינִי *Qēnī*]; but, in any event, it is not of importance to our subject. The name of the city, *the Kain* [הַקַּיִן *Haqqayin*] in Jos. xv 57 is not derived from the name of the Kenite tribe but from a common noun, as is shown by the definite article in front of it. Reference is made to a city in north Canaan called *Qên* or *Qeyn(a)* (*Qi–ya–na* in the Egyptian syllabic writing) in the fourteenth–thirteenth century B.C.E. (Albright, *The Vocalisation of the Egyptian Syllabic Orthography,* New Haven 1934, p. 59, § xvi, part B, Nos. 2, 3); and a river *Qyn* or *Qynȝ* in the vicinity of Megiddo is also mentioned in an Egyptian document belonging to the memoirs of Thotmes III (Yeivin, *Journal of the Jewish Palestine Exploration Society,* iii [1935], p. 162, note 45). Parallels to the name Cain have not been found exclusively among the people of Israel or within the Land of Israel. *Qynw,* the name of a man; *Qynt,* the name of a woman; and *Qynn,* the appellation of a god, occur in the Semitic world (see, for example, Lidzbarski, *Handbuch,* p. 362; idem, *Ephemeris,* ii, pp. 105, 260; iii, pp. 262, 278). Furthermore, *Banu al-Qayn* is the designation of an important and powerful Arab tribe, which, according to some authorities (see, for instance, Nöldeke, *ZDMG,* xl [1886], p. 181) may be identified with the Kenites mentioned in the Bible.

Saying [וַתֹּאמֶר *wattō'mer,* literally, 'and she said'] / The verb is not to be understood as a pluperfect, to wit, that she had said this before she called her son Cain. The Imperfect with *Wāw* consecutive denotes *continuing* action. The meaning is: she called his name Cain, and in explanation of her choice of the name, she made the statement that follows in the text. Analogous passages, e.g. Exod. ii 10, i Sam. vii 12, are to be interpreted in the same way.

On the two different systems of naming children — in the one case the *father* gives the name, in the other the *mother* — see my observations in *La Questione della Genesi,* pp. 251–253, and in *The Documentary Hypothesis,* English Translation, pp. 65–66.

I have created [קָנִיתִי *qānīthī*] *a man* [אִישׁ *'īš*] *equally with the*

Lord [אֶת ה׳ *'ēth YHWH*] / Each of the three parts of this sentence — קָנִיתִי *qānīthī*, אִישׁ *'īš* and אֶת ה׳ *'ēth YHWH* — the translators and expositors have interpreted in different ways; and by various combinations of these interpretations there have been created countless explanations of the verse as a whole. The verb קָנִיתִי *qānīthī* has been understood either according to the usual signification of the stem קָנָה *qānā*, namely, *to acquire;* or in the sense of *to form, give birth to.* The word אִישׁ *'īš* is taken to mean a *male child,* a *man,* or a *husband.* As for the phrase אֶת ה׳ *'ēth YHWH,* many different interpretations have been proposed. The Septuagint renders: *through God* (διὰ τοῦ Θεοῦ); so, too, the Vulgate (*per Deum,* or according to another version, *per Dominum*); Targum Onkelos: *from before the Lord;* Targum Pseudo-Jonathan: *I have gotten for a husband* THE ANGEL OF THE LORD (that is, according to the haggadic view, Samma'el); the Peshiṭta: *I have gotten a man* UNTO THE LORD; R. Saadia Gaon: *from with the Lord* (Allah); Rashi: *with the Lord* (on the basis of the homiletical explanation in Bereshith Rabba); Naḥmanides: *unto the Lord,* that is, *for the service of the Lord;* Dillmann and a number of moderns: *with the help of the Lord;* and so on and so forth. Many commentators are of the opinion that the text should be emended, and have suggested various ways of doing so: some, for example, read: מֵאֵת ה׳ *mē'ēth YHWH* ['from (with) the Lord'] (Budde), or אות ה׳ *'ōth YHWH* ['sign of the Lord'] (Marti), or אֶתְאַוֶּה *'ēth'awwe* ['I yearn for'] (Gunkel in the first and second editions); others delete the word אֶת ה׳ *'eth YHWH* as a gloss written in the margin (אות ה׳ *'ōth YHWH* in connection with *v.* 15), which was afterwards interpolated by mistake in the wrong place; others, again, think that it is no longer possible to determine the original version and leave the nature of the correction unresolved (Holzinger, and Gunkel in the third edition).

In regard to the verb קָנִיתִי *qānīthī,* it appears, especially in view of what we have learnt in recent years about the usage of the root in the ancient Canaanite tongue, that its connotation here is: *I formed (created), gave birth to.* The arguments of Montgomery (*JAOS,* liii [1933], pp. 107, 116, and *HThR,* xxxi [1938], p. 145, end of sec. 1), as well as the added contentions recently put forward by Levi della Vida (*JBL,* lxiii [1944], p. 1, note 1), against attributing this signification to the Semitic stem קני — קנו *qny–qnw* appear to me unacceptable. In many passages in the Ugaritic inscriptions, the meaning of this root is undoubtedly to *form, bear, beget,* and the interpretations of these texts suggested by Levi della Vida are decidedly forced. *'Ašērā,* the mother of the gods, is often designated in the Ugaritic writings *qnyt 'ilm,* the equivalent in Hebrew of קֹנִיַּת הָאֵלִים *qōniyyath hā'ēlīm;* and this title is to be understood not as the *consort of the gods* but, undoubtedly, as *she that gave birth to the gods,* since the gods, on their part, are called the *sons of 'Ašērā.* Of *'Il,* the father of the gods, his sons say (Tablet AB, iii, lines 6–7): *k qnyn 'lm k dr dr(!) dyknn,* that is, 'For he who has made us [exists] for ever, he who establishes us for all generations'. The word that corresponds to *qnyn* in the second line of the verse, which signifies, *who establishes us,* proves that *qnyn* definitely means, *he who made us.* This very pair of synonymous and parallel verbs, קָנָה — כּוֹנֵן *qānā — kōnēn,* is also found in the Bible, in the song הַאֲזִינוּ *Ha'ăzīnū* ['Give ear'] (Deut. xxxii 6): *Is not He your father, who* CREATED YOU [קָנֶךָ *qānekhā*], *who made you and* ESTABLISHED YOU [וַיְכֹנְנֶךָ *wayekhōnenekhā*], just as immediately afterwards, in the continuation of the song (*v.* 7), we find the second pair of synonymous and parallel words of the same Ugaritic verse: *Remember the days of* OLD [עוֹלָם *'ōlām,* rendered in the translation of the Ugaritic text, 'for ever', like the Hebrew לְעוֹלָם *le'ōlām*] *consider the years of many* GENERATIONS [דּוֹר וָדוֹר *dōr wādhōr*] (this collocation, עוֹלָם — דּוֹר (וָ)דוֹר *'ōlām—dōr (wā)d(h)ōr,* occurs very frequently both in the Bible and in Ugaritic poetry; on these and similar word-pairs, which are found in both literatures alike, see my Hebrew article in Tarbiz, xiv, pp. 1–9).

This is also the case with the designation, 'קֹנֵה *qōnē of heaven and earth',* which the Canaanite priest Melchizedek applies to God Most High (Gen. xiv 19). Here, too, unquestionably קֹנֵה *qōnē* means *maker,* as is clear from what we have just noted, and from the parallel expression, *who made heaven and earth* (Psa. cxv 15, etc.). The title 'קֹנֵה *qōnē of heaven and earth'* also passed from the ancient idiom of the Canaanites into the Hebrew language, where it became a designation of the God of Israel, and was couched in exactly the same words (Gen. xiv 22, in the utterance of Abram:

I have sworn to the Lord God Most High, MAKER [קוֹנֵה *qōnē*] OF HEAVEN AND EARTH), or with change of the original Canaanite verb for the synonymous verb עָשָׂה *ʿāśā* ['make'], which is more common in Hebrew: *who made* [עֹשֵׂה *ʿōśe*] *heaven and earth.* See on the whole subject *La Questione della Genesi,* pp. 70–71, 75–77, 373.

Two other verses are worth quoting: Psa. cxxxix 13, *For* THOU DIDST FORM [קָנִיתָ *qānīthā*] *my inward parts, Thou* DIDST KNIT ME TOGETHER [תְּסֻכֵּנִי *tᵉsukkēnī*] *in my mother's womb;* and Prov. viii 22, *The Lord* CREATED ME [קָנָנִי *qānānī*] *at the beginning of His way, the first of His* ACTS [מִפְעָלָיו *miphʿālāw*] *of old;* there, too, the expressions parallel to the verb קָנָה *qānā* (in Psalms, סָכַךְ *sākhakh* — that is, *weave* [*knit together*] — and in Proverbs, פָּעַל *pāʿal* ['do, act']) clearly prove that it signifies *to form, create.* Possibly this was in fact the original and primary meaning of the root in the ancient Canaanite tongue, and from it developed the connotation *to acquire,* just as the verb עָשָׂה *ʿāśā* [literally, 'make'] is often used in this sense; for example, in Gen. xii 5: *and all their possessions which* THEY HAD GATHERED [רָכָשׁוּ *rākhāšū*] *and the persons that* THEY HAD GOTTEN [עָשׂוּ *ʿāśū*] *in Haran,* and in similar verses. In poetic diction, which naturally tends to preserve the archaic elements of a language, the full original signification of the root was also retained, especially in connection with two concepts: Divine creation and parental procreation.

In the light of the foregoing, it is possible to understand the verse with complete clarity: the first woman, in her joy at giving birth to her first son, boasts of her generative power, which approximates in her estimation to the Divine creative power. The Lord formed the first *man* (ii 7), and I have formed the second *man.* קָנִיתִי אִישׁ אֶת ה' *qānīthī ʾīš ʾeth YHWH* [literally, 'I have created a man with the Lord']: *I stand together* [i.e. *equally*] WITH HIM *in the rank of creators.*

The conclusions we have now reached also remove the difficulty presented by the fact that the name קַיִן *Qayin* Cain, derived from the stem קין *qyn,* does not correspond to the verb קָנִיתִי *qānīthī,* which is from the stem קָנָה *qānā.* We have already seen that both the first stem and the second signify primarily *to form.* This is due to the fact that they are two cognate stems, representing two divergent developments from one archaic root; but to the ancient Hebrews, who could not yet grasp fine linguistic distinctions, they appeared as one and the same stem.

Equally with THE LORD [*YHWH*] / Several ancient versions (see above) read here אֱלֹהִים *'Elōhīm* ['God'] instead of ה' *YHWH*. Ostensibly, אֱלֹהִים *'Elōhīm* appears to be the preferable reading, since it is the name אֱלֹהִים *'Elōhīm* that Eve uses in connection with the birth of Seth (*v.* 25), and only subsequently is it stated (*v.* 26): *At that time men* BEGAN *to call upon the name of the Lord.* But, on the other hand, the numerical symmetry of the Divine names occurring in this chapter (see above, § 13 of the Introduction, pp. 191 ff.) confirms the traditional text. This reading, moreover, conforms to the rules that we established earlier (p. 87) in regard to the use of the Divine appellations; for, as a result of her partnership with the Lord [*YHWH*] in the work of creation, Eve feels the personal nearness of the Divine Presence to herself. The significance of the change of the Divine designations in the continuation of the section, we shall discuss below, in our commentary on *v.* 26.

2. *His brother*] Here, and again further on, in *vv.* 21–22, as well as in other parts of the Bible, there appears to be an allusion to an ancient social system that gave the elder brother a certain degree of lordship over his younger brothers — fratriarchy (see on this Gordon's essay, which I have cited above, in the introduction, § 16, p. 196).

Abel [הֶבֶל *Hebhel,* literally, 'breath'] / The word הֶבֶל *hebhel* usually expresses in Hebrew the brevity of human life. We find, for example, in Psa. cxliv 4: *Man is like a* BREATH, his *days are like a passing shadow;* in Job vii 16: *for my days are a* BREATH*;* and similarly in many other passages. Consequently the reader immediately realizes, as he continues to read the section, how appropriate the name is to the fate of Eve's second son. There was no need, therefore, to assign a reason here for the giving of the name as was done in the case of Cain. The Bible implies that whoever called the child's name הֶבֶל *Hebhel,* alluded *unwittingly* to the fate in store for him. We have made a similar observation with regard to the naming of Eve (iii 20). *The name,* according to Talmudic doctrine, *is a determining factor* (B. Berakhoth 7b).

Now Abel was a keeper of sheep, and Cain was a tiller of the ground] The two brothers divided between them the labour necessary for the sustenance of the family. Cattle-rearing and agriculture remain to this day the two main branches of work for the production of our vital commodities; and Scripture, on the principle that 'The acts of the fathers foreshadow those of the children', shows us the first two sons of the first human pair engaged respectively in one of these two occupations. There is a kind of parallel here to what was stated in the previous chapters: the raising of sheep corresponds to the dominion over the living creatures referred to in the story of Creation (i 26, 28), and the tilling of the ground is analogous to what we are told at the beginning and at the end of the story of the Garden of Eden (ii 5, iii 23). By degrees the other occupations will follow in order, according to the development of the material culture of mankind, and will be mentioned, in part, further on in the section.

There is no indication in the text of any conflict between the two vocations: the brothers share equally. *A fortiori* there is not to be read into our section any expression of contempt felt by farmers towards shepherds, as many scholars have thought. On the contrary, it is precisely Abel, towards whom the Bible is sympathetic, who is the keeper of sheep.

This reference to Abel's work as a shepherd does not run counter to what we said in our exposition of i 29–30 (pp. 58 f.), namely, that according to the Torah man should, on principle, have refrained from eating flesh until it was permitted to Noah and his sons (ix 3). In the first place, even one who does not eat meat can still use the milk and wool of the animals, and, after their death, their skins as well. Furthermore, it is certainly not the intention of the Bible to convey the impression that the conduct of the earliest generations was necessarily in accord with ideal standards; Cain's act of murder proves the contrary.

וַיְהִי — הָיָה *way^{e}hī* [Imperfect tense with *Wāw* consecutive; rendered: *Now . . . was*] — *hāyā* [perfect tense; rendered: *was*] / On the change of 'tense' in the two verbs here and in the following verses, see my explanation above, p. 27, on **וַיִּקְרָא — קָרָא** *wayyiqrā'* — *qārā'*.

In this connection, attention should be paid to the construction of the two verses in this paragraph and of the first three verses of the next paragraph. The text refers a number of times to each of the two brothers consecutively, before dealing at length with the older one; and on each occasion it speaks first of the brother who was last mentioned in the previous reference. To begin with it records the birth of Cain, and thereafter, following the chronological order, that of Abel (*v.* 1). Now having concluded with Abel, it immediately proceeds to speak of Abel's occupation, and subsequently of Cain's (*v.* 2). Since Cain was now the last to be mentioned, the next reference deals first with Cain's offering (*v.* 3) and afterwards with Abel's (beginning of *v.* 4). Seeing that Abel's oblation has been referred to, we are next told, in the same verse (end of *v.* 4), that it was accepted, and then (beginning of *v.* 5) that Cain's sacrifice was not accepted. After recounting the rejection of Cain's offering, the Bible immediately goes on to describe (end of *v.* 5) the reaction of Cain. Each time we have a chiastic arrangement. This procedure resembles the method adopted by the Mishnah at the beginning of tractate Berakhoth, as the Gemara notes (B. Berakhoth 2a): 'The Tanna [Mishnah teacher] commences with the evening *(Shema)** and then speaks of the morning *(Shema)*; whilst on the subject of the morning *(Shema)*, he expounds the matters relating to it, and thereafter he reverts to the matters appertaining to the evening *(Shema)*'. By employing this method a number of times consecutively, a chain, as it were, of many interlocked links is created, marked by perfect symmetry.

SECOND PARAGRAPH

THE STORY OF THE MURDER

3. *In the course of time / Cain brought*
of the fruit of the ground / an offering to the Lord,
4. *and Abel, too, brought / of the firstlings of his flock and of their fat portions.*
And the Lord had regard / for Abel and his offering,

* The name, derived from the initial word (שְׁמַע *šemaʿ*, 'Hear!'), of a portion of the Jewish liturgy, recited morning and evening, which comprises the three Pentateuchal passages: Deut. vi 4–9, xi 13–21, Num. xv 37–41.

5. *but for Cain and his offering / He had no regard.*
So Cain was very vexed, / and his countenance fell.

6. *The Lord said to Cain,*
'Why are you vexed, / and why has your countenance fallen?

7. *Surely, if you do well, / you shall be upstanding;*
but if you do not do well, / sin shall be a rōbhēṣ *at your door;*
its desire shall be for you, / but you will be able to master it.'

8. *Cain appointed a place where to meet Abel his brother, / and when they were in the field,*
Cain rose up against his brother Abel, / and killed him.

3. *In the course of time* [מִקֵּץ יָמִים *miqqēṣ yāmīm,* literally, 'at end of days'] / Some explain the phrase to mean, *at the end of a year;* others, *at the end of some time.* The second interpretation is the more probable, since we are not told from when the year is counted. So, too, i Kings xvii 7: *And* AFTER A WHILE [מִקֵּץ יָמִים *miqqēṣ yāmīm*] *the brook dried up.* Similar expressions occur in Jud. xi 4, xv 1: וַיְהִי מִיָּמִים *wayehī miyyāmīm* [literally, 'and it was from days'; rendered: 'After a time', 'After a while']; ibid. xiv 8: *And* AFTER A WHILE [מִיָּמִים *miyyāmīm*] *he returned to take her.*

Of the fruit of the ground] Gunkel comments: 'according to the context, obviously the *choicest* thereof'; most modern commentators take a similar view. Rabbinic exegesis, on the contrary, maintains that Cain brought *produce of the poorest quality* (Bereshith Rabba, xxii 5, and parallel passages; see Aptowitzer, *Kain u. Abel in der Agada,* Wien—Leipzig 1922, pp. 37–41, 142–144). Neither interpretation accords with the natural sense of the verse. On the one hand, it is clear that since in regard to Cain it is stated simply that his offering was *of the fruit of the ground,* and in Abel's case the Bible uses two expressions to emphasize that the oblation was the best of its kind (*of the firstlings . . . and of* THEIR FAT PORTIONS), this distinction is not made pointlessly. On the other hand, it must be noted that although there is a *distinction,* there is no *contrast.* Apparently the Bible wished to convey that whilst Abel was concerned to choose the finest thing in his possession, Cain was indifferent. In other words: Abel endeavoured to perform his religious duty ideally, whereas Cain was content merely to discharge this duty.

To the Lord [*YHWH*] / According to the third rule that we formulated earlier (p. 87) with regard to the use of the Divine appellations, the name *YHWH* ['Lord'] rather than *'Elōhīm* [God] is appropriate here, since the verse deals with sacrifices, and these are offered up specifically to a personal deity. The Talmudic sages already noted correctly that 'in connection with none of the sacrifices mentioned in the Torah is אֱלֹהִים *'Elōhīm* or אֱלֹהֶיךָ *'Elōhekhā* ['your God'] or שַׁדַּי *Šadday* ['Almighty'] or צְבָאוֹת *ṣebhā'ōth* ['Hosts'] mentioned, but only the Specific Name — י״ה *YHWH* (Sifrē Num., § 143, and parallel passages). The exception to this usage in Exod. xviii 12 is intended to stress the fact that it was a stranger who brought the offering, and that, notwithstanding what is stated in the previous verse, he had not yet attained to complete knowledge of the Lord (*YHWH*).

4. *Of the firstlings of his flock and of their fat portions*] This twofold emphasis — on the *firstlings,* which are the best of the flock, and on the *fat portions,* which are their best parts (see the different views on the meaning of the expression *and of their fat portions* in B. Zebaḥim, p. 115a) — underlines, as we have stated, Abel's desire to gratify his Creator, and to honour Him to the best of his ability; his oblation is accompanied by good intent. The customary assertion by modern exegetes that the text does not contain a single word about the devotional intention of the brothers is not correct. On the contrary, Scripture stresses this intention in a manner that is manifest to any one with knowledge of Biblical diction.

And of their fat portions [וּמֵחֶלְבֵהֶן *ūmēḥelbhēhen*] / Since there is a different view, it will not be superfluous to indicate that the pronominal suffix [-הֶן *-hen*] refers to the firstlings [בְּכֹרוֹת *bekhōrōth*], the gender of which is here feminine.

The offering of animal sacrifices does not point to the custom of eating flesh (see above, the commentary on *v.* 3, the penultimate paragraph). On the contrary, it will be noted that the fat and the blood go to the altar, yet they may not be eaten!

And the Lord had regard for Abel and his offering] We have already observed *at the end* of the commentary to the first paragraph that this clause is formally linked to the preceding clause, which emphasizes Abel's intention. The formal connection, in turn, points to an inner relationship: since it was *of the firstlings* of his flock and *of their fat portions* that Abel brought his offering, therefore *the Lord had regard,* etc. See on *v.* 5 below.

5. *But for Cain and his offering He had no regard*] Many conjectures have been advanced by the commentators to explain the difference in God's attitude to the offerings of the two brothers. For example: Cain's oblation of the fruit of the ground did not find favour, because the earth had been cursed in consequence of Adam's sin (Halévy); the Lord likes shepherds and animal sacrifices, but dislikes farmers and offerings of the fruit of the ground (Gunkel); the objective worth of animal sacrifices is greater than that of vegetable offerings (Jacob, and others before him); and many similar suggestions. But all these theories are redundant, if we grasp the significance of the preceding lines of the text and clearly see therein the distinction between Cain's and Abel's intention. Our passage reflects the view that sacrifices are acceptable only if an acceptable spirit inspires them.

How did the two brothers know that the Lord had regard for Abel and for his offering, but for Cain and his offering he had no regard? According to the Greek translation of Theodotion, ἐνεπύρισεν, fire descended from heaven and consumed Abel's offering but not Cain's; a similar explanation is found in late haggadic Midrashim and in a number of medieval commentaries. Others think that the Bible implies that the Lord manifested himself to the two brothers (Skinner, Jacob). Gunkel supposes that the text alludes to a sign that was given in the sacrifices themselves, for instance the appearance of the liver or the like. It is better, however, to understand the verse in accordance with Brock-Utne's suggestion, *op. cit.,* pp. 210–211, to wit, that after the offerings had been made, the Lord bestowed blessing and fertility upon Abel's flocks but not upon the field of Cain.

So Cain was very vexed [literally, 'it was very hot unto Cain'] /— that is, he was grieved; compare xxxiv 7: *and the men were* GRIEVED *and* VERY VEXED.

And his countenance fell] He hung his head like a man who is grieved and crushed.

6. *The Lord said to Cain*] Here and in the rest of the section, the name *YHWH* ['Lord'] and not *'Elōhīm* ['God'] is used,

in conformity with the first rule given above, p. 87, because the passage deals with ethical matters.

Why are you vexed and why has your countenance fallen?] In the Lord's utterance expressions are repeated from the previous narrative verse in accordance with the usual practice followed in our sections.

These are not words of rebuke, as Jacob contends in his commentary, but, on the contrary, an expression of comfort and fatherly counsel, as though to say: My son, you have no reason to be grieved and dejected; bear in mind that *if you do well,* etc.

7. *Surely, if you do well, you shall be upstanding; but if you do not do well, sin shall be a* rōbhēṣ *at your dóor* [הֲלֹא אִם תֵּיטִיב שְׂאֵת וְאִם לֹא תֵיטִיב לַפֶּתַח חַטָּאת רֹבֵץ *hălō' 'im tēṭībh śe'ēth we'im lō' thēṭībh lappethaḥ ḥaṭṭā'th rōbhēṣ*] / This is one of the most difficult and obscure Biblical sentences. In ancient times the Rabbis counted it among the indeterminate verses (B. Yoma, 52a–b, and parallel passages), because of the doubt in regard to the syntactic relationship of the word שְׂאֵת *śe'ēth.* In modern times the expositors have found the text so hard to elucidate that some, like Gunkel and Jacob, have actually abandoned all hope of understanding it, and have left part of it untranslated. The attempts made to interpret the verse in its entirety, or to emend it on the basis of the Septuagint, which is even more obscure than the Masoretic recension, have encountered numerous difficulties. It will not be superfluous, therefore, to make a fresh attempt.

The starting-point must be the word שְׂאֵת *śe'ēth* [literally, 'to lift, carry'] — the first of the problem words in the sentence. Some have connected it with the expression, *bring* [שְׂאוּ *śe'ū*] *an offering* (Psa. xcvi 8), the meaning being: 'whether you bring a fine offering or not, sin couches at the door'. But this interpretation is difficult not only on account of the structure of the sentence, as we shall show later, and because the thought expressed in the verse, according to this conjecture, is neither clear nor probable, but also — and chiefly — for the reason that the crucial word *offering* is missing. The same applies to the other suggestion based on the passage, *then you will lift up* [תִשָּׂא *tiśśā'*] *your face without blemish* (Job xi 15), which would imply an antithesis here to *the falling of the countenance* mentioned in the previous verses; but just the vital word *face* is wanting! The verb נָשָׂא *nāśā'* has, when used absolutely, a *general* signification, and only in conjunction with an object or some other complement is it capable of acquiring specific meanings such as those referred to — *to bring an offering* or *to lift up the face.* Likewise the explanation of our word in the sense of *to forgive iniquity* (Targum Onkelos: *it will be forgiven you*) is open to the same objection; for although the verb נָשָׂא *nāśā'* has this connotation even without the word *iniquity* (e.g. xviii 24: *and wilt Thou not forgive the place?* [E.V. 'spare it']; ibid., *v.* 26: *I will forgive* [E.V .'spare'] *the whole place*), yet in that case the *one who is being forgiven* his sin must be mentioned. It has also been proposed to interpret שְׂאֵת *śe'ēth* in the sense of 'rank, eminence' — cf. *pre-eminent of rank* [שְׂאֵת *śe'ēth*] *and pre-eminent in power* (xlix 3); but this, too, is not free from difficulty, since the concept of rank and eminence does not suit the context. More explanations still have been advanced, but there is no need to detail them.

It is impossible to find the meaning of this obscure word and of the verse as a whole unless we approach the problem methodically. First, we must determine the structure of the sentence and the signification of the expression אִם—וְאִם *'im — we'im* [literally, 'if — and if']. The sense of the verse cannot be: *whether you do . . . or whether you do not . . . ,* for in that case the word תֵּיטִיב *tēṭībh* [literally, 'do good, well'] should not have been repeated by itself, but the sentence should have been framed in one of the following two ways: either the phrase תֵּיטִיב שְׂאֵת *tēṭībh śe'ēth* should have been reiterated in full, thus: וְאִם לֹא תֵיטִיב שְׂאֵת *we'im lō' thēṭībh śe'ēth,* or the clause should have been reduced, the second time, to וְאִם לֹא *we'im lō'* [literally, 'and if not'] only. According to the present form of the verse the contrasted conditions are: (a) אִם תֵּיטִיב *'im tēṭībh* ['if you do well'], (b) אִם לֹא תֵיטִיב *'im lō' thēṭībh* ['if you do not well'], and the word שְׂאֵת *śeēth* is not part of the protasis but constitutes the apodosis. In the event of your doing well, then — שְׂאֵת *śe'ēth;* but in the event of your not doing well, then — לַפֶּתַח חַטָּאת רֹבֵץ *lappethaḥ ḥaṭṭā'th rōbhēṣ.*

Having established this point, let us proceed to the next step. Just as the second condition, אִם לֹא תֵיטִיב *'im lō' thēṭībh,* is the exact opposite of the first, אִם תֵּיטִיב *'im tēṭībh,* so the end of the verse undoubtedly contains a contrast, that is, the word שְׂאֵת *śeʾēth* must be the antithesis of the conclusion of the second condition, namely, לַפֶּתַח חַטָּאת רֹבֵץ *lappethaḥ ḥaṭṭāʾth rōbhēṣ.* Now we have not to go far to find in the Biblical idiom an example of antithesis between the verb נָשָׂא *nāśāʾ* in its general signification, without a predicate, and the verb רָבַץ *rābhaṣ.* In one verse it is written: *he stooped down,* HE COUCHED [רָבַץ *rābhaṣ*] *like a lion, and as a lioness who dares* ROUSE HIM UP [יְקִימֶנּוּ *yeqīmennū*]? (xlix 9); and in another we read: *Behold, a people! As a lioness* IT RISES UP [יָקוּם *yāqūm*], *and as a lion* IT LIFTS ITSELF [יִתְנַשָּׂא *yithnaśśāʾ*] (Num. xxiii 24). The verb נָשָׂא *nāśāʾ* ['to lift up'] corresponds to קוּם *qūm* ['to rise up'] in the second verse, and קוּם *qūm* is the antonym of רָבַץ *rābhaṣ* ['to couch'] in the first verse; when a lion rests on the ground we say that it *couches,* when it stands up on its feet, we say that it *rises up* or that it *lifts itself.* Precisely the same antithesis we can find in our verse. If you do well, that is, if you behave well and perform good deeds, you will be able to rise up and stand firmly on your feet, but if you do not do well, (the *Wāw* of וְאִם *weʾim* means *but*) the opposite will befall you: not upstanding but couching on the ground.

The exact meaning of this couching we must determine by examining the clause, לַפֶּתַח חַטָּאת רֹבֵץ *lappethaḥ ḥaṭṭāʾth rōbhēṣ.* To begin with, it suffers from a grammatical irregularity: the discord between חַטָּאת *ḥaṭṭāʾth* ['sin'], which is feminine, and רֹבֵץ *rōbhēṣ,* which is masculine. It has already been pointed out by several exegetes that the Akkadian word *rābiṣu,* which is the participle of the stem *rbṣ* — just like the word רֹבֵץ *rōbhēṣ* in our verse — denotes a kind of *demon,* that is, a specific class of demons; they have accordingly suggested that the word רֹבֵץ *rōbhēṣ* should not be regarded as a participle but as a substantive, and that the phrase should be interpreted thus: sin is a kind of *rōbhēṣ.* Generally speaking, this conjecture may be correct, but the following two points have to be added:

(a) The Akkadian word referred to has other meanings (see, for instance, the function of the *rābiṣu* in judicial matters; Walther, *Das altbabylonische Gerichtswesen,* Leipzig 1917, pp. 169–173), and of these one fits our context well: the *rābisu* is a kind of government official, not necessarily one of the highest order, but one of the most hated by the people. Possibly, it is this connotation that is specifically intended here, since it is stated afterwards, *its desire is for you,* that is, it [sin] wishes to master you and to have dominion over you like the state officials who seek to impose their authority over the people.

(b) Seeing that of all the synonyms denoting various kinds of officials the name *rōbhēṣ* and not another was chosen, the choice cannot have been accidental; conceivably, the appellation was chosen because it carries the nuance of *couching,* of lying upon the ground, of clinging to the ground, in contrast to the upstanding position implicit in the word שְׂאֵת *śᵉʾēth.* The verb רָבַץ *rābhaṣ* in the Bible not only signifies to lie down in order to rest, but also to bow down beneath a heavy burden. In Exod. xxiii 5 it is written: *lying* [רֹבֵץ *rōbhēṣ*] *under its burden,* and in Num. xxii 27: *she lay down* [וַתִּרְבַּץ *wattirbaṣ*] *under Balaam.* There is an allusion to this sense in the word רֹבֵץ *rōbhēṣ* of our verse. The *'rōbhēṣ',* which is sin, will long for you *(its desire shall be for you),* that is, it will endeavour to have dominion over you, to keep you near to itself, and to make you couch on the ground just as it does. If once you start to sin, sin will draw you to itself more and more. It is similar to the thought expressed in the rabbinic aphorism: 'one transgression leads to another'.

There is no need to cite here in detail the various expositions of חַטָּאת רֹבֵץ *ḥaṭṭāʾth rōbhēṣ* (it symbolizes the evil impulse; the analogy is that of an animal lying in wait for its prey, or of a curse settling on someone, etc.); it is similarly unnecessary to mention all the interpretations offered in regard to the preceding expression, *at the door* (portals of the heart, door of the house, door of the sanctuary, entrance of the grave, and the like). The verse simply says *door (entrance),* and the commentator is not called upon to determine what Scripture leaves undetermined. It means, apparently, *your door* in a general sense, that is, the place through which you are wont to go in and out constantly; in other words, it will always be found in your path.

Now, having explained each difficult expression in the Divine utterance to Cain separately, we shall be able to grasp the connection between them, and the sense of the address as a whole: Why, my son, are you grieved, and why do you hang your head?

There is no cause for it; you have only to do well and then you will be able to stand firmly on your feet, with upright stature. But if you fail to do well and begin to sin, then the sin shall become a 'רֹבֵץ' '*rōbhēṣ*' unto you, and this *rōbhēṣ* will long to bring you low and cause you to couch upon the ground like itself. Nevertheless you are not delivered into its power, and if only you have the desire, you can oppose it and overcome it and free yourself from its influence *(but you will be able to master it).*

Its desire [תְּשׁוּקָתוֹ *t^ešūqāthō*] *shall be for you, but you will be able to master it*] The significance of these words in relation to what precedes we have already explained in the lines above. But we still have to elucidate their connection with the similar sentence in the story of Paradise (iii 16): *yet your desire shall be for your husband, and he shall rule over you.* Most contemporary commentators suspect the authenticity of this part of our verse just because of the verbal repetition, and think that it has suffered from scribal attentions. More probable is the view that this repetition is a case in point of the influence exerted by the epic style on narrative prose, examples of which I have discussed at length in my Hebrew essay 'Biblical literature and Canaanite literature', which was published in *Tarbiz,* xiii, pp. 197–212; xiv, pp. 1–10; and in my Hebrew article 'Israelite Epic Poetry', which appeared in *K^eneseth* dedicated to the memory of H. N. Bialik, viii, pp. 121–142. As I stated there, we may assume that the narrative prose of the Israelites, like that of other peoples, developed from epic poetry, and hence the former still shows traces of the rhetorical characteristics and the stylistic devices commonly found in Canaanite and the oldest Hebrew epic poetry, just as we find in Greek literature that the logographers — the first chroniclers — and even Herodotus, the 'father of history', still use many expressions that were customary in Greek epic poetry; likewise the earliest French historians, to cite an example also from the Middle Ages, continued to employ stereotyped phrases that were common in the French epos that preceded them. Now epic poetry — both Eastern and Western — shows a predilection for verbal repetitions, and this phenomenon is bound up with the essential nature of the epic, which was primarily intended to be heard and not read. The people who gathered to listen to epic poems sung by the minstrel were particularly enchanted when he began a stanza with which they were familiar and which was an old favourite of theirs; they found it easier then to listen to the minstrel and, as it were, to share in his song. Similarly Hebrew narrative prose is given to repetitions. Nevertheless, prose, which is designed for reading rather than recitation, endeavours as a rule to change the phrases slightly, avoiding word-for-word repetition, so as not to weary the *reader* (a point with which we have already dealt a number of times in the course of our commentary). But sometimes, when the subject is technical and does not lend itself to variations, such as the construction of the Tabernacle, which is twice described (Exod. xxv–xxxi, xxxv–xl), or the offerings of the princes (Num. vii 12–83), then even in prose we find the *ipsissima verba* reproduced. This obtains also in other instances where literal repetition is suited also to prose style. In the story of Creation we noted the expression, *and there was evening and there was morning, such-and-such a day,* which occurs six times, at the end of six consecutive paragraphs. Similarly here; the Bible wished to give expression to a thought resembling one that it had already stated on an earlier occasion, and to this end it employed the same wording that it had used the first time, in accordance with the usual practice in such cases in epic poetry.

Here, too, in conformity with what we have noted in iii 16, several ancient versions read תְּשׁוּבָתוֹ *t^ešūbhāthō* ['its return'] instead of תְּשׁוּקָתוֹ *t^ešūqāthō* ['its desire'], and here, just as there, this reading is unacceptable.

8. *Cain* APPOINTED A PLACE WHERE TO MEET [וַיֹּאמֶר *wayyō'mer*] *Abel his brother*] In the Lord's words to Cain there is no reference to Abel, nor any appraisal of his actions and intention; nevertheless Cain does not forget that the Lord had regard for Abel and his offering, whilst for him and his offering he had no regard, and he is jealous of his brother.

This verse raises a difficult problem: it states, *and he* [*Cain*] *said* [the usual meaning of וַיֹּאמֶר *wayyō'mer*], but we are not told what he said. The verb אָמַר *'āmar* is not used absolutely — without an object—as is the verb דִּבֵּר *dibbēr* ['he spoke']. The few passages where such a usage of the verb אָמַר *'āmar* might possibly be claimed (Gen. xxii 7; Exod. xix 25; Hos. xiii 2; Psa. lxxi 10; Esther i 18; ii Chron. ii 11 [Hebrew, *v.* 10]; *ibid.*, xxxii 24) are doubtful. An ancient exegetical tradition, reflected in the old versions, completes the verse by attributing to Cain the additional words: *Come, let us go forth into the field* or some similar sentence. For example, Targum Pseudo-Jonathan: 'Come, let us both go out *into the field*' [לְבָרָא *lebhārā'*]; so, too, the Fragmentary (Jerusalem) Targum [reading: לְאַפֵּי בָרָא *le'appē bārā'*, literally, 'towards the field'] (likewise in the fragment cited by Kahle, *MdW*, Pt. ii, p. 6 — לְאַפֵּי בָרָא *le'appē bārā'*); Septuagint: διέλθωμεν εἰς τὸ πεδίον ['Let us go out into the plain']; Peshiṭta: 'Let us go into the open country'; Vulgate: *egrediamur foras* ['let us go out of doors']. Similarly, the Samaritan Pentateuch reads: 'Let us go into the field'; this is also the rendering of the Samaritan Targum. The divergences between these recensions and translations prove that we have here not a common original reading, but a common exposition; and this exposition derives, it seems, from the continuation of the verse, which states: *and when they were* IN THE FIELD (Naḥmanides: 'to my mind, it [the clause, *and Cain said* (וַיֹּאמֶר *wayyō'mer*) *to Abel his brother*] is connected with *and when they were in the field;* for he [Cain] said to him [Abel], "Let us go forth into the field", and he killed him there secretly'). It is to this interpretation that we also owe the fact that some MSS and printed editions note before the clause, *and when they were in the field,* that there is 'a *pisqa* ['space'] in the middle of the verse' — in other words, the mark of a lacuna — although the ancient Masoretes recognize no such break here.

Other attempts have also been made to determine the nature of Cain's words to his brother Abel. Rashi, after alluding to the well-known haggadic stories about the contentions that broke out between the two brothers, adds that in his view the natural explanation of the verse is that Cain started to quarrel and strive with his brother in order to have an excuse for killing him. Some expositors take the view (so, for example, Ibn Ezra, Qimḥi and other exegetes down to our own time) that the meaning of our text is that Cain related to Abel what the Lord had said to him, or a part thereof. All these interpretations are forced. There are commentators who suggest reading another word in place of וַיֹּאמֶר *wayyō'mer,* for example: וַיִּשְׁמֹר *wayyišmōr,* 'and he watched' (Knobel and others), or וַיֶּמֶר *wayyemer,* that is, 'he strove' (Gunkel), or וַיֵּמַר *wayyēmar,* 'he became bitter' (also Gunkel); but these are only desperate attempts to overcome the difficulty.

But there may be a more authentic solution to the problem, namely, to explain the verb וַיֹּאמֶר *wayyō'mer* not in the usual sense of 'speaking', but according to another signification. The Arabic words امر *'amarun,* امار *'amārun,* إمارة *'imāratun* signify a *sign* or *token,* and, more particularly, تُؤمور *tu'mūrun,* denotes a heap of stones placed one on top of the other to indicate the way in the desert, like the Hebrew תַּמְרוּרִים *tamrūrīm,* Jer. xxxi 21 [Hebrew, *v.* 20] (see Gesenius-Buhl, *sub* תמר). In Ethiopic the verb *'mr,* in the intensive conjugation, signifies *to show, to indicate.* All this is related, apparently, to the regular sense of the verb *amāru* in Akkadian, *to see.* It should also be noted that the word امار *'amārun* sometimes means 'an appointed place, a rendezvous', and is used as a synonym of موعد *maw'idun* ['appointed place' or 'time']. Accordingly, we may understand the word וַיֹּאמֶר *wayyō'mer* in our verse (as a play on the word וַיֹּאמֶר in *vv.* 6, 9, 10, 13, 15, 23) in the sense of *fixing a place for meeting*: Cain arranged to meet Abel his brother, and when they were in the field, in the place that he had appointed for this meeting, Cain rose up etc. (after I had written these lines, I found a similar exposition, based on the word امار *'amārun,* in the Hebrew book *'Or Mimmizrāḥ* ['Light from the East'] by David Moyal, Tel-Aviv 1941, p. 10).

When they were in the field] — far from their father and mother, in a place where no people would see or hear them. Compare Deut. xxii 25–27: *But if* IN THE OPEN COUNTRY [literally, 'in the field'] *a man meets a young woman who is betrothed, and the man seizes her ... in the young woman there is no offence punishable by death, for this case is like that of* A MAN RISING AGAINST HIS NEIGHBOURS AND MURDERING HIM; *because he came upon her* IN THE OPEN FIELD, *and though the betrothed young woman cried for help* THERE WAS NO ONE TO RESCUE HER.

Cain rose up against [אֶל *'el*] *his brother Abel*] This is a recapitulation of the words found at the beginning of the verse: *and Cain appointed a place where to meet* [וַיֹּאמֶר...אֶל *wayyō'mer ... 'el*] *Abel his brother.* First *he made the appointment* and afterwards *he rose up;* first he arranged the meeting and then he turned the meeting into an assault. To mark the repetition, אֶל *'el* [literally, 'to'] occurs here after וַיָּקָם *wayyāqom* ['rose up'] instead of עַל *'al* ['upon, against']. The reiteration further emphasizes the words *Abel his brother* — it was *his brother* whom he slew!

THIRD PARAGRAPH

THE MURDERER'S SENTENCE

9. *Then the Lord said to Cain,*
'Where is Abel your brother?'
He said,
'I do not know; / am I my brother's keeper?'

10. *And He said,*
'What have you done? / Hark! your brother's blood
is crying to Me / from the ground.

11. *And now you are cursed / from the ground,*
which has opened its mouth / to receive your brother's blood
from your hand.

12. *When you till the ground, / it shall no longer yield to you*
its strength;
a vagrant and a wanderer / shall you be on the earth.'

13. *Cain said to the Lord,*
'My iniquity is too great / to be forgiven.

14. *Behold, Thou hast driven me out / this day*
from the face of the earth; / and from Thy face I shall seek
to hide;
and I shall be a vagrant and a wanderer / on the earth,
and everyone who finds me / will seek to slay me.'

15. *Then the Lord said to him,*
'Therefore, if any one slays Cain / sevenfold shall he be
avenged.'
And the Lord set / a sign for Cain,
so that any one who came upon him / would not slay him.

16. *Then Cain went away / from the presence of the Lord,*
and dwelt in the land of Nod ['Wandering'], / east of Eden
[qidhmath 'Ēdhen].

9. *Then the Lord said to Cain, 'Where is Abel your brother?'*] Immediately after the murder, Cain rose up and fled (had he still been standing next to Abel's corpse, the question *'Where is Abel your brother'?* would have been out of place); but before he had gone far, he heard the Lord's voice calling him to account for his deed. No human being had seen what had happened, but the Lord saw and knew. In Deut. xxi 1 it is written: *If in the land . . . anyone is found slain, lying* IN THE OPEN COUNTRY [literally, 'in the field'], *and it is not known who killed him* — people do not know, but the Lord knows; before Him everything is revealed and foreseen. This, too, is what the Torah wishes to teach us here by placing the words *the Lord said* in juxtaposition to *and killed him;* no sooner had the murder been committed than *the Lord said to Cain . . . .* Gunkel (pp. 44–45) thinks that according to the text the Lord became aware of what occurred only because the blood of Abel cried unto Him. Had this been the purport, Scripture would have written in conformity with its usual narrative diction: 'and he [Cain] killed him, and the blood of Abel cried unto the Lord from the ground, and the Lord said unto Cain', etc. The cry of Abel's blood is not mentioned till later, *as a reason for the punishment.*

Where is Abel your brother?] This question, as we have seen earlier (pp. 155 f.), is rhetorical, implying rebuke: Why is not your brother, who but a little while ago was walking beside you, with you now? See, he is no more, and you are to blame for it.

I do not know; am I my brother's keeper?] Cain's conscience is now aroused to the full enormity of his deed. It is he, none other, who brought it about that his brother Abel, who had sucked his own mother's breasts, *is no more* (*Where is Abel your brother?*). He makes a desperate attempt to silence the voice that confronts him with this terrifying question and to free himself from the burden of responsibility for his crime by brazen words that reject this responsibility. *I do not know,* etc. This matter is not my concern.

The two motifs to be heard in Cain's words, that of *knowledge* and that of *guarding,* are, as we have seen, the fundamental motifs of the previous section — an interesting parallel.

10. *And He said, 'What have you done?'*] Cain's effort is quite

in vain; it is impossible to silence that mighty voice. It is the voice of the Judge, who responds to the cry of the blood that has been shed. It continues to ask: '*What have you done?*', etc. The significance of the words *What have you done?* — a rhetorical question resembling an interjection — we have explained before (p. 158). The thought is: See now what you have done! How could you do so terrible a thing? This question also contains a parallel to the preceding section.

Hark! [קוֹל *qōl,* literally, 'a voice'] *your brother's blood* [plural in the Hebrew] *is crying to Me from the ground*] Just as a man who is wronged cries to the judge on account of his oppressors, so the shed blood of the murdered man, even though he can no longer speak, cries before the Heavenly Court.

Shed blood is sometimes called דָּמִים *dāmīm* (in the plural), particularly in rhetorical and poetic diction; compare, for example, I Kings ii 5, 31; Isa. i 15; ix 5 [Hebrew, *v.* 4]; and other passages. In the Samaritan Pentateuch, here and in *v.* 11, דָּם *dām,* the singular, is used. The word קוֹל *qōl* also provides a parallel to the previous section.

11. Above I have so divided this verse as to emphasize the parallelism between it and the preceding verse. Two hemistichs of *v.* 10 end with the word *your brother's blood* and *from the ground;* here, in reverse order (of which we have already encountered several examples), we find two hemistichs that conclude with the words *from the ground* and *your brother's blood.* The significance of this parallelism we shall see immediately below.

At the end there comes a word that stands alone, and its very isolation at the conclusion of the verse lends it emphasis: *from your hand,* from the hand of the murdered man's *brother!*

And now] This phrase usually serves to introduce the *conclusion.* Since the charge was brought before My court, it is compelled to pronounce its sentence.

You are cursed] This is the third time that a *curse* is uttered: first it was pronounced upon the *serpent* (iii 14), then upon the *ground* (iii 17), and here upon Cain himself. Because of the first man's sin, the *soil* was cursed; Cain's transgression, which is far graver, brings down a curse on the transgressor himself. The word *you* is emphatic.

From the ground] The parallelism, indicated above, between this and the preceding verse shows that the principle of measure for measure is applied here, and that the expression *from the ground* in this verse must be understood in the very same sense in which it is used in the previous verse. Hence it is not to be interpreted, with some commentators, as meaning *more than the ground* (so, for instance, Rashi, and now Sellers in *JAOS,* 50 [1930], p. 336), or *by means of the ground* (Michaelis and others), or *far from the* [*cultivated*] *ground* (almost all contemporary exegetes); nor is it to be deleted as a duplication taken over from *v.* 10, the remaining words being arranged differently, as Glueck has proposed in *JPOS,* xiii (1933), pp. 101–102. The correct explanation is: your curse shall come upon you from the ground, just as the cry of your brother's blood came to me from the ground (Ibn Ezra: 'through the ground').

Which has opened its mouth to receive your brother's blood from your hand] To understand the full implication of these words, we must take account of the concepts to which they are related and of the terminology that is normally used in Biblical and Canaanite literature to express them. The identical phrase occurs in the episode of Korah and his company: AND THE GROUND OPENS ITS MOUTH, *and swallows them up, with all that belongs to them* (Num. xvi 30); and thereafter: *and the earth opened* ITS MOUTH *and swallowed them up, with their households,* etc. (ibid., *v.* 32); again in Deut. xi 6: HOW THE EARTH OPENED ITS MOUTH *and swallowed them up, with their households, their tents,* etc.; and in Psa. cvi 17: THE EARTH OPENED *and swallowed up Dathan,* etc. The netherworld, that is, *Sheol* (Num. xvi 33: *So they and all that belonged to them went down alive into* SHEOL) is depicted as swallowing up the people in its jaws and drinking their blood thirstily. As a rule, it swallows up the departed; the engulfment of Korah and his company whilst they were still alive was an exception to the rule. In Isa. v 14 it is written: *Therefore Sheol has enlarged its appetite and* OPENED ITS MOUTH *beyond measure, and her* [Jerusalem's] *nobility and her multitude go down, her throng and he who exults in her;* in Hab. ii 5: *His greed is as wide as Sheol; like death he has never enough;* compare also Prov. xxvii 20, xxx 15–16. I have cited additional texts and details bearing on this subject in the *Bulletin of the Jewish Palestine Exploration Society,* ix (1942), pp. 46–49; here I mention only what is necessary to the elucidation of our verse. For this purpose it should further be noted: (a) that the word אֶרֶץ *'ereṣ* ['earth'], like *erṣetu* in Akkadian, sometimes has the sense of *Sheol,* and that in this sense, too, the word אֲדָמָה *'ădhāmā* ['ground'], which is synonymous with it, and is substituted for it in the section of Korah, must at times be understood; (b) that the concepts alluded to date back to an early period in the history of Israel, who inherited them from the Canaanites. In their poems the Canaanites were accustomed to identify Môt, the god of death and the king of Sheol, with his realm, Sheol; and of one who went down to Sheol they used to say that he entered the mouth of Môt and descended into his gullet (see the quotations from the Ugaritic epics that I have cited in *BJPES,* ibid., p. 48). In one of these poems (tablet I* AB, col. i, lines 14–22) it is related that Môt was wont to boast of his achievements thus: 'As the lioness yearns for the wilderness, as the sea-horse longs for the seas, as the wild oxen crave for the pools and as the hart panteth after water, even so is my desire to kill, to kill; I long to slay heaps; lo, with both my hands I devour; behold, seven portions they cut for me, yea, they pour me out a cup [big] as a jug'. The similes are clear: just as every creature longs for what it needs and is naturally suited to it, so Môt yearns constantly to kill, to pile up a great number of corpses on top of one another, heaps upon heaps, multitudes of them; and he swallows up the dead, but knows no satiety; with both hands he brings them to his mouth, and he drinks their blood in a cup the size of a jug. Among the Israelites, needless to say, in accord with their monotheistic outlook, Môt typifying death, was reduced from the status of a deity to that of a demon — of the *angel of death,* to use a later term. However, his essential nature and the fundamental character of Sheol, his domain, remained unchanged, as is clearly to be seen from the verses I have quoted above and from many other verses that I have cited in *BJPES, loc. cit.* Now, our verse is connected with these concepts and this traditional phraseology; Cain slew his brother, and the netherworld greeted his deed with joy, greedily opening its mouth to drink his brother's blood from his hand.

12. *When you till the ground, it shall no longer yield to you its strength*] This shall be your curse *from the ground*. After the earth had been cursed on account of your father's sin, it yielded its produce only exiguously and as a result of hard toil; nevertheless, it was possible to subsist thereon, and you were the very person who gained a livelihood by tilling the soil (*v.* 2). But from now on, the earth will give *you* nought. You and the ground became partners in the act of violence: you gave it your brother's blood, and it accepted this from your hand; therefore the punishment shall be made to fit the crime, and all connection between you and the ground shall be severed.

A vagrant and a wanderer [נָע וָנָד *nāʿ wānādh*] *shall you be on the earth*] This does not connote, as Budde and others have thought, that Cain would be constrained to live a nomad's life. The life of wandering shepherds was certainly not considered a curse; see what is stated in *v.* 2 about Abel and in *v.* 20 regarding Jabal. *A vagrant and a wanderer* does not describe the wandering shepherd, who moves his tent periodically from place to place according to his needs, but one who never finds rest for the sole of his foot and is a vagabond all his days, because he can nowhere obtain his livelihood. In the fearful imprecation of Psalm cix (*vv.* 9–10) it is said: *May his children be fatherless, and his wife a widow! May his children* WANDER ABOUT [נוֹעַ יָנוּעוּ *nōăʿ yānūʿū*] *and beg; and let them seek their bread out of their desolate places,* etc.. Cain's curse was like that put upon these children. Compare also Amos ix 9, where the verb *to wander* [נוע *nūaʿ*] is used to describe the exile of the people of Israel among *all the nations*. The concept of a *vagrant and a wanderer* will be further clarified in our annotation to *v.* 14.

The question may be asked here: why was not Cain sentenced to death like any other murderer? To find the answer to the question we must consider the special circumstances of this episode. First, it must be realized that the purpose of capital punishment is not only to purge the world of existing evil, but to serve also as a preventive example: *and all the people shall hear and fear.* Now in our case there were in the world, apart from Cain, only Adam and Eve; there were as yet no *people* who could learn the lesson of the murderer's death. On the other hand, if people still to be born would see the bitter fate that Cain endured throughout his days, they might possibly draw the moral therefrom. Furthermore, what kind of death penalty could have been imposed in this instance? Death at the hands of Heaven is not the penalty for murder, and, in any case, it would not have been right for the Lord to have slain Cain as well, and thus to have inflicted on Adam and Eve, who were guiltless, a twofold tragedy. Judicial execution is indeed the usual punishment of the murderer, but at that time there were no established courts of law. To be put to death by the blood-avenger is a method of punishment to which the Torah is opposed, as we have already stated, and as we shall note in greater detail later. Where the court cannot sentence the murderer to death because he did not kill wittingly, the Torah imposes on the slayer, as we know, the penalty of banishment to one of the cities of refuge. Similarly in this case, since the death-sentence does not apply to Cain for the reasons mentioned, it is replaced by exile.

13. *My iniquity is too great to be forgiven* [גָּדוֹל עֲוֺנִי מִנְּשׂוֹא *gādhōl 'ăwōnī minneśō'*] / It is not possible to regard these words as a plea for the mitigation of the sentence, as though Cain said: 'The punishment for my crime is greater than I can bear' (so Ibn Ezra and many moderns), because עָוֺן *'āwōn* ['iniquity'] is, as a rule, used with נָשָׂא *nāśā'* [literally, 'lift', 'carry'] in another sense, namely, 'to forgive iniquity'. According to the homiletical exposition of the Rabbis, we have here a rhetorical question (B. Sanhedrin, p. 101b: 'Is my iniquity greater than that of the sixty myriads [Israelites] who are destined to sin before Thee, yet wilt Thou pardon them!'). Although this is not the actual meaning of the verse, there is no doubt that the idea of forgiveness is suited to the context. Naḥmanides gives the correct interpretation: 'My iniquity is too great to be forgiven.' Cain's heart is now filled with remorse; he realizes the enormity of his crime, and accepts the judgement. We shall immediately see in the following comment how this confession links up with the succeeding verses.

14. *Behold, Thou hast driven me out this day from the face of the earth* [אֲדָמָה *'ădhāmā*] / According to the generally accepted opinion to-day, the meaning is: Behold, Thou hast driven me out this day *from the cultivated ground into the desert.* But no one with a sound and sensitive feeling for the Hebrew tongue could

agree with this view. It is true that, in agricultural terminology, the language prefers אֲדָמָה *'ădhāmā* [literally, 'ground'] to its synonym אֶרֶץ *'ereṣ* ['earth']; but the word אֲדָמָה *'ădhāmā,* used absolutely, also signifies the *earth* as a whole, and serves as a synonym of אֶרֶץ *'ereṣ* in all its connotations. It will suffice to mention, for example, the verses that we quoted earlier from the story of Korah, where the two nouns are interchanged (Num. xvi 30: *and the* GROUND [אֲדָמָה *'ădhāmā*] *opens its mouth;* ibid., *v.* 32: *and the* EARTH [אֶרֶץ *'ereṣ*] *opened its mouth*). Hence, in a general expression, such as *to drive out from the face of the* אֲדָמָה *'ădhāmā,* the word must be understood in a general sense: 'from the face of the earth'. It is this general meaning, moreover, that fits the context. In consequence of the Lord's decree, Cain cannot find rest anywhere; no sooner does he arrive at any place than he feels that he cannot remain there. He is ever conscious of being an outcast — cast out from the whole earth. Further proof: in the parallel clauses, *You shall be a vagrant and a wanderer on the earth* (*v.* 12), *and I shall be a vagrant and a wanderer on the earth* (in the continuation of our verse), it is written *on the earth* and not *in the desert.* The expression *on the earth* is a general term that includes also inhabited parts. The parallelism in our verse is synonymous not antithetic; אֶרֶץ *'ereṣ* and אֲדָמָה *'ădhāmā* are identical.

This day] — by the sentence that you have passed on me *this day.* We shall see further on why Cain emphasizes this point.

And from Thy face I SHALL SEEK TO HIDE [אֶסָּתֵר *'essāthēr,* literally, 'I shall be hidden'] / This clause is usually interpreted by contemporary exegetes in accord with their exposition of the preceding sentence, and on the supposition that the Lord was regarded as the God of the Land of Israel, that is, cultivated land; to be hidden from His face means, in their view, to leave inhabited country and wander in the wilderness. But there can be no doubt that, according to the concept prevailing in the Book of Genesis, God's dominion extends over the entire world, over the desert as well as the cultivated regions. It will suffice to recall what is stated in the first story of Hagar (xvi 7): *The angel of the Lord found her by a spring of water in the* WILDERNESS, and in the second narrative (xxi 14–21): *And she departed, and wandered in the* WILDERNESS *of Beer-sheba ... And God heard the voice of the lad . . . for God has heard the voice of the lad where he is . . . And God was with the lad, and he grew up; he lived in the* WILDERNESS, *and became an expert with the bow. He lived in the* WILDERNESS *of Paran.* This apart, the interpretation referred to militates against the requirements of simple logic, for if Cain entered a region where the Lord has no power, he would have been freed thereby from the penalty that the Lord had imposed upon him. The somewhat similar explanation advanced by R. Judah Hallevi in the *Book of the Kuzari* (ii 14) of the verse, *Then Cain went away from the presence of the Lord* (*v.* 16), the meaning of which, in his view, is that Cain left the Land of Israel, is of a haggadic rather than a scientific character. The natural sense of our text requires it to be understood in accordance with our interpretation of the previous sentence (attention should also be paid to the parallelism: *from the* FACE *of the earth — and from Thy* FACE . . .). אֶסָּתֵר *'essāthēr* means, *I shall seek to hide* (auxiliary verbs are not expressed in classical Hebrew): I shall constantly flee from Thy presence, but wherever I go I shall find Thee also there, and so I shall have to flee from that place, too, in my continual and desperate endeavour to hide from Thy face. The thought resembles that of Psa. cxxxix 7–12: *Whither shall I go from Thy Spirit? Or whither shall I flee from* THY PRESENCE [literally, 'face']? *If I ascend to heaven, Thou art there! If I make my bed in Sheol, Thou art there!,* etc.. Compare further Amos ix 2–4, and the unsuccessful attempt of Jonah son of Amittai to escape.

And I shall be a vagrant and a wanderer on the earth] This follows from his preceding words. Since I shall find myself everywhere in the position of an outcast, and I shall constantly have to flee from Thy presence, I shall be a vagrant and a wanderer on the earth all my days and I shall find no rest. The explanation we gave earlier of the expression, *you shall be a vagrant and a wanderer on the earth,* thus finds corroboration. Cain acquiesces in all this as a just punishment for his crime, and to indicate his submission to the judgement he repeats the words of the Lord's decree. The Lord had said: *you shall be a vagrant and a wanderer on the earth;* Cain says: *and I shall be a vagrant and a wanderer on the earth.*

And everyone who finds me will seek to slay me [literally, 'will slay me'] / The meaning is: Although I acquiesce in the punishment that you decree upon me *this day* (now we understand why Cain stressed the words, *this day*), yet I am afraid lest *in the future* something over and above what you decree will befall me: lest everyone that finds me will slay me. In order to understand this apprehension of Cain, we must pay attention to the word *everyone*. Obviously, Cain can be slain only once; and if any one of those who encounter him should kill him, no one else could put him to death. Hence it is clear that *will slay me* means, *will wish to slay me, will seek to slay me* (compare our explanation of אֶסָּתֵר *'essāthēr* ['I shall seek to hide']). Not enough that I shall constantly have to flee from every place upon earth in my endeavour to hide myself from Thy presence, but I shall also be compelled to conceal myself from every human being, since they will *all* desire to kill me and will attempt to do so, for the reason that they will *all* be relatives of the murdered man. There are, and there will be, in the world none save Abel's father and brothers and his brothers' children and children's children, and all of them will wish to avenge his blood, notwithstanding that the murderer also belongs to their family. A similar situation is described in II Sam. xiv 5–7.

This verse also contains parallels to the previous section; in the latter, too, we are told of man's hiding himself from the presence of the Lord God (iii 8) and of his banishment (iii 24).

15. *Therefore*] The force of the word is: In order to remove this apprehension from your mind, and to assure you that only what I said would come to pass, and what I did not say would not happen, I decree and proclaim that *if any one slays Cain,* etc..

If any one slays Cain, etc.] It is forbidden to slay Cain; it is prohibited to take blood revenge. Here the Torah expresses its *opposition to blood-revenge,* which was practised in the ancient East. Only the Lord, the Judge of the whole earth, and human judges who judge in His name, are permitted to pass sentence on the murderer; not the relations of the murdered man in the heat of their anger. See my remarks on this subject in the introduction, § 5, pp. 184 f.

The verse says, *if any one slays* CAIN, not *if anyone slays* YOU, because this is a proclamation addressed to all mankind. The Lord informs Cain (*Then the Lord said to* HIM) of His decree and His proclamation.

The words כָּל־הֹרֵג קַיִן *kol-hōrēgh Qayin* [literally, 'any one slaying Cain'; rendered: *if any one slays Cain*] are not the subject of יֻקָּם *yuqqām* [which in that case would mean: 'vengeance shall be taken on him'], but constitute a separate, dependent clause [*casus pendens*], signifying: if any one will slay Cain, then Cain shall be avenged sevenfold. Compare, for example, i Sam. ii 13: *when any man offered sacrifices* [literally, 'every man sacrificing a sacrifice'], *the priest's servant would come,* etc. (Gesenius—Kautzsch [2], § 116 w.).

Sevenfold [שִׁבְעָתַיִם *šibhʿāthayim*] / This is not to be understood literally. Obviously the meaning is not whoever slays Cain will be punished seven times as much as one who kills any other person; such a penalty would not be in accord with justice. *Seven* [שֶׁבַע *šebhaʿ*] is the number of perfection (see above, pp. 12 ff.); and שִׁבְעָתַיִם *šibhʿāthayim* — that is, seven times — connotes *in perfect measure,* with the full stringency of the law. Compare Psa. xii 6 [Hebrew, *v.* 7]: *purified* SEVEN TIMES; ibid., lxxix 12: *Return* SEVENFOLD *into the bosom of our neighbours.* He who slays Cain will deserve to be punished with the utmost severity, because he will be guilty of a dual offence: the crime of shedding blood, and the sin of contemning the Lord's judgement by augmenting the Divine punishment.

Shall he be avenged [יֻקָּם *yuqqām*] / This is an established legal term, signifying: his slayer shall be punished. Compare Exod. xxi 21: *But if he* [*the slave*] *survives a day or two, he is not to be* AVENGED; *for he* [*the slave*] *is his* [*the master's*] *money.* Similarly ibid., *v.* 20: HE SHALL SURELY BE AVENGED [נָקֹם יִנָּקֵם *nāqōm yinnāqēm*]. The expression derives, it seems, from the practice of *blood-revenge.* The punishment imposed on the murderer at the instance of the court takes the place of blood-revenge; hence the term was transferred from one sphere to the other. Here in the sentence passed by the Judge of the whole earth, the word is used in its juridical sense, as in Exod. xxi 21. In the song of Lamech (*v.* 24), the same expression occurs in a different meaning, apparently; see on this below.

And the Lord set a sign [אוֹת *ʾōth*] *for Cain*] On the explanation of this *sign* as a tribal mark and the objections to which this interpretation is open, see my earlier remarks in the introduction, pp. 180 ff. It appears that the sign is intended specifically for Cain alone, and not for his offspring. Had it been ordained for succeeding generations, this fact would have been explicitly stated, as we find in the case of Abraham in connection with the *sign of the Covenant* between God and himself and his seed after him (xvii 9–12).

From the continuation of the verse we learn to what end the sign was given: *so that any one who came upon him* WOULD NOT KILL [לְבִלְתִּי הַכּוֹת *lebhiltī hakkōth*] *him.* But this clause does not state the *purpose* only; had that been the intention of the text, it would have been formulated thus: 'so that any one who came upon him *should not kill* [לְבִלְתִּי יַכֶּה *lebhiltī yakkē*] *him'*. In addition to explaining the object of the token, it contains an *assurance* to Cain; the אוֹת *'ōth* serves as a warning to others not to slay Cain, and as a promise to Cain that no man would arise to kill him. Other *signs* of this kind are mentioned in Scripture. Such, for example, is the *sign* on the houses of the children of Israel in Egypt: *The blood shall be a* SIGN *for you, upon the houses where you are . . . and no plague shall fall upon you to destroy you, when I* SMITE *the land of Egypt* (Exod. xii 13; compare also *ibid. v.* 23). There is also the sign of the scarlet cord that the spies gave to Rahab at her request (*and give me a sure* SIGN, Jos. ii 12), in order that the children of Israel should not slay her nor her father's house during the conquest of Jericho. Having submitted to the sentence, Cain is entitled to be delivered from blood-revenge. Also in the instances that have been cited, the word אוֹת *'ōth* ['sign'] has a *Lāmedh* [the preposition לְ־ *le*–'to', 'for'] prefixed to it, as in our case: *for* Cain, and not *in* [בְּ־ *be*–] Cain. *To set a sign* IN *someone* means to bring an affliction on a person, intended to serve as an example to others, for instance: *and what signs I have done* AMONG THEM [בָּם *bhām;* literally, 'in them'] (Exod. x 2); *and I will set a sign* AMONG THEM [בָּהֶם *bhāhem;* literally, 'in them'], *and from them I will send,* etc. (Isa. lxvi 19); *when He wrought His signs* IN EGYPT (Psa. lxxviii 43), and the like. *To set a sign* FOR *someone* signifies to appoint a token for a person's good and benefit (compare Exod. xv 25: *There He made* [literally, 'set'] *for them a statute and an ordinance*).

What the sign was is not stated in the text. The rabbinic explanations are known (a horn, a dog, and so forth), but they do not represent the actual meaning of Scripture. According to the plain exegesis of the passage there is no hint as to the nature of the אות *'ōth,* and it is not possible to guess what the text does not tell us.

So that any one who came upon him would not slay him] On the form of the verb — the infinitive, not the imperfect — see the preceding note. The text has הַכּוֹת *hakkōth* [literally, 'smite'] and not הֲרֹג *hărōgh* ['kill'], in order to include an assault that does not cause death. Although the verb הַכּוֹת *hakkōth* can be used as a synonym for הֲרֹג *hărōgh,* it may also signify a simple beating.

16. *Then Cain went away from the presence of the Lord*] After the conclusion of the judgement, Cain left the presence of the Judge; henceforth, as we have explained, he would constantly flee from before Him.

And dwelt in the land of Nod [*'Wandering'*] / Two interpretations have been suggested: (a) Cain dwelt in a land called Nod (in the Septuagint, Ναίδ), which cannot be identified; (b) he abode in a land of 'wandering'; that is, his residence was never permanent but one of constant roaming from place to place. The second explanation is preferable.

קִדְמַת עֵדֶן *Qidhmath 'Edhen* [literally, 'in front of'] / — *east of Eden* (Ibn Ezra). Again Eden and קֶדֶם *qedhem* ['east'] are linked together, as we have noted twice already in the foregoing section (ii 8; iii 24).

FOURTH PARAGRAPH

THE DESCENDANTS OF CAIN

17. *Cain knew / his wife,*
and she conceived / and bore Enoch,
who became a city-builder; / and he called the name of the city
after the name of his son, / Enoch.

18. *To Enoch was born / Irad;*
and Irad / was the father of Meḥujael,

and Meḥijael / the father of Methushael,
and Methushael / the father of Lamech.

19. *And Lamech took unto him / two wives;*
the name of the one was Adah, / and the name of the other Zillah.

20. *Adah bore / Jabal;*
he was / the father of those who dwell in tents and have cattle.

21. *His brother's name / was Jubal;*
he was / the father of all those who play the lyre and pipe.

22. *Zillah, she also / bore Tubal-cain,*
the instructor / of every worker in bronze and iron.
The sister of Tubal-cain / was Naamah.

17. *Cain knew his wife, and she conceived and bore,* etc.] On the parallels to the other paragraphs of this section, and also to the preceding section, see above, the introduction, pp. 178 f., and the commentary on *v.* 1.

His wife] One of his sisters, of course, is meant (v 4: *and he had other sons and daughters*); this explanation is given by all the commentators from Talmudic times to our own day.

Enoch [חֲנוֹךְ *Ḥănōkh*] / The name occurs thrice again in the Book of Genesis. It is also borne by one of the progenitors of the human race descended from Seth (v 18–24); by one of the sons of Midian, the son of Abraham (xxv 4); and by the first-born of Reuben, the son of Jacob (xlvi 9). Both here and in the last mentioned case, the name belongs to the eldest son of the first-born of the founder of the family, that is, to the one by whom the third generation was *inaugurated* [מִתְחַנֵּךְ *mithḥannēkh*]. But possibly the name is associated here with the idea of *dedication* [חֲנֻכָּה *ḥănukkā*] — the dedication of the first city to be built in the world.

And he became a city-builder] In the same way as in *v.* 2, after the sentence, *And again, she bore his brother Abel,* it is stated, *Now* [literally, 'and'] *Abel was a keeper of sheep,* so here after the words, *and she conceived and bore Enoch,* we are told in similar phrasing, *who became* [literally, 'and he was'] *a city-builder.* Hence, just as in the earlier sentence the subject of the verb וַיְהִי *wayᵉhī* [literally, 'and was'] is the son that was born, so in our verse, too, this is the case. Our text refers not to Cain but to his son, Enoch (in *v.* 2 the name of the son [Abel] is expressly emphasized in contradistinction to that of Cain, but there is no need for this here). By using the construction וַיְהִי בֹּנֶה עִיר *wayᵉhī bōne ʿīr* [literally, 'and he was building a city'; rendered: *and he became a city-builder*] rather than וַיִּבֶן עִיר *wayyibhen ʿīr* ['and he built a city'], the Bible, it seems, does not intend to record a single event—the fact that once Enoch built a city—but to tell us what his occupation was over a long period, thus paralleling the earlier statement about the work of Cain and Abel, and the information given subsequently about the pursuits of the three sons of Lamech.

Of all that the ancient tradition narrated concerning Cain's descendants (and undoubtedly the traditional material appertaining to them was abundant and variegated), the Torah cites a few details that prove that, in contrast to the fate of Cain, who was a vagrant and a wanderer on the earth all his days, a many-sided material culture developed among his scions. The importance of all this we have seen in the introduction (pp. 188 f.). Israel's neighbours used to attribute the development of civilisation to their gods, and from the statements of Philo Byblius it is apparent, despite his euhemeristic interpretation, which regards the figures of the gods as supermen whom popular belief deified, that it was the Canaanites, the closest neighbours of the Israelites, who in particular used to assign the innovations and inventions that promoted civilization to the gods and their offspring. The Torah is uncompromisingly opposed to all the beliefs of this idolatrous environment. It is not satisfied with a rationalistic explanation of these beliefs, such as Philo Byblius sought to offer later; it rebuts and negates them completely. It teaches that human culture was created only by mortals, by ordinary human beings, who were no different from the rest of mankind. In conformity with its usual method (see above, pp. 7, 11 f., 39, 50 ff., 76 etc.) the Torah does not controvert or argue; it quietly states the position according to its viewpoint, and sets at nought the opposing opinions by its silence.

For detailed discussion, see below, in the continuation of our commentary. Likewise on the connection between this subject and the section as a whole, note, in addition to what I have stated in the introduction, my remarks at the end of the annotation to *v.* 24.

After the name of his son] — a play upon words בְּנוֹ *b^enō* ['his son'] — בֹּנֶה *bōne* ['builder'].

18. Without doubt, the ancient tradition also gave a detailed account of the generations between Enoch and Lamech; but these particulars were not, apparently, of importance to the Torah's purpose and therefore the text disposes of them summarily — summarily, but in no dry or jejune manner. Despite the brevity of the language, this verse is constructed with artistic perfection, in accordance with the rules governing the division of sentences and the parallelism of the parts, and the phrasing has beauty and balance. For the use of the particle אֶת *'eth* [sign of the accusative] with a verb in the passive, see Gesenius–Kautzsch [2], § 121 a, b. Regarding the distinction between יָלַד *yāladh* [*Qal*: 'bear, beget'] and הוֹלִיד *hōlīdh* [*Hiph'il*: 'beget'], see my observations in *La Questione della Genesi,* pp. 102–104, and in *The Documentary Hypothesis,* English translation, pp. 45–47. On the occurrence of the word יָלַד *yāladh* three times consecutively, see the introduction, end of § 13.

The etymology of the names mentioned in this verse is in doubt. We must also consider the possibility that they are not Hebrew names but have their origin in another language, and that they were modified, to a greater or less degree, when they assumed a form suited to the Hebrew tongue. I shall mention briefly, in each case, the best interpretations that have been advanced, and I shall state what I regard as the most probable theory.

Irad [עִירָד *'Irādh*] / It is explained to mean 'flight' (so ערד *'rd* in Aramaic and Arabic), or to be related to עָרוֹד *'ārōdh* ['wild ass'] (Job xxxix 5), or to signify 'power, strength' (likewise on the basis of Arabic); or it is thought to be an erroneous version of יֶרֶד *Yeredh* [E.V. *Jered*] (v 15–20), formed under the influence of the word עִיר *'īr* ['city'] above.

The following suggestion is perhaps somewhat better grounded. The form of the name in the Septuagint, Γαιδάδ, indicates that the initial letter is not an ordinary *'Ayin* but a *Ghayin,* corresponding to the Arabic غ (the first δ is clearly a mistake: *Dāleth* instead of *Rēš*); and seeing that the Arabic word غرد *ghardun* means a 'cane-hut', we may perhaps regard our passage, which narrates that

Enoch *built* the first *city* and *dedicated* it, and that his son was called by a name signifying *cane-huts,* as providing a parallel to the Canaanite theogonic tradition mentioned by Philo Byblius, according to which *Šemē Mārōm* ['High Heavens'] (this appears to be the correct form of his name) appointed *Tyre* as his dwelling-place and invented *huts of cane* (καλύβας ἀπὸ καλάμων), reed grass and papyrus. The two names *Enoch* and *Irad* constitute, according to this conjecture, a pair of parallel designations of related meaning, just as the two names that follow, *Meḥujael* and *Methushael,* also form a pair, being similar in form and possibly, as we shall see further on, in meaning.

Meḥujael [מְחוּיָאֵל *Meḥūyāʾēl*]—*Meḥijael* [מְחִיָּיאֵל *Meḥīyā(y)-ʾēl*] / In the Septuagint the name appears in various forms, some corresponding to מְחוּיָאֵל *Meḥūyāʾēl,* some to מְחִיָּיאֵל *Meḥīyā(y)ʾēl* and others to מַהֲלַלְאֵל *Mahălalʾēl* [E.V. *Mahalel*] (v 12–17). In the Samaritan Pentateuch the form מְחִיָּאֵל *Meḥīyāʾēl* [with one *Yōdh*] occurs twice.

This name, too, has received a number of different interpretations: whom God blots out, fattens, *smites, quickens,* and others. Possibly it may be explained on the basis of the Akkadian word *maḫḫû* (from the root *mḫḫ;* a *qaṭṭūl* form), which denotes a certain class of priests and seers. The form מְחוּיָאֵל *Meḥūyāʾēl* (**maḫûyu*) may represent a Canaanite *qāṭūl* form, and the vowel *a* after the *Yōdh* is explicable as a fossilized relic of the accusative termination. The meaning of the word will accordingly approximate to *the priest of God, the seer of God.*

The second time, the name is spelt מְחִיָּיאֵל *Meḥīyā(y)ʾēl* (the *Yōdh* is written twice to emphasize the vowel *ī*); instead of מְחוּי *Meḥūy* we have here מְחִי *Meḥī,* a *qāṭīl* formation, like נָקִי *nāqī.* It does not seem likely that מְחִיָּיאֵל *Meḥīyā(y)ʾēl* is a scribal error, which should be emended to מְחוּיָאֵל *Meḥūyāʾēl,* as many scholars do; no scribe would have made so noticeable a mistake as to vary the spelling of the same word occurring twice in succession. Ineluctably we must conclude that the two different forms were fully intended. Nor is this an isolated example. On the contrary, such divergences are due to a common practice, in general use, which accords with oriental principles of thought and literary taste, although incongruous with European intellectual and aesthetic criteria. When two variant traditions exist, they are both quoted, side by side, so as not to invalidate one of them. Not only can there be no objection to this thesis — contrary to the opinion of several scholars whose judgement is moulded by European ways of thinking, to which they are habituated — but we may go further and regard the practice referred to as the customary and favourite method followed by Scripture. Whenever it is possible to vary the phrasing, the Bible endeavours to do so in order to avoid monotony, and such variation is considered a mark of literary elegance. Even the repetitions, which are a heritage from oral epic poetry (see above, pp. 212 f.), are not, in the written books, *literal,* if a change of formulation is at all possible. What has been said of the *form* applies also to the *content.* In the next section we shall discuss an interesting example of two traditions differing from each other in *content;* and countless other instances may be found in Biblical and Talmudic literature. With reference to variations in form, which are also numerous, it will suffice to mention two examples: the name *Peniel* and *Penuel* (xxxii 31–32), and the refrains at the end of the stanzas in the Psalms, which in the majority of cases do not recur in exactly the same wording, but alter their phrasing slightly from time to time.

Methushael [מְתוּשָׁאֵל *M^ethūšā'ēl*] / — in the Septuagint Μαθουσαλά that is, מְתוּשֶׁלַח *M^ethūšelah* [E.V. *Methuselah*]. An explanation of the name has been proposed on the basis of the Akkadian words, *mutu,* 'men', *ša,* 'of', and *ilu,* 'God', that is, *the man of* 'El, *of God.* But since not only the known substantives — מת *mt* (e.g. in the phrase עִיר מְתִים ['city of men']) and אֵל *'El* ['God] — but also the middle element, *ša,* with the signification 'of', are found in the Canaanite idiom (see *Tarbiz,* xii, p. 170 [Hebrew]), there is no need to go beyond it, for this language also permits us to understand the name in the sense indicated. Thus the names מְחוּיָאֵל *M^eḥūyā'ēl* and מְתוּשָׁאֵל *M^ethūšā'ēl* are analogous not only in form but also in meaning.

Lamech [לֶמֶךְ *Lāmekh*] / It is suggested, by reference to the Arabic word يلمك *yalmakuṇ,* that the name means a *strong youth.* Possibly, in agreement with what we have noted in connection with the names *M^eḥūyā'ēl* and *M^ethūšā'ēl,* it may be related to the Mesopotamian word *lumakku,* which signifies a certain class of priests.

19. Now that we have reached *Lamech,* the *seventh* generation from Adam, Scripture speaks of him at length. The text not only mentions the name of his first-born son, but tells us who were his wives, who were the sons that each one bore, what these sons originated, and also the wording of a famous song that Lamech sang to his wives.

The name of the one was Adah [עָדָה *'Adhā*] *and the name of the other Zillah* [צִלָּה *Ṣillā*] / Both names are mentioned here because the Bible desires, as we have stated, to tell the story of Lamech's family in detail. At the same time the reader incidentally learns something that enables him to understand the opening words of the poem in *v.* 23: *Adah and Zillah, hear my voice.* This is one of the graces of the consummate narrative skill that characterizes the text.

As a rule the name עָדָה *'Adhā* (which occurs also in xxxvi 2f.) is connected with the word עֲדִי *'ădhī* ['ornament (s)'], and צִלָּה *Ṣillā* with צֵל *ṣēl* ['shadow, shade'] (for other interpretations see the commentaries). The explanation of the first name is acceptable: a pretty little girl is born, the *ornament* [עֲדִי *'ădhī*] of the family; so her parents call her עָדָה *'Adhā.* The derivation, however, of the name צִלָּה *Ṣillā* from the word צֵל *ṣēl* is not, on the face of it, quite so probable; but we must bear in mind the pleasantness of the rest and ease that wayfarers find in *the shade of trees* when the day grows hot (xviii 4: *and rest yourselves under the tree*). An alternative possibility seems more probable, namely, to connect the name צִלָּה *Ṣillā* with the word צִלְצוּל *ṣilṣūl* ['tinkle'] and not with צֵל *ṣēl* — Arabic صلّ *ṣalla* ['to sound'], not ظلّ *ẓalla* ['to give shade'] — and to interpret it as an allusion to the sweetness of the female voice. If this be correct, the names of the two women form an excellent parallel, pointing to the two charming femine attributes mentioned in Canticles ii 14: *let me see your face, let me hear your voice, for your voice is sweet, and your face is comely.* Compare also the name of Zillah's daughter *Naamah* (*v.* 22), and our remarks on this name in its context, particularly the quotation from the Ugaritic poem that we shall cite later (Tablet V AB i, lines 19–20): *'cymbals in the hand of the musician* [*n'm*], *the sweet-voiced hero sings'.*

20. *Jabal* [יָבָל *Yābhāl*] / — in the Septuagint Ἰωβέλ or Ἰωβήλ.

This name and also the names of his two brothers are derived from the same stem, יָבַל *yābhal.* Apparently these names are intended to point to the important יְבוּל *y^ebhūl* ['yield, produce'] that resulted from the inventions and work of Lamech's sons.

It is of interest that in the case of each of the three sons of Lamech there is some allusion to the name of their ancestor, Cain [קַיִן *Qayin*]. Of Jabal it is said that *he was the father of those who dwell in tents and have* CATTLE [מִקְנֶה *miqne*]; Jubal is called *the father of all those who play the lyre and pipe,* a description that suggests the idea of קִינָה *qīnā* ['dirge'], which originally meant simply a poetic *composition;* as for the third son, Tubal-*cain,* Cain actually forms a part of his name. So, too, *Naamah,* the name of Lamech's daughter, can be connected with the concept of song and קִינָה *qīnā,* as we explained earlier, and as we shall note again further on.

He was] This expression, which recurs in *v.* 21, corresponds to the words *and Cain was,* which introduce the reference to Cain's profession.

The father of those who dwell in tents and have cattle [literally, 'of him that dwells in a tent and cattle'] / — that is, the father of tent-dwellers and cattle-rearers. The verb *dwells,* which is appropriate to *tent* but not to *cattle,* applies to both nouns by the rhetorical usage called by the Greeks *zeugma.* The meaning is that Jubal originated the mode of living in tents and renewed the industry of sheep-rearing, which fell into desuetude and became completely forgotten after Abel died without leaving sons or disciples. The word *father* has here both the literal meaning of *forbear* — that is, the children and children's children of Jabal continued to practise his occupation — and also the sense of *teacher* and founder of the customs, practices and ways of life of a given class. Philo Byblius informs us that *Amunos* and *Magos* were the first to dwell in villages and to rear sheep. On the meaning of their names, see Clemen, *Die phönikische Religion nach Philo von Byblos,* Leipzig 1939, pp. 54–55.

According to the present text, the teachings and occupation of Jabal, as well as those of his brothers, were apparently transmitted to mankind after the Flood through Noah and his sons. Similarly, there is a Babylonian story about books that were hidden before the Flood in the ground beneath the City of the Sun, Sippar, in order to save them from the water, and were disinterred after the Flood.

21. *His brother's name*] See my observations above, on the words *his brother,* at the beginning of the commentary to *v.* 2.

Jubal] Compare my remarks on the name *Jabal* in *v.* 20.

He was] On this, too, see the annotation on the preceding verse.

The father of all those who play the lyre and pipe] — that is, the father of musicians and the originator of their art. On the word *father,* see the note to the previous verse.

Lyre [כִּנּוֹר *kinnōr*] / This is not, of course, the instrument that bears the name כִּנּוֹר *kinnōr* ['violin'] today, but the *lyre,* apparently. See the article by Sellers in the *Biblical Archaeologist,* iv (1941), pp. 36–38.

Pipe [עוּגָב *'ūghābh*] / Needless to say this, too, is not what is known today as עוּגָב *'ūghābh* ['organ'], but a kind of *pipe* (Targum Onkelos and Targum Pseudo-Jonathan: אַבּוּבָא *'abbūbhā'* ['reed, flute']). See Sellers, *op.cit.,* pp. 40–41.

In the Canaanite inscriptions mention is made of one of the gods who was famed as a musician and singer. Thus, for example, in the verses that I quoted in part above (Tablet V AB I, lines 18–20): 'He rose, began and sang, the musician holds the cymbals, the sweet-voiced hero sings'. See my observations on the subject in *Bulletin of the Jewish Palestine Exploration Society,* x (1943), p. 51 [Hebrew].

22. *Zillah, she also bore*] Compare *v.* 26, x 21, and many more examples of this kind.

Tubal-cain [תּוּבַל קַיִן *Tūbhal Qayin*] / — to be read as one word, according to the eastern Masoretes: תּוּבַלְקַיִן *Tūbhalqayin.* For the name *Tubal* see my remarks on Jabal in *v.* 20. The addition of קַיִן *Qayin* may be an allusion, as several commentators surmise, to Tubal's craft, and signifies: 'Tubal the smith, Tubal the artificer'. According to others (Halévy, etc.), the intention is to distinguish between this Tubal, *Tubal the son of Cain,* and *Tubal the son of Japhet* (x 2); but this is hardly probable. Others, again, are of the opinion that the Tubal of our section is after all to be identified with Tubal the son of Japhet, and it is he who is the eponym of the people, mentioned several times in the Bible, whose name is identical with his (see: Isa. lxvi 19; Ezek. xxvii 13; xxxii 26;

xxxviii 2, 3; xxxix 1). The reason for this identification is the statement in Ezekiel xxvii 13: *Javan,* TUBAL *and Meshech traded with you; they exchanged the persons of men and* VESSELS OF BRONZE *for your merchandise.* According to the sequence of the sections before us, this identification must be ruled out, since only Noah and his sons were delivered from the waters of the flood. Furthermore, in Ezekiel xxvii 13, the vessels of bronze constitute only one of the articles of merchandise, and Tubal is but one of the peoples engaged in this trade.

The instructor [לֹטֵשׁ *lōṭēš,* literally, 'sharpener'] *of every worker* [חֹרֵשׁ *ḥōrēš*] *in bronze and iron*] Generally speaking, the meaning is clear: he invented and perfected the manufacture of bronze and iron articles (not necessarily the making of weapons, as some expositors think, for there is not the slightest reference to this in the text). But the word לֹטֵשׁ *lōṭēš* [E.V. *forger of*] is difficult. We should have expected, instead, אֲבִי *'ăbhī* ['the father of'], as in the previous verses; and some commentators believe this to have been the original reading. This conjecture, however, is improbable; for had this been the original text, it is unlikely that so simple a reading would have been corrupted by the copyists and changed to an obscure one. Rashi and many moderns explain the word חֹרֵשׁ *ḥōrēš* in the sense of 'vessel, instrument'; but this, too, is difficult, because forging is only a single process in the making of instruments, and not necessarily the most important one. The same objection applies also to the proposal to read 'forger of *vessels of* [כְּלֵי *kelē*] bronze and iron', or the like. Perhaps we should regard our verse as presenting a play upon words similar to that in Prov. xxvii 17: IRON SHARPENS IRON, *and one man* SHARPENS *another;* that is, Tubal-cain used to *sharpen* the sharpeners, to wit, the workers in bronze and iron.

We know from the Ugaritic writings that the Canaanites used to attribute the craft and art of metal-work to one of the gods called *kṯr wḫss,* which means, *Fit-and-understanding;* and Philo Byblius mentions two brothers who discovered iron and invented the method of processing it; the name of one of them Χουσώρ (this is the correct reading, found in two MSS), that is, *kṯr.*

The sister of Tubal-cain] See my note above, at the beginning of the commentary to *v.* 2, on *his brother.*

Naamah [נַעֲמָה *Na'ămā*] / The text tells us nothing about her, save her name; but without doubt the ancient tradition had much to relate concerning her. Whether the tradition that identifies her with Noah's wife (Bereshith Rabba xxiii 3) is likewise old, it is impossible to say. Possibly we may deduce from the meaning of the name that the ancient tradition already depicted her as the leader of the female players and singers (Targum Pseudo-Jonathan: 'the mistress of *dirges* [קִינִין *qīnīn*] and songs'; Bereshith Rabba, *loc. cit.,* according to the Sages: 'she made music on the drum for idolatry') for the stem נעם *n'm* is frequently used in connection with singing and playing in both the Canaanite and Hebrew languages. I have already quoted above the passage from the Ugaritic poems in Tablet V AB, in which the god that sings and plays before Baal is designated by the title *n'm* ['musician']. So, too, in another Ugaritic poem (Tablet II D, col. vi, lines 31–32), the verb *šyr* is found next to a noun or adjective from the stem *n'm*. Compare in the Bible: Psa. lxxxi 2 [Hebrew, *v.* 3]: *Raise a* SONG, *sound the* TIMBREL, *the* SWEET [נָעִים *nā'īm*] LYRE *with the harp;* ibid., cxxxv 3: *sing to His name, for He is* נָעִים NA'IM [E.V. *for it is pleasant*]; cxlvii 1: *For it is good to* SING PRAISES *to our God; for He is* נָעִים NA'IM [E.V. *for it is pleasant*]; *a song of praise is seemly;* so, too, in ii Sam. xxiii 1: *the* נָעִים NA'IM *of the psalms of Israel* [E.V. *the sweet psalmist of Israel*], which should not be emended, as some exegetes have suggested, nor should נָעִים *nā'īm* be understood in the sense of 'a delightful and beloved person'; its meaning is, apparently, 'one who *made pleasant* [or *sweet*] *the songs,* one who composed them with *sweetness*'. In view of this, Naamah, the younger (female) child of Zillah, corresponds to Jubal, the younger (male) child of Adah.

Regarding a Canaanite goddess called Naamah, see Baethgen, *Beiträge zur semitischen Religionsgeschichte,* Berlin 1888, p. 150; Albright's essay on 'Islam and the Religions of the Ancient Orient', in *JAOS,* 60, No. 2 (1940), in which he refers to this goddess, I have not yet been able to see, as this number did not reach Jerusalem.

FIFTH PARAGRAPH

LAMECH'S SONG

23. *Lamech said to his wives:*
Adah and Zillah, / hear my voice;
you wives of Lamech, / give ear to my speech;
For a man I slew, / as soon as I wounded (him),
Yea, a young man, / as soon as I bruised (him).

24. *If sevenfold / Cain shall be avenged,*
then Lamech / seventy-sevenfold.

23. *Adah and Zillah*] The metre proves that these words are part of the poem proper. It is incorrect, therefore, to regard the word *hear,* in accordance with the suggestion of some commentators, as the commencement of the song.

Hear my voice — give ear to my speech] In order to gain a clear understanding of the characteristics of the traditional rhetoric used in the Bible, it should be noted: (a) that the paired verbs *hear* [שָׁמַע *šāma'*] — *give ear* [הֶאֱזִין *he'ězīn*] occur frequently in the exordium of a poem or an address as an invitation to hearken to the words of the poet or speaker, or, at the beginning of a prayer, to ask God to deign to listen to the voice of the worshipper (for such 'invocations' in general, see Yellin, *K^e^thābhīm Nibhḥarim* ['Selected Writings'], Vol. ii, Jerusalem 1939, pp. 1–2 [Hebrew]); (b) that also the two synonyms *voice* [קוֹל *qōl*] — *speech* [אִמְרָה *'imrā*] are regularly coupled in the literary tradition. In other passages, too, both pairs of expressions are sometimes found *together,* just as in our verse. We read in Isa. xxviii 23: GIVE EAR AND HEAR MY VOICE, *hearken* AND HEAR MY SPEECH; ibid., xxxii 9: *Rise up, you women who are at ease,* HEAR MY VOICE; *you complacent daughters,* GIVE EAR TO MY SPEECH. There are also analogous verses, for instance, Psa. xvii 6: INCLINE THY EAR TO ME, HEAR MY SPEECH; Jer. ix 20 [Hebrew, *v.* 19]: *Yea,* HEAR, *O women, the word of the Lord, and let* YOUR EAR *receive the word of his mouth.* Further examples of the coupling of *hear* and *give ear* are: Num. xxiii 18: *Rise, Balak,* AND HEAR; GIVE EAR *to me, O son of Zippor;* Deut. xxxii 1: GIVE EAR, *O heavens, and I will speak; and let the earth* HEAR *the words of My mouth* (and *ibid., v.* 2: MY SPEECH); Judges v 3: HEAR, *O kings;* GIVE EAR, *O princes;* Isa. i 2: HEAR, *O heavens, and* GIVE EAR, *O earth;* ibid., *v.* 10: HEAR *the word of the Lord, you rulers of Sodom!* GIVE EAR *to the teachings of our God, you people of Gomorrah!;* Hos. v 1: HEAR *this, O priests!* . . . GIVE EAR, *O house of the king!;* Joel i 2: HEAR *this, you aged men,* GIVE EAR, *all inhabitants of the land!;* Psa. xlix 1 [Hebrew, *v.* 2]: HEAR *this, all peoples!* GIVE EAR, *all inhabitants of the world;* ibid., liv 2 [Hebrew, *v.* 4]: HEAR *my prayer, O God;* GIVE EAR *to the words of my mouth;* ibid., lxxxiv 8 [Hebrew, *v.* 9]: *O Lord God of hosts,* HEAR *my prayer,* GIVE EAR, *O God of Jacob! Selah.;* ibid., cxliii 1: HEAR *my prayer, O Lord;* GIVE EAR *to my supplications!;* Job xxxiv 2: HEAR *my words, you wise men, and* GIVE EAR *to me, you who know.*

Akkadian provides similar examples (Albright, *JBL,* lix [1940], p. 304). In Ugaritic, *šmʿ* ['to hear'] — *byn* ['to understand'] are found coupled; compare Tablet II AB, col. v, lines 121–122: *šmʿ lʾalʾin bʿl, bn lrkb ʿrpt,* that is: '*Hear,* O ʾAlʾin Baʿal, *understand,* O thou who ridest upon the clouds'. The word-pair *voice—speech* occurs also in other contexts; see, for instance, Isa. xxix 4: *your* VOICE *shall come from the ground like the voice of a ghost, and your* SPEECH *shall whisper out of the dust.*

For [כִּי *kī*] / Opinions differ regarding the function of this word. It has been suggested: (1) that it indicates a question; (b) that it introduces *oratio recta;* (3) that it is an interjection, like the word הִנֵּה *hinnē* ['lo, behold!']; (4) that it gives a reason for the preceding statement. The last explanation is to be preferred, the sense being: It is fitting, therefore, that you should listen to me, since I have slain a man, etc.. Another possible rendering is: Hear this thing, to wit, that I have, etc..

A man I slew, as soon as I wounded (him) [לְפִצְעִי *lephiṣʿī*], *and a young man, as soon as I bruised (him)* [לְחַבֻּרָתִי *leḥabbūrāthī*] / These words have been the subject of a multitude of varied interpretations, beginning with the well-known Midrashic story concerning the slaying of Cain and Tubal-cain and culminating with the conjectures of modern scholars, such as the view that Lamech's utterance is a kind of 'Sword Song', which eulogizes the achievements of the weapons fashioned by Tubal-cain; or that Lamech sang this song on returning from battle, his garments stained with the blood of his foes; or that we have here a song of general braggadocio (*I have slain* connotes: I am wont to slay). There is no need to consider all the theories one by one; we shall endeavour to unravel the meaning of the verse by a methodical approach.

In the ancient tradition, this poem was apparently connected with the account of a specific event; the past tense of the verb *I slew* points to an actual happening. The Torah passed the incident over in silence, and contented itself merely with quoting the song; this implies that the episode was not of importance to the Torah's purpose, the poem being sufficient. Consequently, we must base our interpretation only on a detailed examination of the wording of the song. From this study we may possibly learn, in broad outline, the story that constitutes the factual background of the poem. But we cannot guess the details, and in any case they are not of importance to us, since our text saw no need to mention them.

The words *man* and *young man* are placed at the beginning of the sentence, that is, they are emphasized (the reverse order is found in xlix 6: *for in their anger they slay* MEN [literally, *a man*]): it was actually a *man* [אִישׁ *ʾîš*] that I slew, etc.; it was indeed a *young man* [יֶלֶד *yeledh*] that I killed, etc.. אִישׁ *ʾîš* means a warrior; יֶלֶד *yeledh* [literally, 'boy'] signifies a lad, a youth; not an old man whose powers have declined, but a young man in the fulness of his strength. Apparently, not two persons are intended; the יֶלֶד *yeledh* is the same as the אִישׁ *ʾîš*, in accordance with the rules of parallelism. In the same way, for instance, it is written in xlix 11: *Binding his* FOAL *to the vine and his* ASS'S COLT *to the choice vine,* the ASS'S COLT being identical with the FOAL; similar examples are frequently to be found in Scripture. Indeed, the usage is characteristic of Semitic poetry generally, quite apart from the Bible. Thus we read in Tablet I* AB of the Ugaritic poems, col. v, lines 18–19: '(Baal) loved a *heifer* in *dbr,* a *young cow* in the field of *šḫlmmt'*; it is manifest that the heifer and the young cow are one and the same thing.

The words לְפִצְעִי *lephiṣʿī* and לְחַבֻּרָתִי *leḥabbūrāthī* are usually interpreted to mean: in order to avenge myself for the wound and the bruise that I received. At first sight this exposition seems correct, since *v.* 24 speaks specifically of revenge. But this argument is not decisive; it is possible that our verse merely reports the killing, and Lamech only afterwards, in *v.* 24, states that he did this because he is accustomed to avenge himself on his enemies. On the other hand, the explanation cited does not accord with the wording of the text, for to express the sense suggested not the preposition *Lāmedh* [לְ־ *le*–] but *Bēth* [בְּ־ *be*–] is required, for example, ii Sam. xiv 7: *that we may kill him* FOR THE LIFE OF [בְּנֶפֶשׁ *benepheš*] *his brother whom he slew;* furthermore, it is not the way of braggarts to emphasize the thrashing given them by their foes.

Also another interpretation has been proposed: '*through* the wound and bruise that I inflicted upon him.' But this, too, is difficult, because for this meaning, likewise, the preposition *Bēth* and not *Lāmedh* is necessary; moreover, it is not clear in which way these extensions of the predicate — לְפִצְעִי *lephiṣʿī* and לְחַבֻּרָתִי *leḥabbūrāthī* — come to amplify the verb *slew.*

In order to understand the passage, we must bear in mind that 'wounds' and 'bruises' do not as a rule prove fatal, nor are they grave injuries, as we can see from Exod. xxi 23–25: after mentioning *life for life* and thereafter *eye for eye, tooth for tooth,* etc., followed by *burn for burn,* then only does Scripture refer to *wound for wound, bruise for bruise* [E.V. *stripe*]. Hence the preposition *Lāmedh* in our verse is to be understood in the sense of the *Lāmedh* in Isa. vii 15: *When he knows* [לְדַעְתּוֹ *ledhaʿtō,* literally, 'At his knowing'] *to reject the bad and choose the good.* There, as I stated earlier, it is doubtful whether the *Lāmedh* has a simple temporal signification, the more probable interpretation being: AS SOON AS *he knows to reject the bad and choose the good.* Here Lamech's words mean: See, my wives, how great is my strength; a mere tap from my hand suffices to slay a young and powerful man! I touched my enemy only lightly — with my finger tips — yet so soon as I inflicted a wound or bruise, I killed him.

What happened, generally speaking, was this: Lamech wounded a certain youth, who was his foe, and slew him; he then boasts with great bravado of this cruel murder.

In the words, *a man I slew, as soon as I wounded* (*him*), one senses a kind of antithetic parallelism to the statement at the beginning of the section: *I have created a man equally with the Lord.*

Eve gloried in the fact that she had formed and given birth to a *man;* Lamech prides himself on having cut off the life of a *man.* The earlier vaunt was *with the Lord;* the later, *against the Lord.*

The words *wound* and *bruise* are also frequently paired in the literary tradition (see my previous observations on *hear my voice — give ear to my speech*). Apart from the verse already quoted, *wound for wound, bruise for bruise,* compare also Isa. i 6: *wounds and bruises,* etc.; Prov. xx 30: BLOWS THAT WOUND [literally, 'bruises of a wound'] *cleanse away evil.*

24. *If sevenfold Cain shall be avenged*] There is an allusion here, of course, to the Lord's utterance in *v.* 15, but apparently with a difference of meaning. The word יֻקָּם *yuqqām* ['avenged'] when used by the Divine Judge connotes, as we have seen, judicial punishment, but Lamech employs it in the sense of personal vengeance. Of my ancestor it was said that he would be avenged sevenfold, but I shall take vengeance on my enemies seventy-sevenfold; whoever wrongs me in the least forfeits his life.

Seventy-sevenfold [literally, 'seventy-seven'] / — that is, *seventy-seven times as much.* The number, needless to say, is not to be taken literally. *Sevenfold* means in perfect measure (see above, on *v.* 15); *seventy-sevenfold* signifies in overflowing measure, more than is due, many for one. The Canaanites also used this phrase to express hyperbole, and in order to enhance the exaggeration they would augment the number and say: *eighty-eightfold.* Thus, for instance, it is written in Tablet I* AB, of the Ugaritic poems, col. ii, lines 19–21: *škb ʿmnh šbʿ lšbʿm tš*[ʿ]*ly ṯmn lṯmnyn,* that is (so I rendered it in *Tarbiz,* xii, p. 177 [Hebrew]): 'he lay with her seventy-seven times, she had intercourse eighty-eight times.' Compare also Tablet II AB, col. vii, lines 9–10.

Just as *Lamech the son of Methusael,* the seventh generation from Adam, is especially linked with the number *seven,* so the number *seven* occurs particularly in association with *Lamech the son of Methuselah,* the *seventh* generation from Enosh (the name *Enosh* corresponds, it will be noted, to *Adam* [both mean *'man'*]); later on (v 31) we are told that he lived *seven hundred and seventy-seven years.* See further on this below.

So ends the Torah's account of the descendants of Cain. After mentioning their original contribution to human culture, the Bible quotes the song of Lamech, which shows that material progress did not go hand in hand with moral advancement. Not only did violence prevail in the world, but it was precisely in deeds of violence that those generations gloried. The very qualities that are ethically reprehensible, and are hateful in the sight of the Lord, were esteemed in the eyes of men. In such circumstances, the Judge of the whole earth could not but execute judgement. All the achievements of material civilization are not worth anything without moral virtues, and cannot protect man from retribution. We have here a kind of prelude to the decree of the Flood.

SIXTH PARAGRAPH

THE BIRTH OF SETH AND ENOSH

25. *And again Adam knew / his wife,*
and she bore a son / and called his name Seth:
'For God has appointed for me / another child [she said]
instead of Abel, / for Cain slew him.'

26. *And to Seth, to him also, a son was born / and he called his name Enosh.*
Then men began once more / to call upon the name of the Lord.

25. *And again Adam knew his wife,* etc.] After completing the genealogy of the sons of Cain, who are not to appear again in the rest of the book, nor even to exist in the world, Scripture proceeds to give a detailed account of the descendants of Seth, the ancestor of all those who will henceforth be mentioned in the book and of all postdiluvian humanity throughout the generations. It was fitting, moreover, to record the beginning of this genealogy already here, at the close of our section, in order to preserve the symmetry of the narrative, which requires that the ending should contain some allusion to the opening theme, and that the section should conclude on a happy note. See on the whole subject my observations in the Introduction, p. 191. At the same time, this paragraph marks the transition to the next section.

The parallels to the beginning of the section stand out clearly.

There:	*Here:*
Now Adam knew Eve his wife; and she bore;	*And again Adam knew his wife; and she bore;*
the child is named by the mother;	the child is named by the mother;
the name is explained by reference to the *Lord* [*YHWH*];	the name is explained by reference to *God* [אֱלֹהִים *'Elōhīm*];
Cain and Abel mentioned;	Cain and Abel mentioned;
two births recorded;	two births recorded;
אֶת ה' *'eth YHWH* ['equally with the Lord'].	בְּשֵׁם ה' *bᵉšēm YHWH* ['upon the name of the Lord'].

The verbal resemblances are indicative of the similarity of the subject-matter. For parallels to the other paragraphs see above, pp. 178 f.

Adam] For this use of the word as a proper name, without the definite article, see pp. 166 f.

And called his name Seth] The name *Seth* [שֵׁת *Šēth*] signifies *foundation* (Isa. xix 10: *And* HER FOUNDATIONS [שָׁתוֹתֶיהָ *šāthōthehā*] *shall be crushed;* Psa. xi 3: *if the* FOUNDATIONS [שָׁתוֹת *šāthōth*] *are destroyed*); this son was to be the foundation of new life for the family and for humanity.

For God HAS APPOINTED [שָׁת *šāth*] *for me another child*] If we interpret שָׁת *šāth* in the simple sense of 'appoint, give', the purport of the verse will be similar to that which we noted in connection with the names *Eve* and *Abel,* where each name was appropriate to the person concerned not only in that it reflected the intention of the one who assigned it in the first instance, but also in the light of the subsequent destiny of the individual (in this case: the *foundation of life,* as we stated). Possibly we may even understand the verb שָׁת *šāth* to mean 'set *foundations*', as it is written (i Sam. ii 8): *For the pillars of the earth are the Lord's and on them* HE HAS SET [וַיָּשֶׁת *wayyāšeth*] *the world.*

This time Eve does not give voice to feelings of joy and pride such as she expressed when her eldest son was born. Her mood is one of mourning and sorrow for the family calamity, and her words are uttered meekly, with humility and modesty. On the first occasion, she gloried in her creative power and her collaboration with the Lord; this son she now regards purely as a gift vouchsafed to her by Heaven. In the former instance, she mentioned the name of the Lord, the Tetragrammaton, which signifies the Godhead in His personal aspect and direct relationship to His creatures (see above, p. 87); now, in the hour of her mourning, it seems as if God is far removed from her, in the supernal heights of Heaven, as the supranatural Creator of nature, as that transcendental Power denoted by the appellation אֱלֹהִים *'Elōhīm* (see *ibid.*). Hence, she uses only the name אֱלֹהִים *'Elōhīm*. An analogy to this may be found in Amos (vi 10) in connection with people who are mourning: Hush! *For* WE MUST NOT MENTION THE NAME OF THE LORD.

Instead of Abel, for Cain slew him] All three sons are mentioned in this verse, which comes, as it were, to summarize briefly at the end the entire contents of the section.

26. *To him also*] See my previous remarks on *v*. 22.

And he called] The subject is Seth (on the son being named by the father see above, p. 198), or possibly it is impersonal: 'he that called called', that is, 'they called his name', or 'his name was called'. Here, too, there is a parallel to *v*. 2.

Enosh] — a synonym for *Adam*. This son would be the founder of the *human race* belonging to the line of Seth, which was destined to survive upon earth, just as Enoch was the *inaugurator* of the branch of mankind descended from Cain, whose days were not prolonged.

Then men began once more to call upon the name of the Lord] — an example of paronomasia: above we read, *and he called his name Enosh*. There is a parallelism of both language and theme here: a human being is called by a name suited to him — *Enosh;* and God is called by a name befitting Him — *Lord* [*YHWH*].

I shall not mention here all the numerous and varied expositions that have been advanced through the years in regard to אָז הוּחַל *'āz hūḥal,* etc. [rendered: *Then men began once more,* etc.], from the Midrashic explanation, which connects the word הוחל *hūḥal* with the term חֻלִּין *ḥullīn* ['profane, secular things'] and sees in our verse a reference to the inception of idol-worship in the world, to the view usually favoured today, according to which this sentence, which emanates from source J, states that in the time of Enosh people began (or Enosh himself began, if the reading זֶה הֵחֵל ['this one began'], found in several ancient versions, be adopted) to use the name *YHWH* ['Lord'] in worship. Nor shall I deal with the theories belonging to the sphere of religious history that are based on this interpretation, or with the objections that can be raised against it in view of the occurrence of the name *YHWH* in the preceding paragraphs, which are also attributed to J. I shall only give my own views on the subject.

The expression *to call upon the name of the Lord* does not necessarily imply a ritual act. It is a general phrase that conveys only the idea of calling, without indicating either the significance or the purpose of the invocation. These may vary with circumstances and can be determined only by reference to the context. It is possible to say even of God Himself that He *calls upon* [E.V. *proclaims*] *the name of the Lord* (Exod. xxxiii 19; xxxiv 5–6), and it is obvious that such an invocation has not the same character as that uttered by human beings. In the present case, too, the expression is to be understood according to the context. Cain could not teach his offspring to know the *Lord* and to *call* upon His name, that is, to address Him by His particular designation and to feel His personal proximity, for he was compelled, as stated, to *hide himself* constantly *from the face of the Lord.* The antithesis seen by the Israelites between *calling upon the name of the Lord* and *being estranged from the Lord's face* [i.e. presence] is demonstrated by Isa. lxiv 7 [Hebrew, *v.* 6]: *There is no one that calls upon Thy name . . . for Thou hast hid Thy face from us.* As for Adam and Eve, we have already noted in our commentary on the previous verse why they were unable, during their period of mourning, *to call upon the name of the Lord,* and were forced to restrict themselves to the name אֱלֹהִים *'Elōhīm.* But on the birth of Enosh, when Adam and Eve perceived that not only had a third son been born to them to replace the first two sons whom they had lost, but that, as additional compensation, they had also been vouchsafed a grandson through their third son, forming the beginning of a new generation and bringing incipient hope for the future, they were comforted from their mourning. They again felt, because of the blessing that rested upon their home, the nearness of the Lord, and once more they were able *to call upon the name of the Lord* in religious joy.

This interpretation is well suited to the wording of the verse. The adverb *Then* cannot refer, as is usually held, to the lifetime of Enosh, but only to what has been previously mentioned, namely, the *time* when Enosh *was born.* With respect to the verb הוּחַל *hūḥal,* it should be borne in mind that in classical Hebrew no distinction is made between the initial performance of an action and its reiteration. Just as the verb בָּנָה *bānā* can mean both to *build* and *rebuild,* so the verb הֵחֵל *hēḥēl* can signify to *commence* and *recommence;* here it connotes *recommence.*

Then men began once more to call upon the name of the Lord — a happy ending and a parallel to the close of the next section (vi 8): *But Noah found favour in the eyes of the Lord.*

SECTION FOUR

THE BOOK OF THE HISTORY OF ADAM

(CHAPTER V, VERSE 1 — CHAPTER VI, VERSE 8)

INTRODUCTION

§ 1. *Delimitation of the Section.* The commencement of the section is indicated by the heading, *This is the book of the history of Adam,* but its termination is not marked with equal clarity. As a rule it is assumed that *the book of the history of Adam* extends only as far as the end of chapter v; the first four verses of chapter vi are regarded as an independent passage or as a prologue to the section of the Flood, whilst verses 5–8 are held to be the exordium of that section. To me it seems that the whole forms one integrated section as far as vi 8, and that the section of the Flood begins only at vi 9. My reasons are as follows:

(a) Only in vi 9 do we find the new rubric, *This is the history of Noah,* which corresponds to the previous heading.

(b) The last verse of chapter v does not give the impression of being the conclusion: it mentions Noah and the birth of his sons and then leaves the subject suspended, as something to be completed later.

(c) On the other hand, the verse, *But Noah found favour in the eyes of the Lord* (vi 8), is a very fitting ending: in accordance with the customary practice of stating in general terms what is subsequently to be recounted in detail, it reverts to Noah and tells us briefly the gist of the story concerning him that will be narrated at length in the next section.

(d) From another aspect, too, this verse forms a suitable conclusion: it provides the story with a *happy ending,* which is likewise in keeping with the prevailing technique of the narrator's art.

(e) The paragraph vi 5–8 contains a number of parallels to the first paragraph of the section; this conforms to the literary principle that requires the closing passage to allude to the opening theme. Thus, at the beginning of the section it is stated, *In the day that God* CREATED MAN (v 1), HE CREATED THEM (*ibid., v.* 2), *in the day when* THEY WERE CREATED (*ibid.*); and here, MAN WHOM I CREATED (vi 7). In the first paragraph we read, HE MADE *him* (v 1); and here, THAT HE MADE MAN ON THE EARTH (vi 6), THAT I HAD MADE THEM (*ibid. v.* 7). In the initial passage it is written, AND HE BLESSED THEM (v 2); and here, *But Noah* FOUND FAVOUR IN THE EYES OF THE LORD, an allusion to the fact that at the time of the universal retribution the benison bestowed upon Adam found fulfilment in Noah and his sons, as we are explicitly informed later on (ix 1f.), *And God* BLESSED *Noah and his sons, and said to them*: 'BE FRUITFUL AND MULTIPLY, AND FILL THE EARTH', etc. — precisely the same terms in which the first man was blessed (i 28).

(f) There are further analogies and links between the paragraphs; worthy of particular note are the parallels existing between the eleventh paragraph and those preceding it, and also the one following it, as we shall see further on, in § 9, and subsequently in the continuation of the commentary; attention should also be paid to our remarks on vi 6.

(g) Numerical symmetry of the kind that we found in the previous sections (pp. 13 ff., 94, 191 ff.) can be observed in our section only if we take the whole of it, from v 1 to vi 8, into consideration (see on this below, § 11).

§ 2. Within the limits that we have determined, this section, like the previous one, comprises several different topics. These are:

(a) *The list of generations from Adam to Noah* (v 1–32). This part consists of ten paragraphs, one for each of the ten generations.

(b) *The story of the sons of God and the daughters of men* (vi 1–4).

(c) *How retribution was decreed on the generation of the Flood, and Noah found favour in the eyes of the Lord* (vi 5–8).

§ 3. Let us, to begin with, consider the first topic: *the list of generations from Adam to Noah.*

Three sons of the first man are mentioned by name in the Torah. One of them, Abel, died childless. A brief genealogy is presented of his elder brother, Cain, in the preceding section, and the subject is closed. The offspring of Cain were all overwhelmed by the waters of the Flood and did not survive; hence the Torah is content to dismiss them with a summary account. After chapter iv they remain outside our purview. The third son, Seth, is the most important of them for the genealogy of mankind, since from him was descended Noah, the father of resuscitated humanity after the Flood, and the inheritor of the first man's blessing. Consequently, it is proper that the pedigree of man through the line of Seth should be given at greater length. All this accords, as we explained in our introduction to the story of Cain and Abel, with the usual method adopted in the Book of Genesis. We observe a similar procedure in connection with the family of which the children of Israel were an offshoot: the genealogy of the sons of Keturah and Ishmael (xxv 1–18) is recorded briefly, but a detailed account is subsequently given of the descendants of Isaac (xxv 19ff.), whilst Ishmael and the sons of Keturah, who are not relevant to the ancestry of the Israelites, are not mentioned again, save indirectly. Esau's offspring are listed succinctly (chapter xxxvi), then the story of the heirs of Jacob, the father of the Nation, is recounted at length (xxxviiff.), but Esau is never again referred to in the whole book. The *children* of Noah are treated in the same way: a concise pedigree of Noah's sons is given in chapter x, followed by a more elaborate account of the scions of Shem (xi 10–32), from whom stemmed Abraham, the ultimate progenitor of the children of Israel and the spiritual ancestor of humanity (*the father of a multitude of nations*), and a source of blessing to all the families of the earth.

Most modern commentators call chapter v the *Sethite Genealogy, Sethitenstammbaum;* but this is not correct. It is the genealogy of *the children of the first man* through the line of Seth: the superscription, *This is the book of the history of Adam,* is proof of it.

§ 4. Of each one of the founding fathers of the world mentioned in the section, we are given the following details: his name; his age at the birth of his eldest son (or, in the case of Adam, his most important son relative to the history of mankind and the preservation of the human species); the name of this son; the number of years he lived after the son's birth; a general intimation that he had other sons and daughters; his age at the time of his death. *Noah,* however, is an exception, for mention is made not only of his first-born but of all his three sons, and his vital statistics extend only as far as the birth of his sons, the rest being given later. For the other patriarchs, the text employs an unvarying formula — unvarying, that is, in its essential form, but not in all particulars. On the general similarity between all the paragraphs, as well as the differences between them, I shall have something to say later on (§ 8).

The record of the age of each patriarch at the time when the first-born or the most important son was born is of interest in that it marks the date of the inauguration of the new generation; it enables us to determine, by simple addition, all the dates of birth and death from the creation of the world to the birth of Noah's children. If we take into consideration what is stated subsequently (vii 6, 11; viii 13) regarding Noah's age at the time of the Flood, we can also calculate the date of the Flood, which marks the end of the first epoch of the life of man upon earth. According to the existing text, the Flood began in the year 1656 after the creation and ended in 1657.

On examining the genealogy, we are confronted by a number of difficult questions. Those appertaining to specific verses we shall discuss in the notes to the respective passages, in the continuation of our commentary. Here we shall deal with the problems relating to the genealogical chapter as a whole, namely:

(a) How is the astonishing longevity of the ancestors of the world to be understood?

(b) What is the relationship of our text to the parallel traditions of the ancient Orient?

(c) How are we to explain the divergences between the Masoretic recension and the Samaritan and Septuagint texts in regard to the chronological data, and which is the original tradition?

(d) What is the relation between the genealogy given here and that of the children of Cain recorded in the preceding section?

§ 5. With the first two questions — namely, the longevity of the patriarchs and the connection between our passage and the parallel lists of the ancient East — I have dealt fully in a separate essay that is due to be published soon in the *Louis Ginzberg Jubilee*

Volume [Hebrew section]; here, then, I can be brief. Any one wishing to make a detailed study of the subject, will find the material in the aforementioned article. In the present discussion, too, I shall consider the two questions together, since they are interdependent.

Every one who reads our section is amazed at the great ages attained by the patriarchs of the world, which far exceed the normal bounds of human life. Apologists have, indeed, attempted in various ways to lend credibility to the figures, but these attempts cannot be regarded seriously. To this category, for instance, belongs the hypothesis that the years mentioned here are not years of twelve months each, but much shorter periods of time. It cannot be questioned that words like *nine hundred years* mean, quite literally, what they state. Nor can it be doubted that a specific significance, in accordance with the Torah's system, attaches not only to the genealogical chapter as a whole but also to the individual figures listed therein. Certainly, Scripture did not intend to satisfy the curiosity of idle inquirers who wish to know how many years one man lived, or how old another was when his eldest son was born. Assuredly, it wishes to inculcate some lesson in keeping with its general spirit and aim.

However, the numerous proposals put forward by contemporary scholars with a view to elucidating the subject and determining the Torah's intention in this chapter also fail of their purpose, and their conclusions are unconvincing. In my essay, mentioned above, I have cited the most important of them; here, then, I shall content myself with a brief reference to the following:

(a) Von Gutschmidt (in Nöldeke, *Untersuchungen zur Kritik des Alten Testament,* Kiel 1869, pp. 111–112) surmised that the object of the Bible was to show that the Exodus occurred in the year 2666 of Creation, after the completion of two thirds of a world cycle of 4,000 years.

(b) Bousset (*ZAW,* xx [1900], pp. 136–147) took part of the chronological data from the Masoretic text and part from the Samaritan Pentateuch and Septuagint, and, with the help of the composite recension thus achieved, he obtained interesting figures for the dates of certain important events: the Exodus from Egypt, for example, took place, according to this scheme, in the year 2501 of Creation, the dedication of the First Temple in the year 3001, and so forth.

(c) Jepsen (*ZAW*, xlvii [1929], pp. 251–255) accepted the Samaritan chronology in chapter v and the Masoretic dating in chapter xi, and concluded accordingly that the First Temple began to be built in 2800 *anno mundi*, only the Samaritans altered chapter xi in order to prove that their sanctuary on Mount Gerizim was built in 2800, and the Jews emended chapter v to show that the Second Temple was erected in 3600.

All these conjectures, as well as others that I have mentioned in my essay, are based on involved calculations and encounter many difficulties, as I have explained there; to go over the ground again in detail would be superfluous. But here, too, we must take full cognizance of one point, namely, that it is not possible to solve the problem without investigating the traditions current in antiquity among the eastern peoples on matters of this kind.

A tradition concerning *ten* heads of primeval generations are found among many peoples of the ancient Orient: the Babylonians, the Egyptians, the Persians, the Indians, and others. The closest parallel to the Biblical tradition is the Babylonian concerning *the ten kings who reigned before the Flood*. It is to this tradition, which was undoubtedly known in the environment in which the ancestors of the people of Israel lived, that we must devote particular study.

Until 1923 this Babylonian tradition was unknown to us except from the Greek account of Berossus; but even the late testimony of Berossus was sufficient to make us aware of remarkable parallels between the Biblical record and the Babylonian tradition that he cites. In the case of both we find that the earliest generations are divided into two groups, one antediluvian and the other post-diluvian; that the antediluvian period comprises a series of *ten* notable individuals; that an amazing longevity (the Babylonian figures far exceed those of the Torah, an average of myriads of years being allotted to each monarch prior to the Deluge) is attributed to the important personages living before and after the Flood; that the length of life gradually decreases after the Flood until it reaches the normal span of today. To this it was also possible to add, at the time when we knew only the evidence of

Berossus, a few parallels among the proper nouns. Some of the names appearing in the Greek text of Berossus were regarded as Akkadian, and were explained according to etymologies appertaining to that language; as a result of these interpretations, parallels were found between the signification of these names and that of several names occurring in our section. The discoveries made in recent years, of which I shall speak later on, have proved that these names are not of Akkadian but Sumerian origin, and consequently the etymological derivations — and with them, the parallels between the names — were shown to be erroneous (*Adamu,* the second name on the list of Assyrian kings published by Poebel, does not fall within our discussion). Nevertheless the analogies that we have indicated above (and they have been corroborated by the new discoveries) suffice to demonstrate that there is a similarity here that cannot be considered fortuitous.

At the time when only the evidence of Berossus was available to us, Oppert endeavoured (in *GGN,* 1877, pp. 205–209, 214–220, and also in *The Jewish Encyclopaedia,* s.v. 'Chronology') to elucidate with its help the chronology of our section. He found by computation a definite relationship to exist between the length of time from the Creation to the Flood according to our text, namely 1656 years, and the period covered by the reigns of the antediluvian kings according to Berossus — a total of 432,000 years. These two numbers are exactly divisible by 72 and are related to one another in the ratio of 23 to 6,000. Now 23 solar years, each consisting of 365¼ days, contain 8,400 days or 1,200 weeks. Thus 1,200 weeks in the Biblical chronology correspond to 6000 years in the Babylonian reckoning. The Biblical total is equivalent to 72 units of 23 years, that is, $72 \times 1{,}200$ weeks; whilst the Babylonian figure is the sum of 72 units of 6,000 years; or, if we divide the years into five-year periods, it is the same as $72 \times 1{,}200$ lustrums. In other words, the Babylonian source has 86,400 lustrums as against 86,400 weeks in the Bible.

But this theory is also unsatisfactory. At first sight, it is true, the parallel between the 86,400 lustrums of the Babylonian chronology and the 86,400 weeks of the Biblical dating may appear remarkable and attractive. But ultimately we must realize that this parallelism is achieved by Oppert only by means of complicated calculations (what I have cited above is the simplest part of them); nor should we forget that the numbers easily yield to much manipulation, if care is not taken to avoid the introduction of imaginary factors into the computations. Formerly, I was inclined to the view that it was possible to detach the number 86,400 from the complicated calculations referred to, and to regard it simply as a characteristic figure of the sexagesimal system in use among the Sumerians (60 × 60 × 24, which is the number of seconds in a day), and to conjecture, on this basis, that there was a common tradition in the ancient East concerning 86,400 units of time that elapsed before the Flood, and that these units were, according to the Babylonians, periods of five years, whereas the Torah, in contradistinction to this view, considered them to be weeks. But after further study I was convinced that even this restricted hypothesis was not acceptable, for the following reasons:

(a) Our chapter contains not the slightest allusion to a *hebdomadal unit,* and it is hard to imagine that the Torah, when adopting a new chronological system in contrast to that of the Babylonians, would not have been at pains to draw the attention of its readers in some way to the principle underlying its chosen method of dating.

(b) On the other hand, the unit of *five years,* the *assumed* basis of the Babylonian chronology, is conspicuous in our chapter, as I shall show later, and precisely, it may be added, as the underlying principle of the *Torah's own* chronology, not as that of an alien system to which Scripture is opposed.

This apart, account must be taken of the ancient Babylonian records recently discovered, and of their chronological data, *which differ from those of Berossus.*

These archives were published in 1923 by the English Assyriologist Langdon, from the Weld-Blundell collection. They consist of two documents in the Sumerian language, belonging to the end of the third or the beginning of the second millenium B.C.E. One, referred to as W.B. 62 is very short, containing the list of the ten kings who reigned before the Flood, and the length of each reign. Langdon first printed it in *JRAS,* 1923, pp. 251–259. The other, identified as W.B. 444, was first published by Langdon in the second volume of *The Weld-Blundell Collection,* Oxford 1923, pp. 1–27, and pls. I–IV. It comprises a long list of kings extending almost to the end of the dynasty of Isin, at the head of which are recorded the names of the antediluvian kings — eight in all, in accordance with the tradition that the inscription reflects — and the number of years that they ruled respectively (pp. 8–9 and pl. I). In my essay, cited previously, I included a bibliography of the articles dealing with Langdon's publications; there is no need, therefore, to do so again here. I shall only mention the fact that in 1939 Jacobsen published, on the basis of these and other documents, a fundamental and comprehensive work on the Sumerian king list (cited above, p. 188) in which he proved *inter alia*: (a) that the long Sumerian king list did not originally include the monarchs who reigned *before the Flood,* but commenced with the first dynasty after the Deluge; (b) that the roll of antediluvian kings originally came from another source, namely, the mythological epic belonging to the city of Eridu; (c) that it was transferred from that epos and placed at the beginning of several recensions of the long list, such as W.B. 444, and possibly of other lists, too; or it was reproduced as an independent summary, like the one in Tablet W.B. 62. Jacobsen also succeeded in identifying a fragment of the original version of the epic, in Tablet K. 11,624 of the British Museum, which contains only a few incomplete lines.

As I indicated earlier, all the parallels that could be established on the basis of Berossus' statements, except those that rested on illusory etymologies of proper names, have been corroborated by these ancient texts. The antediluvian kings numbered only eight according to W. B. 444, but according to W. B. 62 there were actually *ten,* as Berossus states. The matter was apparently a disputed point among the Babylonian scholars; but, be that as it may, what interests us is the fact that the tradition underlying one of the two ancient archives, as well as the later evidence of Berossus, gives the number as *ten,* the same as that of the founding fathers of the world enumerated in our chapter.

We must now investigate the chronological data of all the Babylonian sources, and see whether they can help us to solve the problem of the chronology of our chapter. To be convincing, the solution must satisfy all the following requirements:

(a) It must not depend on complicated calculations, but should be quite simple.

(b) It must be based on a numerical system commonly used by the Torah, and consequently one that is known to its readers.

(c) The requisite information should all be found in the text itself.

(d) It must explain not only the interval of time between Creation and the Deluge, but also another matter, which the scholars dealing with our problem have almost wholly neglected, although it plays an important role in our chapter, to wit, the life-span of the ten patriarchs.

(e) It should also be able to elucidate the chronology of the Babylonians.

We shall endeavour to see if we can find a solution that will satisfy all these conditions.

Both in the two ancient Sumerian documents and in Berossus the chronology is founded on the Sumerian *sexagesimal system.* According to this method of reckoning, sixty years constitute a time-unit called *šūš;* ten *šūš,* that is, 600 years, equal a *nēr;* sixty *šūš,* that is, 3,600 years, equal a *šar;* sixty *šar,* that is, 216,000 years, equal a *great šar* [*šūššar*].

The chronological data in the three sources in our possession are not identical, but upon examination we shall find that despite the differences there are elements common to all three of them. In W. B. 444, after the separate figures relating to the reign of each individual king, it is explicitly stated (col. i, line 38) that the total length of the monarchic period preceding the Deluge was a *great šar* plus *seven šar* (i.e. 241,200 years). In W. B. 62, the total is not expressly mentioned, but if we add together the years that all the kings reigned (with the minor emendation correctly proposed by Dhorme in *RB,* xxxiii [1924], p. 549), the total will come to *one hundred and twenty šar* plus *seven šar* (i.e. 457,200). According to Berossus, the sum of all the individual reigns is exactly *one hundred and twenty šar* (i.e. 432,000 years). Thus, in all three documents we find a round number of *šars* — either *sixty* or *a hundred and twenty* (twice *sixty*) — with the addition, in the case of two of them, of the sacred number *seven.*

These two elements, the *sexagesimal system* and the number

seven, are common also to the Israelite way of reckoning. I have already indicated above (p. 192) that many round figures based on the sexagesimal system occur very frequently in Biblical literature and in Talmudic and Midrashic works; for example, one hundred and twenty, three hundred, six hundred, one thousand and two hundred, three thousand, six thousand, twelve thousand, thirty thousand, sixty thousand, six hundred thousand or sixty myriads, and so forth. They all signify: a great number or an exceedingly great number.

As regards the number seven, I have shown earlier (pp. 13 ff., 94, 191 ff.) how it prevails in each of the three preceding sections. This is equally true of the whole of the rest of the Book of Genesis (see my remarks, written eighteen years ago, in *GSAI,* New Series, i [1925–1926], pp. 224–228; subsequently in *La Questione della Genesi,* p. 332, and in *The Documentary Hypothesis,* 1942, English translation, p. 96. Gordis in his essay in *JBL,* lxii [1943], pp. 17–26, overlooked what I had already stated before him). The *addition of seven* to round numbers of the sexagesimal system, such as we observed in the two aforementioned Sumerian documents, also obtained among the Israelites. *One hundred and twenty,* for example, means a *large number;* when *seven* is added it connotes *an even greater number.* Thus the years of Sarah's life not only reached the round number of *one hundred and twenty,* but exceeded it by *seven* (xxiii 1). The number of provinces in the Persian kingdom, which is given as *a hundred and twenty* in the Book of Daniel (vi 2), totals *one hundred and twenty seven* in the *Book of Esther* (i 1; viii 9; ix 30).

And another point. A detailed study of the chronology of the entire Book of Genesis makes it apparent that all the numbers of years listed therein (apart from a few exceptions, which prove the rule, since they are due to special circumstances) can be grouped under two heads: (a) multiples of *five,* that is, numbers exactly divisible by five, whose last digit is 5 or 0; (b) multiples of *five* with the addition of *seven.* Now a lustrum is part of the sexagesimal system, since it comprises *sixty months.*

It clearly follows that the chronology of the Book of Genesis as a whole is also founded on the dual principle of the *sexagesimal system* and the *addition of seven.* Let us take, for instance, the chronological data appertaining to the patriarchs of the people of Israel.

Abraham: his age when he left Haran was 75; when Isaac was born, 100; when he died, 175. Sarah: at Isaac's birth her age was 90; at her death, 127 (120+7, as explained). Isaac: when he married Rebecca he was 40; when Jacob and Esau were born, 60; when he died, 180. Jacob: his age when he went down to Egypt, 130; at his death, 147 (140+7). Joseph: he was sold at the age of 17 (10+7); when he stood before Pharaoh he was 30; he died at 110.

The use of this system is also to be found outside Genesis, in other books of the Bible; but we cannot go into details here.

Now let us examine the ages in our chapter. To facilitate our study, I shall arrange them in a special table (in square brackets I give the figures derived from other parts of Genesis: vii 11; ix 28–29).

	Age when first son was born	*Remaining years of life*	*Total*
Adam	130	800	930
Seth	105	807	912
Enosh	90	815	905
Kenan	70	840	910
Mahalalel	65	830	895
Jared	162	800	962
Enoch	65	300	365
Methuselah	187	782	969
Lamech	182	595	777
Noah	500	[450]	[950]

We see at once that all the numbers in this table likewise belong to one of the two categories previously mentioned: they are either exact multiples of *five,* or else multiples of *five* with the addition of *seven* (one number, the years of Methuselah's life, was twice augmented by seven, one septennium having been added to his age when his eldest son was born, and another to the remaining years of his life). And since there are five such additions (one for Seth, one for Jared, two for Methuselah, one for Lamech), it follows that the sum of the last column is also a multiple of five

It should also be noted that the numbers *five* and *seven* are specially stressed in the text, in a way calculated to attract the reader's attention. The composite numbers in our chapter are arranged almost wholly in ascending order, that is, the units precede the tens, and the tens the hundreds (on the ascending and descending order of composite numbers see *La Questione della Genesi,* pp. 166–171, and *The Documentary Hypothesis,* English translation, pp. 51–53). Consequently, the units *five* and *seven* are mentioned first whenever they occur, and hence they are conspicuous. In the enumeration of Lamech's years — *seven and seventy* years, and *seven* hundred years (*v.* 31) — the emphasis given to the number *seven* is even more manifest.

We have already seen that the total number of years that elapsed from the creation of the first man to the *end* of the Flood, that is, until the beginning of the era of the new humanity, was, according to what is stated here (and later in viii 13), 1657. This figure does not, by itself, convey anything; but since the number of days in a solar year — 365 — is clearly alluded to in our chapter, in the length of Enoch's life (*v.* 23: *five and sixty years and three hundred years*), it is worth seeing if the number of days in 1657 years is significant. Possibly the number 365 in *v.* 23 is intended by Scripture to provide us with the key to the understanding of our subject, as though to say: Pray do not forget that every year has 365 days. In point of fact, if we calculate the number of days, we again find the familiar use of the *sexagesimal system augmented by seven.*

Of the round numbers referred to, which are composed according to the sexagesimal system, one is 600,000 — sixty myriads — a high figure that indicates an exceedingly large amount. Now 600,000 days make 1643 solar years of 365 days each. If we add seven plus seven, as was done in the case of Methuselah's years, we obtain exactly 1657. We have here, then, a pattern similar to that of the Babylonian chronology: a number based on the *sexagesimal principle* with the *addition* of twice times *seven.*

The fact that the total of 600,000 days is not expressly mentioned is not a valid objection. The omission is characteristic of the Torah. The number of the seventy nations enumerated in chapter x was, without doubt, purposely contrived (it will suffice to recall the allusion in Deut. xxxii 8), yet it is not expressly mentioned in the text. Similarly the number of bulls offered up during the Festival of Tabernacles was clearly fixed at seventy by deliberate design, nevertheless it is only by computation that we are able to arrive at the figure.

Our method of interpretation also offers a satisfactory explanation of the aggregate of years lived by the world's ten founding fathers. If we add together the years of their lives up to the end of the Flood — that is, until the six hundred and first year of Noah's life — the total comes to 8226 years. Now *three million* days (this, too, is one of the globular numbers — half of *six hundred myriads*) is equivalent to 8219 years, and by *the addition,* as usual, *of seven* years, we obtain 8226 exactly.

In the same way all the individual numbers in our chapter, without exception, conform to this system, as we shall show in detail in the continuation of our commentary to each verse.

It is inconceivable that all this should be accidental. Undoubtedly these numbers have a specific significance. What is it? What was the aim of the Torah in giving us these ages? At this stage we approach the focal point of the problem under discussion, to wit, the inquiry into the Torah's intention in our chapter.

For this purpose, we must pay particular attention to the *divergences* between the Babylonian and Biblical traditions.

The Babylonian tradition was essentially, as we have seen, of a mythological epic character. It told of the ancient kings, the representatives of the monarchy that 'descended from heaven' (W.B. 444, col. i, lines 1, 41), kings who were in part divinities, or demi-gods, or human beings who had become deities; and it linked their memory with various mythological legends that are still reflected in the account of Berossus. To these kings was attributed an excessively exaggerated longevity, tens of thousands of years, on the average, to each one. The Torah sets itself in opposition to all this. Scripture did not consider it right to invalidate completely all the existing traditions on the subject, or to pass them over in silence, since they could be of value for its didactic purpose. However, it sought to purify and refine them, and to harmonize them with its own spirit. As usual, this disapproval of the alien tradition does not find expression in polemic or argument. The Torah states its own view quietly, setting the contrary opinion at nought by the calm exposition of its own concepts. It is correct — the Bible comes to tell us — that there lived before the Flood ten generations of notable personages; but they were only ordinary mortals, not gods, or demi-gods, or even men transformed into divinities, and they had no mythological associations whatsoever. They were born, they begot sons and daughters, and in the end they died; that is all. Even about Enoch, concerning whom wonderful tales were undoubtedly recounted among the Israelites (we shall deal with this subject later on), the Torah gives us no details. It only varies the phrasing slightly when speaking of him, as though to hint at the special importance attaching to him among the earliest patriarchs; but the Bible conceals more than it reveals, so as not to validate by its authority the fabulous stories current among the masses. This apart, these persons are never alluded to as *kings,* but simply as heads of families. There is no reference here to *kingship that descended from heaven,* only to Adam (*Man*) and the children of 'Adam who were formed from the ground. Neither monarchy nor might is important in the eyes of the Torah, for God's pleasure is not in the power of man. These individuals are notable only on account of the fact that they are the *fathers* of humanity; their genealogy explains how the stream of life that God had created in His world flowed generation after generation, and teaches us that all the children of men are actually the children of *Man* [*Adam*], the scions of the first man by his wife Eve, the descendants of one pair, and that there is no distinction between them. We are not to believe that some of them belong to the seed of divine royalty, whom the rest of the human race is destined to serve; we must realise that they are all the offspring of one father and mother, and are all kin to one another.

This is what the Torah seeks to inculcate in opposition to the Babylonian tradition. Similarly with regard to its chronology, Scripture wishes to negative the fantastic figures, which attribute to each king a longevity that is unnatural to human beings and makes them almost godlike. The Torah does, indeed, accept and confirm the thesis that these generations, since they were still near to the time of their creation, exceeded the life-span of our generations, but they did so in human, not in divine, measure. Not one of them attained the age of a thousand years, the day of the Almighty (Psa. xc 4). It is true that their epoch was a long one, its days totalling sixty myriads with the addition of twice times seven years, and that the aggregate of the days of their lives came to a far greater number still — to half of six hundred myriads plus seven years; but they were *days,* not *years,* and *a fortiori* not longer periods of time, like the units of the Babylonians who measured the reigns of their kings in *šars,* that is, in units of 3600 years. Although the ages in our section may appear high compared with the normal human life-span, yet if we bear in mind the notions prevailing in the environment in which the Torah was written, and the impression that the reading of this section must have left on its ancient readers, they will seem, on the contrary, low and modest. Scripture sought to diminish the exaggerated traditions current in the ancient East, and at the same time to preserve the harmony of the numbers, which pointed to the harmony that ruled in the world.

§ 6. Let us now pass on to the *third problem.*

The chronology of the Samaritan recension differs from that of the Masorah, and the dating of the Septuagint deviates from both. Following are the divergences in the Samaritan Pentateuch.

The years of *Jared's* life are given as 847, of which 62 preceded and 785 followed the birth of Enoch; *Methuselah* lived 720 years, 67 before and 653 after the birth of Lamech; *Lamech's* years came to 653, consisting of 53 before the birth of Noah and 600 thereafter.

In the Septuagint, the total years of each life-span does not differ from the Masoretic record except in the case of *Lamech* (753 years). On the other hand, the figures for the years prior to the birth of the first son show divergences in most instances, and only the ages of *Jared* and *Noah* (according to some MSS also of *Methuselah*) agree with those of the Hebrew text. For *Adam, Seth, Enosh, Kenan, Mahalalel and Enoch,* the number is higher than that of the Masorah *by a century,* and for *Lamech by six years.* In the case of *Methuselah* there is a deviation only in a few MSS, which give his age at the birth of Lamech as 167 years (twenty years less than the Masoretic figure), but apparently this is a mistake, for according to this reckoning Methuselah would have survived the Flood. The number 187 found in the other MSS is not a later correction to make it accord with the Masoretic text, but the original reading of the Septuagint. The error may derive from the number 67 in the Samaritan text. There is no need for us to deal here with the chronology of the Book of Jubilees nor with that of Josephus Flavius, since the former is dependent on the Samaritan recension and the latter on the Septuagint.

What is the cause of the divergences between the three texts, and which recension has preserved the original figures? Much has been written on this subject, and the answer remains in dispute. Having regard to the results of our investigation in the preceding subsection [§ 5] concerning the correspondence between the Masoretic chronology and the ancient system obtaining in the Babylonian documents, we may conclude, it would seem, that it is the Masoretic chronology that is the original, and that the differences in the other recensions were brought about by later alterations. It is possible to explain these modifications as due to the tendency to follow fixed, systematic schemes, which is frequently to be observed both in the Samaritan Pentateuch and in the Septuagint; we have already noted earlier a number of examples of changes resulting from this trend, and immediately below, in § 7, we shall meet with yet another instance. In the Masoretic text, the numbers that give the age of begetting do not form an ordered series: although at first the figures steadily decrease, from Adam to Mahalalel (130, 105, 90, 70, 65), yet subsequently they increase (Jared 162), drop again (Enoch 65), rise once more (Methuselah 187), and again diminish (Lamech 182), before the enormous jump in the case of Noah (500). But in the Septuagint the numbers grow progressively smaller until we reach *Jared* (signifying: 'going down'!), and thereafter they increase steadily (230, 205, 190, 170, 165, 162, 165, 187, 188, 500). What the Septuagint attains by *raising* the ages, the Samaritan Pentateuch achieves by *reducing* them (a hundred years for *Jared,* and one hundred and twenty for *Methuselah*). The order of the latter recension is similar to that of the Septuagint (130, 105, 90, 70, 65, 62, 65, 67, 53, 500), with a solitary exception in the case of Lamech (53), which was necessitated by the year fixed for the Flood. According to the Samaritan system, Jared and Methuselah and Lamech died together in the year of the Deluge.

§ 7. Let us now turn to the *fourth problem,* the question of relationship between the genealogy of *the sons of Cain* (iv 17–22) and that of *the sons of Adam belonging to the line of Seth* (v 1–32).

The names of the founding fathers of the world in our chapter, beginning with *Enosh,* bear a remarkable resemblance to the names that appear in the family-tree of the sons of Cain. *Enosh* corresponds to *Adam,* Cain's father (the two names have the same signification ['man']); *Kenan* [קֵינָן *Qēnān*] is the equivalent of *Cain* [קַיִן *Qayin*]; the series *Mahalalel — Jared — Enoch* parallels, in reverse order, the series *Enoch — Irad — Meḥujael; Methuselah* is the counterpart of *Methushael;* thereafter *Lamech* appears in both pedigrees. The parallelism is even more exact in the Septuagint, which reads *Methuselah,* in chapter iv, instead of *Methushael,* and, according to some texts, even *Mahalalel* in place of *Meḥujael.* These variant readings are to be explained in the light of the tendency towards stereotyped patterns, on which we have already remarked in several places, including the previous subsection [§ 6]. Be that as it may, even according to the Masoretic text the similarity is striking, and cannot be regarded as fortuitous. The customary analysis, based on the documentary theory, which attributes the genealogy of the sons of Cain to source J, and the genealogy in our chapter to source P, does not solve the question of the relation of the two sections.

Our exegetical approach provides a satisfactory explanation of the problem, consistent with what we have noted among the Babylonians. There existed divergent Babylonian traditions relative to the kings who reigned before the Flood. According to one tradition, these kings numbered *ten,* according to another, *eight;* most of their names were common to both sources. A similar position, apparently, obtained among the Israelites in antiquity: one tradition referred to *ten* antediluvian generations, from Adam to Noah, and another to *eight* generations, from Adam to the sons of Lamech; the majority of the names of the heads of the generations were to be found in both versions. Thereupon the Torah adopted a similar method to that mentioned earlier, in our commentary on iv 18 (pp. 232 f.), and accepted both accounts, placing them side by side. Generally, when the Torah makes use of earlier sources, it has no intention to subject them to historical criticism, and to investigate, for example, if two traditions germinated from a single seed or not. This is not of importance to Scripture, whose purpose is to inculcate, by means of traditional sagas, religious, ethical and national truths. This applies also to the present case. The two accounts — the one listing eight generations from Adam to Jabal and his brothers, and the other ten generations from Adam to Noah — could easily be linked together as the offspring of two families who were descended from two sons of the first man; and it was possible to make the whole subject an important object-lesson that is apparent to the reader who studies the text attentively. The two families, which from one aspect develop side by side along parallel lines, differ from each other in another aspect that is of the utmost importance. The offspring of Cain, as we have already noted, could not inherit from their father the knowledge of the Lord, since he was constantly hiding from the Lord's presence; and so they were able to promote in their circle only material culture, which does not suffice to serve as a shield against retribution, and in consequence they were all destroyed by the Flood. On the other hand, the descendants of Seth were heirs (not all, in truth, but the elect among them) of the knowledge of the Lord, a fact that is alluded to both at the beginning of their genealogy, in connection with the birth of Seth's first son (iv 26), and also at the end, in the words of Lamech the son of Methuselah (how different is this Lamech from Lamech the son of Methushael, the scion of Cain!), who, when his eldest son was born, set high hopes on him in the name of the Lord (v 29); and afterwards, again, in connection with Shem the son of Noah, we read (ix 26): *Blessed be the Lord, the God of Shem.* Now the knowledge of the Lord and the moral attributes based thereon bring to man the blessing that all material civilisation cannot bestow; it is they that cause Noah, *a wholly righteous man in his generations,* to find favour in the eyes of the Lord, and to be saved with his entire family from the waters of the Flood.

§ 8. I have indicated earlier, at the beginning of § 4, that, although all the paragraphs in chapter v resemble one another in their essential construction, they are not absolutely identical. It is worth while examining the matter, at this point, in detail.

The *first* paragraph is distinguished from the others by its special exordium (the second part of *v.* 1, and *v.* 2), as well as by a number of other expressions, for example: *and he begot a son in his own likeness, after his own image* (*v.* 3); *and he called his name* (ibid.); *and the days of Adam were* (*v.* 4) instead of *and Adam lived;* and in the end, *that he lived* (*v.* 5).

The *seventh* paragraph, concerning *Enoch,* also employs distinctive phraseology: *Enoch walked with God* (*vv.* 22, 24), followed by *and he was not, for God took him.*

The *ninth* — penultimate — paragraph corresponds to the first in the use of expressions like *and he begot a son* (*v.* 28), *and he called his name* (*v.* 29); and in making mention of God (*ibid.*). Another distinguishing feature is the fact that the *reason* for the name given to the son is stated (*ibid.*).

These three paragraphs — the first, the seventh and the ninth — are further differentiated from the remaining paragraphs by their exalted and almost poetic style.

The *tenth* paragraph (*v.* 32) is exceptional in that it commences, *and Noah was . . . old* instead of *and Noah lived,* and also in that it mentions not only the first son but the three sons of Noah, yet after acquainting us with their birth it records nothing more. The rest of Noah's life-story is left untold, so that Scripture may revert to it later.

There remain six paragraphs (2, 3, 4, 5, 6, 8) that are almost identical in form. But even in their case the repetitions do not resemble the typical instances of literal recapitulation, such as those found in connection with the construction of the Tabernacle (Exod. xxv–xxxi, xxxv–xl) and the offerings of the princes (Num. vii 12–83). In the description of the work of the Tabernacle, the entire account is repeated word for word, except for the change of tenses (*and you shall make* — *and he made,* and the like), and in the record of the offerings of the princes, both the sacrifices and the weights are identical, likewise the quantities, and only the names of those who bring the offerings change. In our passage even the numbers change; nor are they accidental figures devoid of significance for the reader, but on the contrary they evoke associations and present new ideas in every paragraph. We need only mention, for instance, the 365 years of Enoch's life, corresponding to the days of the solar year, or the 777 years that Lamech lived; in regard to the other numbers, see below in the continuation of the commentary.

Even in minor details, there is discernible the desire to introduce as much variation as possible. We have already seen that instead of *and Noah lived,* our wording is (*v.* 32), *and Noah was . . . old;* so, too, although as a rule it is stated, and all the days of *so-and-so* WERE [וַיִּהְיוּ *wayyihᵉyū*], yet twice — with respect to *Enoch* and *Lamech* — our text has וַיְהִי *wayᵉhī* ['and was' (singular)] for וַיִּהְיוּ *wayyihᵉyū* [plural]. This stylistic trait has its parallel in the recurring verses of certain Psalms, to which we have referred earlier (p. 233).

§ 9. The *eleventh* paragraph, which tells *the story of the sons of God and the daughters of men* (vi 1–4), is one of the obscurest in the Torah. The elucidation of its content and significance depends largely on the interpretation of its individual words and phrases; we shall not, therefore, deal with this matter here in the introduction, but at the end of the commentary to the passage, after it has been annotated in detail, point by point. For the present we shall only consider the relationship between this paragraph and the other parts of the section.

In the first place, why does the paragraph come at this particular juncture? The answer to the question is very simple. Since the Torah desired to mention the subject, this was the most suitable place for it. The story belongs to the period preceding the Deluge; hence it could be recorded only after the general survey of the antediluvian generations, and before the paragraph that informs us of the Divine decision to bring the Flood upon the earth. The Torah declares that *in those days* (vi 4), that is, in the days of the generations mentioned in Chapter v, this episode occurred.

Not only the phrase *in those days* constitutes a link between this paragraph and those preceding; but also in the opening words, *And it came to pass, when* MEN *began* TO MULTIPLY *on the face of the ground* (vi 1), a reference is to be seen to the *increase* of *man's* offspring, recorded above in the clause that occurs nine times in succession: *and he begot sons and daughters.* The allusion to this clause is still clearer in the continuation of the verse: *and daughters were born to them.*

Just as there is a connection with what precedes, so there is also a link with what follows. Here, at the beginning of the paragraph, it is written, *to multiply* [לָרֹב *lārōbh*], and further on, at the commencement of the next paragraph, *that* [*the wickedness of man*] WAS GREAT [רַבָּה *rabbā*] (*v.* 5); here (still in *v.* 1) we have, *on the face of the ground,* and later (in *v.* 7), *from the face of the ground;* here we read (*v.* 2), *and* [*the sons of God*] *saw,* and subsequently (*v.* 5), *and* [*the Lord*] *saw;* here we find (*v.* 2), *that they were fair* [literally, 'good'], and below (*v.* 5), *that the wickedness of man was great* (*good looks* are contrasted with *bad morals*). In the middle of both paragraphs there occur, with identical meaning, the words *and the Lord said.* To these verbal parallels may be added further analogies of theme with which we shall deal in the continuation of the commentary.

Most exegetes see in the episode narrated in this paragraph the reason for the Deluge, but this is incorrect; there is not the slightest indication in the text of such a connection. We shall revert to this point later.

§ 10. The *twelfth* paragraph (vi 5–8) tells us of the Divine decision to bring retribution upon the generation of the Flood on account of their wickedness. The nature of their wickedness we have already learnt from the song of Lamech: it was usual in that period to commit acts of violence and then to *boast* of them (see above, pp. 243 f.). Later it will be expressly stated: *and the earth was filled with* VIOLENCE (vi 11); and again, *for the earth is filled with* VIOLENCE *through them* (ibid. *v.* 13). Here the Bible informs us that not only the sons of Cain but even the sons of Seth were almost wholly, save for the elect few in their midst, men of violence. The world, which had been created with paternal love, was filled with enmity and wrong-doing to such a degree that it was impossible to reform it, and there was no option but to destroy it.

The passage describes the position in general terms only; it is content to hint lightly, at the end of its account of the antediluvian period, to the decree that put an end to this epoch. The details will be given in the next section, in accordance with the usual method of providing *first a general outline and then a detailed account.*

However, the section could not close thus. A fitting conclusion must end on a *happy note* (see above pp. 190 f.). Therefore we are told in the last verse that Noah found favour in the eyes of the

Lord. Here, too, there is a slight allusion to events to be recounted in detail later. This reference suffices, however, to show the reader a ray of light in the darkness, and to give the section a happy ending.

§ 11. The numerical symmetry, which was clearly discernible already in each of the three preceding sections (see pp. 13 ff., 94, 191 ff.), constitutes here, in paragraphs 1–10 of our section, a basic element, and an important part, too, of the content itself, as we noted in § 5, and as we shall see again further on. Nor is this all: this harmony of numbers is reflected also in the general structure of this section not less than in the earlier sections. The word אָדָם *'ādhām* ['Adam, man'], which expresses the principal theme of *the book of the history of Adam,* occurs fourteen times in the section — twice times *seven.* The name אֱלֹהִים *'Elōhīm* ['God'] is mentioned *seven* times; so, too, the synonymous verbs בָּרָא *bārā'* ['created'] and עָשָׂה *'āśā* ['made'] appear jointly *seven* times. Alongside the number *seven,* the symmetry of the sexagesimal system is also in evidence in the over-all pattern of the section. The name of the Lord [*YHWH*] is mentioned in the section *six* times; the verb יָלַד *yāladh* ['bore, begot'], *thirty* times — five times *six;* the nouns בֵּן *bēn* ['son'], בָּנִים *bānīm* ['sons'], בָּנוֹת *bānōth* ['daughters'] — apart from the figurative usage, *son of five hundred years* [i.e. 'five hundred years old'] — occur *twenty-four* times, that is twice *twelve.* And the number of paragraphs into which the section is clearly and unmistakably divisible is precisely *twelve.*

§ 12. The relation betwen our section and the one preceding is similar to that between the story of the Garden of Eden and the account of Creation. In the same way as the making of man which is first described in the story of Creation in general outline as the formation of one of the world's creatures, is retold in full detail in the story of the Garden of Eden as a basic theme of that section (see pp. 90 ff.), even so the account of the birth of Seth and Enosh, which has already been narrated in summary form at the end of the story of Cain and Abel as the conclusion of the episode that occurred in the family of the first man, is here repeated at greater length, with all its chronological details, as the foundation of the genealogy of man upon earth. At the same time, there recur here, at the commencement of our section, several expressions appertaining to the creation of man that we have already encountered in the Creation story or at the beginning of the narrative of the Garden of Eden. Overleaping the personal and family episodes in the lives of Adam and Eve and their children, chronicled in chapters ii, iii and iv, they link this section, whose theme embraces all humanity, with what is related in the first pages of the Book concerning the creation of the world and the genesis of mankind therein. This recapitulation, too, is in keeping with the normal practice followed at the beginning of the 'histories', as we shall explain in detail further on, in the opening lines of the commentary to the first paragraph. On the verbal parallels to the preceding section see below, in the notes to v 3, 29.

§ 13. *Special bibliography for this section.* In accordance with the method I adopted in connection with the previous sections, I append here a bibliographical list of publications, appertaining to this section, that appeared after the year 1934, in so far as these are known to me despite wartime conditions.

Junker, 'Zur Erklärung von Gen. 6, 1–4', *Biblica,* xvi (1935), pp. 205–212; Kuhn, 'Die Lebenszahl Lamechs, Gen. 5 31', *ZAW,* liv (1936), pp. 309–310; Closen, *Die Sünde der "Söhne Gottes", Gen. 6, 1–4,* Roma 1937; Wright, 'Troglodytes and Giants in Palestine', *JBL,* lvii (1938), pp. 305–309; Kroon, 'De Hemelvaart van Henoch', *Studiën,* cxxxi (1939), pp. 397–403; Lewy, 'Nāḫ et Rušpān', *Mélanges Syriens offerts à M.R. Dussaud,* Paris 1939, pp. 273–275 (compare *JBL,* lv [1936], p. xviii); Morgenstern, 'The Mythological Background of Psalm lxxxii', *HUCA,* xiv (1939), pp. 76–114; Joüon, 'Les unions entre les "Fils de Dieu" et les "Filles des Hommes" (Gen. 6, 1–4)', *Rech. Sc. Rel.,* xxix (1939), pp. 108–112; Guillaume, 'A Note on the meaning of Gen. vi 3', *AJSL,* lvi (1939), pp. 415–416; Graham, 'Adam and Enosh', *Expository Times,* li (1939–1940), p. 205; Ben-Mordecai, 'B'shaggam: an Obscure Phrase in Gen. vi 3', *AJSL,* lvii (1940), pp. 306–307; Albright, *From the Stone Age to Christianity,* Baltimore 1940, pp. 226–228; Pfeiffer, *Introduction to the Old Testament,* New York–London 1941, pp. 199–202, 204–205; Cassuto, '*Maʿăsē b^{e}nē hāʾĕlōhīm ūbh^{e}nōth hāʿādhām*', in *Essays Presented to J. H. Hertz, Chief Rabbi,* pp. 35–44 [Hebrew]; Bamberger, 'The Rebel Angels' (summary), *JBL,* lxiii (1944), p. iv.

RUBRIC OF SECTION

CHAPTER V

1. *This is the book of the history of Adam.*

1. *Book* [סֵפֶר *sēpher*] / This noun is a loan-word from the Akkadian language (*šipru,* from the root *šapāru,* 'to send'); originally it denoted a missive that was *sent* from one place to another, and subsequently it came to mean anything in writing. Stories such as those narrated in the preceding chapters can be recorded in writing in a book, or they may be recited by heart; but the present section which includes so many numbers, is conceivable only in *writing.* Hence it is called a book.

The history of Adam] Here the word אָדָם *'Adhām* is used as a proper noun, signifying: the First Man. This is the book that recounts the history (תּוֹלְדוֹת *tōl^edhōth*) of the first man and his children and children's children, for as long as they trace their ancestry to him. After the Flood the people will claim descent from Noah, and will be called the *children of Noah.* The phrase בְּנֵי אָדָם *b^enē 'ādhām* (also בְּנֵי הָאָדָם *b^enē hā'ādhām*) [literally, 'sons of man' or 'sons of the man'] means *children of the human species* and not *children of Adam.*

FIRST PARAGRAPH

ADAM

[1. continued] *In the day that God created / man,*
in the likeness of God / He made him.

2. *Male and female He created them, / and He blessed them,*
and called their name Man, / in the day when they were created.

3. *And Adam lived / thirty and a hundred years,*
and he begot [one] in his own likeness, after his image, / and called his name Seth.

4. *And the days of Adam were, / after he begot Seth,*
eight hundred years; / and he begot [other] sons and daughters.

5. *Thus all the days / that Adam lived*
were nine hundred years / and thirty years;
and he died.

In the opening sentences of the paragraph (the second part of *v.* 1, and *v.* 2) the text reverts to the creation of man. Just as in the case of each of the other patriarchs of mankind mentioned in the section it is stated when his father begot him, so here, in regard to the first man, who had neither father nor mother, we are told how the Creator formed him. The recapitulation of the story of man's creation, which had already been recounted previously, corresponds to what is normally found at the beginning of the 'histories'. Thus, after we have been apprised that *Noah begot Shem, Ham and Japheth* (*v.* 32), we are again informed (vi 9–10): *This is the history of Noah . . . And Noah begot three sons, Shem, Ham and Japheth.* We find the same in many subsequent instances; for example, after the statement that *Terah begot Abram, Nahor and Haran* (xi 26), it is further recorded (*ibid.* 27): *Now this is the history of Terah. Terah begot Abram, Nahor and Haran.* Similarly, Scripture writes of Ishmael: *This is the history of Ishmael, Abraham's son, whom Hagar the Egyptian, Sarah's handmaid, bore to Abraham* (xxv 12), thus repeating the particulars that had been narrated earlier. So, too, relative to Isaac: *This is the history of Isaac, Abraham's son: Abraham begot Isaac* (ibid. 19).

The details that are duplicated here are precisely those that have a special importance for the main theme of our chapter, which is the continued existence of the human race, created in the Divine image, and its dispersion upon the face of the earth. We shall deal with this point in detail later.

The exordium begins with the words, *In the day that God created man*, and ends, . . . *Man, in the day when they were created* — a chiastic parallel between the beginning and the end. Compare above (ii 4): *the heavens and the earth when they were created — in the day when the Lord God made the earth and the heavens*, and my comments on that verse (pp. 98 f.).

In the day that God created] This phrase, as well as that below, *in the day when they were created*, belongs to the ancient Creation tradition relative to the Garden of Eden, which is reflected both in the Book of Genesis and in the Book of Ezekiel (see above, pp. 75, 99).

God [אֱלֹהִים *'Elōhīm*] / Since every statement of this exordium, apart from the clauses: *in the day that... created* and *when they were created,* recapitulates what was narrated in the story of Creation (i 26–28), the name *'Elōhīm,* and not *YHWH* [*'Lord'*], is used here in conformity with the exclusive use of *'Elōhīm* in the story of Creation. This apart, the expression *in the likeness* could not fittingly be linked with the Tetragrammaton.

Man] As we see clearly from *v.* 2, the substantive אָדָם *'ādhām* serves in this opening passage as a common noun in accordance with its signification in i 26–27; and here, as there (*him, them*), the pronoun referring to it occurs first in the singular and then in the plural, because of the word's collective meaning.

In the likeness of God He made him] This circumstance is again noted here in order to provide a preliminary basis for what we shall subsequently be told concerning *the generations of the children of men.* It is stated later (*v.* 3): *he begot in his own likeness after his image;* thereby Scripture declares that since Adam, who was created *in the likeness of God,* begot his children *in his likeness,* it follows that also Adam's children were formed *in the likeness of God.*

Although earlier it is written (i 26): *in our image, after our likeness,* and so, too, further on (*v.* 3): *in his own likeness, after his image,* here we have *in the likeness* alone (similarly, in i 27, we find only *in His own image, in the image*), on account of the rhythm of the verse.

On the parallelism, בָּרָא *bārā'* — עָשָׂה *'āśā,* compare ii 4.

2. *Male and female He created them* [בְּרָאָם *berā'ām*] / — previously (i 27): *male and female He created them* [בָּרָא אֹתָם *bārā' 'ōthām*]. This fact is mentioned here, because the continued existence of the race is dependent thereon. The use of בְּרָאָם *berā'ām* in stead of בָּרָא אֹתָם *bārā' 'ōthām* [both forms signify: 'He created them'] is due to the rhythmic requirements of the sentence (3+2; 3+2).

And he blessed them] — above (i 28): *And God blessed them,* etc. The blessing is recorded here because it refers to procreation, as I have explained previously (pp. 51 f., 58).

And called their name Man] This was not reported before; but since the other patriarchs who are to be mentioned later will receive their names from their parents, it was appropriate to state here who named Adam. Thus we have here a parallel, both in theme and phrasing, to *vv.* 3, 29, and to the commencement and conclusion of the preceding section, as well as to the giving of names in chapters i–iii.

In the day when they were created] The close of the exordium corresponds to the opening. See above on *In the day that God created* (*v.* 1).

3. *Lived — begot*] The meaning is not, as Gunkel holds, that when Adam was so-and-so many years old, he begot, etc.. If that were the sense, the wording would have been, as in *v.* 32: And Adam was a hundred and thirty years old, and he begot. The order of the verbs before us requires us to understand the text thus: *After* Adam had lived a hundred and thirty years, he then begot.

Adam [אָדָם *'ādhām*] / Here it is a proper noun: the First Man.

Thirty and a hundred years] The ages of begetting recorded in our chapter range between 65 and 187 (save in the exceptional case of Noah). They correspond in detail to the chronological structure of the chapter as a whole, of which I have spoken in § 5 of the introduction, that is, they are round numbers belonging to the *sexagesimal system,* to which, at times, *seven is added.* The lowest number, 65 years, consists of *sixty years and sixty months* (the unit of five years, which forms the basis, as I have shown earlier, of the entire chronology of the Book of Genesis, equals sixty months); and the highest figure, 187 years, comprises three times *sixty years* plus *seven years.* Here the number appertaining to Adam — 130 years — is made up of *twice* times sixty years with the addition of *twice times sixty months.*

And a hundred years [מְאַת שָׁנָה *me'ath šānā*] / On the difference in the use of the two forms מֵאָה שָׁנָה *mē'ā šānā* and מְאַת שָׁנָה *me'ath šānā,* see my remarks in *La Questione della Genesi,* pp. 158–163. Similarly, with reference to the repetition of the word *šānā* in each part of the composite numbers, see *ibid.,* pp. 163–166. Concerning the ascending or descending order of the components of the composite numbers, compare *ibid.,* pp. 166–171, and *The Documentary Hypothesis,* English translation, pp. 51–53 (and above, p. 261).

He begot [*one*] *in his own likeness, after his image*] In the Babylonian account of Creation, i, 16, we read: '*And Anu begot Nudimmud* in his likeness (*tamšilašu*).'

On the use of the verb יָלַד *yāladh* in the *Hiph'il* in our chapter, see *La Questione della Genesi,* pp. 102–104, and *The Documentary Hypothesis,* English translation, pp. 43–47. In regard to the expression *in his own likeness, after his image,* see above, on *in the likeness of God* in *v.* 1.

On account of the pronominal suffix [וֹ- *-ō*] in the word שְׁמוֹ *šemō* ['his name'] several scholars (like Olshausen and Gunkel) have suggested the addition of the word *son* after *begot;* but such an addition would spoil the beauty of the diction and the rhythm of the verse. The pronominal suffix of שְׁמוֹ *šemō* refers to the object that is implied — even if not expressed — in the verb *begot.*

Seth] Regarding this name see on iv 25.

It does not follow from the statement here that, according to our chapter, Seth was the first-born son of Adam, as many suppose. In this genealogy, which seeks to set out the chronology of the generations from Adam till after the Flood, it was essential to mention specifically that son of Adam from whom Noah was descended. This is also the case at the beginning of the Book of Chronicles.

4. *And the days of Adam were, after he begot Seth*] From the genealogical viewpoint, a man's life is divisible into two separate parts: in the first, he lives only his personal life; the second begins from the moment that he bequeaths life to a new generation.

Eight hundred years] The figures for the second period of life (excluding the cases of Enoch and Lamech, which are affected by special circumstaces, as we shall see subsequently) are approximately the same throughout the chapter: in two instances (Adam and Jared) they are exactly eight hundred years; in four cases (Seth, Enosh, Kenan, Mahalalel), slightly over eight hundred; and there is one example (Methuselah) of a little under eight hundred. *Eight hundred years* comprise 160 units of five years (i.e. of 60 months, as I have explained); in other words, 6,000 months and another 60 × 60 months.

5. *Thus* [literally, 'And'] *all the days that Adam lived*] The meaning is: from what has already been stated, it follows that all Adam's days, in the aggregate, came to so-and-so many years.

The expression אֲשֶׁר חַי *'ăšer ḥay* ['that he (i.e. Adam) lived'] does not recur in the whole chapter.

Nine hundred years and thirty years] The total ages enumerated in our chapter — apart from those for Enoch and Lamech, which are abnormal — are all close to 900 years. Now *nine hundred years* comprise 60+60+60 units of five years, that is, of sixty months. The sexagesimal system undoubtedly obtains here, too. In the case of Adam, there have been added thirty years, which are equal to six units of 60 months.

It is interesting to note that similar figures are also to be found in the Sumerian list of kings of the first postdiluvian dynasty (before the Flood, as we have seen, the Babylonian ages are much higher, amounting to myriads of years for each king). The monarchs of this dynasty number twenty-three, but in the case of two of them the duration of their reigns is not stated. Now of the 21 figures given, five are precisely 900, two are 960 (900 plus 60!) and three are 840 (900 less 60!).

And he died] The sense is: and after Adam had lived nine hundred and thirty years, he then died. There is no intention here, as Jacob supposes, to emphasize the words, *and he died.*

SECOND PARAGRAPH

SETH

6. *And Seth lived / five years and a hundred years,*
and begot Enosh.

7. *And Seth lived / after he begot Enosh*
seven years / and eight hundred years,
and begot sons and daughters.

8. *Thus all the days of Seth were / twelve years / and nine hundred years;*
and he died.

After the first paragraph, which is marked by an exalted and almost poetic diction, the text continues in a simple style; but this, too, has dignity and grace, despite the multiplicity of numbers.

6. *Five years and a hundred years*] — comprising 1,200 months plus another 60 months.

Enosh] Regarding this name, see above, on iv 26.

7. *And Seth lived,* etc.] Compare the expression — somewhat different in form, but similar in meaning — in *v.* 4.

Seven years and eight hundred years] — the basic number of 800 years with the addition of *seven* years.

8. *Twelve years and nine hundred years*] To the fundamental number of 900 years there has been added here a unit of five years (60 months), as well as a unit of *seven* years.

THIRD PARAGRAPH

ENOSH

9. *And Enosh lived / ninety years,*
and begot Kenan.

10. *And Enosh lived / after he begot Kenan*
fifteen years / and eight hundred years,
and begot sons and daughters.

11. *Thus all the days of Enosh were / five years / and nine hundred years;*
and he died.

9. *Ninety years*] 6+6+6 units of 60 months.

Kenan] With reference to this name, see above, on iv 1.

10. *Fifteen years and eight hundred years*] The basic figure of 800 years has been augmented here by three units of 60 months.

11. *Five years and nine hundred years*] To the fundamental number of 900 years there is added here a unit of 60 months.

FOURTH PARAGRAPH

KENAN

12. *And Kenan lived / seventy years,*
and begot Mahalalel.

13. *And Kenan lived / after he begot Mahalalel*
forty years / and eight hundred years,
and begot sons and daughters.

14. *Thus all the days of Kenan were / ten years / and nine hundred years;*
and he died.

12. *Seventy years*] — the well-known round number: ten times *seven;* or: twice times seven units of 60 months.

Mahalalel] — a distinctly Hebrew name: מַהֲלַלְאֵל *Mahălal-'El* ['Praise of God'] (it is also found in Nehemiah xi 4). Among the sages of the Mishnah occurs the name Akabya son of Mahalalel.

13. *Forty years and eight hundred years*] To the basic age of 800 years have been added 360+120 months.

14. *Ten years and nine hundred years*] The fundamental number of 900 years has been augmented by 120 months.

FIFTH PARAGRAPH
MAHALALEL

15. *And Mahalalel lived / five years and sixty years,*
and begot Jared.

16. *And Mahalalel lived / after he begot Jared*
thirty years / and eight hundred years,
and begot sons and daughters.

17. *Thus all the days of Mahalalel were / five and ninety years / and eight hundred years;*
and he died.

15. *Five years and sixty years*] — that is, 60 years and 60 months.

Jared] — in Akkadian (*w*)*ardu*, 'a slave' (Albright in *JBL*, lviii [1939], p. 17, note 9 a).

16. *Thirty years and eight hundred years*] — the fundamental age of 800 years plus 6 units of 60 months.

17. *Five and ninety years and eight hundred years*] — the basic number of 900 years, which, as I have stated, equals 60+60+60 units of 60 months, less one unit.

SIXTH PARAGRAPH
JARED

18. *And Jared lived / two and sixty years / and a hundred years,*
and begot Enoch.

19. *And Jared lived / after he begot Enoch*
eight hundred years / and begot sons and daughters.

20. *Thus all the days of Jared were / two and sixty years / and nine hundred years;*
and he died.

18. *Two and sixty years and a hundred years*] — thirty units of sixty months plus another 60 months, and the further addition of *seven* years.

Enoch] For this name, see on iv 17.

19. *Eight hundred years*] — the exact basic number.

20. *Two and sixty and nine hundred years*] 60+60+60+6+6 units of sixty months, less one, plus *seven* years.

SEVENTH PARAGRAPH
ENOCH

21. *And Enoch lived / five and sixty years,*
and begot Methuselah.

22. *And Enoch walked with God / after he begot Methuselah*
three hundred years, / and begot sons and daughters.

23. *Thus all the days of Enoch were / five and sixty years / and three hundred years.*

24. *And Enoch walked with God, / and he was not;*
For God took him.

21. *Five and sixty years*] — that is: 60 years and 60 months.

Verse 15 reads: *five* YEARS *and sixty years*. On the difference see *La Questione della Genesi*, pp. 164–165, § α.

Methuselah [מְתוּשֶׁלַח *Mᵉthūšelaḥ*] /—a composite name: מְתוּ־שֶׁלַח

Mᵉthū-šelaḥ. מְתוּ *mᵉthū* [Akkadian *mutu*], as we know, signifies *man* (see the note on iv 18). The meaning of שֶׁלַח *šelaḥ* is in doubt. One suggestion is that it is the name of a deity, another that it is the name of a place, and according to yet another theory it is a common noun (denoting *weapons* or something else); it is impossible to decide which view is correct. שֶׁלַח *Šelaḥ* [E.V. *Shelah*] also occurs by itself as the name of a man (x 24; xi 12–15; i Chron. i 18, 24).

22. *And Enoch walked with God*] In regard to Enoch, Scripture uses exceptional expressions. Instead of *And Enoch lived* it is stated here, *And Enoch walked with God.* So, too, in *v.* 24, in place of *and he died,* the text has: *And Enoch walked with God, and he was not; for God took him.* Also the length of his life — 365 years — is abnormal. All this is indicative of the special character and significance that the Masorah attributed to Enoch. He is the head of the *seventh* generation from Adam; hence his importance as well as his right to enjoy a unique status. The rabbinic sages already drew attention to this, when they declared: 'All sevenths are favoured . . . of the generations, the seventh is favoured: Adam, Seth, Enosh, Kenan, Mahalalel, Jared, Enoch — *And Enoch walked with God'* (*Pesiqta deRab Kahana,* ed. Buber, pp. 154b–155a; *Wayyiqra Rabba,* xxix 9, and parallel passages).

In the Babylonian tradition, the seventh king in the list of antediluvian kings — who thus corresponds to the Biblical Enoch, the son of Jared — is likewise distinguished from the other monarchs. His name appears as *Enme(n)duranna* in the list of kings; as *Enmeduranki* in another document, belonging to the worship of the diviner-priests (K. 2486); and as Εὐεδώραγχος (this is apparently the correct reading) in Berossus. The inscription K. 2486 records all sorts of wonderful tales about this king. Although the text has been badly damaged, the essential subject-matter, despite the obliterations, is clear, to wit, that *Enmeduranki* was *beloved* of the gods Anu, Bēl, Šamaš and Adad, and that these deities, or some of them, (made him) an associate of theirs, (placed him) on a throne of gold, and transmitted to him their secrets, the secrets of heaven and earth, and gave him possession of the tablets of the gods, the cedar rod, and the secret of divination by means of pouring oil upon water (a method of divination that was also known among the Israelites; see Daiches, *Babylonian Oil Magic in the Talmud and in later Jewish Literature,* London 1913). *Enmeduranki* was regarded as the father of the diviner-priests — their father in the sense that he was the originator of their doctrine, and also in the physical connotation of the term (cf. my note on *father* in iv 20); every diviner-priest (*bārû*) claimed descent from him.

It seems that the Israelites recounted about Enoch similar legends to those that the Babylonians narrated concerning this king. But the Torah, in accordance with its principles, refused to accept these myths, which were akin to alien idolatrous beliefs. It obliterated all the mythological elements, and indicated how the existing traditions about the father of the seventh generation were to be understood in keeping with its spirit. Twice Scripture says of him: *And Enoch walked with God,* and apparently the meaning of this sentence is not identical in the two instances. On the first occasion, when the expression refers to Enoch's *lifetime,* and is used instead of *and he lived,* the sense is clearly established by what we are told subsequently concerning Noah (vi 9): *Noah was wholly righteous in his generations; Noah walked with God.* The parallelism there shows that 'walking with God' signifies walking in God's ethical ways and cleaving to the virtues of a wholly righteous man. How the verse has to be interpreted the second time, we shall endeavour to explain later.

In *v.* 21, we find *and he lived* and not *and he walked,* etc., because the childhood years of Enoch are included in the period mentioned.

Although excluded from the Torah, the ancient sagas concerning Enoch were not forgotten by the children of Israel. They continued to exist as folk-tales, and in the last centuries before the Christian era, they assumed a literary form and came to occupy an important place in the Pseudepigrapha, which contain numerous stories about Enoch similar to those that the Babylonians used to relate in regard to the seventh king (to wit, that on account of his righteousness he became an intimate of the Deity; that he was translated to heaven; that he was given a seat on the left hand of God; that the tablets of heaven were shown to him; that he was instructed in sublime and mystic wisdom concerning all that exists in heaven and on earth, and touching all that was and will be; that he did not die but became the Scribe of the heavenly court for ever; and similar fables). From these books, which, although composed at a late date, were doubtless based on ancient material, it is possible to gain an idea of what the early Israelite tradition narrated about Enoch before the Torah was written down, and of the attitude adopted by Scripture thereto.

It is interesting to note that when the mythological legends were accepted as part of the Pseudepigrapha, and in consequence were given a new lease of life, the attitude of the authoritative and official Jewish circles towards them was similar to that of the Torah relative to their earliest form. Mostly, the Jewish sages preferred to pass them over in silence (in the whole of the Tannaitic literature and in both Talmuds there is no mention of Enoch); sometimes they briefly noted the simple meaning of the relevant Biblical passage (see my earlier observations on the favoured sevenths); and occasionally they expressed open opposition and not only refuted those who declared that Enoch never knew death (Bereshith Rabba, xxv 1; cf. Targum Onkelos on *v.* 24, according to the original version: 'for the Lord slew him'), but they even interpreted the text to his discredit, asserting that Enoch was not inscribed in the Book of the Righteous but in the Book of the Wicked (Bereshith Rabba, *ibid.*); or at least that he was a hypocrite, at times righteous and at times wicked, and the Holy One blessed be He said: 'Whilst he is righteous, I shall translate him (*ibid.*).

Nevertheless, despite all opposition, the mythological legends did not lose their popularity with the masses, and lived on in their midst. When the pseudepigraphical writings were forgotten by the Jewish people, these sagas found new literary expression in the mystical literature and the late Midrashim (see also Targum Pseudo-Jonathan). In truth, Enoch's status then rose higher than ever through his indentification with Meṭaṭron, the prince of the Presence, and it reached the stage where he was assigned the title of 'Little Lord'. This demonstrates the vitality of the folk myths.

Three hundred years] — sixty units of sixty months each.

23. *Thus all the days of Enoch were*] We have here, for stylistic reasons, a slight change of form וַיְהִי *wayᵉhī* [the singular; literally, 'and was'] instead of וַיִּהְיוּ *wayiheyū* [the plural: 'and were'] etc.,

found in most of the paragraphs (see the introduction, § 8); so, too, in *v.* 31. Possibly this variation was intended to bring more strikingly to the reader's notice the two anomalous numbers — 365 and 777 — as though each one constituted a distinct unit.

Five and sixty years and three hundred years] — corresponding to the days of the solar year, as many exegetes have pointed out.

24. *And Enoch walked with God*] After being told in the previous verse that Enoch lived 365 years — that is, that the account of his entire life was concluded — we cannot assign to the expression here the same meaning as in *v.* 22 (see above, on *v.* 22). Since Enoch had already been taken from the world, there is no point in referring again to his ethical conduct. It would appear that there is a word-play here, and that the phrase is repeated in a different connotation from that which it had in the earlier verse. The whole of verse 24 — not just from the words, *and he was not,* etc. — is a substitute for *and he died* in the other paragraphs. The reference here to walking with God signifies, apparently, removal from the world, forming a parallelism with what is stated at the end of the sentence: *for God took him.* There is an echo here of the ancient traditions about Enoch's translation to the Divine sphere, but only a faint echo. The Torah, as we have observed, conceals more than it reveals, and is unwilling to give explicit assent to what is not in harmony with its spirit.

And he was not [וְאֵינֶנּוּ *we'ēnennū*] / Since he walked with God, *he was not. He was not* is the customary way of saying, *he departed from the world,* without mentioning the dread word *death.* Compare, for example, Psa. xxxix 13 (Hebrew, *v.* 14): *Look away from me, that I may know gladness, before I depart* AND BE NO MORE [וְאֵינֶנִּי *we'ēnennī*]; ibid. ciii 16: *For the wind passeth over it,* AND IT IS GONE [וְאֵינֶנּוּ *we'ēnennū*]; Prov. xii 7: *The wicked are overthrown* AND ARE NO MORE [וְאֵינָם *we'ēnām*]; Job vii 21: *For now I shall lie in the earth; Thou shalt seek me* AND I SHALL NOT BE [וְאֵינֶנִּי *we'ēnennī*]; ibid. viii 22: *and the tent of the wicked* WILL BE NO MORE [אֵינֶנּוּ *'ēnennū*]; and so forth.

For God TOOK [לָקַח *lāqaḥ*] *him*] The commentators cite, on the basis of Ges. – Buhl s.v. לָקַח *lāqaḥ,* two parallels: the ascent of Elijah (ii Kings ii 3, 5, etc., in which the verb לָקַח *lāqaḥ* occurs a number of times), and the ascent of Utnapištim in the Gilgameš

Epic (in that narrative, too, the verb *laqû,* which corresponds to לָקַח *lāqaḥ,* is used).

To this may be added:

(a) That if we examine the continuation of the verse in the Epic of Gilgameš (Tablet XI, 196) we shall find there an even more interesting parallel, which reads thus: 'And they took me (*ilquinnima*), and set me *in the mouth of the rivers.*' Now in the Ethiopic Book of Enoch, xvii 8, it is stated that when the angels took Enoch on a tour of inspection of the entire world, he saw, among other things, *the mouth of the rivers* (on the expression, *mouth of the rivers,* see Albright, *AJSL,* xxxv [1919], pp. 161–195).

(b) That also in the Bible there is a more important parallel, namely, Psa. xlix 15 [Hebrew, *v.* 16]: *But God will ransom my soul from the power of Sheol, for* HE WILL RECEIVE ME [יִקָּחֵנִי *yiqqāḥēnī*]. *Selah.* (cf. also Psa. lxxiii 24: *and afterward,* THOU WILT RECEIVE ME [תִּקָּחֵנִי *tiqqāḥēnī*] *to glory*). The Torah's intention, apparently, is not to convey that Enoch did not die (it is written: *and he was not!*), but only that his death was not like the death of other people, and that when he died he did not descend to Sheol, but God redeemed him from the power of Sheol. How this redemption was carried out, we are not told, either in our verse or in Psa. xlix.

On the use of the name אֱלֹהִים *'Elōhīm* ['God'] in this paragraph, see *The Documentary Hypothesis,* English translation, p. 35.

EIGHTH PARAGRAPH

METHUSELAH

25. *And Methuselah lived / seven and eighty years / and a hundred years,*
and begot Lamech.

26. *And Methuselah lived / after he begot Lamech*
two and eighty years / and seven hundred years,
and begot sons and daughters.

27. *Thus all the days of Methuselah were / nine and sixty years / and nine hundred years;*
and he died.

25. *Seven and eighty years and a hundred years*] — 6×6 units of 60 months, plus *seven* years.

Lamech] Regarding this name see above, on iv 18.

26. *Two and eighty years and seven hundred years*] — the basic number 800, less 3×6. Methuselah lived another 60 months after the death of his son Lamech (777+5=782).

27. *Nine and sixty years and nine hundred years*] — 60+60+60 +6+6 units of 60 months, less one, with the addition of twice times *seven years*. Methuselah lived longer than any other founding father of the world, but further his life could not be extended, because 969 years after his birth the Flood came upon the world. This implies either that he perished in the Flood, or that he died shortly before the Deluge (in the Rabbinic view, he lived to such an advanced age because he was a righteous man; and he died a few days before the Flood in accordance with the verse, *the right eous man is taken away before* [E.V. *from*] *the calamity*).

NINTH PARAGRAPH

LAMECH

28. *And Lamech lived / two and eighty years / and a hundred years,*
and begot a son.
29. *And he called his name Noah, / saying,*
'This one shall bring us comfort from our labour / and from the toil of our hands,
arising from the ground, / which the Lord has cursed.'
30. *And Lamech lived / after he begot Noah*
five and ninety years / and five hundred years,
and begot sons and daughters.
31. *Thus all the days of Lamech were / seven and seventy years / and seven hundred years;*
and he died.

This paragraph records the birth of the man who completed the line of antediluvian patriarchs, and became the father of postdiluvian humanity; hence the Torah speaks of him at length, and resumes the exalted, almost poetic, diction that it used in the first paragraph.

28. *Two and eighty years and a hundred years*] — 35 units of 60 months, plus another *seven* years. The number 35 (i.e. 5×7) occurs frequently in the numerical scheme of our sections; see pp. 14, 192.

And he begot a son] Here Scripture does not immediately mention the son's name, so that it may be dealt with specifically in the next verse; the reader, meanwhile, is kept in suspense to learn what the nature of this son will be.

29. *And he called his name*] This corresponds to the first paragraph, *vv.* 2, 3; see my observations there.

Noah [נֹחַ *Nōaḥ*] / — from the root נוח *nūaḥ* ['to rest'], according to the usual view, which, despite the defective spelling [omission of *Wāw*], appears to be correct. Lewy (see the bibliography, p. 272) thinks that there may have been an Amorite god *Nāḫ,* who is to be identified with Noah.

This one shall bring us comfort] This etymology does not fit the root נוח *nūaḥ.* As far back as Rabbinic times (Bereshith Rabba xxv 2) it was observed that 'the explanation does not correspond to the name nor the name to the explanation. The text should have either, *Noah — this one* WILL GIVE US REST [יְנִיחֵנוּ *yenīḥēnū*]; or, *Nahman* [נַחְמָן *Naḥmān*] — *this one* WILL BRING US COMFORT [יְנַחֲמֵנוּ *yenaḥămēnū*].' However, we find an allusion to the root נָחַם *nāḥam* already in early sources; in a fragment of a Hurrian version of the Gilgameš Epic, the hero of the Flood seems to have been called *Naḥmūlel* (see Burrows, in *JRAS,* year 1925, pp. 281–282). Apparently two traditions were current among the Israelites with regard to the name of the righteous man who was saved from the waters of the Flood: according to the one his name was *Noah,* according to the other his name was *Menahem* [מְנַחֵם *Menaḥēm*] or *Nahman,* and the Torah, following the principle that we have discussed earlier (p. 232), accepted the first view but did not wish to disregard the second. The Septuagint reading יְנִיחֵנוּ *yenīḥēnū* arose, it seems, as a result of the harmonizing tendency that we have several times noticed in that version (see my remarks on p. 265).

Both traditions are recorded in the late Haggada. It is stated in

סֵפֶר הַיָּשָׁר *Sēpher Hayyāšār,* ed. Goldschmidt, p. 14: 'And Methuselah called his name Noah, saying, "the earth rested and ceased from acting corruptly in his days"; but his father Lamech called him Menahem, saying, *"This one will bring us comfort"'*, etc..

Scripture makes several allusions later on to the name Noah in word-plays: *But Noah found* FAVOUR [חֵן *ḥēn*] (vi 8); *and the ark came to* REST [וַתָּנַח *wattānaḥ*] (viii 4); RESTING-PLACE [מָנוֹחַ *mānōaḥ*] *for the sole of her foot* (viii 9); *the* PLEASING [נִיחֹחַ *nīḥōaḥ*] *odour* (viii 21); a slight assonance suffices. In our verse, too, there is a similar play on words. The meaning is: Lamech set comforting hopes on this son of his, and subsequent events proved that the appellation was appropriate to him, though in a different sense from that intended by his father (see my notes on the names *Eve, Abel* and *Seth*). To the root נָחַם *nāḥam* there is a very interesting parallel in the last paragraph (vi 6); see my comment there.

From our labour and from the toil of our hands] — that is, from our work, which is being done with the toil of our hands. There is an allusion here to what had been said to Adam (iii 17): *cursed is the ground because of you; in* TOIL *you shall eat of it all the days of your life.*

Arising from the ground] — a parallel to the preceding section (iv 11; see my annotation there). Unto Cain a curse came out of the ground; for the rest of mankind only *toil* issued from it, the curse resting on the ground alone.

Which the Lord [YHWH] has cursed] For the use of the Tetragrammaton in this verse see *The Documentary Hypothesis,* English translation, p. 35.

30. *Five and ninety years and five hundred years*] — 600 years less 60 months.

31. *Thus all the days of Lamech were*] See the commentary to *v.* 23.

Seven and seventy years and seven hundred years] — *seven* hundreds and *seven* tens and *seven* units. See above, p. 243. Kuhn attempted to show in his aforementioned essay a number of other links with the number *seven,* but his calculations are unduly complicated and appear improbable.

TENTH PARAGRAPH
NOAH

32. *And Noah was / five hundred years old;*
and Noah begot / Shem, Ham and Japheth.

32. The usual formula is not completed here; the concluding passage appears only later (ix 28–29). The Torah temporarily interrupts its genealogical account in order to describe in detail what occurred at this time, and particularly what befell Noah and his three sons. By this break in the narrative, the Bible arouses the attention of its readers, who await intently to learn the rest of the story.

Five hundred years] — 100 units of 60 months.

And Noah begot] The subject *Noah* is repeated on account of the rhythm of the verse. In the Samaritan version it is omitted.

Shem, Ham and Japheth] The meaning is not that they were born at the same time, but that in the five-hundredth year of his life Noah became a father, his eldest son being born (Dillmann).

The various explanations suggested with regard to the etymology of the three names are all doubtful; see on the subject the modern commentaries.

ELEVENTH PARAGRAPH
THE STORY OF THE SONS OF GOD AND THE DAUGHTERS OF MEN

CHAPTER VI

1. *And it came to pass when men began / to multiply on the face of the ground,*
and daughters were born to them,

2. *that the sons of God saw / the daughters of men*
that they were fair;
and they took them wives / of whomsoever they chose.

3. *Then the Lord said,*
'My spirit shall not abide / in man for ever,
in as much as he, too, is flesh,
but his days shall be / a hundred and twenty years.'

4. *The Nephilim were on the earth / in those days,*
and also afterward,
when the sons of God came in / to the daughters of men,
and they bore children to them.
These were the mighty men that were of old, / the men of renown.

This paragraph, as has been stated, is one of the obscurest in the Pentateuch. I devoted a special expository essay to the passage, which was printed in *Essays Presented to J. H. Hertz, Chief Rabbi,* London 1943, pp. 35–44 (Hebrew; regrettably with many typographical errors). I shall give a resumé of that article here, adding whatever is necessary for the elucidation of those matters that fell outside the scope of the essay.

1. *And it came to pass when* MEN [הָאָדָם *hā'ādhām*] *began to multiply on the face of the ground*] — as we were told in the previous chapter; a clear link with chapter v.

The word אָדָם *'ādhām* [literally, 'man'] is used here as a common noun in a collective sense; hence, as at the beginning of the first paragraph, the pronoun appears first in the singular and then in the plural.

On the face of the ground — as in *v.* 7, thus establishing a connection with the next paragraph.

And daughters were born to them] — as the Bible had stated: *and begot sons and* DAUGHTERS. Here, too, is an obvious nexus.

2. *The sons of God* [בְּנֵי הָאֱלֹהִים *b^e^nē hā'ĕlōhīm*] / All the expositions, both ancient and modern, that regard *the sons of God* as a distinct group of human beings (I have cited these expositions in detail in my aforementioned essay, p. 36) are unsatisfactory. Several commentators have already noted:

(1) That the expression *the sons of God* is used here in contradistinction to *the daughters of men,* and these words — *daughters* and *men* — cannot be understood in this verse in a different sense from that which they have in *v.* 1, which definitely refers to the

human species as a whole; hence 'the sons of God' must be entities existing outside the sphere of humankind.

(2) That wherever the terms בְּנֵי (הָ)אֱלֹהִים *bᵉnē (hā)'ĕlōhīm* or בְּנֵי אֵלִים *bᵉnē 'ēlīm* ['sons of God' or 'the mighty'] occur, the reference is definitely to *angels,* (Psa. xxix 1; lxxxix 6 [Hebrew, v. 7]; Job i 6; ii 1; xxxviii 7; so, too, Deut. xxxii 8, according to the reading of the Septuagint). Consequently, it appears more correct to explain these expressions to mean *angels* or the like. The interpretation in the sense of angels is the oldest in the history of exegesis (for expositions of this kind see my essay, pp. 35–36, 37–38), to which approximate the views of most contemporary scholars, who hold that we have here a mythological narrative, a kind of relic of the ancient mythological sagas, which was preserved as an alien element in the Book of Genesis (see on these interpretations my remarks *ibid.,* p. 36, note 6).

There are, however, three objections to this interpretation. The first is that the episode recorded here is not consonant with the character of the angels who are mentioned in other sections of the Book of Genesis. Elsewhere they are depicted as pure and exalted beings, who represent the Lord, speak in His name and carry out His mission; but here we are confronted by personalities that act on their account, and not necessarily with overmuch purity.

The second problem is this: if the text refers specifically to angels, why does it not use the normal terms for them, מַלְאֲכֵי אֱלֹהִים *mal'ăkhē 'Elōhīm* [literally, 'messengers of God'] or מַלְאֲכֵי ה' ['messengers of the Lord'].

The third is that the Torah, as we have seen in many instances in the previous chapters, is systematically opposed to any kind of mythology; how then can we presume that our passage is connected with a mythological legend?

But all these difficulties can be explained. With regard to the first objection, we must consider the origin and development of the expressions בְּנֵי (הָ)אֱלֹהִים *bᵉnē (hā)'ĕlōhīm* and בְּנֵי אֵלִים *bᵉnē 'ēlīm*. It is not sufficient to state that just as the expression בְּנֵי הַנְּבִיאִים *bᵉnē hannᵉbhī'īm* ['sons of the prophets'] signifies the men belonging to the prophetic class, so the phrase בְּנֵי הָאֱלֹהִים *bᵉnē hā'ĕlōhīm* denotes the entities appertaining to the Divine sphere. Since the Hebrew linguistic and literary tradition is but a continuation of the linguistic and literary tradition of the Canaanites, we must make the latter our starting-point. In the Ugaritic writings the term *bn 'il* (i.e. *sons of* 'IL ['god']) indicates the gods collectively and the phrase *mpḫrt bn 'il* or *pḫr bn 'ilm* (בְּנֵי אֵלִים *bᵉnē 'ēlīm*) connotes the congregation and assembly of the gods. In a Phoenician inscription we read: *mpḥrt 'l gbl qdšm,* that is, 'the congregation of the holy gods of Byblus'. On the other hand, the theology of the Israelites, which recognizes only one God, concentrates in the Lord or in His messengers all the forces and tasks that the pagan peoples used to attribute to the various deities, as, for example, the administration of the heavenly hosts or the other phenomena of nature. Hebrew religious doctrine attributes them to the Lord Himself, if they are matters befitting the Divine glory, and if not, it transfers them to His envoys and angels. Since the angels, accordingly, take the place of the Canaanite deities, the terms that formerly denoted the collectivity of gods and their congregational assembly changed their meaning in conformity with this trend. The expressions בְּנֵי אֵלִים *bᵉnē 'ēlīm* or בְּנֵי (הָ)אֱלֹהִים *bᵉnē (hā)'ĕlōhīm* — so, too, עֲדַת אֵל *'ădhath 'ēl* ['Divine council'], קְדוֹשִׁים *qᵉdhōšīm* ['holy ones'], סוֹד קְדוֹשִׁים ['council of the holy ones'] — became in the Bible designations for the heavenly household, the angel congregation standing before the Lord to serve Him. This explains why in Job xxxviii 7 the words *the sons of God* בְּנֵי אֱלֹהִים *bᵉnē 'ĕlōhīm* form a parallel to *the morning stars;* the stars, which were deities in the idolatrous cult, were transformed into servants of the Lord in Israel's religion (likewise in Ugaritic, the phrase *pḫr kbkbm,* that is, *congregation of the stars,* corresponds to *bn 'il* ['sons of God']; and the assembly of *the sons of God* that came to present themselves before the Lord in Job i 6 and ii 1 is paralleled by the gathering of *the host of heaven* in i Kings xxii 19. Similarly we find in Psa. ciii 20–21: *Bless the Lord, O you His* ANGELS . . . *Bless the Lord, all His* HOSTS!; and *ibid.* cxlviii 2: *Praise Him all His* ANGELS, *praise Him all His* HOSTS!

According to the Israelite conception, the angels are, of course, divided into different ranks: there are higher and lower angels; some angels are close to the Lord, like those who were called in a later epoch 'ministering angels', and there are others that were termed 'demons' or 'destroying angels' ('demons' denote the gentile gods in Deut. xxxii 17, Psa. cvi 37). Although Scripture has no elaborate angelology like that which developed at a subsequent period, yet it is clear that already in Biblical times categories similar to those we have mentioned were distinguished. In our paragraph, it is apparent from the context that not angels sublime and pure, but those of a degraded type, are referred to. The Talmudic sages also held (B. Ḥagiga 16a), that, although the ministering angels do not beget offspring, the demons do procreate.

Hence (and this resolves the *second problem*) the text does not employ the word *angels* *, which throughout the Book of Genesis denotes the high-ranking angels, who represent the glory of the Divine Presence, but prefers the general term בְּנֵי הָאֱלֹהִים *bᵉnē hā'ĕlōhīm,* since it is common to all the Lord's ministers, the superior and the inferior, the good and the evil, including also demons and destroying angels. In the Book of Job even Satan is counted among בְּנֵי הָאֱלֹהִים *bᵉnē hā'ĕlōhīm.* So, too, in Deut. xxxii 8, according to the Septuagint reading, the expression בְּנֵי אֵל *bᵉnē 'ēl* or בְּנֵי הָאֱלֹהִים *bᵉnē hā'ĕlōhīm* simply means the guardian angels of the seventy nations. The third objection we shall discuss later.

That they were FAIR [טֹבֹת *ṭōbhōth;* literally, 'good'] / Numerous expositions of a fanciful nature have been given of the word טֹבֹת *ṭōbhōth,* even in modern commentaries; but its meaning is simply, *good in appearance, beautiful;* compare the Biblical expression: *and when she saw that he was a goodly* [טוֹב *ṭōbh,* literally, 'good'] *child* (Exod. ii 2).

And they took them wives, etc.] According to the traditional rabbinic interpretation as well as the view of most modern exegetes, the Torah refers here to grave offences, or opposition to the world-order approved by the Lord; and this was the reason for the punishment meted out to the generation of the Flood. But this exposition does not appear to fit the language of the text. *And they took them wives* is simply the usual expression for legal marriage. The passage contains not a single word, either here or in the Lord's speech in *v.* 3, alluding to rape or adultery or to any act against the Lord's will. And even if we concede that the *sons of God* sinned, why

* Hebrew, מַלְאָכִים *mal'ākhīm.*

should the *sons of men* suffer retribution? According to the plain meaning of the text, it would seem that proper, honourable wedlock is intended. The sons of God mentioned here do not belong to the group of ministering angels, who do not propagate their species, but resemble in this respect human beings. It is not surprising, therefore, that they took wives unto themselves.

Of [-מִ *mi-*] *whomsoever they chose*] Here, too, it does not appear to be the Bible's intention to condemn the actions of the sons of God, as though they took all the women they wanted — by force. The *Mēm* in the word מִכֹּל *mikkōl* [literally, 'of all'] is regarded by many commentators as the explicative *Mēm,* as in, *whatsoever* [מִכֹּל *mikkōl;* literally, 'from all'] *was in the dry land died* (vii 22). But this seems incorrect. It is more likely that the sense is this: each one of them took a wife *from among* those women who in general found favour in their eyes.

3. *Then the Lord said*] The Lord did not actually speak to any one, but He resolved, decided. We find the same in *v.* 7; in this respect, too, the two paragraphs are parallel. Regarding the use of the name Lord [*YHWH*] in this verse, see *The Documentary Hypothesis,* English translation, p. 35.

My spirit shall not abide [יָדוֹן *yādhōn*] in man for ever] The interpretations proposed with regard to these words are legion, but, without exception, they are forced. All the suggestions that have been advanced on the assumption that the verb יָדוֹן *yādhōn* is derived from an *ʿAyin–Wāw* or *ʿAyin–Yōdh* stem (דִּין *dīn* or דּוּן *dūn* in Hebrew, دوم *dwm* in Arabic) encounter a serious objection in the vocalisation with a *Ḥōlem* [וֹ *ō*], and the attempts made to explain this pointing (as that of the jussive form, or of a verb conjugated after the manner of יָבוֹא *yābhō'*, יָאוֹר *yā'ōr*) are not particularly satisfactory. The same applies to the emendations that have been proposed (יָדוּם *yādhūm,* יָדוּר *yādhūr,* יָלוּן *yālūn,* יִכּוֹן *yikkōn,* etc.). It appears that the word can only be derived from the stem דָּנַן *dānan.* Vollers in *ZA,* xiv (1899), pp. 349–356, explained it, on the basis of the Akkadian verb *danānu,* as meaning *to be strong;* but this interpretation does not suit the context. Recently Guillaume pointed out in *AJSL,* lvi (1939), pp. 415–416, that the Arabic دَنَّ *danna* signifies in the fourth conjugation *to remain, to exist.* To this may be added:

(a) That in Akkadian there occurs a second root *danānu,* found in the substantives *dinnû, dinnūtu, madnanu,* which connote a *couch* or *bed.*

(b) That the word דַּן *dan*, which denotes a jar, with a sharp bottom rim, that is thrust into the ground so that it may stay there permanently, is found not only in Arabic but also in Akkadian, Syriac, Talmudic Aramaic, and possibly also in Hebrew (see my observations in the above-mentioned essay, p. 42, note 35, concerning the Talmudic expression דן דני *dn dny* or דוני דני *dwny dny* [rendered: 'be strong, O ye barrels'!], and the bibliography *ibid.,* and also note 36).

(c) That the verb דָּנַן *dānan,* in the stated sense of *to remain* or *exist perpetually in a given place,* occurs not only in a secondary conjugation, which could be regarded as a denominative formation from the noun דַּן *dan,* but is found also in the *Qal* conjugation in Talmudic Aramaic, and possibly in Hebrew, too (see my remarks *op. cit., ibid.*). In the light of all this, and taking into account the fact that according to the early exegetical tradition reflected in the ancient versions, the word in our verse has precisely this signification, to wit, *to abide permanently,* it seems that we shall not err if we consider this to be the correct interpretation. The whole passage is then easily explained. The Lord said: My spirit, the spirit of life that I breathed into man's nostrils, shall not abide in man for ever, that is, the children born from the union of the sons of God with the daughters of men, since they are human on their mother's side, shall not be immortal like their fathers, but shall die when their time comes like all members of the human race.

In as much as he, too, [בְּשַׁגַּם *bešaggam*] *is flesh*] The vocalisation בְּשַׁגָּם *bešaggām,* found in some editions and manuscripts, has nothing to support it. In the MSS of Ben Asher, the word is pointed בְּשַׁגַּם *bešaggam.* All the expositions based on the pointing with *Qāmeṣ* (meaning: 'through their erring') are not only unsuited to the context, but do not even accord with the grammatical form of the word. In respect to this word, too, it appears that the correct interpretation is that of the ancient versions: בַּאֲשֶׁר גַּם *ba'ăšer gam* ['in as much as, also']. It is precisely in the Book of Genesis that we find בַּאֲשֶׁר *ba'ăšer* twice in the sense of *in as much as* [E.V.

because] (xxxix 9, 23). Here, for reasons of poetic style, Scripture has chosen the form -שַׁ *ša*–, which is found also in the Song of Deborah (Jud. v 7), in preference to the form אֲשֶׁר *'ăšer.* If the Bible had written בַּאֲשֶׁר גַּם הוּא בָשָׂר *ba'ăšer gam hū' bhāšār,* the language would have been prosaic; whereas בְּשַׁגַּם הוּא בָשָׂר *bešaggam hū' bhāšār* is a line of poetry. The meaning is: My spirit shall not abide for ever in the children born of these marriages, who belong, on their mother's side, to the species of man, *in as much as he, too, is flesh,* that is, because man, even though he transcends the earthly creatures, *is also* flesh like them (for the significance of גַּם *gam* ['also', 'too'] see Naḥmanides). It is possible, perhaps, to explain the phrase to mean: *also because he is flesh;* but despite the accents the previous interpretation appears to me preferable.

But his days shall be a hundred and twenty years] Two explanations of this clause have been suggested:

(a) until one hundred and twenty years I shall be forbearing with them; but if they do not repent, I shall bring a deluge upon them (so Rashi);

(b) the length of human life upon earth shall henceforth be a hundred and twenty years.

The first interpretation is ruled out, not only because the wickedness of the generation of the Flood, as we pointed out, has not yet been mentioned, but also because in the continuation of the passage there is no mention of the fact that the time-limit had passed without the sinners repenting. As for the second explanation, how does the question of human longevity arise here, if we follow the conventional interpretations? In the light, however, of my exposition of the preceding part of the verse, everything is clear: they are human on their maternal side; hence they will not enjoy immortality, since man, too, is flesh, and his life is destined gradually to reach the stage where those who live the longest will attain the age of a hundred and twenty years. The sense of the passage is apparently this: the earliest generations, which were the strongest on account of their nearness to the Divine source, lived almost to a thousand years, the day of the Almighty; but the span of life was diminishing from generation to generation, and in the end would be stabilized at the point where the healthiest person, if he did not suffer illness or any calamity, would be able to live only a little more than a hundred years — a hundred and twenty years according to the round figure of tradition. This would be the fate of all who belong to humankind, be they ordinary people or offspring of the mixed marriages of the sons of God with the daughters of men.

This interpretation finds corroboration in the expression, *and the days of so-and-so were,* which recurs frequently in the preceding paragraphs. It should also be noted that according to the Sumerian list of kings, the first postdiluvian monarch reigned precisely 1,200 years.

4. *The Nephilim*] — that is, the giants (compare Num. xiii 33). Regarding the etymology of this word, various improbable theories have been advanced. The correct explanation appears to be that they were called thus because, according to the story related of them, they all *fell* [נָפְלוּ *nāph^e lū*] by the sword and descended to Sheol abode of the dead. In the book of Ezekiel, xxxii 20f., reference is made to the גִּבּוֹרִים *gibbōrīm* ['mighty'] in Sheol (גִּבּוֹרִים *gibbōrīm* is the very word used here in the continuation of our verse), and the verb נָפַל *nāphal* ['to fall'] occurs there several times (*vv.* 20, 22, 23, 24, 27).

At a later period, this word became the basis of the legend concerning the angels who fell from heaven (see the bibliography on this myth in my essay, p. 37, note 17), and in order to express their opposition thereto our sages declared that by *the sons of God* are meant the sons of the great men and princes of mankind — בְּנֵי רַבְרְבַיָּא *b^e nē rabhr^e bhayyā'* ['sons of the great'] or בְּנֵי דַיָּנַיָּא *b^e ne dhayyānayyā'* ['sons of judges'] (see my essay, p. 36).

Were on the earth in those days] They were born of the union of the sons of God with the daughters of men, and *in those days* — that is, before the Flood — they were still *upon the earth* and had not yet descended into Sheol (the expression *on the earth* means here, *in the land of the living*).

And also afterwards, etc.] After the Flood, too, there were to be found, in exceptional instances, a few individuals of this race, *when* [אֲשֶׁר *'ăšer* (literally, 'which', 'who') in the sense of כַּאֲשֶׁר *ka'ăšer* ('as', 'when')] some of the *sons of God came* and were intimate with *the daughters of men,* and the daughters of men *bore unto them* children.

These were the MIGHTY MEN [גִּבּוֹרִים *gibbōrīm*] / The word גִּבּוֹרִים *gibbōrīm* occurs also in Ezekiel, *loc. cit.*

That were of old] — that lived in ancient generations and now are no more. God's word was fulfilled in them: the spirit of life did not abide in them *for ever* [לְעוֹלָם *le*ʿ*ōlām*] (*v.* 3), but *of old* [מֵעוֹלָם *mē*ʿ*ōlām*] already they had ceased to exist.

The men of RENOWN [הַשֵּׁם *haššēm,* literally, 'the name'] / It is true that they had acquired a name for themselves in the world, but now nought but the name was left of them. The reason for the emphasis given by Scripture to these phrases — *that were of old* and *the men of renown* — we shall see later. Possibly the last expression echoes, as a word-play, the name of *Shem* [שֵׁם *Šēm*], the son of Noah, mentioned at the end of the preceding paragraph.

With regard to the internal structure of the paragraph, the chiastic parallels between its opening and close should be noted. At the beginning the wording is: *were born to them . . . the sons of God; the daughters of men;* and at the end: *the sons of God to the daughters of men, and they bore children to them.*

Now, having annotated the paragraph in detail, let us endeavour to grasp its meaning as a whole.

Among the ancient peoples, as we know, various myths were current telling of sexual relations between gods and daughters of men, and of the children born from these unions, who were regarded as half-gods or were raised to the full status of deities. Also among the Canaanites, who were closest to the Israelites, there existed legends of this kind, as the Ugaritic inscriptions testify. Although the Ugaritic poems on *the pleasant and beautiful gods* are not clear in detail, yet this at least is certain, that they refer to the father of the gods, *'El,* as having married two daughters of men and begotten from them two sons, *šḥr* and *šlm,* who both became divinities. An obscure allusion to a similar topic is found in the work of Philo of Byblus (see Clemen, *op. cit.*, pp. 21–22, 44–45). The Torah, in the paragraph under consideration, takes up an attitude towards these myths and the concepts flowing from them. The reader who has come thus far might ask: I have now learnt how the human families, the offspring of Adam and Eve by the natural process of procreation, were born and multiplied and became ramified; but I know that in the past there lived upon earth giants, men of far greater stature and strength than ordinary people, and we have a tradition from our forbears that when they entered the Land they still found there some of the surviving giants. What was their origin, seeing that they did not resemble human beings like ourselves? To this question, which might arise in the reader's mind, the Torah proceeds to give an answer in our paragraph.

The explanation it offers contradicts the gentile legends we have mentioned. Following its usual practice, Scripture does not engage in any polemic or argument here; it merely explains, in harmony with its outlook, the origin of the titans, and from the affirmations one may deduce the negations. These colossi are in no way related — Heaven forfend! — to the *Deity,* but only to 'the sons of God', that is, to the members of the Divine household, to God's *ministers,* more particularly to the lowest orders among them. The subject is treated with extreme brevity. Of set purpose, the Torah compresses its words into a few sentences, as though it wished to convey that it finds the entire topic wholly uncongenial, and that the subject is mentioned not for its own sake but in order to disabuse the reader's mind of certain notions. The declaration in *v.* 3, *My spirit shall not abide in man,* etc. implies: Do not believe the heathen tales about human beings of divine origin, who were rendered immortal; this is untrue, for in the end every man must die, *in as much as he, too, is flesh.* The sons that were born from the intercourse of the sons of God with the daughters of men were, in truth, gigantic and mighty, yet they did not live *for ever* [לְעוֹלָם *le'ōlām*], but had *long ago* [מֵעוֹלָם *mē'ōlām*] become extinct. And when they lived, it is *on the earth* that they lived; even before their descent to Sheol, they were only *on the earth,* and were never translated to heaven. They were *the men of renown;* indeed, men of *renown,* but even so they were *men,* not more than men.

Thus we see that we have not here, as is generally supposed today, a surviving fragment from the mythological sagas of the peoples of the ancient East, which has been preserved in the Book of Genesis as a misplaced anachronism. On the contrary, the Torah's intention is to *counteract* the pagan legends and to reduce to a minimum the content of the ancient traditions concerning the giants.

Of that content only so much was retained as was innocuous to Israel's monotheistic faith, and did not in the least detract from the glory of God, or even the dignity of His closest ministers.

TWELFTH PARAGRAPH

PUNISHMENT IS DECREED ON THE GENERATION OF THE FLOOD BUT GRACE IS SHOWN TO NOAH

5. *The Lord saw / that the wickedness of man was great / in the earth;*
and that every device of the thoughts of his heart / was only evil continually.

6. *And the Lord was sorry / that He had made man / on the earth,*
and it grieved Him to His heart.

7. *So the Lord said,*
'I will blot out man whom I have created / from the face of the ground,
man and beast and creeping things / and flying creatures of the air,
for I am sorry / that I have made them.'

8. *But Noah found favour / in the eyes of the Lord.*

5. *The Lord saw that the wickedness of man was great in the earth*] In the first section it is stated, of almost every one of the Divine acts, that God saw it and appraised it (*And God saw that it was good*); and in conclusion, after the completion of His works, Scripture declares, *And God saw everything that He had made, and behold, it was very good* (i 31). Similarly with regard to the deeds of the children of men, after we have been informed, by examples such as those of Cain and Enoch, that God saw them and assessed them, we are told here, at the end of the first ten generations of mankind (הָאָדָם *hā'ādhām* [literally, 'the man'] signifies here: 'humanity') that the Lord reviewed their actions as a whole and passed righteous judgment upon them. However, the impres-

sion that the Lord gained of human deeds was the diametrical opposite of that created by His own works: earlier the Bible says, AND BEHOLD, IT WAS VERY GOOD, but in our verse it testifies THAT THE WICKEDNESS *of man was* GREAT *in the earth.*

It is not stated of *man* in the first section that *he was good* (see my remarks on this point on pp. 59 f.), since he was enabled to be good or bad, according to his choice. Although this special privilege was a good thing from the standpoint of the over-all design of the world (of *all* that God had made, taken as a whole, the Torah says, *and behold, it was very good*), and raises man to a higher plane than that of the other creatures, yet it can be a source of terrible danger to him, and it is, indeed, related here that the majority of men actually chose evil. The Bible has already prepared the reader for this conclusion by the Song of Lamech and by the expression, *he walked with God,* which is used exceptionally of Enoch, as we have explained previously. The word *saw* does not denote sudden perception but the consideration of a state of affairs that had long been in existence, and on account of which a decision has to be taken. Compare xxx 1: *When Rachel* SAW *that she bore Jacob no children,* etc.; ibid. *v.* 9: *When Leah* SAW *that she had ceased bearing children,* etc.; l 15: *When Joseph's brothers* SAW *that their father was dead,* etc.; and so forth.

I have already indicated above the parallels that connect this verse with the beginning of the preceding paragraph: here it is stated, *that the wickedness of* MAN *was* GREAT [רַבָּה *rabbā*] *in the* EARTH, and, in like manner, we are told there, that MEN *began* TO MULTIPLY [לָרֹב *lārōbh*] *on the face of the* GROUND. The verbal parallelism indicates a correspondence of theme; in this case, too, there is an antithesis between God's and man's deeds. God blessed mankind that they should be fertile and fill the earth (i 28), and He implemented His promise: men began to *multiply* on the face of the *ground.* Man, however, was an ingrate: he, too, *increased,* but it was *evil-doing* that he increased; truly, he filled *the earth,* but he did so with *violence* (vi 11, 13). The same applies to the parallel between *v.* 2, *the sons of God* SAW *the daughters of men that they were* FAIR [literally, 'good'], and our verse, which speaks of the WICKEDNESS of man. The Creator had blessed man with good-looking daughters, but man requited evil for good.

And that every DEVICE [יֵצֶר *yēṣer*] *of the thoughts of his heart was only evil continually* (cf. viii 21)] The word יֵצֶר *yēṣer,* needless to say, is not used here in the sense of יֵצֶר הָרָע *yēṣer hārā'* ['evil impulse'], which is its usual signification in later Hebrew, but in the meaning of יְצִירָה *yeṣīrā* ['formation', 'creation']. Not only what man actually did with his hands, but what he *formed* [i.e. devised] with his mind was nought but evil, continually (literally, *all the day*). For the thought compare Micah ii 1; and for the wording, Jer. xviii 11: *Behold, I am* SHAPING [יוֹצֵר *yōṣēr*] *evil against you and devising a plan against you.* Here, too, the text expresses an antithesis between the Creator's work, which was *very good* even *on the day of its creation* (v 1, 2), and that of man, which was only evil continually.

6. *And the Lord was* SORRY [וַיִּנָּחֶם *wayyinnāḥem*] *that He had* MADE [עָשָׂה *'āśā*] *man . . . and it* GRIEVED [וַיִּתְעַצֵּב *wayyith'aṣṣēbh*] *him,* etc.] There are three verbs in this sentence, נחם *nāḥam* [*Niph'al*: 'be sorry', 'regret'; *Pi'el*: 'to comfort', 'console'], עָשָׂה *'āśā* ['do', 'make'], עָצַב *'āṣabh* ['grieve', 'suffer']; and all three of these stems have already appeared, in precisely the same order, in the opening words of Lamech (v 29): *This one* SHALL BRING US COMFORT [יְנַחֲמֵנוּ *yenaḥămēnū*] FROM OUR LABOUR [מִמַּעֲשֵׂנוּ *mimma'ăśēnū*] AND FROM THE TOIL [וּמֵעִצְּבוֹן *ūmē'iṣṣebhōn*] *of our hands.* This is certainly no coincidence. At the least, we have here a parallelism of form linking the two paragraphs together; and possibly there is also an antithesis of thought. Lamech had hoped that his son would be a source of *consolation* from the *travail* resulting from manual *labour* of people who perform hard work on the accursed ground; but he did not consider that just as the works of human beings in the field of physical toil brought them pain, so their deeds in the moral sphere caused suffering to their Creator; and that just as men were yearning to be *comforted* for the *sorrow* caused them by their material work, so the Creator, out of His heart's *grief, regretted* that He had *made* man upon the earth. The hopes that Lamech set on his son were realized in a manner far different from that which he had imagined (see my earlier observations on the naming of *Noah*).

On the earth [בָּאָרֶץ *bā'āreṣ*] / — corresponding to the word בָּאָרֶץ *bā'āreṣ* in the previous verse (note how I have divided the verses above), and to בָּאָרֶץ *bā'āreṣ* in paragraph eleven (*v.* 4).

And it grieved Him to His heart] Man's deeds and the thoughts of his *heart* (*v.* 5) bring grief to the *heart* of the Lord.

As a rule the commentators dwell at length on the problems connected with the anthropopathic expressions in this verse. These questions arise only from later conceptions, and it is superfluous to discuss them, if one's aim is purely to understand the Torah-text. The Torah was not intended specifically for intellectuals but for the entire people, which is not concerned with philosophic or theological speculations. It uses ordinary language, plainly and without sophistication, and pays no heed to the inferences that later readers, who are accustomed to ways of thinking wholly alien to the Bible, may draw from its words.

7. *So the Lord said*] — as in *v.* 3, and having the identical meaning.

I will blot out [אֶמְחֶה *'emḥe*] / It is usually interpreted in the sense of אַשְׁמִיד *'ašmīdh* ['I will destroy']. But the verb מָחָה *māḥā* has not a general signification like that of הִשְׁמִיד *hišmīdh* ['he destroyed']; in order to grasp the meaning of the verse it is necessary to define the connotation of this verb exactly. Mostly, it signifies the erasure of writing from a book. Thus it is expressly stated in Num. v 23: *Then the priest shall write these curses in a book, and* WASH THEM OFF [מָחָה *māḥā*] *into the water of bitterness.* In metaphorical expressions: Exod. xxxii 32: BLOT ME [מְחֵנִי *meḥēnī*], *I pray Thee, out of Thy book which Thou hast written*; ibid., *v.* 33: *Whoever has sinned against Me,* HIM WILL I BLOT OUT [אֶמְחֶנּוּ *'emḥennū*] *out of My book;* Psa. lxix 28 [Hebrew, *v.* 29]: LET THEM BE BLOTTED OUT [יִמָּחוּ *yimmāḥū*] *of the book of the living.* So, too, whenever the Bible speaks of blotting out anyone's name or memorial, it means its erasure — literal or figurative — from the books of remembrance or kinship (Exod. xvii 14; Deut. ix 14 [with regard to the same episode as in Exod. xxxii 32–33]; *ibid., vv.* 19–20; Jud. xxi 17; ii Kings xiv 27; Psa. ix 6; cix 13); and whenever reference is made to the blotting out of iniquities or acts of lovingkindness, their expunction from the Heavenly Court's book of remembrance is intended (Isa. xliii 25; xliv 22; Jer. xviii 23; Psa. li 3, 11; cix 14; Neh. iii 37; xiii 14; an analogous case occurs in Prov. vi 33). If we consider all these passages, as well as Isa. xxv 8: *and the Lord God* WILL WIPE AWAY [ומָחָה *umāḥā*] *tears from all faces,* and Ezek. vi 6: *and your works* WIPED OUT [וְנִמְחוּ *wenimḥū*], etc. (that is, the images and altars that you made for idolatrous worship would be purged from the earth) we shall see that generally speaking the meaning of the verb is to rub out and remove one thing from off another. From this emanates a secondary meaning: to cleanse and purify something from what was on it before (ii Kings xxi 13: AND I WILL WIPE [ומָחִיתִי *ūmāḥīthī*] *Jerusalem as* ONE WIPES [יִמְחֶה *yimḥe*] *a dish,* WIPING [מָחָה *māḥā*] *it and turning it upside down;* Prov. xxx 20: *she eats* AND WIPES [ומָחֲתָה *ūmāḥăthā*] *her mouth*). In our verse, and further on in the section of the Flood (vii 4, 23), the verb signifies to *expunge* from the face of the ground, just as one rubs off writing from a book, or, generally, one thing from another.

Since the wickedness of man was universal, his punishment likewise had to take the form of universal obliteration. The righteous exceptions were so few that they could not protect the whole race, and only saved themselves. Compare what the Bible states later on concerning Sodom, and Ezek. xiv 12f.

Whom I have created] This is one of the parallels between the close of the section and its opening (see above, pp. 249 f.); there is no reason to regard it as a later interpolation, as do many of the modern expositors, who attribute these verses to source J and hold that the term בָּרָא *bārā'* is characteristic of source P. We have already seen that the verb בָּרָא *bārā'* belongs to the most general and the most ancient poetic tradition (cf. pp. 75, 99); see also my observations on this verse on p. 98).

From the face of the ground] This expression is connected with the verb אֶמְחֶה *'emḥe* ['I will blot out'], as we have noted. The parallel to *v.* 1 is clear.

Man and beast and creeping things and flying creatures of the air] All these words, too, are usually considered a later addition, because they appertain to the vocabulary attributed to P, and because they are not a logical specification of the preceding word הָאָדָם *hā'ādhām* ['man']. But they are all such common words that it is impossible to regard them as confined to any particular source or school, and their use to be prohibited to all other Israelite writers. As for the connection between them and the preceding word הָאָדָם *hā'ādhām,* it is undoubtedly true that if they came to detail its content, this specification would be illogical; but there is no need to assume that their purpose is to particularize. On the contrary, they come to *augment* what has preceded, as though to say: And not man only, but in general all living creatures upon earth, man and beast and creeping things, etc.. The proof is to be seen in the subsequent statement (vii 23): *He blotted out every living thing that was upon the face of the ground, man and animals and creeping things and flying creatures of the air,* exactly as it is written here. The two verses parallel each other; the second describes the execution of the decree stated in the first. Since the implementation must correspond to the edict, the words used there must also occur here. The difference between the two verses (here: *man whom I have created;* there: *every living thing*) was necessitated by the context. In the present verse, the starting-point is the wickedness of man, and on account of it the Lord decides to bring a deluge on the earth; hence it was necessary to begin by stating: *I will blot out man whom I have created;* that was the essential point. An inevitable consequence of the Flood would be that together with man the other living creatures on earth would also perish, as we are apprised later (*v.* 13): *behold, I will destroy them* WITH THE EARTH. In the final description of how the decree was carried out, seeing that it had actually come to pass as foretold and the other living creatures as well as man were overwhelmed, it was proper to employ at the outset a term that would embrace them all; consequently the phrase used there is: אֶת־כָּל־הַיְקוּם *'eth-kol-hay^eqūm* ['every living thing'].

For I am sorry that I made them] Here recur the two verbs that appeared at the beginning of *v.* 6. The same expressions as are found at the commencement of the passage are repeated at the end.

8. *But* [־וְ *w^e-*] *Noah found favour in the eyes of the Lord*] Utter destruction, in truth, had been decreed upon the world, *but* Noah (the *Wāw* of וְנֹחַ *w^eNōaḥ* [literally, 'and Noah'] is antithetic) found favour in the Lord's eyes. Not the material civilization that had developed among the sons of Cain (iv 17, 20–22), nor the multitude of the children of men (ch. v; also vi 1), nor the might of the mighty men (vi 4), nor the fame acquired by the mighty men because of their might (*ibid.*), could be of avail

in the hour of retribution; only the righteousness of the righteous man was able to save the world. Only *Noah,* who was, as the Torah stresses immediately afterwards (*v.* 9), a wholly righteous man in his generations and walked with God, *found* FAVOUR [חן *ḥēn*] *in the eyes of the Lord* (note the word-play [anagram]: נח *Nōaḥ* —חן *ḥēn*), and was chosen so that the blessing bestowed on the first man should be realized in him and in his seed after him: *Be fruitful and multiply, and fill the earth* (see p. 250). All this will be recounted in detail later; but already at this stage the Bible wishes to inform us that at the very moment that the Lord decreed punishment on the wicked, He prepared, by means of the righteous man, salvation for the world and the fulfilment of His promises to mankind. Thus the section ends on a note of grace.

INDEXES*

I. Biblical References **

GENESIS

I:1–II:3 7–19 (Introd.) *19–70*
I:1 *19–20* 88 97 167 197
2 *21–25*
3 *25 f.*
4 *26*
5 *26–30* 92 130
6 *31–33*
7 *33 f.* 70
8 *34* 92 130
9 *35–39*
10 *39–40* 92 130
11–12 89
11 *40 f.*
12 *41* 108
14–15 *42–44*
16 *45 f.* 70
17–18 *46 f.*
20–21 89
20 *48 f.*
21 *49–51*
22 *51 f.*
24–25 89
24 10 *53 f.*
25 11 *54 f.* 70 144
26–27 275
26–28 275
26 *55–57* 70 92 127 203 275
27 11 *57 f.* 70 88 92 127 275 (twice)
28–29 164
28 51 *58* 92 162 203 275 302
29–30 40 *58 f.* 203
29 122 171
30 11 122 144
31 *59 f.* 92 127 301
II:1–3 *see* I:1–II:3
1 *61*
2 *61–64* 70
3 60 *64–70*
4–III:24 71–96 (Introd.) *96–177*
4 75 88 89 90 *96–100* 274 275
5–6 88
5 73 74 89 90 92 *100–103* 168 169 173 203
6 73 *103 f.* 114 f.
7 89 *104–106* 131 169 (twice) 173 201
8 76 93 *107 f.* 121 174 (twice) 228
9 74 80 89 93 *108–114* 130 147 176
10–14 93 121
10 104 *114 f.*
11–14 *115–121*
11–12 79
11 30
15 76 93 *121–123* 175
16–17 144
16 *123 f.*
17 *124 f.* 133 145 (twice) 154 (twice) 161 170
18 73 92 *126 f.*
19–20 92 139
19 21 89 90 *127–131*
20 21 128 *131–133* 166 167
21–22 89 128
21 *133 f.*
22 73 92 *134 f.*

* References are to pages.

** Numbers printed in italic refer to the pages in which the commentary on the verse is given.

23	73 94 *135 f.*
24	*136 f.* 166
25	*137* 148 149 171
III:1–7	94 *138 f.*
1–5	84 88
1	21 *139–144* 158 197
2–3	*144 f.*
3	73 110
4	*145 f.*
5	111 112 *146 f.* 148
6	73 74 78 *147 f.* 157 158
7	112 137 139 *148 f.* 157 171 (twice)
8	110 *150–155* 156 225
9	*155 f.*
10	*156 f.*
11	112 *157*
12	*157 f.*
13	*158*
14–19	73
14	139 *158–160* 168 218
15	139 *160 f.* 164 166
16–19	92
16	137 160 *161–166* 168 171 197 212 213
17–19	171 173
17	165 *166–168* 169 171 218 289
18	90 102 *168 f.*
19	75 94 102 105 106 136 *169 f.* 173
20	*170 f.* 197 202
21	58 139 149 163 166 167 *171*
22	109 111 112 123 f. 146 *172 f.*
23	94 102 105 122 136 *173* 203
24	73 108 110 123 125 *173–177* 225 228
IV:1–26	178–196 (Introd.) *196–248*
1–2	185 f.
1	21 163 167 *197–202* 204 245 279
2–5	27
2	58 *202–204* 221 (twice) 229 230
3–16	183 ff.
3	204 *205 f.*
4	58 204 *206 f.*
5	204 *207*
6	*207 f.* 215
7	161 (twice) *208–213*
8	*213–216*
9	155 215 *217*
10	152 156 158 215 *217 f.*
11	*218–220* 289
12	*221 f.* 223
13	215 *222*
14	*222–225*
15	180 189 199 215 *225–228* 243
16	174 *228*
17–22	186 ff. 265 ff.
17	180 *229–231* 281 306
18	21 *231–233* 282 287
19	*234*
20–22	306
20	221 *234–236*
21–22	202
21	*236*
22	180 234 *236–238*
23–24	189 f.
23	215 234 *239–243*
24	226 241 f. *243 f.*
25–26	190 f.
25	167 202 *244–246* 277
26	202 236 *246–248* 267 279
V:1–VI:8	249–272 (Introd.) *273–307*
V (passim)	167 306
1	97 *273–275* 276 277 303
2	58 75 *275 f.* 288 303
3	275 (twice) *276 f.* 288
4	*277* 279
5	*277 f.*
6–9	*279*
10–14	198
10–11	*279*
12–17	232 *280*
18–24	229
18–20	*281*
21	*281 f.* 283
22	*282–284*
23	*284 f.* 289
24	*285 f.*
25–27	*287*

28 *288*
29 267 276 *288 f.* 303
30 *289*
31 243 285 *289*
32 274 276 *290*
VI:1–8 *see* V:1–VI:8
1 *291* 305 306
2 *291–295* 302
3 294 *295 ff.* 299 300 304
4 *289–300* 304 306
5 60 140 189 *301–303* 304
6 289 *303 f.* 306
7 98 291 295 *304–306*
8 248 289 *306 f.*
9–10 274
9 283 307
11 189 270 302
13 189 270 302 306
18 148
VII:4 305
6 252
7 148
11 252 260
16 21
19 21
22 295
23 305 306
VIII:4 289
9 289
13 252 261
20 58
21 60 140 289 303
IX:1 52
3 58 203
26 267
28–29 260 290
X 251 261
2 236
6 119
7 118
8 21
9 21
13 21
15 21
21 236
24 21 282
26 21
29 118 119
XI:7 56
9 132
10–32 251
12–15 282
12 21
14 21
26 274
27 274
XII:5 201
18 155 158
XIII:1 148
10 74 76 104 108 117
14 21
XIV:13 175
19 200
22 200 f.
XVI:7 223
XVII:9–12 227
16 52
20 52 132
22 61 f.
XVIII:1 153 f.
4 234
13 144
17 21
18 21
23 144
24 144 209
26 209
XIX:33–34 28
XX:4 21
6 145
9 155 158
XXI:1 21
14–21 223 f.
15 102
XXII:1 167
7 213
17 52
23 21
XXIII:1 259
XXIV:11 153
19 62
50 113
60 52
XXV:1–18 251
4 229
12 274
18 118
19 ff. 251

19 274
23 115
XXVI:3–4 52
9–10 155
10 158
11 145
XXVII:30 62
XXVIII:3 52
5 91
6–9 91
10 ff. 91
XXIX:14 135
XXX:1 147 302
9 147 302
XXXI:24 113
29 113
XXXII:31–32 233
33 (E.V. 32) 136
XXXIV:7 145 207
XXXV:9–11 52
XXXVI 251
2 f. 234
13 99
17 99
18 99
19 99
XXXVII ff. 251
8 45
XXXIX:9 297
23 297
XLI:40 131
XLIII:2 62
XLVI:9 229
XLVIII:3–4 52
15–16 52
XLIX:3 209
6 241
9 210
11 241
13 40
25 52
33 62
L:15 302

EXODUS

II:2 294
10 198
III:12 122
VI:1 173
IX:30 101
X:2 227
XI:1 173
XII:13 227
15 60
18 29
23 227
XV:25 227
XVII:14 304
XVIII:12 206
XIX:25 213
XX:8 64
9–10 63
10 60 68
11 63 65
XXI:20 226
21 226 (twice)
23–25 242
XXII:19 (E.V. 20) 167
XXIII:5 211
12 63 69
XXV–XXXI 213 268
XXVIII:9 120
12 120
17–20 120
XXIX:29 122
XXX:18 122
XXXI:17 63
XXXII:32–33 304
32 304
33 304
XXXIII:19 247
XXXIV:5–6 247
10 69 70
21 63
XXXV–XL 213 268
XXXVIII:3 106
XXXIX:3 31
6–7 120
10–13 120
XL:33–34 62

LEVITICUS

XI:19 f. 49
42 159
XVII:13 129
XXIII:32 29
XXVI:12 152

I. BIBLICAL REFERENCES

NUMBERS

III:1 99
V:23 304
VII:12–83 213 268
84 99
XI:7 119 120
XIII:33 298
XV:38–39 45
XVI:30 69 219 223
32 219 223
33 219
XXI:17 103
XXII:27 211
XXIII:18 239
24 210
XXVIII:2 122
XXXII:38 130

DEUTERONOMY

I:39 112 f.
IV:44 110
V:14 68 f.
15 69
IX:14 304
19–20 304
XI:6 219
XXI:1 217
XXII:25–27 215
XXIII:15 (E.V. 14) 152
XXV:8 155
XXXII:1–2 239 f.
6 200
7 200
8 261
8 (Septuagint) 292 294
11 25
17 294
XXXIII:13–15 168

JOSHUA

II:12 227
XV:57 198

JUDGES

III:22 134
V:3 240
7 297
17 40
24 159
VI:38 28
IX:2 135
XI:4 205
XIV:8 205
XV:1 205
13 146
XX:33 116
XXI:4 28
17 304

I SAMUEL

II:4 51
8 245
13 226
III:2–4 20
VII:12 198
XV:7 118
33 159
XIX:11 28
XXVI:16 156
XXVIII:19 28 f.

II SAMUEL

I:24 171
V:1 135
24 151
XIV:5–7 225
7 242
17 113 172
20 113 172
XIX:13 (E.V. 12) 135
14 (E.V. 13) 135
36 (E.V. 35) 112
XXI:16 197
XXII:1 100 165
11 175
XXIII:1 238
XXIV:14 55

I KINGS

II:5 218
31 218
XIV:6 151 f.
XVII:7 205
XXII:19 55 293

II KINGS

II:3 285
5 285

VI:32 152
XIV:27 304
XXI:13 305
XXIII:34 130
XXIV:17 130

ISAIAH

I:2 240
6 243
10 240
15 218
V:14 219
26 130
VI:2–8 55
VII:15–16 112
15 153 242
VIII:6–7 118
IX:4 (E.V. 5) 218
XI:7 59
15 118
XII:3 118
XIX:10 245
XXV:8 305
XXVII:1 50 141 160
XXVIII:23 239
XXIX:4 240
16 105
XXX:22 130
XXXII:9 239
XXXIV:11 22
XL:12 9 f.
21 f. 9 f.
XLII:5 46 106
XLIII:25 304
XLIV:22 304
24 46
XLV:7 26
9 105
XLIX:23 160
LI:3 74 76
9 f. 24 37 50
LIV:6 144
16 69
LVII:19 69
LVIII:3 168
LXIV:6 (E.V. 7) 247
7 (E.V. 8) 105
LXV:25 59 160
LXVI:19 227 236

JEREMIAH

IV:23 22
V:22 37 38
IX:19 (E.V. 20) 239
XIII:12 146
XVIII:1–14 105
11 303
23 304
XXVI:1 19
XXVII:1 19
XXVIII:1 19
XXX:11 146
XXXI:20 (E.V. 21) 215
XLVI:22 152
L:11 116

EZEKIEL

I:13 80
VI:6 305
XIV:12 ff. 305
XXI:35 (E.V. 30) 69
XXVII:13 236 237 (twice)
XXVIII:11–19 75
13 75 77 78 99 120
14 73 75 76 79 123
15 75 81 99
16 76 79 81 123
17 81
18 75 81
19 81
XXXI:8 f. 75 80
8 77
16–18 75
18 80
XXXII:2 116
20 ff. 298 f.
22 298
23 298
24 298
26 236
27 297
XXXVI:35 74
XXXVIII:2 f. 237
XXXIX:1 237
XLVII:1–12 115

HOSEA

I:2 19
V:1 240

VI:7 148
X:8 169
XIII:2 213

JOEL

I:2 240
II:3 74
IV:18 115

AMOS

I:11 181
II:7 161
VI:10 246
VIII:4 161
IX:2–4 224
8 146
9 221

MICAH

II:1 303
IV:10 116
VII:17 160

NAHUM

III:18 116

HABAKKUK

I:18 116
II:5 219

ZECHARIAH

XIV:8 115

MALACHI

III:20 (E.V. IV:2) 116

PSALMS

VIII:6 113 f.
IX:6 304
XI:3 245
XII:7 (E.V. 6) 226
XVII:6 239
XVIII:1 100 165
11 (E.V. 10) 175
XXIX:1 292
XXXVI:9 107
XXXIX:14 (E.V. 13) 285
XLVI:5 (E.V. 4) 115
XLIX:2 (E.V. 1) 240
8 f. (E.V. 7 f.) 146
16 (E.V. 15) 286
LI:3 (E.V. 1) 304
11 (E.V. 9) 304
12 (E.V. 10) 69
LIV:4 (E.V. 2) 240
LXIII:3 (E.V. 2) 70
LXIX:29 (E.V. 28) 304
LXXI:10 213
LXXII:9 160
LXXIII:24 286
LXXIV:13 f. 50
13 37
LXXVIII:24 119
43 227
55 174
LXXIX:12 226
LXXXI:3 (E.V. 2) 238
LXXXIV:9 (E.V. 8) 240
LXXXVI:8 167
LXXXIX:7 (E.V. 6) 292
11 (E.V. 10) 37
XC:2 101
4 263
XCVI:8 208
CIII:14 170
16 285
20 f. 293
CIV:3 f. 175
3 10 32
4 176
6 23
7–9 37
29 170
CV:40 119
CVI:17 219
37 294
CIX:9 f. 221
13 304
14 304
CXV:15 200
16 20
CXIX:73 105
CXXVII:2 168
CXXXV:3 238
CXXXVI:5 46
6 46
7 45
8 f. 45 f.

CXXXIX:7–12 224
13 201
CXLIII:1 240
CXLIV:4 202
CXLVII:1 238
CXLVIII:2 293
7 20 51

PROVERBS

III:18 74 109
V:10 168
VI:33 304
VIII:22 201
27–29 37
27 25
X:22 168
XI:30 74 109
XII:7 285
XIII:12 74
XIV:23 168
XV:4 74 109
XX:30 243
XXVII:17 237
20 219
XXX:15 f. 219
20 305

JOB

I–II 55
I:6 292 293
II:1 292 293
IV:19 105 170
VII:12 37 50
16 202
21 285
VIII:22 285
IX:8 10
13 37
X:8 105
9 105 170
XI:15 208
XIII:12 105
XXVI:10–12 38
10 25
12 46
13 50
XXVIII:5 f. 78
16 78
XXX:19 105
XXXI:33 155
XXXIII:4 24 106
6 105
XXXIV:2 240
15 170
XXXVI:27 73 103
XXXVIII:4–7 9
7 11 292 293
8–10 38
8 116
XL:23 116

CANTICLES

II:8 152
14 234
V:2 152

LAMENTATIONS

IV:5 107

ECCLESIASTES

I:18 113
III:20 170
XII:7 170

ESTHER

I:1 259
18 213
VIII:9 259
IX:30 259

DANIEL

VI:2 259

NEHEMIAH

III:37 304
XI:4 280
XIII:14 304

I CHRONICLES

I:1 277
8 119
9 118
18 282
23 118 119
24 282
XI:1 136

II CHRONICLES

II:10 (E.V. 11) 213
XXXII:24 213
XXXVI:4 130

II. Other Literary References
(Ancient and Modern)

Abravanel 134 152 165
Albright, W. F. 19 77 104 114 116 175 196 198 238 240 272 280 286
Apocrypha and Pseudepigrapha 2 139 283 284; Book of Jubilees 61 265; Ethiopic Book of Enoch 286
Aptowitzer, V. 205
Aquila *see* Bible translations, ancient
Astruc, J. 84

Baethgen, F. 238
Bamberger, B. J. 272
Barton, G. A. 83
Ben Asher MSS 296
Ben Mordechai, C. A. 272
Berossus 32 106 254 ff. (passim) 282
Bertholet, A. 18
Bible translations, ancient 41 213
- Aquila 103
- Peshiṭta 44 61 103 166 199 214
- Septuagint 33 34 35 41 49 61 92 103 120 127 129 166 174 199 208 214 228 231 232 233 234 252 253 **264 f. 266 288 292 294**
- Targum, Fragmentary (Jerusalem) 214
- Targum Jonathan 103
- Targum Onkelos 103 111 199 209 236 284
- Targum Pseudo-Jonathan 120 199 214 236 238 284
- Targum, Samaritan 214
- Theodotion 207
- Vetus Latina 166
- Vulgate 44 92 103 127 199 214

Bibliographical references, started from 1934 3; not up to date 5; Creation 18 f.; Garden of Eden 94 f.; Cain and Abel 195 f.; History of Adam 272
Böhl, F.M.T. 98
Böhmer, J. 95
Bornstein, H. J. 28
Bousset, D. W. 253
Brock-Utne, A. 95 181 182 185 196 207
Budde, K. 34 124 153 193 199 221
Buhl, F. *see* Gesenius
Burrows, E. 288

Cabbala 38 50
Cassuto, U.
- Baʿal and Môt in the texts of Ugarit, *BJPES* IX [Hebrew] 220 (3 times)
- Biblical Literature and Canaanite Literature, *Tarbiz* XIII, XIV [Hebrew] 2 12 f. 16 49 200 212
- La creazione del mondo nella Genesi, *Annuario di Studi Ebraici* I 15 18 31
- The Death of Baʿal (Tablet I* AB from Ras-Shamra), *Tarbiz* XII [Hebrew] 233 243
- *The Documentary Hypothesis and the Composition of the Pentateuch* 2 58 85 86 101 198 231 259 261 276 277 286 289 295
- Eden, the Garden of God, *Schorr Festschrift* [Hebrew] 73 80
- Israelite Epic Poetry, *Keneseth* VIII [Hebrew] 9 16 37 50 73 141 212
- Il nome divino El nell'antico Israele, *SMSR* VIII 167
- Il palazzo di Baal nella tavola I* AB di Ras Shamra, *Orientalia* N.S. VII 78
- Psalm LXVIII, *Tarbiz* XII [Hebrew] 141
- *La Questione della Genesi* 2 18 40 85 86 93 94 96 101 167 198 201 231 259 261 276 277 281
- The Reception of Baʿal in the Ugaritic Tablet V AB, *BJPES* X [Hebrew] 91 236
- The Sons of God and the Daughters of Man, *Hertz Festschrift*

[Hebrew] 272 291 f. 296
Studi sulla Genesi, *GSAI* N.S. I 259
The Ten Generations from Adam to Noah, *Ginzburg Festschrift* [Hebrew] 252 ff.
Chiera, E. 83
Christian Church exegesis 111 187
Clemen, C. 235 299
Closen, G. E. 195 272
Cross, E. B. 196

Daiches, S. 282
Danthine, H. 95 f.
Deimel, A. 18
Dhorme, P. 175 258
Dillmann, A. 28 59 69 101 111 133 144 (twice) 199 290
Dornseiff, F. 111* 139
Dumaine, H. 18

Ehrenzweig, A. 180 182
Eissfeldt, O. 18

Feigin, S. J. 18
Fischer, J. 95
[Freytag, G. W.] 23

Geiger, A. 56
Gesenius, W.–Buhl, F. 30 215 285
Gesenius, W.–Kautzsch, E. 145 226 231
Ginzberg, L. 39
Glueck, N. 219
Gordis, R. 95 111 259
Gordon, C. H. 196 202
Graham, A. C. 272
Groot, J. de 95
Guillaume, A. 272 295
Gunkel, H. 28 34 44 69 111 133 144 180 182 193 194 199 (twice) 205 207 (twice) 208 214 215 217 276 277

Haggada 140 160 199 207 214 224 288
Halévy, J. 207 236
Heidel, A. 18
Heinisch, P. 69
Hoffmann, G. 28
Holzinger, H. 28 124 199
Hooke, S. H. 196
Hornblower, G. D. 196
Humbert, P. 18 93 95 109 112

Ibn Ezra, Abraham 19 28 69 101 111 131 144 146 214 219 222 228
Ibn Gi'at, Isaac 30

Jacob, B. 28 69 131 133 144 145 153 166 171 207 (twice) 208 (twice)
Jacobsen, T. 188 189 257
Jean, C.-F. 18
Jepsen, A. 254
Jewish Liturgy 30
Jewish Medieval commentaries 103 152
Jewish mystical literature 284
Josephus Flavius 265
Joüon, P. 272
Juda Hallevi 224
Junker, H. 272

Kahle, P. 214
Kautzsch, E. *see* Gesenius
King, L. W. 80
Knobel A. 214
König, E. 88
Kraeling, E. G. 18 65
Krappe, A. H. 18 58
Kroon, J. 272
Kuhn, G. 272 289

Landsberger, B. 18 65
Langdon, S. H. 18 65 83 256 f.
Levi della Vida, G. 199 200
Lewy, H. 19
Lewy, J. 19 65 272 288
Lidzbarski, M. 198

Marcus, R. 96
Marti, K. 199
May, H. B. 18 26 96
McClellan, W. H. 196

* Reference is to the work cited on p. 139.

II. OTHER LITERARY REFERENCES

Michaelis, J. D. 219
Midrash 38 50 192 240 246 259 284; *see also* Rabbinic literature
Midrash Rabba:
Bereshith Rabba 199
III 1, 25
IV 8, 34
VIII 1, 57
3–7, 55
XI 8, 13
XIII 9–10, 104
9, 103
XVI 2, 120
5, 122
8, 121
XIX 1, 159
7, 152
8, 152 f.
XX 2, 171
11, 170 f.
XXII 5, 205
XXIII 3, 238
XXV 1, 284
2, 288
Wayyiqra Rabba
XXIX 9, 282
Pesiqta de Rab Kahana (ed. Buber) 282
Sifre Num. 143, 206
Sifre Deut. 32:2, 108
Miklik, J. 95
Mishnah 204; Aboth V 1, 14; *see also* Rabbinic literature
Mishnah of R. Eliezer b. R. Jose the Galilean (ed. Enelow) 92
Montgomery, J. A. 199
Morgenstern, J. 272
Mowinckel, S. 93 95 180 193 196
Moyal, D. 215

Naḥmanides 30 34 49 69 101 111 131 136 153 199 214 222 297
New Testament 139
Nöldeke, T. 198 253

Obbink, H. T. 124
Olshausen, J. 277
Oppenheim, A. L. 19
Oppert, J. 255
Perrot, N. 95
Peshiṭta *see* Bible translations, ancient
Pfeiffer, R. H. 18 193 272
Philo of Byblus 22 188 230 232 235 237 299
Pirke Rabbi Eliezer V 38
Poebel, A. 255
Proksch, O. 101
Pseudepigrapha *see* Apocrypha and Pseudepigrapha

Qimḥi 214

Rabbinic literature 2 26 33 39 43 50 91 f. 187 211 227 f. 287 294; *see also* Midrash, Mishnah, Talmud
Rashbam 28
Rashi 19 40 92 99 101 111 130 136 144 174 199 214 219 237 297
Reggio, Isaac Samuel 131
Reisner, E. 95
Renz, B. 95
Robertson, E. 95
Rost, L. 18

Saadia Gaon 103 199
Samaritan Pentateuch 61 129 130 214 218 232 252 253 254 264 f. 290
Schill, S. 69
Schulz, A. 18 95
Schwally, F. 58 98
Sellers, O.R. 219 236 (twice)
Sēpher Hayyašar (ed. Goldschmidt) 289
Septuagint *see* Bible translations, ancient
Sforno, R. Obadiah 135 137
Skinner, J. 207
Speiser, E. A. 84
Stade, B. 179 f. 181 182
Staerk, W. 95
Sutcliffe, E.F. 18

Talmud 14 38 50 61 82 134 140 192 259 284; *see also* Rabbinic literature
B. Berakhoth 2a 204
4a 30
7b 202
61a 57

Shabbath 30b–31a 139
ʿErubin 18a 57
Rosh Hashana 32a 14
Yoma 52a–b 208
72b 110
75a 120
Taʿanith 9b 103
Megilla 21b 14
Hagiga 12a 24 38
16a 294
Kethuboth 10b 107
Soṭa 9b 140
Qiddushin 30b 110
Baba Bathra 74b 38
Sanhedrin 101b 222
Zebaḥim 115a 206
Tannaitic literature 284; *see also* Mishnah
Targum *see* Bible translations, ancient
Theodor, J. 13 25 104 120 159 171
Theodotion *see* Bible translations, ancient
Torczyner, N.H. 18 54 78 95 155
translations of the Bible, ancient *see* Bible translations, ancient

Vetus Latina *see* Bible translations, ancient
Vincent, L.H. 175
Vollers 295
Von Gutschmidt 253
Vriezen, T.C. 83 95 109 114 175
Vulgate *see* Bible translations, ancient

Walther, A. 210
Ward, W.H. 160
Weiser, A. 95
Wellhausen, J. 111
Witter, H.B. 84
Witzel, M. 83 95
Wolfe, R.E. 19
Wright, G.E. 272

Yalon, H. 55
Yeivin, S. 198
Yellin. D. 239

III. Notabilia

Ab, first nine days of 67
Adad 282
Adamu 255
Adapa, myth of 83
αἴτια 139
Akkadian 13 23 46 74 80 81 82 105 109 134
Amalek 180
Amenhotep IV 8
Amunos 235
ʿAnat 80
Ancient Near East 1 7 f. 9 11 26 36 43 49 56 73 74 76 86 104 114 175 252; *see also* Akkadian, Assyria, Babylonia, Canaan, Egypt, Hurrian, Mesopotamia, Phoenician, Sumerian, Ugaritica
angels 55 61 81 f. 146 172 292 ff.; angel of death 220; destroying angels (demons) 294; *see also* cherubs
Anu 277 282
Anunnaki 82 123
Arabic literature (example) 189
archaeological data 1 *and passim*
Aruru 82 105
ʾAšērā 200
Assyria 105 117 *see also* Mesopotamia
Assyrian Calendar 66
Aten 8

Baʿal 36 49 80 107 179
Βάαυ 22
Babylonia 117; legends 26 f. 32 36 43 91 122 235 f. 254 ff. 277 278 282 298; records 256 ff.; seal 84
Banu al-Qayn 198
Bārû (diviner-priest) 283
Ba-u 22
Bel 32 282
blood-revenge 184 f. 195 222 225 227
brotherhood 83

Canaan, legends 36 49 179 220 230

232 238 299; theogony 188 232; tongue 56 199; *see also* Ugaritica
cherubs 73 f. 80 ff. 83 110 123 175
Χουσώρ 237
Creation, Ancient East 7 f.; Babylonia 26 f. 32 36 43 91 122 277; Israelite (stories supposed to exist prior to the Biblical account) 8 ff. 104 f. 150 274 f.; Pentateuch *see* Index to Biblical References; relationship between ch. I and ch. II 84 ff.
Creation of mankind, Ancient East 104; Akkadian literature 82 105 134; Egyptian literature 82; Pentateuch 82 f. *see also* Index to Biblical References; Prophets 104 f.; Sumerian literature 82; Ugaritic literature 134

Day of Atonement 29
Day-reckoning 28
Days, festival 29
demons *see* angels
Dighlath 121
Divine Names 84 ff. 206 246 275 295 *and passim*
dragon 49 50 141

Eden 71 ff. 275; comparison with Ezek. XXVIII and XXXI 75 f.
Edom 181
Egypt 8 49 82 104 106 116 f. 179 198
Enki 82
Enkidu 105
Enlil 82
Enmenduranki 282 f.
Enme(n)duranna 282 f.
Enoch, in Israelite legend 263 283 ff.; king corresponding to Enoch in Babylonian tradition 282
epic poetic traditions of Israel *see* traditions, Israelite
epic poetry, Ancient Near East 11 26 36 43 49 74; *see also* Gilgameš, Ugaritica
Eridu 257
Εὐεδώραγχος 282 f.
Euphrates 115 f. 117 f. 121
examples: Arabic literature 189; earliest French historians 212; Greek literature 212; Medieval Jewish writers 189
Exodus from Egypt 253

festival days 29
first generations stories, Ancient East 255 ff.; Israelite 266 f.
fratriarchy 202
fratricide 179
French historians, earliest (example) 212

gan (hā)ʾElōhīm 76
gardens of the gods 76 108
genealogical trees 186 f.
genealogy of Cain, relation to the genealogy of Adam through Seth 190 252 265 ff.
Gerizim, Mt., Sanctuary on 254
Giḥon, spring 116
Gilgameš epic 74 77 78 80 82 105 108 109 285 f. 288
grammatical and stylistical remarks 10f. 19 20 21 26 27 34 46 54 55 f. 60 61 91 98 f. 100 109 110 130 135 143 145 f. 148 151 153 165 166 f. 197 198 201 f. 203 204 212 224 227 231 235 242 248 274 276 299
Greek literature (example) 212

Hebrew, post-Biblical 144
Ḥeḳet 106
Herodotus (example) 212

Id 104
Idiglat 121
Idol-worship 246 f.
Israelite traditions, ancient *see* traditions, Israelite
Kenites 179 f. 182 198
Khnum 82 106
king lists, Mesopotamian 187 188 189 254 ff. 278 298
Kingu 123

Leviathan, ancient Israelite tradition 141; Biblical 50; Ugaritic 49
lightning 26 79 f. 176

literary tradition 2 10 46 72 ff. 78 135 243 293
logographers (example) 212
lyric poetry of Israel *see* traditions, Israelite

Magos 235
Manna 119
Marduk 32 36 43 82 91
matriarchy 137
Medieval Jewish writers (example) 189
Mesopotamia 22 32 36 49 64 65 67 68 104 122 160 187; *see also* Akkadian, Assyria, Babylonia, Sumerian
Meṭaṭron 284
method used in this commentary 3 f.
Midian 180 182
Môt 49 179 220
mountain of God 76 ff.

Naamah 238
Nāḫ 288
Naḫmūlel 288
names 26 f. 39 92 130 f. 136 170 191 198 202 229 231 ff. 245 ff. 268 276 288 f.; *see also* Divine Names
Nannaru (Sin-Nannaru) 43 65
narrative prose of the Bible 212 f.
Near East *see* Ancient Near East
ʿnḫ (Egyptian sign of life) 106
Nile 116 f.
Nudimmud 277
number eight 243
number five 259 ff. 276
number seven 12 ff. 26 61 94 136 191 f. 226 243 258 f. 271 276 282
number three 14 61 62 f. 65 100 107 131 135 157 165 193 231
numbers, ascending and descending order of components 261 276; sexagesimal system 192 f. 256 258 ff. 271 276 278 ff.
numerical harmony 12 15 94 191 193 202 250 264 271

Osiris 179

Passover 29
Persians, dualistic doctrine 26
Phoenician inscriptions 171 293
poetry in the Bible 8 11 39
potter's wheel 82 105 106
Prophets 8 39 104 f.; *see also* Index to Biblical References
Purattu 121

Rahab 8 11 24 36 37 38 46 50
Ramman 80
rivers, primeval 114
Romulus and Remus 181

Šabattu or Šapattu 18 64 65 ff.
Sabbath 13 15 18 29 63 ff.
Samael 139 199
Šamaš 282
Satan 139 294
sea, personified, Ancient East 49; Ancient Israelite poetic tradition 39 49 141; Bible 8 11 12 36 37 50; Ugaritic 49
seals, Mesopotamian 84 160
serpent 83 88; Ancient Near East 140 160; Ancient Israelite 141; Bible 50; Ugaritic 49
Seth (Egyptian legend) 179
Sethite genealogy 251
sexagesimal system *see* numbers
Sheol 81 123 219 220 286 298 300
Shiloah 118
Siduri 74 77 78
signs, of Cain 180 182 226 f.; of Covenant 227; on houses in Egypt 227; of life in Egypt (ʿnḫ) 106; of Rahab 227
Sin-Nannaru *see* Nannaru
Sippar, city of the Sun 236
smiths 180 182 197 f. 236
Sodom 305
sources of the Book of Genesis 2 15 28 84 ff. 93 96 98 190 193 f. 266 305 *and passim; see also* traditions
stones of fire 79 f.
stylistical remarks *see* grammatical and stylistical remarks
Sumerian inscriptions 83; king lists 188 189; language 256; literature 82; numerical system 192 256

III. NOTABILIA

Tabernacles, Festival of 261 f.
Tâmtu 32
temple of Jerusalem 115 117 f. 254
Tepe-Gawra, excavations 84
Thamte 32
themes-tradition *see* traditions, Israelite
Thotmes III 198
Tiamat (Akkadian) 23 32 36
Tigris 121
Tihāmat (Arabic) 23
traditions, Israelite, before the Torah, epic 11 f. 21 f. 23 f. 36 f. 39 46 50 72 ff. 75 f. 86 90 105 129 141 150 254 189 212 241; lyric 189; thematic 1 f. 36 46 49 73 74 93 123 141 175 176 178 ff. 182 183 186 230 f. 241 266 283 299; *see also* Creation, Israelite; Eden
traditions, literary *see* literary tradition
trees, of the knowledge 74; of life among other Semitic peoples 109; of the gardens of the gods 108; miraculous 77 f. 109

Ugaritica 13 22 25 36 49 74 80 91 107 134 200 234 236 237 238 240 241 243 293 299; *see also* Canaan
Utnapištim 285

vegetarianism 59 171 203 206

wisdom literature, international 9; of Israel 9 12 72 86 110
World-Egg 24 f.
World-Ocean, primeval 23 24 32